ఇ‍ "Quite frankly [this is such a] little gem and so reasonably [priced, anyone] could and should afford to own it. In addition to providing a wide range of definitions, descriptions and identifications, it devotes space to informative discussions of such general subjects as Symphony, Concerto and Song. There are brief explanations of numerous individual works, many of which are indexed by programmatic titles (which never fail to interest the layman) and many opera plots are given in brief detail.

ఇ‍ "The text is concise, clear and straightforward, and never too technical. And there are a number of musical examples and drawings of important musical instruments (both old and modern) which perfectly clarify or illustrate the text. Willi Apel, who is one of the foremost musicologists in the country, made an important contribution to the musical world with his larger 'Harvard Dictionary of Music,' reprinted many times since 1944. With Professor Daniel's assistance this new volume is equally fine for another type of reader."

—GEORGE KENT BELLOWS, *The Baltimore Sun*

THE
HARVARD
BRIEF
DICTIONARY
OF
MUSIC

WILLI APEL AND RALPH T. DANIEL

PUBLISHED BY POCKET BOOKS NEW YORK

POCKET BOOKS, a Simon & Schuster division of
GULF & WESTERN CORPORATION
1230 Avenue of the Americas, New York, N.Y. 10020

ISBN: 0-671-43475-6

First Pocket Books printing November, 1961

30   29   28   27   26   25   24   23   22

POCKET and colophon are trademarks of Simon & Schuster.

Printed in the U.S.A.

Preface

As early as a few years after its appearance, I came to realize that the *Harvard Dictionary of Music,* useful though it turned out to be for many readers, overwhelmed some of them. At that time I had the opportunity of teaching evening courses to groups of adult people with a lively interest in music. Not a few of them, anxious to obtain additional information on one subject or another, consulted the Dictionary, but complained to me that they were not sufficiently prepared for the lengthy and sometimes rather too "scholarly" explanations given there. Looking at the matter from their standpoint, I could not help agreeing with them. What they needed was a book of similar character, but more limited in scope and more elementary in approach.

When, about ten years later, Harvard University Press invited me to write such a book, I did not hesitate to accept the offer. I was encouraged by some of my friends and colleagues, among whom was Ralph T. Daniel, the subsequent coauthor of this book. I was very fortunate to find a collaborator whose special field of interest and knowledge complemented mine to a most satisfactory degree. He contributed most of the articles dealing with the more recent developments in music, many of which were not included in the original Dictionary. It goes without saying, however, that the present book is a joint enterprise in the strictest sense of the word. Both he and I have worked on and are responsible for all its contents.

It is hoped that the *Harvard Brief Dictionary of Music* will serve the audience for which it was written: adults who have an active interest but no specialized training in music and young people just beginning their study. We can only wish that this new dictionary will be accepted and judged, not as a rival and by the standards of its elder and bigger brother, but as a reference book in its own right and, I hope, with its own merits.

August 1960

Willi Apel

ACKNOWLEDGMENT

The sketch of the seating plan of the Boston Symphony Orchestra (Fig. 80) was drawn from information kindly supplied by the Librarian of the BSO, Mr. V. Alpert.

THE
HARVARD
BRIEF
DICTIONARY
OF
MUSIC

Note

Approximate pronunciations of many foreign words and titles have been informally suggested by respelling for readers of English and using capital letters for accented syllables. Thus: *Al fine* (ahl FEE-nay) means that the syllables are to be read as English words, with the accent falling on "fee." Some sounds are almost impossible to indicate in English spelling: *ui* has been used to represent the French *u* (*musique:* mui-ZEEK) and the German *ü* (*Rührtrommel:* RUIR-trom-mel), and *nh* to represent the nasal sound in French (*enfant:* ahnh-FAHNH). It is assumed that the reader will pronounce a syllable consisting of a single *o* as *oh*, but to avoid confusion other long vowels have generally been represented as follows: *a* as in *father* by *ah*; *a* as in *fate* by *ay*; *e* as in *feet* by *ee*; *i* as in *like* by *eye*. Ordinarily, unless appearing in these forms, *a*, *e*, and *i* are short. The pronunciation of Latin words has been left to the reader.

An asterisk (°) preceding a word indicates that there is an article under that word.

The method used for indication of octaves is explained under *Pitch names*, Fig. 89.

A

A. As absolute pitch, see under *Pitch.* —For a 2, see *A due.*

A battuta (ah bah-TOO-ta: It., at the beat). Indication to return to strict tempo after a free passage.

Abbreviations. The most common abbreviations used in musical notation are indicated in Fig. 1, which gives the sign as written, followed by the indication of how it is to be played. See also *Ornaments.*

Abduction from the Seraglio, The (*G., Die Entführung aus dem Serail*). Comic opera by Mozart (libretto by C. F. Bretzner, adapted by G. Stephanie), produced in Vienna, 1782. The action takes place at a Turkish castle (seraglio) where Belmont (tenor) and his servant Pedrillo (tenor) seek Constanze (soprano) and her maid Blondchen (soprano), who are held captive by the Pasha Selim (speaking part), and guarded by the terrible Moor, Osmin (bass). Pedrillo has obtained a post as a gardener in the castle, and tries to introduce Belmont as an architect. The situation becomes serious when Selim demands the love of Constanze, and Osmin that of Blondchen. Pedrillo contrives to make Osmin drunk so that the two couples can escape, but they are trapped and brought back. Selim condemns the lovers to death, but, touched by their love and grief, finally pardons them.

Fig. 1

Except for *Bastien and Bastienne*, a small work written when he was only twelve, the *Abduction* was Mozart's first opera in the German language, and stands as the first really significant German opera. It was written during Mozart's courtship of Constanze Weber, whom he married one month after its first performance. It reflects the happiness of this period in its long array of ingratiating arias and its scenes of irresistible charm and humor.

Abegg Variations. Robert Schumann's Variations for Piano, op. 1, dedicated to his friend, Meta Abegg, whom he playfully designated as "Mademoiselle Pauline Countess Abegg." The first notes of the theme, a-b♭-e'-g'-g', spell her name (B-flat is called B in German).

Absolute music. Music which is free from extramusical implications, in distinction from *program music. The term generally excludes vocal music, especially that type in which the music is clearly influenced by the text (e.g., songs by Schubert). The suites and fugues of Bach or the sonatas and symphonies by Haydn and Mozart are examples of absolute music.

Absolute pitch. Usually the term denotes what should more correctly be called "absolute judgment of pitch," i.e., the ability to identify immediately a musical sound by name, or to sing any tone at will. This faculty is a manifestation of tonal memory which is sometimes inborn, but can also be acquired by training. It is found chiefly in persons possessing some degree of musical experience or aptitude, but can by no means be considered a measuring stick or indication of musical talent. Many instrumentalists have absolute pitch (probably acquired through years of training), but among outstanding composers and performers it is probably as often lacking as not. Absolute pitch may be a valuable asset to a musician, but it may also prove a real inconvenience, e.g., when music must be transposed to another key. See *Relative pitch.*

Abstract music. Same as *absolute music.

Academic Festival Overture (G., *Akademische Festouvertüre*). An orchestral composition by Brahms, op. 80, written for the University of Breslau in appreciation of the degree of Doctor of Philosophy conferred on him in 1879. It is based upon several German student songs, skillfully arranged and connected.

A cappella (ah ka-PEL-a: It., in or for the chapel). Designation for choral music without instrumental accompaniment. Originally the phrase referred to unaccompanied church music such as was written in the 16th century by Palestrina. Today it is used for all unaccompanied choral music whether sacred or secular.

Accelerando (ah-chel-er-AHN-do: It.). Becoming faster.

Accent. Emphasis or stress on one tone or chord. Normally, a main accent falls on the first note of a measure, with secondary accents occurring, e.g., on the third beat in 4/4 meter, or on the fourth and seventh beats in 9/8 meter. Frequently, however, irregular accents are found on weak beats (see *Syncopation*). An accent is called *dynamic* if it results from greater volume; *tonic*, if from higher pitch; *agogic*, if from longer duration of the stressed notes. The dynamic accent is the most common type.

Acciaccatura (at-chak-ka-TOO-ra: It., crushing). An ornament used in harpsichord and organ music (especially *c.* 1675–1750) which consists of one or more dissonant notes, for instance, c-e-f#-g *or* c-e-g#-a (dissonant notes in bold face), struck together with a chord, but immediately released, leaving the consonant notes sounding. Today the term is often incorrectly used in the meaning of the short *appoggiatura.

Accidentals. The signs used in musical notation to indicate chromatic alterations or to cancel them. The five signs are # (sharp), which raises by a semitone; b (flat), which lowers by a semitone; X or ※ (double-sharp), which raises by two semitones; bb (double-flat), which lowers by two semitones; and ♮ (natural), which cancels a previous alteration. Compound signs (♮#, ♮b, ♮♮) are frequently used to cancel partly or completely a previous ※ or bb, but the simple signs #, b, ♮, are sufficient for this purpose. These accidentals apply to the note before which they appear, as well as to all the notes of the same pitch (but not in different octaves) within the same measure. Modern composers frequently add bracketed accidentals in order to clarify the situation.

Accompaniment. The musical background provided for a principal part. For instance, in piano music the left hand often plays chords which serve as an accompaniment for the melody played by the right hand. Similarly, a solo singer or instrumentalist may be accompanied by a pianist or by an orchestra.

Accordion. A portable musical instrument consisting of two rectangular headboards connected by a folding bellows. Inside the headboards are free-beating metal tongues which vibrate when the bellows is compressed or expanded. On the right-hand headboard there is a keyboard, like that of the piano, on which the melody is played. On the left side there are buttons which produce the bass notes and full chords. The earliest instruments of this type were made about 1830.

A similar instrument, preferred in England and considered superior to the accordion, is the *concertina*. This is of hexagonal shape and has studs on each side, those to the left producing chords, those to the right sounding single tones. The *bandoneon* is an Argentine variety with buttons on each side, for single tones only.

Acis and Galatea (AY-sis and gal-a-TEE-a). A dramatic cantata composed by Handel (about 1720) for the Duke of Chandos. Originally designated as Masque, Pastorale (pastoral play), or Serenata (evening entertainment), it was intended to be sung in costume but without action. Based on the Greek legend, the work includes some selections for a chorus that plays the role of commentator like the chorus in ancient Greek drama.

Acoustics. The science of sound which, therefore, forms the scientific basis of music, furnishing the explanation for many of its elementary facts. Among these are (1) the nature of musical sound; (2) intervals; (3) the physical properties of sound-producing media; and (4) overtones.

(1) *The nature of musical sound.* A sound is invariably generated by the vibration of an elastic body, such as a stretched string, a tuning fork, or an enclosed column of air (in wind instruments). A simple vibration is characterized by its *frequency* (number of vibrations per second) and by its *amplitude* (extent of its vibration, as in the back-and-forth movement of a plucked string); these characteristics are directly related to two basic properties of the resulting sound, namely its pitch and its loudness. The greater the frequency, the higher the pitch; the greater the amplitude,

quency can be indicated more specifically than by saying merely that greater frequency means higher pitch. The relationship is governed by specific laws, some of which were discovered by the Greek philosopher Pythagoras. If the frequency of a tone be designated as 1, that of its higher octave will be 2. Thus the ratio of the two tones in an octave is 2:1; of the fifth, 3:2; and of the major third, 5:4. From these intervals all the others of so-called *just intonation can be derived by the rule: intervals are added by multiplying the corresponding ratios (or, of course, intervals are subtracted by dividing the corresponding ratios). For instance, the double octave (c'') of c is $2 \times 2 = 4$; the double fifth (d'') is $3/2 \times 3/2 = 9/4$, hence *its* lower octave (d') is $9/4:2 = 9/8$, etc. Here follow the frequencies for the C-major scale, with ratio relationships for $c' = 1$ and frequency relationships for $c' = 24$ (the number 24 has been chosen because it is the smallest number leading to integers for all the frequencies).

	c'	d'	e'	f'	g'	a'	b'	c''
$c' = 1$:	1	9/8	5/4	4/3	3/2	5/3	15/8	2
$c' = 24$:	24	27	30	32	36	40	45	48

the louder the sound. Each pitch is determined by a definite number of vibrations per second. For instance, the tone a' of the present system of tuning (see under *Pitch*) is fixed in the United States at 440 vibrations (cycles) per second. The tones of the piano range from about 30 to about 4000 cycles.

(2) *Intervals.* The relationship between pitch and fre-

(3) *The physical properties of sound-producing media.* For tones produced by pipes (organ pipes, wind instruments), the following law applies: the frequency of a pitch is in inverse proportion to the length of the pipe producing the sound. If, therefore, a pipe for the tone c' (ratio 1) is one yard in length, the one required for its upper octave (ratio 2) would be 1/2

yard long, and that for the fifth (ratio 3/2), 2/3 yards. This law is the basis for the foot measurement of organ pipes (see *Foot*), as well as for the length, position of finger holes, etc., in wind instruments. The law also applies to strings, provided they are all of the same thickness and tension (see *Monochord*).

(4) *Overtones.* The acoustic effect produced by a vibration as described above (i.e., one determined by a given frequency) is called a pure sound. All musical instruments, however, produce composite sounds resulting from the simultaneous sounding of many pure sounds. The lowest of these is the so-called *fundamental* (or *first partial*), and this is the one identified by the ear as the pitch of the musical tone. In addition to the fundamental, there are the so-called *overtones* or *upper partials*, which are not heard distinctly because their intensity (amplitude) is much less than that of the fundamental. Nevertheless, they are extremely important, since they account for the different tone colors produced when the same pitch is played on different instruments, e.g., a violin and an oboe. The frequencies of the upper partials (overtones) are always exact multiples of the fundamental (or first partial). Thus a tone of 100 cycles will have upper partials of 200, 300, etc., cycles. The second partial is the upper octave, the third partial the upper twelfth, the fourth partial is the double octave, etc. Fig. 2 shows the first 16 partials of the tone C. It will be seen that if the numbers of any two partials be written in ratio form, the ratio will be that of the interval

formed by the two partials. For example, 6 (g') over 4 (c') equals $6/4 = 3/2$, the ratio of the perfect fifth. The series of tones in Fig. 2 is also known as the *overtone series* or *harmonic series*.

Fig. 2

Since the intervallic relationships between overtones are the same for any fundamental, the question may well be raised as to how different tone colors can result from them. They result not from the overtones as such, but from their varying amplitudes, i.e., the varying degrees of their volume. For instance, in a tone produced by an oboe, the first three overtones are practically absent, while the fourth and fifth are rather strong. In a flute tone, on the other hand, the

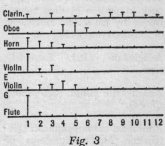

Fig. 3

first two overtones are prominent, and the higher ones practically negligible. Fig. 3 shows diagrams of the relative strength of the overtones in various instrumental sounds.

Action. Any kind of mechanism used in instruments in order to transmit the motion of the fingers (or the feet) to the sound-producing parts. On keyboard instruments the action consists of the keys and the mechanisms operated by them. Wood-wind instruments also have an action consisting of metal levers (keys) which serve to cover and to open finger holes. The action of the harp is controlled by the feet.

Actus tragicus (L.). An early cantata (no. 106) by Bach, composed in Weimar (1708–17) for an occasion of mourning. The German title is *Gottes Zeit ist die allerbeste Zeit* (God's Time Is Best).

Adagietto (It.). (1) A tempo slightly faster than *adagio*. — (2) A short *adagio* (composition in slow tempo).

Adagio (It., *ad agio*, i.e., at ease). (1) A slow tempo, between *andante* and *largo* (see *Tempo marks*). — (2) A composition written in slow tempo, frequently the second movement of sonatas, symphonies, etc.

Adagissimo (It.). Extremely slow.

Added-sixth chord. See under *Chords*.

Additional accompaniment. Designation for enlargements of earlier orchestral scores, especially those of Handel and Bach. The most familiar example is Mozart's arrangement of Handel's *Messiah*. Today such methods are justly considered falsifications rather than im-provements, and are therefore generally abandoned.

Adelaide. A famous song by Beethoven (op. 46) composed in 1795 or 1796 to words by F. von Matthisson.

Adélaïde Concerto. A violin concerto attributed to Mozart, and edited by Marius Casadesus from a violin part dedicated to the French Princess Adélaïde. The orchestral accompaniment was added by Casadesus. Although it is known that Mozart did write such a piece for the Princess, it has not been proved that this is the work.

Adeste Fideles (L.). A Latin hymn usually sung today in the English translation beginning "O come, all ye faithful." The words and music are attributed to John F. Wade, and it was published in 1750 for use in the English Roman Catholic College in Lisbon; hence, the tune name "Portuguese Hymn."

Adieux, Les (layz ah-DYEU: F.). See *Farewell Sonata*.

Ad libitum (L., at will). An indication giving the performer the liberty to vary from strict tempo, to add or omit a part, or to include a cadenza in a concerto (cadenza ad libitum). Abbreviated *ad lib*.

A due (ah DOO-ay: It., for two). A direction indicating that two instruments written on one staff (e.g., Flutes 1 and 2) should play in unison (°*all' unisono*). However, the term is also used in the opposite meaning, more clearly indicated by °*divisi*.

The same ambiguity exists with the equivalent French term *à deux.* — *A due corde,* see *Due corde.* — *A due mani,* for two hands. — *A due voci,* for two voices.

Aeolian. See under *Church modes.*

Aeolian harp (ee-O-lee-an: from Gr. *Aeolos,* the god of the winds). A sound-producing contrivance (not an instrument, since it is not played by man) consisting of a long narrow box with a number of strings inside which are exposed to the wind, e.g., in an open window. The sound varies considerably with the changing force of the wind and produces a highly romantic, mysterious effect. The instrument was much in vogue about 1800. Its intimate charm is most beautifully described in E. Mörike's poem, *Die Aeolsharfe,* and in its musical settings by Brahms and Hugo Wolf. Chopin's Etude, op. 25, no. 1, is sometimes called the "Aeolian Harp" Etude because of its shifting sonorities.

Aerophones. See under *Instruments;* also under *Harmonium* (*Aerophone*).

Affettuoso (ahf-fet-too-O-zo: It.). Affectionate, with warmth.

Afternoon of a Faun, The (F., *L'Après-midi d'un faune*). Symphonic poem by Debussy, composed in 1894 as a musical interpretation of a poem by Mallarmé. It portrays a faun (a creature of Roman mythology, half man, half goat) dozing in the warm sunshine of the Apen-nines, his dreams being interrupted by a vision of fleeing nymphs. The complete title, *Prélude à l'après-midi d'un faune,* has been interpreted to mean that Debussy had planned it as a prelude for additional sections of music. The work, in which the sensuous atmosphere of the poem is captured with consummate skill, is one of the first and most convincing realizations of musical °impressionism.

Agitato (a-ji-TAH-to: It.). Agitated, excited.

Agnus Dei (L., Lamb of God). The last item of the Ordinary of the °Mass.

Agogic accent. See under *Accent.*

Agréments (F.). °Ornaments.

Aida (ah-EE-dah). Grand opera by Verdi (libretto by A. Ghislanzoni), commissioned by the Khedive of Egypt to celebrate the opening of the Suez Canal, and produced in Cairo in 1871. The scene is laid in ancient Egypt, and the plot centers around the love of the Egyptian warrior Radames (tenor) for the captive Ethiopian princess Aida (soprano), and the jealousy of Amneris (mezzo-soprano), daughter of the king of Egypt (bass). Amonasro (baritone), the king of Ethiopia and also a captive, prevails upon his daughter Aida to learn the Egyptian battle plans. After Radames has innocently revealed the plans, Aida and Amonasro flee, leaving Radames to be condemned to death for treason. In the tomb where he is buried alive, Radames finds Aida, who has returned to die with him.

Aida was Verdi's last work written in the traditional style of Italian grand opera. After a long period, it was followed by the two late operas, *Otello* (1887) and *Falstaff* (1893). A striking feature in *Aida* is the brief atmospheric prelude which replaces the conventional overture.

Air (F.). (1) Song, aria, sometimes used as a synonym for "tune." — (2) In the Baroque suite (Bach), a movement of an essentially melodic character, not in the dancelike style of the other movements.

Albert Herring. Comic opera by Benjamin Britten (libretto by Eric Crozier after a story by Maupassant), produced in Glyndebourne, 1947. The town of Loxford, being unable to find a sufficiently virtuous girl to serve as May Queen, appoints a naïve young man, Albert, as May King. He is not happy with the choice, but his overbearing mother drives him to accept it. Emboldened by some rum slipped into his lemonade by a friend, Albert takes the prize money and steals away to a nearby town to sow his first wild oats. The townspeople of Loxford, believing him dead, are interrupted in the midst of their mourning by Albert's return. Made more manly by his experience, he asserts his independence of his mother.

Alberti bass. Stereotyped broken-chord figures used frequently as accompanimental patterns in piano music of the late 18th century (Haydn, Mozart). They are named after Domenico Alberti (*c.* 1710–1740) who was one of the first to use the patterns extensively.

Fig. 4

Alborada (al-bo-RAH-da: Sp., dawn). "Morning music," especially characteristic of northwestern Spain, where it is played on a rustic bagpipe accompanied by a small drum. Ravel's "Alborada del gracioso" (see *Miroirs*) derives certain features from the Spanish model.

Albumblatt (AHL-boom-blat: G.). Album leaf, a fanciful name for short pieces such as might be used as a contribution for an autograph album. The title was especially popular among piano composers of the 19th century.

Alceste (ahl-SEST [F.], ahl-CHES-tay [It.]). Opera in three acts by Gluck (libretto by Calzabigi), produced in Vienna, 1767. The story, based loosely on the drama by Euripides, tells of the heroic queen Alceste (soprano) who offers to die in place of her husband, the king Admetus (tenor). Admetus prepares to follow her to Hades, but both are saved by the intervention of Hercules (bass) and subsequently blessed by Apollo (baritone).

Written in a simple, nonvirtuosic style, *Alceste* was one of the first of Gluck's "reform" operas, embodying his theories regarding the proper relation of drama and music. In its French version (1776) it touched off the famous quarrel between the "Gluckists" and the "Piccinists" (supporters of Niccolo Piccini) who favored the traditional Italian operatic style.

Al fine (ahl FEE-nay: It.). To the end. See under *Da capo; Sin' al fine.*

Alla (It.). In the manner of; e.g., *alla turca* (Turkish), *alla zingarese* (gypsy).

Alla breve (AH-la BRAY-vay: It.). A tempo mark, indicated by the sign ¢, for quick duple time, i.e., with the half note rather than the quarter note as the beat. In other words, 2/2 instead of 4/4. See under *Time signature.*

Allargando (ahl-lar-GAN-do: It.). Slowing down and increasing volume.

Allegretto (It.). (1) A tempo between allegro and andante (see *Tempo marks*). — (2) A short piece in a lively tempo.

Allegro (It., cheerful). (1) Indication for fast tempo (see *Tempo marks*). — (2) Used as the title for a movement or a composition in fast tempo, often for the first or the last movement of a sonata, symphony, etc.

Alleluia (Latinization of Hebrew *halleluyah,* praise ye the Lord). (1) The third item of the Proper of the *Mass. — (2) Nickname of Haydn's Symphony no. 30, in C major (composed in 1765), which uses a portion of a plainsong Alleluia as part of its thematic material.

Allemande (ahl-MAHNHD: F., German [dance]). (1) The first dance movement in the *suites of Bach and his predecessors. It is in very moderate 4/4 time, with a short upbeat (eighth or sixteenth note), and in a richly ornamented style with sixteenth note figurations passing from one voice to another. — (2) In the late 18th century the name was used for quick waltzlike dances in 3/4 or 3/8, e.g., Beethoven's "A l'Allemande" (*Bagatellen,* op. 119).

Allentando (ahl-len-TAHN-do: It.). Slowing down.

All' ottava (ahl-ot-TAH-va: It.). See under *Ottava.*

All' unisono (ahl-oo-nee-SO-no: It.). In orchestral scores, indication that two instruments notated on the same staff (e.g., Flutes 1 and 2) should play in unison, i.e., the same notes. See remark under *A due.*

Alphorn, alpine horn. A primitive wind instrument, in the shape of a long wooden tube resting on the ground, which is still used by the herdsmen in the Alps both for calling their cattle and for rendering simple melodies (see *Ranz des vaches*).

Alpine Symphony, An (G., *Eine Alpensinfonie*). A large symphonic poem in one movement by R. Strauss, op. 64 (1911–15), describing a day of mountain climbing in the Alps. It is subdivided into sections such as "Night," "Ascent," "Dangerous Moment," "Summit," etc. Particularly noteworthy for its time is the extreme dissonance and daring use of instruments in the section entitled "Vision."

Al segno (ahl SAY-nyo: It.). See under *Segno*.

Also sprach Zarathustra (AHL-zo shprahkh zar-rah-TOOS-tra: G.). See *Thus Spake Zarathustra*.

Alt. (1) Term for the notes above the treble staff, from g" to f''', which are said to be the notes "in alt" (from It. *in alto*, high up), while those of the next octave, from g''' to f'''', are said to be "in altissimo." — (2) German for a contralto singer or part (*Altstimme*).

Alteration. The raising or lowering of a note by means of a sharp or a flat (chromatic alteration). See *Accidentals*.

Altered chord. A chord having one or more chromatically altered tones, as in the diminished seventh chord. See under *Chords*.

Alternativo (It.), **Alternativement** (F.). Indication for a section alternating with another section, as in an A B A structure (ternary form). In the suites of Bach, *Bourrée I, alternativement, Bourrée II* indicates repetition of the first bourrée after the second section. Schumann occasionally used the term as a designation for an internal section.

Altissimo. See under *Alt* (1).

Alto (It., high). (1) Same as °contralto, the second highest part in choral music (see under *Contratenor*). — (2) A high-pitched male voice, produced in falsetto. It was universally used in early vocal music (14th to 16th centuries), and is still utilized by Anglican church choirs. Elsewhere it is replaced by the female contralto. — (3) French for viola.

Alto clef. See under *Clefs*.

Alto Rhapsody. Composition by Brahms, op. 53 (1869), for contralto, men's chorus, and orchestra, based on a fragment from Goethe's *Harzreise im Winter* (Winter Journey through the Hartz Mountains).

Alzati (ahl-TZAH-tee: It., lifted). In music for violins, etc., indication to remove the mutes (*sordini alzati*).

Amahl and the Night Visitors. Opera in one act by Menotti, produced in New York on Christmas Eve, 1951, as the first opera commissioned specifically for television. Amahl, the small, crippled son of a destitute shepherdess living in the Italian mountains, is gifted with a vivid imagination. This makes his mother distrust him when he tells her that the Three Holy Kings have arrived in front of their house. They have indeed, however, and are invited to come in for a rest. To their gifts for the Christ child Amahl adds his crutch, and the use of his leg is restored as if by a miracle. He joins the kings on their journey to see the Christ child.

Ambitus (L.). See under *Church modes*.

Ambrosian chant. The liturgical chant in use at the cathedral of Milan (Italy), therefore also called Milanese chant. It was named after St. Ambrose (c. 340–397), bishop of Milan. Usually believed to represent an older tradition than *Gregorian (Roman) chant, recent investigations make this assumption very doubtful. The Ambrosian melodies are often more highly melismatic and ornate than the Gregorian.

Ambrosian hymns. The hymns written by St. Ambrose, or other hymns of the same type written by his successors. They are poems consisting of eight four-line stanzas, each line with eight syllables in iambic meter (e.g., Deús creátor ómniúm). Sung to simple melodies which are repeated for each stanza, they are probably the earliest examples of *strophic song. They are used in the Gregorian as well as in the Ambrosian rites. The name "Ambrosian Hymn" is sometimes used for the *Te Deum which, however, has no connection with St. Ambrose or with his hymns.

Ambrosian modes. See under Church modes.

American in Paris, An. A symphonic poem by George Gershwin, commissioned by Walter Damrosch and first performed in New York in 1928. The music undertakes to describe the reaction of an American tourist — Gershwin's own situation at the time of the writing of the work — to various scenes in the French capital. There are touches of realism such as the inclusion in the score of four French taxicab horns.

American organ. See under Harmonium.

American Quartet. Nickname for Dvořák's String Quartet in F major, op. 96. Composed while Dvořák was living in the United States, the work is based upon melodies of an American Negro character.

Am Frosch (ahm frosh: G., near the frog). Indication to use that portion of the violin bow nearest the right hand.

Am Griffbrett (ahm GRIF-bret: G., near the finger board). In violin playing, bowing near the finger board (*sul tasto). See Flautando.

Amor brujo, El (el a-MOR BROO-kho: Love the Sorcerer). A ballet by Manuel de Falla, produced in Madrid, 1915. The story deals with the love of Candelas, a gypsy maid who is hindered from any further happiness in mortal love by the phantom of her former lover. A gypsy witch flirts with the phantom, lets him kiss her, and thus dispels his supernatural powers. The music includes numerous dance pieces inspired by folk dances, the best known being the "Ritual Fire Dance." A unique feature is the inclusion of two songs for the ballerina.

Amore dei tre re, L' (lah-MAW-ray day-ee TRAY RAY: The Love of Three Kings). Tragic opera by Montemezzi (libretto by Benelli), produced in Milan, 1913. The story deals with the disastrous attempt of a medieval king to discover the lover of his daughter-in-law. In his rage, he strangles her and places her body on an open bier. The lover steals in to bid her farewell and is killed by poison the king has placed on her lips. Her husband, the king's son, dies in a similar manner and the father is left with nothing. Father, son, and lover are all kings, hence the title.

Am Steg (ahm shtayg: G., near the bridge). Same as *sul ponticello*, bowing near the bridge.

Anche (ahnsh: F.). Reed. Also reed instruments (oboe, clarinet), e.g., *trio d'anches*, trio for reed instruments.

Andante (ahn-DAHN-tay: It.). The term, literally translated "going" or "walking," indicates a moderate speed, between allegretto and adagio (see *Tempo marks*). It is usually understood as being a slow tempo, so that *più* (more) *andante*, means slower than andante, while *meno* (less) *andante* means a slightly faster tempo. Some composers (particularly Brahms) consider it as a fast tempo, in which case *più* or *molto andante* would mean faster than normal andante. *Andantino* (diminutive) is generally understood as indicating a tempo faster than *andante*.

Andantino (It.). See *Andante* above.

An die ferne Geliebte (ahn dee FAYR-ne ge-LEEP-ta: To the Distant Beloved). Song cycle by Beethoven, op. 98 (1816), consisting of six songs to poems by A. Jeitteles.

Andrea Chénier (ahn-DRAY-a shay-NYAY). Opera in four acts by Umberto Giordano (libretto by Luigi Illica), produced in Milan, 1896. The story takes place in Paris at the time of the French Revolution. The main characters are Chénier (tenor), a poet who has offended the revolutionists; Madeleine (soprano), a member of the nobility; and Gerard (baritone), formerly Madeleine's servant but now an official in the revolutionary party.

Anglaise (ahnh-GLAYZ: F., English [dance]). A dance type of the 17th and 18th centuries, occasionally found in the optional group of the *suite. About 1800 the term was used for the *country dance or the *écossaise.

Anglican chant. The music employed in the Anglican Church for the Psalms, canticles, and other unmetrical texts. It developed in the 16th century from the *Psalm tones of the Roman Catholic service. Like those, it is essentially a recitation on one note with cadential formulas, but it differs (aside from the English text) in the use of four-part harmony and of metrical divisions, as illustrated in Fig. 5.

Années de pèlerinage (ahn-NAY de pel-er-in-AHZH: Years of Pilgrimage). Collective title for three volumes of piano music by Liszt. Each volume contains several pieces with descriptive titles. See *Dante Sonata*.

Answer. The second (and fourth) statement of the theme in a *fugue. Also the imitation part of a *canon.

Antar (AHN-tahr). A symphonic suite (op. 9) composed in 1868 by Rimski-Korsakov. In four movements, it is a descriptive piece based upon the legend of Antar, an Arabian hero of the 6th century.

Antecedent. See under *Fugue*.

Anthem (from *antiphon). A choral composition, usually accompanied by the organ, written to English words from the Scriptures or to some other religious text, and performed in the service of most Protestant churches. In the Anglican Church, it is usually sung during the Offertory immediately after the sermon. If

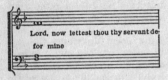

Fig. 5

it includes sections for solo singers, it is called *verse anthem* (see under *Verse*), otherwise, *full anthem*.

The anthem developed in the latter part of the 16th century, after the Reformation, as a counterpart of the *motet of the Roman Catholic rites. Particularly outstanding are the anthems of William Byrd (1543–1623).

The second flowering of the anthem came after the Restoration, under John Blow (1649–1708), Henry Purcell (1659–1695), and Handel (1685–1759), whose grandiose anthems were written mostly for special occasions (see *Chandos Anthems; Coronation Anthems*). An outstanding composer of anthems during the 19th century was Samuel Sebastian Wesley (1810–1876).

Anticipation. See under *Nonharmonic tones* (1).

Antiphon. In Gregorian chant, short texts from the Scriptures or elsewhere, set to music in a simple syllabic style, and sung before and after a Psalm or a canticle. The term is also used for some other chants, not connected with Psalm singing, of greater extension and elaboration. Among these are the four Antiphons of the Blessed Virgin Mary (B.V.M.), of which the *Salve regina* is the most famous. In the 15th and 16th centuries they were frequently composed polyphonically, for voices or for the organ.

The term antiphon comes from a Greek word, *antiphonia* (literally, counter sound), denoting the interval of the octave. In early Christian worship it came to mean singing by alternating choruses, probably because the second chorus consisted of women who answered in the higher octave. Hence, the term *antiphonal singing* for singing in alternating choruses. Antiphonal chants are chants performed by two choruses, as opposed to responsorial chants, in which there is alternation between a soloist and the whole chorus (see under *Gregorian chant*). In early antiphonal psalmody a short sentence was sung in alternation with the verses of the Psalm. It was this short sentence (later sung only at the beginning and end of the Psalm) which finally came to adopt and retain the name antiphon. The *Antiphonal* (noun; also *Antiphoner, Antiphonary*) is the collection of all the chants for the Office hours, as opposed to the *Gradual* which contains all the chants for the Mass.

A piacere (ah pee-a-CHAY-re: It.). At pleasure, i.e., freely performed.

Apollo Musagetes (ah-POL-lo mew-SA-je-teez: Apollo, Leader of the Muses). A ballet for string orchestra by Stravinsky, produced in Washington, D. C., 1928. It consists of a prologue depicting the birth of Apollo, a group of allegorical dances in classical ballet style, and a final apotheosis in which Apollo leads Terpsichore and the Muses to their eternal home on Mt. Parnassus.

Appalachia. Variations for orchestra and chorus by Frederick Delius, composed in 1902. The title stands for North America in general, and the theme is a Negro slave song.

Appalachian Spring. A ballet composed by Aaron Copland in 1943–44 for Martha Graham. The subject is a pioneer celebration around a newly built farmhouse in the Pennsylvania hills. The bride-to-be and the young farmer are the principals

and are joined by groups of neighbors, including a wise old woman and a revivalist. The original score is for a chamber orchestra of thirteen instruments. A suite for full orchestra, completed in 1945, includes much of the music in a continuous movement of eight sections. An interesting feature is the set of variations on a traditional Shaker melody, "The Gift to be Simple."

Apparebit Repentina Dies (Suddenly Shall the Day Appear). Cantata for full chorus and brass instruments by Hindemith, commissioned in 1947 for the Harvard Symposium on Music Criticism. The text is a medieval Latin poem describing the day of judgment. The music is in a series of neoclassic forms and includes a lengthy recitative for the entire bass section of the chorus.

Appassionata (ap-pas-syo-NAH-ta: It., impassioned). Nickname for Beethoven's Piano Sonata in F minor, op. 57 (1806), adopted from an early publication (by Cranz) where it was called *Sonata appassionata*. This famous work may be said to form the "dark" companion piece to the °Waldstein Sonata composed two years earlier. Strikingly contrasted in character, the sonatas are similar in structure: each consists of three movements, the first and the last very extended, the second forming a lyrical interlude leading directly into the final movement. In both sonatas, as well as in the °Emperor Concerto dating from the same period (1809), these transitions are among the most admirable tokens of Beethoven's genius. Forms of the movements of op. 57: sonata form — variations — sonata form.

Appoggiatura (ap-poj-a-TOO-ra: It., from *appoggiare,* to lean). Generally the term denotes the temporary replacement of a note by its upper or lower neighbor note, an effect aptly described by the phrase "to lean." For the modern appoggiatura, see under *Nonharmonic tones* (2).

Originally (17th, 18th centuries) the appoggiatura was an ornament, indicated by a special sign (little hook or diagonal dash placed before the main note: see under *Ornaments*) or by a grace note. In music up to 1750 this is always the *long* appoggiatura, in which the ornamenting (inserted) note falls on the strong beat, taking away from the main note one half or, in triple time, even two thirds of its value. After 1750 there appeared the *short* appoggiatura (often called *acciaccatura) which is performed as a quick grace note before the main note, without tak-

ing away from the latter's position or value. In the works of Haydn, Mozart, and Beethoven both types occur, the latter being occasionally (though not always reliably) indicated by a little stroke drawn across the stem of the grace note. Fig. 6 shows four examples from the works of Mozart and Beethoven, all calling for the long appoggiatura.

Appreciation of music. See *Music appreciation.*

Apprenti sorcier, L'. See *Sorcerer's Apprentice.*

Après-midi d'un faune, L'. See *Afternoon of a Faun.*

Arabesque. An ornamentation in Arabic architecture. The word has been used by Schumann and others as a title for pieces probably meant to be regarded as "beautiful decorations."

Aragonaise. Same as *Jota aragonese.

Arcato (ar-CAH-to: It.). Bowed, after a passage in *pizzicato. Arcata in giù,* down stroke; *arcata in su,* up stroke.

Archduke Trio. Nickname of Beethoven's Piano Trio in B-flat, op. 97 (1811), dedicated to the archduke Rudolph. Its four movements are Allegro (sonata form), Scherzo, Andante (variations), and Allegro moderato (rondo).

Archlute. A large lute, e.g., a *theorbo.

Fig. 6

Arco (It.). Bow. *Coll' arco,* with the bow, after a passage in *pizzicato.

Aria (It.). An elaborate composition for solo voice (occasionally a duet) with instrumental accompaniment, which figures prominently in operas, oratorios, and cantatas beginning about 1600. Arias, in contrast to songs, are characterized by a vocal part of considerable complexity, often including elements of virtuosity. They may also be called °absolute vocal music, owing to their high degree of formal organization and their regard for purely musical design rather than for dramatic continuity. For this reason they were banished from the opera by Gluck and Wagner. Nevertheless, they represent a highly important musical development, including such excellent examples as the arias in Bach's cantatas, Handel's oratorios, and Mozart's operas. An aria is usually preceded by a °recitative, which serves to carry on the story, whereas the aria gives the singer an opportunity to convey feelings and emotions.

The standard type of the Baroque period is the *da capo aria*, consisting of two sections, the first of which is repeated after the second, thus producing the ternary form A B A. The nearly exclusive use of this type of aria started with A. Scarlatti (1660–1725). During the 18th century there developed certain conventional types of aria, categorized according to their expressive character, such as the *aria cantabile* (slow, lyrical), *aria di bravura* (fast, virtuosic), *aria di carattere* (characteristic affection), etc. About 1750 and later (Porpora, Hasse), whole operas consisted of nothing but recitatives and conventionalized arias. This abuse was the main point of attack by Gluck (1714–1787), who replaced the aria with songs in a simple, expressive style. Nevertheless, arias have remained in the favor of operatic composers although they have been made a more integral part of the drama as a result of the reform initiated by Wagner during the last half of the 19th century.

Ariadne auf Naxos (ahr-ee-AHD-ne owf NAHX-os). A curious parody-opera by Richard Strauss (libretto by Hofmannsthal), originally (1912) intended as an entr'acte of Molière's play, *Le Bourgeois Gentilhomme*, for which Strauss wrote the incidental music. In 1916, it was produced in Vienna as an independent work, with the addition of an introductory scene representing the stage rehearsal of the work.

Arietta (It.). A short aria in simple style, more like a song, and usually lacking the second part which is characteristic of the aria.

Arioso (It.). Properly *recitativo arioso*, that is, a °recitative of a lyrical and expressive quality, rather than of a declamatory nature. Bach used the *arioso* repeatedly at the end of a recitative to emphasize an important thought or feeling.

Arlésienne, L' (lar-lay-ZYEN: The Girl from Arles). Incidental music by Bizet for A. Daudet's play, composed in 1872. It is usually played in the form of two orchestral suites.

Arpa (It.). Harp.

Arpeggio (ar-PEJ-o: It., harplike). The playing of a chord with its notes sounded in succession, rather than simultaneously. This term is used either for written-out figurations of various patterns (see *Broken chord*) or for an ornament in which the notes of the chord are played in rapid succession, starting with the lowest note. The ornament is indicated by either grace notes or a wavy line (occasionally also a vertical bow) placed in front of the chord (see Fig. 7a). There

Fig. 7

are two ways of performing an ornamenting arpeggio, i.e., either with its first or with its last note falling on the beat and, consequently, receiving the accent (see Fig. 7b, c). In older music (Bach, probably also Mozart) execution as under 7b is mandatory. In 19th-century music the situation is more flexible. The present-day practice shows a strong, if not exclusive, preference of method 7c (see the general remarks under *Ornaments*). However, there are many examples, e.g., in Chopin, where method 7b is preferable because

of its more expressive, less incisive character.

In piano music a wavy line extending through both staves usually indicates that both hands perform one continuous arpeggio, with the right hand beginning just after the left finishes. If there are separate lines on each staff, it means that both hands should start simultaneously.

Arpeggione (ar-pe-JO-ne). A stringed instrument the size of a violoncello, but with a guitarlike body, a fretted neck, and six strings tuned E, A, d, g, b, e'. It was invented in 1823 by G. Staufer, and is remembered today only through Schubert's *Arpeggione Sonata,* composed in 1824 for that instrument and pianoforte.

Arrangement. Also **Transcription.** The adaptation of a composition for a medium different from that for which it was originally written, in such a manner that the musical substance remains essentially unchanged. One may distinguish between arrangements made chiefly for study purposes and others destined for public performance. To the former class belong the customary piano arrangements (often four-hand) of operas, symphonies, string quartets, etc. To the other class belong Bach's arrangements of Vivaldi's violin concertos for the harpsichord or the organ, Liszt's piano arrangements of Schubert's songs, and the numerous recent arrangements of Bach's organ works either for the piano (Busoni) or for the orchestra (Respighi, Stokowski), some of which are open to criticism because they bestow upon Bach's organ works a coloristic lushness or Romantic exuberance inconsistent with the intrinsic clarity of his style.

Ars antiqua (L., the old art). Designation for the music of the late 12th and 13th centuries, in distinction from that of the 14th (see *Ars nova*). At the beginning of the *ars antiqua* stands the School of Notre Dame in Paris, represented by Leoninus (c. 1130–1190) and Perotinus (c. 1150–1220). Both composed mainly *organa. Perotinus and his colleagues also wrote a great number of *clausulae, which became the point of departure for the *motet, the chief form of the 13th century. Another important form of the period is the *conductus. Although musical activity centered in France, it also spread to England, Spain, and Italy. The main achievements of the *ars antiqua* are (1) the establishment of regular meter based upon the strict patterns of the six *rhythmic modes, and (2) the transition from two-part writing to composition in three and occasionally in four voices. Simultaneously with the development of polyphonic music there was a great flowering of monophonic song; see *Troubadours; Trouvères; Minnesingers; Cantigas; Lauda.*

Arsis and thesis. Greek terms for "lifting" and "setting" of the foot in dancing, applied respectively to the unaccented and the accented syllables of a verse. Although the meanings are erroneously reversed in modern English poetic scansion, the original implications are retained in conducting: *arsis* refers to the up-

ward motion of the hand (or the weak beat), *thesis* to the downstroke (or accented part of the measure).

Ars nova (L., the new art). Designation for the music of the 14th century (see *Ars antiqua*). The outstanding composer in France during the period was Guillaume de Machaut (1300–1377) who composed *motets as well as polyphonic secular songs (see *Ballade; Rondeau; Virelai*). A parallel development of polyphonic music took place in Italy, mainly in Florence, where such men as Giovanni da Florentia and Jacopo da Bologna (c. 1350) wrote two-part *madrigals. The outstanding later composer was Francesco Landini (1325–1397) who preferred the *ballata. Another form of special interest cultivated in Italy was the *caccia.

Art of Fugue, The (G., *Die Kunst der Fuge*). The last composition of J. S. Bach, written in 1749–50. It contains some twenty fugues and canons, all based on the same theme (Fig. 8), in

Fig. 8

which all the devices of imitative counterpoint, such as inversion, stretto, augmentation, diminution, canon, double and triple fugue, etc., are employed in a most ingenious manner. The last, unfinished, fugue was planned as a quadruple fugue, with *B-A-C-H as one of its four themes. The chorale "Wenn wir in höchsten Nöten sein" (When we are in greatest distress), which was given at the end of the first printed edition, does not belong to the work. While *The Art of Fugue* was formerly regarded as a theoretical manual of advanced counterpoint, it has become generally recognized as one of the greatest masterpieces of musical art. Bach did not specify any instruments, but it has been transcribed for string quartet, small orchestra, and keyboard.

Art song. A song of serious artistic intent written by a trained composer, as distinct from a *folk song.

A. S. Abbreviation for *Al segno,* or "to the sign." See *Segno.*

As (G.). A-flat (see under *Pitch names*).

ASCAP. American Society of Composers, Authors, and Publishers, a society founded in 1914 by Victor Herbert mainly to protect copyrights and performing rights. About 3000 composers and authors and more than 400 publishing firms belong to it.

Assai (ahs-SAH-ee: It.). Very, e.g., *allegro assai,* very fast.
A tempo (It.). Indicates return to normal tempo after some deviation.

Atonality, atonal music. Terms used frequently to denote certain practices in 20th-century music in which a definite tonal center or "key" is purposely avoided. Although the traditional principles of tonality had been considerably weakened about the turn of the century by such composers as Debussy, Scriabin, and Reger, they were not completely abandoned until Arnold Schönberg's *Three Piano Pieces* (op. 11) of 1908, in which, for all practical purposes, all vestiges of a tonal center are eliminated, each of the twelve tones of the chromatic scale having equal rights and being equally admissible in vertical as well as in horizontal relationships (see Fig. 9).

Fig. 9

The discarding of tonal centers or other references of a traditional character (triads, scales, etc.) means that some principles recognizable in tonal music are abandoned, and are replaced by others of a much more intangible nature. While the first ventures in atonality were radical negations rather than constructive contributions, Schönberg began to feel, about 1915, that atonality needed a positive principle and a technique of its own. The *twelve-tone technique was his answer to this problem. Although twelve-tone music is not necessarily atonal, atonality prevails in most compositions written according to that system.

Attacca, attacca súbito (at-TAHK-ka SOO-bi-to: It., attack suddenly). Indication at the end of a movement that the next movement should follow without a pause.

Aubade (o-BAHD: F., from *aube,* dawn). Morning music, in distinction from *serenade, evening music. Used to denote music of a quiet, idyllic character.

Aufforderung zum Tanz (G.). See *Invitation to the Dance.*

Augmentation and diminution. The presentation of a theme in doubled or halved note values, e.g., a quarter note becomes a half note (augmentation) or an eighth note (diminution). There are also instances of triple and quadruple augmentation or diminution. These devices are occasionally used in fugues, usually toward the end, to provide increased breadth or increased density. See, e.g., Bach's *Well-tempered Clavier,* I, no. 8, and II, no. 9. Beethoven, in the final movement of his piano sonata op. 110, uses the theme simultaneously in augmentation and diminution (Fig. 10). Both devices are also found in the develop-

Fig. 10

ment sections of symphonies (Brahms, Bruckner, and others).

Augmented chords, intervals. See under *Chords; Intervals.*

Aulos (OW-los). The most important wind instrument of the ancient Greeks. It is not a flute (as is often stated), but a shrill-sounding oboe. It originated in the Orient, and was associated with the orgiastic rites of the god Dionysus.

Aus Italien (ows i-TAH-lyen: From Italy). A symphonic fantasy by Richard Strauss composed as a result of a visit to Italy in 1886. It is a descriptive work in four movements, each having a programmatic title which suggests the impression Strauss intended the music to convey. The popular Italian song, *Funiculi, funicula,* is used in the last movement.

Authentic cadence. See under *Cadence.*

Authentic modes. See under *Church modes.*

Autoharp. A trade name for an instrument of the *zither family. Simple chords are produced by strumming the strings. Damper bars, upon being depressed, damp all strings except those required for the chord selected.

Auxiliary tone. See under *Nonharmonic tones* (1).

Ave Maria (L., Hail, Mary). A prayer to the Virgin used in the Roman Catholic Church. Also title for songs of similar contents, e.g., by Schubert and by Gounod. In the latter, the first prelude from Bach's *Well-tempered Clavier* is used as a harmonic background for an original melody.

Ayre. A 16th- and 17th-century type of English song (later spelled *air) in a simple homophonic style, the melody being supported either by voices or instruments (lute, viols) or by both.

B

B. In German terminology *B* is equivalent to the English *B-flat*. See under *Pitch names*.

Baborak (BA-bo-rak). A Bohemian national dance, including alternating sections in duple and triple time.

Baby grand. See under *Pianoforte*.

B-A-C-H. The letters forming Bach's name, each of which denotes a tone if the German terminology (see *B; H*) is used. The resulting theme, bb-a-c'-b, has been repeatedly used in compositions, first by Bach himself in his *Art of Fugue*, later by Schumann (*Sechs Fugen über Bach*, op. 60), Liszt (Fantasy and Fugue on B.A.C.H.), Reger, Piston, Honegger, and others. Four fugues on B-A-C-H said to be by Bach are spurious.

Bach trumpet. See under *Clarin trumpet*.

Bachianas Brasileiras (bah-ki-AH-nas brah-sil-AYR-as). Title used by the Brazilian composer Heitor Villa-Lobos for nine compositions written between 1930 and 1945. Scored for various media such as orchestra (nos. 1, 2, 7, 8), piano (no. 4), and soprano with cello octet (no. 5), the works are an attempt to synthesize some aspects of the style of Bach with that of native Brazilian music.

Badinage, badinerie (bah-dee-NAZH, bah-deen-REE: F.). A composition of a playful, jocose character.

Bagatelle (F., trifle). A 19th-century name for a short *character piece, used first and mainly by Beethoven.

Bagpipe. An instrument having several reed pipes (single or double reeds) which are attached to a windbag providing the wind for the pipes. One or two of the pipes, called *chanter* (*chaunter*) pipes, have finger holes and are used for the melody, while the others, of greater length and called *drones*, produce only one tone each and are used for the accompaniment. In some bagpipes the wind in the bag is supplied from the

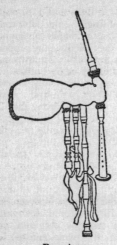

Bagpipe

mouth through a blowing pipe, while in others it is provided by bellows placed under the arm. To the former type belong the old Irish bagpipe and the Highland bagpipe (Scotland); to the latter, the modern Irish bagpipe. See illustration.

Baguette (bah-GET: F.). (1) Drumstick; *baguettes de bois*, wooden drumsticks; *baguettes d'éponge*, sponge-headed drumsticks. — (2) The stick of the violin bow.

Balalaika (bah-lah-LIKE-ah). A popular Russian guitar with a triangular body, a long neck with frets, and (usually) three gut strings tuned in fourths. It is made in different sizes, several of which are often combined to form a balalaika band. See illustration.

Ballad (from L. *ballare*, to dance). Originally a dancing song, the term now denotes a

popular song usually combining romantic and narrative, often adventurous, elements. A great number of English and American folk ballads have been collected. The poems are usually in the so-called *ballad meter* (the common meter of hymns, 4.3.4.3), the lines alternating from four accents (—'—'—'—') to three (—'—'—'). For other connotations of the term, see under *Ballade (2) and (3).

Ballade (bal-LAHD: F.; bal-LAH-de: G.). (1) A form of medieval poetry and music which flourished in the 13th and 14th centuries. The poem usually consists of three stanzas, each of seven (or eight) lines, the last (or the last two) being a *refrain. The music for each stanza has the form A A B, and is the same for all stanzas. The first section, A, provides the melody for the first two lines of the stanza, and this melody is repeated for the third and fourth lines. A second melodic phrase,

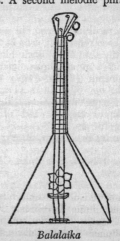

Balalaika

B, serves for the remaining lines of the stanza. Beginning with the late 13th century, ballades were composed polyphonically by Adam de la Halle (c. 1230–1287), Guillaume de Machaut (1300–1377), and others. — (2) In modern German usage, *Ballade* denotes art poems written in imitation of the old English ballads. They usually deal with medieval subjects or with fantastic stories (e.g., Goethe's *Der Erlkönig*). These extended narrative poems were set to music, particularly by Carl Loewe (1796–1869) and Franz Schubert. — (3) Chopin, Brahms, and others have used the term *Ballade* for dramatic piano pieces. Chopin's ballades are said to have been inspired by poems of A. Mickiewicz.

Ballad opera. A popular type of 18th-century English stage entertainment, consisting of spoken dialogue and simple songs adapted from folk tunes or from operas of the period. The earliest ballad opera was A. Ramsay's *The Gentle Shepherd* (1725), followed shortly by the most famous of them all, *The °Beggar's Opera* (1728) with text by John Gay and music arranged by John Pepusch (1667–1752). The style of the ballad opera has been imitated in Vaughan Williams' *Hugh the Drover* (1924) and in Kurt Weill's *The °Threepenny Opera* (*Die Dreigroschenoper*) of 1928, the latter based on the plot of *The Beggar's Opera*.

Ballata (bahl-LAH-ta: It.). A form of Italian 14th-century poetry and music derived not from the French °*ballade* but from the French °*virelai* (also called

chanson balladée). The form was used mainly by Francesco Landini (1325–1397).

Ballet. A theatrical performance of artistic dancing with costumes and scenery, usually accompanied by orchestral music. Ballet originated during the 15th century at the French court where the royal family and other members of the nobility participated in dramatic dancing to celebrate festive occasions such as weddings, birthdays, and victories. The earliest of these court ballets for which music is preserved is *Le Ballet comique de la Royne* (1581). The reign of Louis XIV witnessed the first golden age of ballet under the leadership of the ballet master Beauchamp and the composer Lully (1632–1687). *L'Academie Nationale de la Danse* was founded (1661) and professional dancers appeared, making ballet a spectator art rather than a form of recreation for the nobility.

The French tradition was continued during the 18th century under the leadership of the ballet master J. G. Noverre (1727–1809) with music furnished by such composers as Rameau (*Les Indes galantes*, 1735) and Gluck (*Don Juan*, 1761). During this century the positions and movements identified as "classical" were gradually evolved.

The Romantic movement of the early 19th century was manifested in ballet as in all other forms of art. While the center of greatest activity shifted from France to Italy, the principal spokesman for the new movement was the Frenchman Théophile Gautier, who proclaimed that the new style of dance must be poetic, dramatic, illusional, and, above all, novel. Dancing on the toes, which to most laymen is synonymous with ballet, was a rather sensational novelty introduced at this time and exploited to a degree far out of proportion to its rightful place as just one of many techniques available to the dancer. The Romantic period was also the age of the *ballerina* when male dancers, who had formerly played a primary role, were relegated to a subordinate position. These characteristics are apparent in *Giselle* (1841) by Adolphe Adam, one of the earliest ballets still in the current repertory. During the later 19th century the center of greatest vitality in ballet moved from Italy to Russia, where Tchaikovsky's three famous ballets, *The *Swan Lake* (1876), *The *Sleeping Beauty* (1889), and *The Nutcracker* (1892), represent the culmination of the activities of the Russian Romantic ballet under the leadership of Marius Petipa (1819–1910).

The great flowering period of modern ballet began during the second decade of the present century when a touring company of Russian dancers under the director Sergei Diaghilev and the dancer Michel Fokine transplanted the great Russian tradition, particularly to France, England, and America. Their most outstanding musical collaborator was Igor Stravinsky, who wrote the scores for *The *Firebird* (1910), *Petrushka* (1911), *The *Rite of Spring* (1913), and others. Ravel contributed the music for *Daphnis and Chloë* (1912), Falla for *The *Three-Cornered Hat* (1919), and Milhaud for *Le Train bleu* (1924).

Since about 1920 ballet has become increasingly popular in the United States and has developed a distinctively national flavor and a style which departs markedly from traditional positions, movements, and techniques. The term "modern dance" is sometimes used for ballets in the new style. Among the best known works are Copland's *Billy the Kid* (1938), *Rodeo* (1942), and *Appalachian Spring* (1944); Bernstein's *Fancy Free* (1944); Hindemith's *Nobilissima Visione* (1938); and Morton Gould's *Interplay* (1945). Ballet has also become an important factor in light musical comedy (e.g., *Oklahoma; Brigadoon*).

Balletto (bal-LET-to: It.), **ballet**. Vocal compositions of about 1600, dancelike in character, written in a simplified madrigal style, and frequently provided with a *fa-la refrain. They were popular in Italy (Gastoldi, 1591) and England (Morley, 1598, and others).

Ballo (It.). Dance. *Tempo di ballo*, in a dancelike tempo.

Ballo in maschera, Un. See *Masked Ball.*

Band. An instrumental group composed principally of woodwind, brass, and percussion instruments as distinguished from an orchestra whose nucleus is the string family. Band music is of a somewhat lighter nature (marches, dance music, etc.)

than orchestral music, although since about 1920 many serious composers have considerably enriched the band repertory, and transcriptions of orchestral music have been popular.

Bandoneon. See under *Accordion.*

Banjo. A stringed instrument with a body in the form of a shallow drum, a long fretted neck, and usually six strings. It is the characteristic instrument of the American Negroes, and was frequently used in early jazz music. Very likely it is not an aboriginal instrument of the Negroes, but a modification of the Arabian or European guitar which was imported into Africa. See illustration.

Banjo

Bar. Originally, the vertical line drawn through the staff to mark off measures. Such lines are now usually called bar lines, while bar is used in the meaning of *measure.

Barber of Seville, The (It., *Il Barbiere di Siviglia*). Comic opera by Rossini (libretto by Sterbini, based on Beaumarchais' *Le Barbier de Seville*), produced in Rome, 1816. The scene is 17th-century Seville, where Count Almaviva (tenor) and Dr. Bartolo (bass) are rivals for the hand of Bartolo's rich young ward, Rosina (soprano). The doctor is supported by the singing-master Don Basilio (bass), the count by the resourceful barber Figaro (baritone). Almaviva gains entrance into Bartolo's house by disguising himself, first as a drunken soldier who needs the doctor's aid, then as a music teacher substituting for Basilio who, he says, is ill. In the end a notary, who has come to marry Rosina to Bartolo, is induced to marry her to Almaviva. Bartolo appears too late but is consoled by being permitted to keep Rosina's dowry.

The *Barber* is one of the last examples of the 18th-century type of Italian comic opera and, in particular, the last to use the *secco* *recitative. Figaro's aria "Largo al factotum" is one of the most outstanding examples of *buffo* aria in rapid declamation. The plot of Mozart's *Marriage of Figaro* is based on Beaumarchais' sequel to *Le Barbier de Seville.*

Barbershop harmony. Colloquial term for a type of banal harmony, usually in close position, used in popular American part singing such as was formerly practiced in barber shops. Diminished seventh chords, dominant seventh chords, augmented sixth chords, and triads with added sixths prevail (see under Chords).

Barcarole (BAHR-ka-rol: from It. *barca*, barge). A boat song of the Venetian gondoliers or a composition written in imitation of that type of song. Barcaroles are in 6/8 or 12/8 meter with a uniform accompaniment suggestive of the rocking motion of a boat.

Bard. A medieval poet–musician (°minstrel) of the Celtic nations, particularly the Irish and the Welsh. In the early Middle Ages bards exercised great cultural and political power, serving as historians, heralds, and ambassadors in addition to their activities in poetry and music. They continued to exist in Ireland until 1690, in Scotland until 1748. The congregations of the Welsh bards, the *eisteddfod* (sitting of the learned), were revived in the 19th century and are now held annually as a competition in poetry and music (see *Penillion*).

The main instrument of the ancient bards was the °crwth and, later, the harp. Some bardic music, preserved in manuscripts, has been erroneously claimed to be "not later than the sixth century, and probably much earlier" (Dolmetsch). The pieces in question probably date from the 17th century. Many other claims found in books on the subject are equally unfounded.

Bariolage (bah-ree-o-LAHZH: F., variety of colors). A special effect of violin playing, obtained by shifting rapidly back and forth between two or more strings, the lower strings being used to produce relatively higher

Fig. 11

tones. This technique is used for broken-chord passages (Fig. 11a: Bach, Solo Sonata in E) or for a "coloristic" tremolo (Fig. 11b: Brahms, Symphony no. 4).

Baritone (Gr., low sound). (1) A male voice (see *Voices, Range of*). — (2) In connection with instruments (horn, saxophone), the term indicates a size smaller and of higher pitch than the bass size. — (3) Short for baritone horn (see *Brass instruments*, IId). See also *Baryton*.

Bar line. The vertical line drawn through the staff to mark off °measures.

Baroque music. The music of the period about 1600–1750, following that of the °Renaissance (see also *History of music*). The term Baroque (from Portuguese *barroco*, a pearl of irregular shape) has long been used to denote the contemporary period of painting and architecture (Rubens, Rembrandt, Velasquez, Bernini), and has now been adopted in music as a purely chronological term, without any of the qualitative implications ("grotesque," "in corrupt taste") sometimes attached to the word baroque.

The beginning of Baroque music is marked by the rise of the °monodic style, applied to opera, oratorio, and cantata; its end, by the death of Bach (1750) and Handel (1759). It was an extremely fruitful period, during which Italian, French, German, and English composers contributed to the development, not only of the opera, oratorio, cantata, aria, and recitative, but also of many instrumental forms such as the fugue, concerto, sonata, suite, variations, chorale prelude, passacaglia, chaconne, toccata, and rondeau. From the stylistic point of view, some of the main achievements of this period are the thorough-bass accompaniment, the introduction of contrasting effects (e.g., in the various movements of a sonata), and the rise of an idiomatic style in instrumental music.

Following is a list of the most important Baroque composers: *Italy:* G. Caccini (c. 1550–1618); E. de' Cavalieri (c. 1550–1602); J. Peri (1561–1633); C. Monteverdi (1567–1643); G. Frescobaldi (1583–1643); F. Cavalli (1602–1676); G. Carissimi (1605–1674); P. A. Cesti (1623–1669); G. Legrenzi (1626–1690); A. Corelli (1653–1713); A. Steffani (1654–1728); A. Scarlatti (1660–1725); A. Vivaldi (c. 1675–1741); D. Scarlatti (1685–1757); F. M. Veracini (1690–c. 1750). *Germany:* H. Schütz (1585–1672); J. H. Schein (1586–1630); S. Scheidt (1587–1654); F. Tunder (1614–1667); J. J. Froberger (c. 1616–1667); A. Krieger (1634–1666); D. Buxtehude (1637–1707); H. von Biber (1644–1704); G. Muffat (1653–1704); J. Pachelbel (1653–1706); J. Kuhnau (1660–1722); G. P. Telemann (1681–1767); J. S. Bach (1685–1750). *France:* D. Gaultier (c. 1600–1672); J. C.

de Chambonnières (c. 1602–c. 1672); J.-B. Lully (1632–1687); J.-H. d'Anglebert (1653–1691); F. Couperin (1668–1733); J.-P. Rameau (1683–1764); J. M. Leclair (1697–1764). *England:* M. Locke (c. 1630–1677); J. Blow (1649–1708); H. Purcell (1659–1695); G. F. Handel (1685–1759). *Netherlands:* J. P. Sweelinck (1562–1621).

Barrel organ. See under *Mechanical instruments.*

Bartered Bride, The (Czech, *Prodaná Nevěstá*). Comic opera by Bedřich Smetana (libretto by K. Sabina), produced in Prague, 1866. It is often sung in the German translation, *Die verkaufte Braut.* The opera describes an episode from Bohemian peasant life, centering around the love of Jeník (Hans, tenor) and Mařenka (Maria, soprano). The former agrees to give up his right to Mařenka's hand for a sum of money, under the condition that she marry "the son of Micha," whom everybody believes to be the stuttering Vašek (Wenzel, tenor). In the last scene, however, Jeník is revealed as Micha's eldest son by a former marriage, so the "sales contract" is fulfilled to the satisfaction of everyone.

The Bartered Bride is one of the most successful examples of national opera (see under *Nationalism*), and in times of political oppression has contributed immensely to stimulate Czech patriotism.

Baryton (BAH-ree-ton). An 18th-century variety of the °*viola da gamba*, characterized by the addition of °sympathetic strings (as in the *viola d'amore*). Haydn wrote nearly 200 works for the baryton because his patron, the prince Nicolas Eszterházy, played the instrument.

Bass. See under *Voices, Range of*.

Bass-bar. In violins, etc., a strip of wood glued inside the table (sound board). About eleven inches long and diminishing at either end, it serves to support the left foot of the °bridge and to spread over the table the vibrations of the bridge produced by those of the strings.

Bass clarinet. See under *Clarinet*.

Bass clef. See under *Clefs*.

Bass drum. See under *Drums*.

Basse danse (bahs dahnhs: F.). A slow dance of the 15th and 16th centuries, possibly so called because it was executed with low (*bas*) gliding steps (that is, the feet were not lifted). It was frequently paired with a succeeding faster dance. See also under *Dance music*.

Basset horn. See under *Clarinet*.

Bass fiddle. Colloquial name for the °double bass.

Basso continuo (BAHS-so con-TEE-nwo: It.). °Thorough bass.

Basson (F.). Bassoon.

Bassoon. See under *Oboe*.

Basso ostinato. See *Ground; Ostinato*.

Bass viol. Same as °double bass.

Bastien and Bastienne (bahs-TYANH and bahs-TYEN). A miniature opera by Mozart written when he was twelve, first performed in 1768 in the garden theater of A. Mesmer, the hypnotist, in Vienna. The love of the "shepherd" couple Bastien (tenor) and Bastienne (soprano) is disturbed by the former's admiration of a "city" lady, but is quickly restored when, on the advice of the magician Colas (bass), Bastienne feigns to desert her lover. The utter simplicity of the story (based on a parody of Rousseau's *Le Devin du village*) and the naïve charm of Mozart's immature style combine to make this a truly delightful work, a German counterpart of Pergolesi's *La *°Serva padrona*. See under *Singspiel*.

Baton (ba-TONH: F.). The stick used by a conductor when directing an ensemble. It is now abandoned by many conductors who prefer the more subtle movements of the hand.

Battle of the Huns, The (G., *Die Hunnenschlacht*). A symphonic poem by Liszt (1857), inspired by a painting of Kaulbach.

Battle of Victoria. See *Wellington's Victory*.

Battre (batr: F.). To beat, e.g., *battre à deux temps*, two beats to a measure.

Battuta (bah-TOO-ta: It.). Beat. *A battuta* indicates a return to strict tempo after a deviation. In fast tempo, *battuta* means the strong beat at the beginning of the measure; hence *ritmo di tre* (*quattro*) *battute* indicates that three (four) measures are to be grouped together in a phrase (for example, the Scherzo of Beethoven's Ninth Symphony).

Bauernkantate (G.). See *Peasant Cantata*.

Bay Psalm Book. See under *Psalter*.

Bayreuth Festivals. Annual festivals held in the opera house of Bayreuth (Bavaria) for the performance of Wagner's operas. They originated in 1876 with the first complete performance of the *Ring of the Nibelung*.

BB-flat bass. See *Brass instruments*, IIe.

B.c. Abbreviation for basso continuo (*thorough bass*).

Bear, The. See *Ours, L'*.

Bearbeitung (Be-AR-beye-toong: G.). Arrangement, transcription.

Beat. (1) The temporal unit of a composition, as represented by the (real or imagined) up-and-down movement of a conductor's hand. The duration of such a beat varies depending upon the tempo indication (e.g., *adagio*, *allegro*), with a metronome indication of 80 being a moderate speed (*moderato*). In slow or medium tempo, the 4/4 measure has four beats, the 3/4 has three, the 2/4 has two. In fast tempo there may be only two beats (in 4/4) or even one beat to the measure (see under *Battuta*). — (2) See *Beats*.

Beatitudes, The (F., *Les Béatitudes*). Oratorio by Franck for solo voices, chorus, and orchestra, set to the well-known text from the Scriptures (Sermon on the Mount, *Matt.* v: 3–12). It was completed in 1879. The choral texture is largely homophonic, the polyphonic interest lying almost entirely in the orchestral parts.

Beats. Acoustical phenomena resulting from the interference of two sound waves of slightly different frequencies (pitches). They are heard as minute pulsations at regular intervals. The number of pulsations per second depends on, and is therefore an indication of, the difference in pitch between two sounds. See under *Tuning*.

Beautiful Maid of the Mill, The. See *Schöne Müllerin*.

Bebop. A term coined about 1945 to describe jazz characterized by improvised solo performances in dissonant and complex patterns, often by accentuation of the second and fourth beats in each 4/4 measure and by the 12-bar "blues" phrase structure (typical of all jazz music), and sometimes by the singing of nonsense syllables. The term probably originated from the latter practice. This style of jazz became generally popular after World War II under the leadership of Dizzy Gillespie and Charlie ("Yardbird") Parker.

Becken (G.). Cymbals.

Beggar's Opera, The. Ballad opera with music arranged by Pepusch (libretto by John Gay), produced in London, 1728. The plot is a satirical presentation of life among the lower classes in early 18th-century London, the characters being highwaymen, pickpockets, and harlots. The most successful of all °ballad operas, it has been revived several times (F. Austin, 1920; B. Britten, 1948), with fuller harmonization and orchestration. Another revival, with much the same plot but with new music, is Weill's °Threepenny Opera.

Begleitung (bay-GLEYE-toong: G.). Accompaniment.

Bel (from Alexander Graham Bell). A scientific unit for the measurement of loudness. One tenth of a bel, called *decibel* (*db*), represents about the smallest degree of difference in loudness that can be distinguished by the normal ear. Musical sounds vary from about 25 db (softest violin tone) to about 100 db (fortissimo of the full orchestra).

Bel canto (bel CAHN-to: It., beautiful song). The Italian vocal style and technique most notably developed during the 18th century, emphasizing beauty of sound and ease, flexibility, and brilliancy of performance rather than dramatic or emotional expression. In spite of its inherent danger (exaggeration of the purely virtuoso element), it is a basic vocal ideal and technique, particularly for Italian opera and for Mozart.

Bell. A percussion instrument of metal (alloy of copper and tin), sounded by a clapper placed inside the vessel. The sound of old (European) bells is characterized by a great number of overtones which are noticeably out of tune. Modern bells, mainly in England and America, have five overtones in accurate tuning. The largest bell ever founded was the Tsar Kolokol (Tsar's bell) of the Kremlin in Moscow (1733, damaged in 1737). It weighed about 350,000 pounds. Large modern bells usually weigh from 5,000 to 15,000 pounds. The earliest preserved bells are found in Italy and Germany (11th century). While in continental Europe several bells are often sounded simultaneously, producing a clamorous noise, English and American bells are usually rung in succession, producing a melody. See *Change ringing; Carillon.*

Bell lyra. See under *Glockenspiel.*

Bells, Orchestral. Recent name for either the °glockenspiel or the °chimes.

Belly. The upper surface of violins, etc.

Bémol (bay-MOL: F.), **bemolle** (bay-MAWL-lay: It.). Flat, e.g., *si-bémol,* B-flat.

Berceuse (bayr-SEUZ: F.). Cradle song, lullaby; also instrumental pieces of a like character, e.g., Chopin's Berceuse, op. 57, remarkable for its "monotonous" accompaniment (°ostinato).

Bergamasca (BEYR-ga-mahs-ka). A famous popular tune from the district of Bergamo in northern Italy which was used repeatedly by 17th-century composers as a theme for fugues (canzonas) or variations. The 19th-century bergamasca is a fast dance in 6/8 time, much like the tarantella. See also *Suite Bergamasque*.

Bergerette (bayr-zhe-RET: F., from *berger*, shepherd). An 18th-century type of French popular song, based on pastoral or amorous texts. See under *Chanson*.

Berkshire Festivals. The Berkshire Symphonic Festivals were founded in 1934 at Stockbridge, Mass., by Henry K. Hadley. In 1936 the Boston Symphony Orchestra became the official orchestra of the annual summer festival, and its conductor, Serge Koussevitzky, became the guiding spirit of the whole enterprise which, since 1940, has included a music school. The Festivals are now held at the permanent home of the Berkshire Music Center at Tanglewood near Lenox, Mass.

The Berkshire Festivals of Chamber Music, inaugurated in 1918 by Mrs. Elizabeth Sprague Coolidge, take place in Pittsfield, Mass. Many chamber music works have been commissioned for and produced at the Festivals.

Billy Budd. Opera in four acts by Benjamin Britten (libretto by E. M. Forster and E. Crozier, after the story by Melville), produced in London, 1951. The plot takes place aboard the British warship *Indomitable* during the French Wars in 1797. The main characters are Captain Vere; Billy Budd, a young seaman who is impressed into British naval service; the master-at-arms Claggart, who hates Billy

from the moment he appears; and the corporal Squeak, whom Claggart employs for his scheme of tempting Billy to mutiny. In Act III, Claggart, who has accused Billy of mutiny, is told by Captain Vere to confront Billy with the accusation. The young seaman, who is afflicted with a speech impediment when excited, is struck dumb, and in his rage hits Claggart and kills him. Billy is sentenced by a court-martial to be hanged, a symbol of an innocent victim of evil. The music is somewhat somber in character, and provides an effective background for the dramatic events of the tragic story.

Binary form. A basic musical form, consisting of two sections, A and B, both of which are usu-

Fig. 12

ally repeated: ||:A:||:B:||. Frequently encountered in folk song, it is the standard form for the single movements in the °suites of Bach and his predecessors. It occurs also in many of the themes used for sets of variations (Bach's *Goldberg Variations,* Beethoven's *Diabelli Variations,* etc.), and occasionally in slow movements of °sonatas. Both sections are similar in musical design, the first usually modulating from the tonic to the dominant, the second back to the tonic.

	A		A	B	A	B	A = ||:A:||:B+A:||
Mozart:	16 (8+8)	16	12	8	12	8 (plus coda)
Chopin:	4		4	4	4	4	4 (plus coda)

Three varieties of binary form can be distinguished (see Fig. 12): (a) symmetrical, (b) asymmetrical, and (c) rounded. The *symmetrical* variety is one in which both sections are of equal length, e.g., eight measures. The *asymmetrical* is one in which the second section is longer than the first. The dance movements of the Baroque suites are mostly in symmetrical, sometimes in asymmetrical form. The *rounded* variety is one in which the second section concludes with a restatement (or partial restatement) of the first: ||:A:||:B+A:||. The rounded binary form is of great importance in the music of the Classical period. It is almost mandatory for the minuets (or scherzos) and trios which form the third movements of sonatas, symphonies, string quartets, etc. (see under *Minuet*). One of the many other examples of rounded binary is the theme of the variations forming the first movement of Beethoven's Piano Sonata op. 26.

Sometimes the binary structure is obscured by the fact that the repeats are written out in full so that the second statement may be varied. Two examples in point are the slow movement of Mozart's Piano Sonata in C, K. 309, and Chopin's popular Nocturne in E-flat, op. 9, no. 2. Both are in rounded binary form, as appears in the following scheme (the figures indicate number of measures):

From the historical point of view, rounded binary form is of great importance as the structural plan from which °sonata form directly evolved.

Bind. Same as °tie.

Bitonality. The simultaneous use of two different tonalities (keys), e.g., of B-flat minor in the left hand against F-sharp minor in the right (see Fig. 13a, from

Fig. 13

Prokofiev's *Sarcasmes*), or of C major against F-sharp major (Fig. 13b, from Stravinsky's *Petrushka*). This device has been used to quite an extent by 20th-century composers seeking new tonal effects. It is often referred to as polytonality, although there are rarely more than two keys involved.

Black bottom. A type of slow fox trot characterized by intricate steps.

Black-Key Etude. Nickname of Chopin's Etude, op. 10, no. 5, in G-flat major, in which the right hand uses only black keys.

Blasinstrument (BLAHZ-in-stroo-ment: G.). Wind instrument.

Blech, Blechinstrument (BLEKH-in-stroo-ment: G.). Brass, brass instrument. *Blechbläser*, brass players.

Blessed Damozel, The (F., *La Damoiselle élue*). Debussy's cantata for women's voices (solo and chorus) with orchestra, submitted in fulfillment of his obligation as a holder of the Grand Prix de Rome from 1884 to 1887. Based on a poor translation of portions of Rossetti's poem, the work was accepted by the Institute with serious misgivings, the style being criticized as much too unorthodox.

Blind octaves. A trick device of piano virtuosity, in which both hands alternate rapidly with octaves, the passage (usually a scale, also a trill) being played essentially by the thumbs and doubled by the little fingers, alternately in the higher and in the lower octave. See Fig. 14.

Blockflute, Blockflöte (G.). Recorder.

Blues. A style of jazz, both vocal and instrumental, introduced in the first decade of the 20th century. The principal sources of the blues appear to be Negro work songs and spirituals, but the earliest traceable example is probably the "Memphis Blues" (written in 1909; published 1912) by the Negro musician W. C. Handy. The most persistent characteristic of the blues is a 12-measure pattern, instead of the 8- and 16-measure patterns of ragtime. The blues are further characterized by a smoother, less percussive rhythm and a slower tempo than ragtime. The name is obviously related to the "blue notes," i.e., the third and seventh scale degrees which are used either natural or flatted, and which are frequently played deliberately out of tune.

B-minor Mass. A great Mass by Bach, for soloists, chorus, and orchestra, composed 1733–38 to the (Latin) text of the Roman Catholic *Mass. The five items of the Mass are subdivided into many sections treated as choruses, arias, duets, etc. Several of these are rewritten from earlier cantatas, among them the famous *Crucifixus* (from Cantata no. 12, *Weinen, Klagen*). The fact that the foremost Protestant composer wrote a Catholic Mass has long

Fig. 14

been a matter of special interest and of controversy. Undoubtedly some opportunism was involved when, in 1733, he sent the Kyrie and the Gloria to the Catholic king of Saxony, requesting the title of Court Composer. Whatever the motives, we can only be grateful that denominational considerations are set aside in this magnificent work which stands before us as a testament of one great universal faith.

Boehm system (beum). An improved system of keying woodwind instruments, invented about 1830 by Theobald Boehm, which allows the holes to be cut in the proper acoustical position and size, and yet be within the spread of the average hand. It permits the performance of trills and rapid passages that were impossible on the older instruments in which most of the holes were covered directly by the fingers. Instruments provided with this key system, as is generally the case today, are sometimes called *Boehm flutes*, etc.

Bohème, La (bo-EM: The Bohemian World). Opera by Puccini (libretto by G. Giacosa and L. Illica, based on H. Murger's novel, *La Vie de Bohème*), produced in Turin, 1896. The setting is Paris in the 1840's, and the opera gives a touching though somewhat sentimental description of the life of young artists, centering around the love of the poet Rodolfo (tenor) and of Mimi (soprano), who dies of consumption in the last act. The lighter side of Bohemian life is represented by another couple, Marcello (baritone) and Musetta (soprano).

The opera, one of the best-known examples of °*verismo*, approximates, in its light texture, clarity of orchestration, and lyric style, the French opera rather than the typically Italian opera (Verdi).

Bolero (bo-LAYR-o). A Spanish dance, for a solo dancer or a couple, which includes many brilliant and intricate steps and characteristic motions, such as the sudden stop with one arm held arched over the head (*bien parado*). The music is in moderate triple time with accompaniment of castanets and with rhythms such as shown in Fig. 15. Particularly famous are Cho-

Fig. 15

pin's Bolero for pianoforte, op. 19, and Ravel's for orchestra (1928). The latter, often used for ballet performance, consists of a single theme stated over and over in a long crescendo and presented in a fascinating variety of orchestral colorations.

Bonne chanson, La (bun shahnh-SONH). A song cycle composed by Fauré in 1892, based on eight poems from Verlaine's collection of that title.

Boogie-woogie. Originally a special type of piano °blues, first heard in Chicago in the early 1920's (Jimmy Yancey, "Pinetop" Smith), and later revived about 1935 on commercial recordings, both by pianists (Meade "Lux" Lewis, Albert Ammons, Pete Johnson) and by ensembles (Benny Goodman's "Roll 'em"). It is characterized by a repeated bass figure (*ostinato) against which the right hand improvises freely.

Bop. See *Bebop.*

Boris Godunov (BO-ris gaw-doo-NAWF). Opera by Moussorgsky (to his own libretto, based on Pushkin's drama), composed 1868–69 and produced in St. Petersburg, 1874. The action takes place during the years 1598–1608 in Moscow where Boris Godunov (bass), after having murdered Dmitri, the rightful heir to the throne, rules over Russia. Suffering from a sense of guilt (in the Prologue he is in a monastery in order to gain expiation), and frightened by the appearance of the "false Dmitri" (the young monk, Gregory, a tenor), he admits his crime and, bequeathing the crown to his young son, Feodor (mezzo-soprano), falls dead.

Boris Godunov is the outstanding masterpiece of Russian national opera. Its musical style is remarkably advanced for its time, and many innovations of a more recent date have been traced to this work, e.g., the use of *parallel chords, *modality, and other unconventional devices. Particularly striking is the prominence of the chorus, representing the Russian people, and it has been said that they are the real protagonist of the opera rather than Boris himself.

Boston, Valse Boston. A term hardly known in America, but widely used in Europe, particularly in Germany, during the period after World War I. Called *hesitation waltz" in the United States, the Boston is a slow waltz with a sophisticated rhythm, single beats or whole measures of the accompaniment being suppressed. A good example occurs in Hindemith's *Suite 1922.*

Bouché (F.). See under *Cuivré.*

Bourrée (boo-RAY). A French 17th-century dance, probably from the Auvergne, in quick 4/4 meter and with an upbeat (4/1234/123 . . .). It occurs among the optional dances of the Baroque *suite.

Bow. The implement used for playing on a stringed instrument, consisting essentially of a wooden stick with horsehair stretched from its lower end (called *nut* or *frog*) to the tip. Its name derives from the fact that it was originally shaped much like the bow used in archery. The bow design in present-day use was developed by François Tourte (1747–1833). It has a long, tapering, and slightly inward-curving stick, made from Pernambuco wood, and a screw mechanism for the adjustment of the tension of the horsehair. Although it is now universally used, a 17th-century German type of bow has been recommended for playing Bach (particularly his pieces for unaccompanied violin such as the famous *Chaconne*). On this latter bow it is possible to control the tension of the hairs by pressure of the thumb, and thus the numerous full chords in the *Chaconne* are more easily executed than with the modern bow.

Bowing. The technique of using the bow on stringed instruments (violins, etc.). There are numerous manners of bowing (some of them rather elusive in terminology and description), the most important of which are the following.

(1) *Plain bowing* (*legato*) consists of the two basic strokes, *down-bow* and *up-bow* (indicated by (a) and (b) of Fig. 16). The slur (c) indicates that

Fig. 16

a group of notes is to be taken in a single stroke.

(2) *Détaché.* A broad vigorous stroke applied to single notes of equal value, not too fast. Sometimes indicated as under (d).

(3) *Martelé, martellato.* Literally, a "hammered" stroke, that is, played with very short strokes, usually at the tip of the bow. Indicated as in (e).

(4) *Spiccato.* A short stroke played in rapid tempo in the middle of the bow, so that the bow bounces on the strings. Other terms for much the same thing are *sautillé, saltato, saltando, piqué.* Indicated as in (f).

(5) *Ricochet.* This is done by throwing the bow, in its upper section, on the string so that it will bounce several times on the down-bow. Notation as under (g).

(6) *Staccato.* This is a difficult solo effect, which may be described as a number of *martelé* or hammered notes taken in

the same stroke. Notation as under (h).

See also *sul ponticello, sul tasto* (under *Sul*); *col legno* (under *Col*); *Tremolo.*

Brace. The bracket connecting two or more staves in a score for pianoforte, chamber music, etc. Hence, also the group of staves thus connected.

Brandenburg Concertos. Six concertos written by Bach in 1721 and dedicated to Christian Ludwig, Margrave of Brandenburg. They represent the artistic peak of the Baroque concerto (see *Concerto*). Each consists of three movements, fast–slow–fast, except for the first, which has a Minuet and a Polacca added at the end. Three of them, nos. 2, 4, and 5, are *concerti grossi*, employing a group of solo instruments against the string orchestra.

Brass band. A band consisting ordinarily of cornets, alto saxhorns, trombones, baritones or euphoniums, BB-flat basses, drums, and occasionally trumpets, bugles, and kettledrums (see *Brass instruments* II). The brass band movement is particularly popular in England, where such bands are frequently found attached to high schools, colleges, religious groups (Salvation Army), factories, etc.

Brass instruments. The group of wind instruments made from brass or some other metal and having a cup-shaped mouthpiece. The large number of brass instruments can be conveniently divided into two groups, one comprising those that are standard members of the orchestra, the other those used mainly in bands.

I. *Orchestral Instruments.* The brass section of the modern orchestra consists of the °horn, the °trumpet, the °trombone, and the °tuba. The tuba and the horn are related, both having a conical pipe, and the trombone and the trumpet are related, both having a pipe which, for its major part, is cylindrical and widens into a relatively small bell. Other instruments occasionally used in the orchestra are the Wagner tubas (see under *Tuba*) and the cornet (see under II below).

II. *Band Instruments* (see *Brass band*).

(a) *Cornet.* An instrument similar in shape to the trumpet, but shorter and with a relatively longer conical part of the pipe. It is pitched in Bb and has a range from e to bb" (with a written range from f♯ to c'''; see under *Transposing instrument*). Its tone quality is similar to that of the trumpet, although somewhat less brilliant. Owing to its shorter tube it is capable of considerably greater agility and has, therefore, sometimes been used in the orchestra, especially by French and Italian composers.

(b) *Flügelhorn.* Similar in design and size to the cornet, but with a wider bore, resulting in a sound somewhat like that of the horn, though lacking the latter's mellowness. It has the same range as the cornet.

(c) *Mellophone.* Designed like the French horn, but differing, among other things, in its having three upright pistons, like the saxhorns (see below). The range is a fifth below that of the cornet.

(d) *Baritone, Euphonium.* Larger instruments of the *Flügelhorn* type, and built in two shapes: like a trumpet, with the bell pointing upwards, or oval, with the bell facing backwards. The range of the baritone is an octave below the cornet. The euphonium has a fourth valve for additional bass notes.

(e) *BB-flat Bass.* The largest and lowest pitched of the group, with a range two octaves below that of the cornet. Its normal shape is similar to the baritone, but it also exists in two other shapes: *Helicon*, which is circular and carried over the shoulder; and *Sousaphone* (named after J. P. Sousa, who suggested it), which has a widely flaring bell of a conspicuous shape.

Most of these instruments are derived from the *saxhorns*, a family of brass instruments invented by Adolphe Sax and designed on a uniform model, i.e., upright and with three pistons standing on top of the tube. The bass size is known as *Sax tuba.*

Bratsche (BRAH-tshe: G. From It. *viola da braccio*, arm viol). Viola.

Breve, brevis. See under *Notes and rests.*

Bridge. (1) In stringed instruments (violin, etc.), the wooden support atop the table across which the strings are stretched. It serves to raise the strings and transmit vibrations to the instrument proper. See under *Violin.* — (2) Short for °bridge passage.

Bridge passage. In musical composition, a passage of subordinate importance serving as a connection between two sections or themes, e.g., between the first and second themes in °sonata form.

Brindisi (BRIN-dee-zee: It.). Drinking song, particularly in operas, e.g., Verdi's *La Traviata* ("Libiamo") or Mascagni's *Cavalleria rusticana* ("Viva il vino").

Brio, Con (BREE-o: It.). With vigor and spirit.

Broken chord. The notes of a chord (triad, seventh chord, etc.) played successively, as, e.g., in the °Alberti bass. Chopin's works contain many examples of ingeniously devised broken-chord patterns, also called arpeggios.

Buckwheat notes. See under *Fasola.*

Bühne (BUIH-ne: G.). Stage. *Bühnenfestspiel* (stage festival play) and *Bühnenweihfestspiel* (stage–consecrating festival play) are Wagner's designations for his *Ring of the Nibelung* and *Parsifal* respectively.

Bürger als Edelmann, Der (BUIR-ger ahls AY-del-mahn: G.). German title of Molière's comedy, *Le Bourgeois Gentilhomme,* to which R. Strauss set incidental music. The play, in a shortened version by H. von Hofmannsthal, was performed in connection with the première of Strauss's opera °*Ariadne auf Naxos.*

Buffo (BOOF-fo: It.). A comic character in Italian opera, usually a bass (*basso buffo*).

Bugle. (1) A military instrument, somewhat in the shape of a trumpet, but without valves and therefore capable of producing only the natural tones (for example, g-d'-g'-b'-d'') such as occur in military signals. See illustration. — (2) The term is also used as a generic name for the instruments of the *Flügelhorn* type, described under °Brass instruments, IIb.

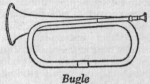

Bugle

Burgundian School. The leading group of composers of the early 15th century, mostly residents of the duchy of Burgundy and represented chiefly by Dufay (*c.* 1400–1474) and Binchois (*c.* 1400–1467). It was formerly called the First °Netherlands School. The music of this period is prevailingly secular (as is that of the 14th century), but Dufay wrote a number of Masses (among them the earliest known Mass on °*L'homme armé*) and other religious works (motets, hymns), thus foreshadowing the trend toward sacred music which appears fully established in the °Flemish School (Ockeghem, Obrecht). Abandoning the exaggerations, dissonances, and rhythmic complexities of the late 14th century, Dufay and Binchois developed, under the influence of the English master Dunstable (*c.* 1370–1435), a musical language of great delicacy and refinement, notable for its transparent beauty and tenderness. Characteristic traits are °fauxbourdon passages and the "Burgundian" cadence (see under *Cadence*).

Burla, burlesca, burletta (It.), **burlesque** (F.), **Burleske** (G.). A composition in a jesting, boisterous mood. Also a light (or even vulgar) comic opera.

Butterfly. See *Madame Butterfly*.

C

C. See under *Pitch names.*

C. a. *Col arco* (see under *Col*).

Cabaletta (cah-bah-LET-ta: It.). A short operatic song in popular style, rhythmically simple in melody and accompaniment. They are frequent in the operas of Rossini. Verdi used the term for the final sections of arias and duets, written in faster tempo (*stretto*) and uniform rhythm.

Caccia (CAHT-cha: It., chase, hunt). A type of 14th-century Italian music (see *Ars nova*) in which a lively text, dealing with hunting, fishing, or other naturalistic subjects, is presented as a two-voice °canon, supported by a free tenor in longer note values.

Cachucha (ca-CHOO-cha: Sp.). A Spanish dance in triple time from Andalusia, similar to the °bolero but faster and more energetic.

Cadence (from L. *cadere*, to fall). A progression of two or more °chords used at the end of a composition, section, or phrase to convey a feeling of permanent or temporary repose.

A cadence is called *perfect* (*final, full*) if the last chord is the °tonic triad (I) with the °root of the chord in both the top (soprano) and bottom (bass) parts, preceded either by the

Fig. 17

*dominant (V) or *subdominant (IV). The term *imperfect* denotes an otherwise perfect cadence where the root of the chord does not appear in the top part.

The formula V-I is called *authentic* cadence (Fig. 17a); IV-I is called *plagal* (Fig. 17b). The authentic cadence usually occurs as a part of longer formulas IV-V-I (Fig. 17c) or IV-I$_4^6$-V-I (17d), sometimes called *mixed* cadences because both IV and V chords are present. *Half cadences* use the same formulas transposed to the dominant (Fig. 17e, f) or subdominant (g, h), their distinctive feature being the absence of the tonic (I) as the final chord. A cadence is called *deceptive* (*interrupted*) if the tonic chord is — deceptively — replaced by some other chord such as VI or III (Fig. 17i, j).

In medieval music (prior to 1450) cadences usually show the melodic progression II-I in the lowest part (Fig. 17k, l). Of particular interest are the "Burgundian" cadence, which is distinguished by two "leading tones" (Fig. 17l), and the so-called *Landini cadence* (Fig. 17m), frequently found in compositions of Machaut, Landini, and the Burgundian masters, and characterized by the melodic progression 7-6-8 in the top part.

Cadenza (ca-DEN-za). A passage or section in the style of a brilliant improvisation, placed near the end of a solo composition such as an aria or, especially, a concerto, giving the performer a chance to exhibit his technical mastery. Normally the cadenza forms a part of the soloist's final cadence (hence the name), being inserted between the chords I$_4^6$ and V (see Cadence, Fig. 17d), as shown in Fig. 18. The cadenzas of concertos make ample use of highly virtuoso passage work, but also draw from the thematic substance of the movement, presenting its subjects in artfully devised modifications or combinations. They usually close with an extended trill on the domi-

Fig. 18

nant (V), after which the orchestra closes the cadenza with the tonic chord (I), followed by a short coda.

Originally (18th century) cadenzas were not written by the composer, but were improvised by the player. This was the case in all the concertos of Mozart and in most of those by Beethoven. Present-day performers use cadenzas written by such artists as Hummel, Moscheles, Reinecke, Joachim (for the violin concertos), and Busoni, or, occasionally, write their own cadenzas. There exist original cadenzas (written later by the composers themselves) to all the Beethoven concertos and to a number of Mozart's, but these are hardly ever used by modern performers because they do not conform to present-day standards of virtuosity. However, from the point of view of musical style they are superior to most of the cadenzas commonly heard, in which considerations of stylistic unity are often treated very lightly. It is not unusual to hear a concerto by Mozart winding up with a cadenza full of the lush harmonies and heavy texture of the late Romantic period.

Beethoven was the first to do away with the optional cadenza, in his last concerto, op. 73 (*Emperor Concerto), by including a written-out cadenza as an integral part of the first movement. His precedent was followed by nearly all the later composers of concertos (Schumann, Brahms, Tchaikovsky).

Caisse (cays: F.). Drum. *Caisse claire*, snare drum; *caisse roulante*, or *sourde*, tenor drum; *grosse caisse*, bass drum.

Calliope (cal-EYE-o-pee). An instrument, invented in America in the 1880's and named after the Muse of Eloquence, which consists of a number of steam-blown whistles played from a keyboard. It can be heard at a great distance and is still occasionally used at fairs, circuses, etc.

Calm Sea and Prosperous Voyage (G., *Meeresstille und glückliche Fahrt*). Orchestral overture by Mendelssohn (op. 27, 1828), based on two short poems by Goethe. The same pair of poems was also set by Beethoven as a cantata for chorus and orchestra (op. 112, 1815).

Calypso. A kind of extemporaneous singing which originated in the Caribbean islands, notably Haiti and Trinidad. Native Calypso singers compete in regular singing contests, where they are given general subjects, usually topical or political in nature, upon which they must extemporize rhymed lyrics, following a highly conventional melodic pattern. The singers employ a peculiar Anglo-French dialect which is sometimes comprehensible only to the natives.

Cambia, cambiano (CAHM-bi-a, cahm-BI-ah-no: It., it changes, they change). Direction in orchestral scores to change instruments or tuning (see under *Muta*).

Cambiata (cahm-bi-AH-ta: It.). See under *Nonharmonic tones,* 1.

Camera (CAH-me-ra: It., chamber). In Baroque music *da camera* indicates domestic music, as opposed to *da chiesa,* i.e., music for the church. For *sonata da camera* and *sonata da chiesa,* see under Sonata, II.

Camerata (cah-me-RAH-ta: It.). Name for a group of distinguished amateurs, writers, artists, and musicians who, shortly before 1600, gathered in the drawing room (*camera*) of Count Bardi at Florence, in order to discuss the possibilities of dramatic music in imitation of the ancient Greek tragedy. These discussions played an important role in the rise of *opera. See also *Nuove musiche.*

Campane (cahm-PAH-nay: It.). Bells; also orchestral chimes.

Campanella (cahm-pa-NEL-la: It.). (1) Title for compositions imitating the sound of bells, especially for Liszt's Transcendental Etude no. 3, based on a theme from the last movement of Paganini's Violin Concerto in B minor in which a bell is used. — (2) Glockenspiel (also *campanette*).

Cancan. A French dance of the last half of the 19th century which developed from the quadrille, introducing features of unrestrained gaiety and of vulgarity.

Cancel. See under *Accidentals*.

Cancrizans (KANG-kri-zanz: L., from *cancer*, crab). In crabwise motion, i.e., °retrograde.

Canon (Gr., law, rule). A contrapuntal device whereby an extended melody, stated in one part, is imitated strictly and for its entire length in one or more other parts. The canon is the strictest species of °imitative counterpoint. While imitation occurs sporadically in a fugue, it is continuously present in a canon. Any motive heard in the leading voice will appear in the imitating voice or voices (see Fig. 19). Various types of canon are distinguished according to the distance of the voice parts (one, two, etc. measures), the interval of imitation (canon of the unison, fifth, etc.), or special devices, as in the canon by augmentation, in which the imitating voice has the melody in doubled note values (see under *Augmentation*).

The earliest examples of canon are the famous °*Sumer is icumen in* (c. 1280) and the Italian °caccias of the 14th century. Several of the Masses on °*L'-homme armé* (15th century) include canons of this melody, and these are interesting as the earliest examples showing the application of canonic imitation to a pre-existing melody, rather than to one devised for this purpose. The most ingenious examples of this type are Bach's *Five Canonic Variations on the Christmas Song* ("Vom Himmel hoch"). The canon has frequently been used in 19th-century symphonies and sonatas, e.g., in Beethoven's Fifth Symphony, which closes with a triumphant canonic presentation of the main theme of the last movement. Similar examples occur in Brahms, Bruckner, Franck, and others. Yet another method of "prescribed" canon is the *canonic variation*, that is, the writing of a canon

Fig. 19

as a variation of a given theme. The most celebrated examples are the ten canons contained in Bach's °Goldberg Variations. The variations by Mozart, Beethoven, and Brahms often include one or two variations of this kind.

A special type of canon, often used for popular entertainment, is the *round. See also Catch.

Cantata. A composite form of vocal music, mainly of the Baroque period, consisting of a number of movements (four to six or more) such as arias, recitatives, duets, and choruses. The text may be either religious or secular. Owing to Bach's activity in this field, the church cantata is particularly well known. Originally, however, the cantata was a secular composition for solo voice and continuo (see Thorough bass) based on love lyrics, and it always retained this character in its native country, Italy, where it developed shortly after 1600 as one of the offspring of the *monodic style (opera, oratorio). Outstanding among the Italian masters of the cantata are Luigi Rossi (1597–1653), Giacomo Carissimi (1605–1674), and Alessandro Scarlatti (1660–1725), whose more than six hundred cantatas usually consist of two arias in contrasting character, each one preceded by a recitative. Similar cantatas, mostly for one singer (solo cantata), were written in France, e.g., by André Campra (1660–1744) and Jean-Philippe Rameau (1683–1764).

The German development of the cantata shows different traits, such as preference for the church cantata and the employment of more varied resources, e.g., choruses, orchestra, and several soloists. Outstanding among the predecessors of Bach are Franz Tunder (1614–1667) and Dietrich Buxtehude (1637–1707). Bach was one of the most prolific writers of cantatas, with about two-hundred sacred and about twenty-five secular works (approximately a hundred are lost). Most of his church cantatas date from the Leipzig period (1723–50) and follow a fairly uniform scheme, beginning with an extended chorus in fugal style, continuing with a number of recitatives and arias for several soloists, and closing with a *chorale (hymn) in four-part harmony. An example is Du Hirte Israel, höre (no. 104). There are also a number of solo cantatas, such as the Kreuzstab cantata (no. 56) for bass and orchestra, as well as *chorale cantatas, e.g., Christ lag in Todesbanden (no. 4). Among his secular cantatas are the *Peasant Cantata, the *Coffee Cantata, and Phoebus and Pan (see under Streit zwischen Phöbus und Pan).

Canticle, canticum. In the Roman and Anglican liturgies, a scriptural text similar to a Psalm but occurring outside of the Psalter of David. The most important ones are the canticle of the Virgin, *Magnificat anima mea Dominum (My soul doth magnify the Lord; Luke 1:46), and the canticle of Simeon, Nunc dimittis servum tuum (Lord, now lettest thou thy servant depart in peace; Luke 2:29).

Cantigas (cahn-TEE-gas). Spanish monophonic songs of the 13th century, mostly in honor of the Virgin, collected (and to a large extent probably written) by the king Alfonso the Wise who ruled from 1252–84. They are mostly in the form of the French *virelai.

Cantillation (can-til-LAY-shun). Chanting in plainsong style, especially with reference to the Jewish service.

Cantor. In the Roman Catholic and Jewish service, the solo singer. In the German Protestant Church, the director of the church music (e.g., Bach was often referred to as *Thomaskantor*, cantor of St. Thomas Church in Leipzig).

Cantus firmus (L., fixed song). A pre-existing melody which is made the basis of a polyphonic composition, contrapuntal voices being added to it. Prior to 1300 practically all polyphonic pieces (except for the *conductus) were cantus-firmus compositions, based on melodies taken from Gregorian chant (see *Organum; Clausula; Motet*). In the 15th century secular melodies were occasionally used as a cantus firmus for Masses, e.g., the *L'homme armé* tune. Most of the liturgical organ compositions (organ hymns, etc.) of the 16th century are based on Gregorian cantus firmi. In the Baroque period, the most important repertory of cantus-firmus compositions is that of the German Protestant *chorale preludes.

Canzona, canzone (cahn-TSO-na, cahn-TSO-nay: It.). (1) Designation for a lyrical song, particularly in Italian operas. — (2) An important type of instrumental music of the 16th and 17th centuries, which developed from the Franco-Flemish chansons of the early 16th century (see *Chanson,* 2). These were reprinted, without text, in Italy under the name of "canzona francese" and became the point of departure for the composition of new instrumental pieces, often called *canzone da sonare.* They are of a lively character and, in their fully developed form, consist of several sections of contrasting design, involving changes of meter, tempo, texture, etc. They were written for either a keyboard instrument (*organ canzona*) or an instrumental ensemble. In the 17th century these two types developed in different directions. In the organ canzona emphasis was placed on the fugal treatment, so that it finally became a lively fugue in three or more sections, all usually based on rhythmic variants of one and the same theme (*variation canzona*). As late as about 1720 Bach wrote such organ canzonas. In the ensemble canzona emphasis was placed on the element of contrast, the short sections being extended into larger parts, and finally into separate "movements." Thus the instrumental canzona led directly to the Baroque sonata of the late 17th century.

Canzonet (can-zo-NET: from It. *canzonetta*, little song). Short vocal pieces in a light vein, much in the character of a dance song, written by the English madrigalists about 1600.

Cappella. See *A cappella.*

Capriccio (cap-REET-cho: It., from *capra,* goat). (1) Title for a composition of a capricious or humorous character. — (2) In the 17th century, name for pieces in a lively fugal style and often involving some special trick, as, e.g., in Frescobaldi's *Capriccio sopra il cucu* in which the call of the woodcock is persistently used. Bach's *Capriccio sopra la lontananza del suo fratello dilettissimo* (c. 1705) is a free program piece picturing in a number of short movements "the departure of his beloved brother" Johann Jacob who went into military service.

Capriccio Espagnol (es-pahn-YOL). A symphonic suite, op. 34, by Rimski-Korsakov, composed in 1887. A masterpiece of brilliant orchestration, the work is in five sections: Alborada, Variations, Alborada, Scene and Gypsy Song, Fandango. Native dance rhythms and melodic figures evoke a Spanish atmosphere.

Capriccio Italien (ee-tal-YEN). A symphonic poem by Tchaikovsky, op. 45, written in 1880 while the composer was visiting in Italy. Italian folk songs provide most of the thematic material.

Capricorn Concerto. A concerto for small orchestra, op. 21, composed by Samuel Barber in 1944 and named for his house, "Capricorn," in Mt. Kisco, N. Y. The instruments are treated in the manner of the Baroque °concerto grosso with the flute, oboe, and trumpet set off both as a group and as individual soloists against the string orchestra.

Card Game, The. See *Jeu de cartes*.

Cardillac (CAR-dee-yak). Opera by Hindemith (libretto by F. Lion, based on E. T. A. Hoffmann's story *Das Fräulein von Scuderi*), produced in Dresden, 1926; extensively revised and produced in Zurich, 1952. Cardillac is a goldsmith who cannot bear to part with his creations, and commits heinous crimes to repossess them. The course of the opera deals with these crimes and with his final destruction. The music has an intricate rhythmic and contrapuntal texture, and makes notable use of choral passages with dramatic effectiveness.

Carillon (CAR-i-yon). (1) A set of bells placed in a tower and played by means of a keyboard or a mechanism. Carillons originated in the Low Countries (Belgium, the Netherlands) where they were known as early as the 15th century. In the 19th century they became popular in England and, more recently, in America. A modern carillon consists of 30 to 50 bells, tuned as a chromatic scale, whose clappers are connected by wires to long wooden keys which form a manual and a pedal keyboard. The manual keys are struck with the fist protected by a glove. Among the largest carillons are those at the University of Chicago Chapel and at the Riverside Church in New York. — (2) The orchestral glockenspiel.

Carmen. French opera in four acts by Bizet (libretto by Meilhac and Halévy, based on a novel by Mérimée), produced in Paris, 1875. The central figure is the gypsy girl Carmen (mezzo-soprano). A sergeant of the guard, Don José (tenor), deserts his regiment and joins Carmen in a band of smugglers. The fickle Carmen soon abandons him in favor of the bull-fighter, Escamillo (bass), to whom she promises herself on condition that he is victorious in a certain bullfight. In a jealous rage, Don José stabs Carmen just as Escamillo emerges triumphant from the arena. The lyric contrast to Carmen is furnished by Don José's former sweetheart Micaela (soprano).

To this dramatic and realistic plot Bizet has written music which, although in a "popular" vein, rises to greater heights of artistic accomplishment than hundreds of more ambitious and more "serious" operas. Although the music has been termed "pseudo-Spanish," *Carmen* represents to most people the essence of Spanish life and Spanish music (see *Flamenco*). It is interesting to note that the opera was only moderately successful at its first performance, and that one of its most popular selections, the °Habanera, is not by Bizet but was taken from a collection of Spanish songs by Yradier. (See *Seguidilla; Comic opera.*)

Carmina Burana (Songs of Beuren). A group of 13th-century Latin secular songs set for soloists, chorus, and orchestra by Carl Orff in 1937. The title refers to the Bavarian monastery of Benedictbeuren where the original manuscript was found. Performed either in concert form or as a "scenic cantata" with scenery and costumes, the work was incorporated by the composer into a three-part dramatic presentation called *Trionfi* in 1953.

Carnaval Romain (car-na-VAL ro-MAYNH: F.). See *Roman Carnival.*

Carnival (original title, *Carnaval*). A piano composition by Schumann, op. 9 (1834), consisting of twenty-one short pieces portraying various characters and scenes which might appear at a masked ball. Among them are Pierrot, Arlequin, Eusebius and Florestan (see *Davidsbündler Tänze*), Chiarina (Clara Wieck, later Schumann's wife), Chopin, and Paganini. It closes with a grandiose "March of the David-leaguers against the Philistines." The subtitle, "Scènes mignonnes sur quatre notes" (Little Scenes on Four Notes), refers to the use of four notes forming the word *Asch* (a town in Bohemia where a girl, a friend of Schumann's, lived), a word which, in German °pitch names, becomes A—E$\flat$(*Es*, facetiously for S)— C—B, or A$\flat$(*As*)—C—B.

These musical mottos appear as the opening notes of most of the pieces, the former in nos. 2 to 9, the latter in nos. 10 to 19 (in no. 2 in the left hand; in no. 5 ornamentally disguised; in no. 10 in the grace notes).

Carnival of the Animals, The (F., *Le Carnaval des animaux*). A "Grand Zoological Fantasy" for orchestra and two pianos by Saint-Saëns, composed in 1886. In a series of brief °character pieces entitled Introduction and Lions, Hens and Cocks, Horses, Tortoises, Elephants, Kangaroos,

Aquarium, Personages with Long Ears (Mules), Cuckoo in the Woods, Birds, Pianists, Fossils, The Swan, and Finale, the composer uses various instruments and sections of the orchestra in descriptive fashion. Best known from this work is the cello solo, "The Swan."

Carnival of Venice. An Italian popular melody of the 19th century which has been used by a number of composers (Paganini, Herz, Benedict) as a theme for variations.

Carol. An English traditional song of a joyful character (Easter carol, May carol), particularly one for Christmas (Christmas carol). The earliest existing examples date from the 15th century. Very likely the carols originally were dancing songs, a surmise suggested not only by the word (from F. *carole*, round dance) but also by the fact that all the old carols have a refrain.

Cassa (CAHS-sa: It.). Bass drum, also called *gran cassa*, or *cassa grande. Cassa rullante*, tenor drum.

Cassation (cas-SAY-shun). An instrumental form of the late 18th century, designed for outdoor performance by a small orchestra. It is very similar to the *divertimento. The name may be derived from It. *cassare*, to say farewell, or from L. *gassatim*, streetlike.

Casse-Noisette (cahs-nwah-ZET: F.). See *Nutcracker Suite.*

Castanets. A percussion instrument consisting of two shell-shaped pieces of hard wood, hinged together by a string which passes over the thumb and the first finger of the player's hand. They are used by Spanish dancers, usually in pairs, one in each hand. The castanets of the modern orchestra (e.g., in Bizet's *Carmen*) have springs and handles which facilitate playing, but which lack the finesse of true castanet playing.

Castrato (cahs-TRAH-to: It.). A male soprano or alto who has been castrated in order to preserve the youthful range and character of his voice. The operation was frequently practiced in Italy during the 17th and 18th centuries, and produced such famous castrati as F. Senesino (*c.* 1680–*c.* 1750), G. Caffarelli (1703–1783), and C. Farinelli (1750–1782). Their voices were greatly admired for their unusually wide range combined with great power and a peculiar, youthful tone color.

Catalog Aria. Famous aria in Mozart's opera *Don Giovanni* in which the servant Leporello gives an inventory of his master's numerous amorous adventures.

Catch. English *rounds of the 17th and 18th centuries. They were particularly in vogue during the reign of Charles II, and it was mainly in this period that they acquired their disreputable distinction, i.e., the indecent, often clearly obscene, nature of their texts. In modern editions (e.g., the Complete Works of Purcell) these texts are altered or replaced by others.

Catechism Chorales. See under *Clavierübung.*

Catgut. The tough chord used for the strings of violins, etc., actually made from the intestines of animals, especially of sheep (not, as its name would imply, of cats).

Cat's Fugue. Popular name of a fugue by Domenico Scarlatti (1685–1757), so called because the theme (Fig. 20) consists of wide and irregular skips in ascending motion, such as might have been (and possibly were) produced by a cat walking on the keyboard.

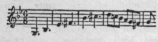

Fig. 20

Cavalleria rusticana (cahv-ahl-e-REE-a roos-ti-KAH-na: Rustic Chivalry). Opera in one act by Mascagni (libretto by Menasci and Tozzetti), produced in Rome, 1890. The setting is a Sicilian village on Easter morning. The young soldier Turiddu (tenor), lover of Santuzza (soprano), turns his attentions to his former love, Lola (mezzo-soprano), now married to Alfio (baritone). In a fit of jealousy, Santuzza tells Alfio of his wife's infidelity, and in the resulting duel between Alfio and Turiddu the latter is killed.

This opera, which was Mascagni's only success, owes its appeal to the concise and dramatic plot as well as to the realistic music. Widely welcomed as a relief from the numerous imitations of Wagner's heroic opera, it inaugurated the movement known as °*verismo* and was responsible for a mushroom crop of one-act operas.

Cavatina (cah-vah-TEE-na: It.). In 18th- and 19th-century operas or oratorios, a simple and short solo song, lacking the elaborate methods of form and style found in the aria. The term has also been applied to songlike pieces for instruments.

Cave of the Heart. See *Medea*.

C. b. *Col basso*, with the bass. Also, *contrabasso*.

C clef. See under *Clefs*.

C. d. *Colla destra*, with the right hand.

Celesta (che-LES-ta: It., heavenly). A percussion instrument, invented by Mustel in the 1880's, resembling in appearance a small upright pianoforte. The hammers act on steel bars and may be considered a °glockenspiel with a keyboard mechanism. The range is from middle C to the highest A of a piano keyboard. It produces delightful, clear, bell-like sounds. The celesta was first used by Tchaikovsky in the "Dance of the Sugar-Plum Fairy" of his *Nutcracker Suite* (1891).

Cello. (CHEL-o). The third-largest member of the violin family, with four strings tuned C G d a. The correct name of the instrument is *violoncello*, which literally means "little big-violin" (°*violone*, big violin; -*cello*, a diminutive suffix of the Italian language). The earliest preserved specimens are two instruments made by Andrea Amati between 1560 and 1570, the same period that violins and violas came into existence.

Cembalo (CHEM-bah-lo: short for *clavicembalo*). Italian and German name for the *harpsichord.

Cent. The unit for the scientific measurement of musical intervals. It is one hundredth of a half tone (semitone); thus the half tone equals 100 cents, and the octave contains 1200 cents. The tones of the chromatic scale (c, c♯, d, etc.) are represented by the numbers 0, 100, 200, etc., quarter tones by numbers such as 50, 150.

Ceremony of Carols, A. A setting for treble voices and harp of nine medieval English carols, composed by Benjamin Britten in 1942. A Latin plainsong processional and recessional enframe the carols which retain their Middle English texts.

C. f. *Cantus firmus.*

Chaconne and passacaglia (sha-KONH, pahs-sah-KAHL-ya). In Baroque music, chaconne (or passacaglia) denotes a composition consisting of continuous variations based on a short theme (four or eight measures) in rather slow triple meter. The theme is not a tune (as is usual in variations), but is essentially a succession of harmonies (often somewhat like a full *cadence, I-IV-I$\frac{6}{4}$-V) which is repeated many times with varied figurations, melodies, etc. A special class is formed by those compositions in which the theme consists of a recurrent melodic progression in the bass. These belong to the general category of *basso ostinato* or *ground bass. Although the Baroque composers used the names chaconne and passacaglia interchangeably, modern writers usually make a distinction, applying the term passacaglia to the more rigid type with an ostinato bass (as, e.g., in Bach's Passacaglia in C minor for organ), the term chaconne to the other type (e.g., Bach's Chaconne for violin solo). Fig. 21a shows a ground consisting of four descending notes which was used by numerous composers, frequently in a chromatic modification, as under Fig. 21b. A famous composition based on such a chromatic ostinato is the "Crucifixus" from Bach's B-minor Mass. Fig. 21c is a schematic presentation of a composition based on a recurring harmonic formula, without a fixed bass line (chaconne).

Fig. 21

Chair organ. Same as *choir organ.

Chamber music. Instrumental ensemble music in which there is one player for each part, as opposed to orchestral music in which there are many more players than parts. According to the number of players (or parts), chamber music is classified as follows: *trio* (three players), *quartet* (four), *quintet* (five), *sextet* (six), *septet* (seven), and *octet* (eight). If the ensemble consists of strings only, the composition is called a *string trio* (vl., vla., vlc.), *string quartet* (2 vl., vla., vlc.), or *string quintet* (2 vl., 2 vla., vlc.). If one of the strings is replaced by another instrument, names such as *horn trio* (horn, vl., vlc.) or *piano quartet* (pf., vl., vla., vlc.) are used. These terms apply to the instrumental groups just described as well as to the compositions written for them, e.g., String Quartet, op. 132, by Beethoven. The sonata for a solo instrument (e.g., violin or violoncello) accompanied by pianoforte is sometimes not considered chamber music because of the markedly soloistic character of the parts. In true chamber music, emphasis lies on the ensemble, not on the single player.

The ensembles described above emerged during the 18th century, and the present-day repertory of chamber music begins with the late string quartets of Haydn and Mozart. In these works were established the formal patterns to which practically all later composers of chamber music have adhered — the basic form is the °sonata in four movements. After Haydn and Mozart the most outstanding composers of chamber music are Beethoven, Schubert, Brahms, Bartok, and Hindemith.

Chamber music, in the widest sense of the word, has existed since the late Middle Ages. Until the Baroque period, however, such music was neither written for nor restricted to specific instruments, but was performed on whatever instruments were available, e.g., viols, recorders, and lutes. The chief type of Baroque chamber music is the °trio sonata in its two varieties, the *sonata da chiesa* and the *sonata da camera*.

Chamber opera. An opera of small dimensions and of an intimate character, accompanied by a small orchestra, e.g., Strauss's °*Ariadne auf Naxos*, Mozart's °*Bastien and Bastienne*, or Menotti's The °*Old Maid and the Thief*.

Chamber orchestra. A small orchestra of about twenty-five players, consisting mainly of a small string section and wood winds.

Chamber sonata. *Sonata da camera*. See under *Sonata*, II.

Chandos Anthems (CHAN-dos). Twelve anthems by Handel, composed 1716–18 for the Earl of Carnarvon, later Duke of Chandos, and performed at his palace. There also exists a Chandos Te Deum and a Chandos Jubilate.

Change ringing. The ringing of a set of bells by a group of men, one for each bell, and in a methodical order according to certain schemes of arithmetic permutation. For instance, a set of three bells, 1 2 3, may be played six ways without repetition: 1 2 3, 1 3 2, 2 3 1, 2 1 3, 3 1 2, 3 2 1. Standard combinations, consisting of a great number of "changes," are known under traditional names such as "Grandsire Triple," "Treble Bob," etc. Change ringing is still widely practiced in England.

Changing note. See under *Nonharmonic tones,* 1.

Chanson (shanh-SONH: F., song). (1) Generally, a song in the French language, e.g., the monophonic songs of the °troubadours and °trouvères (12–13th centuries), the instrumentally accompanied songs by Machaut, Dufay, Binchois (14–15th centuries; see *Ars nova; Burgundian School*), and the vocal chanson (for four or five voices) of the 16th century (Isaac, Josquin, Jannequin, Lassus), with which the early development came to its conclusion. Throughout the 17th, 18th, and the major part of the 19th century, French song continued only on a popular level, under names such as °vaudeville, pastourelle, °bergerette, and brunette. For the modern development, see under *Song.* — (2) Especially, the *polyphonic chanson* of the 16th century, written in the imitative style of the period (see under *Motet,* II), but often with a leaning toward homophonic texture, sectional treatment, repetition of sections, etc. A special type is the *program chanson* of Jannequin, based on picturesque texts such as "L'Alouette" (The Swallow) or "La Guerre" (The War) which provide opportunity for musical imitation of natural sounds.

Chant. General denomination for the various bodies of liturgi-

cal music, such as °Ambrosian, °Anglican, Byzantine, or °Gregorian chant.

Chanter. See under *Bagpipe.*

Chantey, chanty. See *Shanty.*

Character piece. A convenient denomination for a large repertory of short 19th-century compositions, mostly for pianoforte, designed to express a definite mood or character. They often carry titles suggesting smallness or casualness, e.g., *Bagatelle* (Beethoven), *Moment musical* (Schubert), *Impromptu* (Schubert, Chopin), *Fantasy Piece* (Schumann), *Intermezzo* (Brahms). With composers such as Beethoven, Schubert, and Brahms, they represent a by-product (by no means negligible) created in moments of relaxation from the more exacting task of composing sonatas, symphonies, etc. For other composers, however, the character piece became their most successful medium of expression, e.g., Schumann with his *Intermezzi, Scenes from Childhood, Fantasy Pieces,* Chopin with his *Nocturnes, Preludes, Etudes, Impromptus,* and Mendelssohn with his *Songs without Words* and *Children's Pieces.* Schumann also wrote large and demanding compositions consisting of a number of character pieces to be played in succession (character cycle), and representing a unified idea, e.g., in his °*Papillons,* °*Davidsbündler Tänze,* °*Kreisleriana,* and °*Carnival.* Many of the character pieces, particularly those of Chopin and Brahms, are in ternary form, A B A, with A and B representing contrasting moods.

Charles V. (G., *Karl V*). Opera by Křenek (to his own libretto), produced in Prague, 1938. The opera shows the emperor Charles V (1500–1556) on his deathbed, telling his father confessor the events of his life which appear as visions on the stage. The opera was supposed to have political significance, extolling the universalism of the Roman Catholic empire against the destructive forces of nationalism, materialism, and religious indifference. It is the first composition by Křenek which makes consistent use of the *twelve-tone technique.

Charleston. A kind of *fox trot, first popular about 1922–26, and probably named for the city in South Carolina. It was briefly revived about 1950–51.

Chasse, La (shas: F., the hunt). Name for pieces imitating the commotion of a hunt. See also *Hunt Quartet* (Haydn, Mozart); *Hunt Symphony* (Haydn).

Chasseur maudit, Le (shas-seur mo-DEE: The Accursed Huntsman). Symphonic poem by Franck (composed 1882), based on a ballad by Gottfried Bürger (1747–1794) entitled "Der wilde Jäger." It tells the legend of a huntsman who goes hunting on Sunday instead of going to church, and who is therefore bewitched and pursued by demons.

Cheminée du Roi René, La (she-mi-NAY dui rwah re-NAY: The Chimney of King René). A suite in seven movements for woodwind quintet by Darius Milhaud (1942). The title refers to a folk legend concerning a favorite sunning place of the 15th-century King René in the composer's native Aix-en-Provence.

Chest of viols. See under *Viol*.

Chest voice. See under *Register* (2).

Chevalet, au (o she-va-LAY: F., at the bridge). Same as *sul ponticello* (see under *Sul*).

Chiesa (kee-AY-za: It., church). See under *Camera*.

Childhood of Christ, The. See *Enfance du Christ*.

Children's Corner. A set of piano pieces (with English titles) by Debussy, composed 1906–08, including: 1. *Doctor Gradus ad Parnassum* (humorous allusion to Clementi's *Gradus ad Parnassum*); 2. *Jimbo's Lullaby;* 3. *Serenade for the Doll;* 4. *Snow is Dancing;* 5. *The Little Shepherd;* 6. *Golliwogg's Cakewalk*. They were written for Debussy's daughter, Claude-Emma, referred to as "Chou-chou" in the dedication.

Chimes. An orchestral percussion instrument, consisting of a set of about eighteen metal tubes, suspended from a metal frame and tuned chromatically from c' to about f". They are struck with a hammer, and are employed to produce the effect of bells, hence the alternative name, *tubular bells* (or *orchestral bells*). See under *Bells*.

Chinese block. A percussion instrument used in jazz bands, consisting of a hollowed-out wooden block. Played with a drumstick, it produces a dry, hollow sound. Sometimes called *temple block*.

Chinese crescent, Chinese pavilion. See *Crescent*.

Choir. A group of singers. Also used to denote groups of the orchestra, e.g., brass choir.

Choir Organ. Originally a small organ used for the accompaniment of the church choir. Today, the third manual of the °organ, which is designed for this purpose.

Chopsticks. A popular waltz tune played by generations of children. There is a collection of *Paraphrases* by Borodin, Cui, Liadov, Rimski-Korsakov, and Liszt.

Choral. (1, pronounced KO-rel) for a chorus or a choir. — (2, pronounced ko-RAHL) a church hymn, mainly of the German Protestant Church. In order to distinguish between these two different meanings, the spelling *chorale* for the second meaning is preferable and is adopted in this book. Hence: *choral* cantata, a cantata in which a chorus is employed (as opposed to a solo cantata); *chorale* cantata, a cantata based on a German Protestant hymn. Nearly all of Bach's cantatas are choral cantatas, but only some of these are chorale cantatas (e.g., *Christ lag in Todesbanden*). The German word *Choral* (ko-RAHL) always means chorale, i.e., church hymn, the other meaning being indicated by the term *Chor* (*Chorkantate, Choralkantate*).

Chorale (ko-RAHL). A hymn tune of the German Protestant Church. It was introduced into the service by Luther (1483–1546), who wrote the texts and probably also the melodies for some of the oldest and most beautiful chorales, e.g., *Vom Himmel hoch* (From Heaven high) and *Ein' feste Burg* (A mighty fortress).

Chorale cantata. A cantata in which the text (and, as a rule, also the melody) of a chorale is used for movements other than the final one, which is nearly always a harmonized chorale. The only chorale cantata by Bach in which the chorale tune appears in every movement is *Christ lag in Todesbanden*. Others make use of the chorale in some movements only, e.g., *Wachet auf* and *Ein' feste Burg*.

Chorale prelude. An organ composition based on a °chorale and designed to be played during the service, before the chorale is sung by the congregation. Outstanding among the numerous composers who contributed to this repertory are Samuel Scheidt (1587–1654), Dietrich Buxtehude (1637–1707), Johann Pachelbel (1653–1706) and, above all, J. S. Bach (1685–1750), who wrote c. 140 chorale preludes. Brahms revived the tradition in one of his latest works (*Eleven Chorale Preludes*, op. 122, 1896).

There are various traditional methods of treating the chorale melody, such as the *cantus-firmus chorale*, which has the melody in long notes (usually in the tenor or bass), accompanied by contrapuntal voices in quicker motion; the *chorale motet*, in which each line of the chorale is treated in fugal style; the *chorale fugue*, in which the first line only is treated in imitation, in the manner of a short fugue; the *melody chorale*, with the chorale in the upper part, accompanied by contrapuntal voice parts; the *ornamented chorale*, in which the chorale appears in the soprano with expressive ornamentating figures; the *chorale canon*, involving canonic presentation of the melody; the *chorale fantasy*, in which the chorale is presented in a free, improvisatory style; and the *chorale variations*, consisting of a number of variations on the melody. Bach arranged a number of his chorale preludes in collections; see *Clavierübung* III; *Orgelbüchlein*; *Schübler Chorales*; *Eighteen Great Preludes*.

Choral Symphony. The name commonly used for Beethoven's Ninth Symphony, in D minor, op. 125 (1823–24), which in the last movement uses a chorus (and four soloists) in addition to the orchestra. The formal plan of the symphony is: I. Allegro (sonata form); II. Scherzo with Trio; III. Adagio (A B A' B A" Coda — A' and A" are variations of A); IV. Introduction (with quotations of themes from the preceding movements), Allegro assai (with chorus on Schiller's *Ode to Joy*). In many respects this work may well be considered the culmination of Beethoven's symphonic writing.

Chords. A chord is the simultaneous sounding of three or more tones (two simultaneous tones are considered an °interval

rather than a chord). The most important chords, as shown in Fig. 22, with numerical identification in the key of C, are:

1. *Triad* (Fig. 22a) with its first and second inversions, the former (Fig. 22b) also called

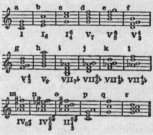

Fig. 22

sixth chord, the latter (Fig. 22c) *six-four chord*. See also *Triad*; *Harmonic analysis*.

2. *Seventh chord* (Fig. 22d) with three inversions (e, f, g). It occurs mostly on the fifth degree of the scale as the *dominant seventh chord*. The name "seventh chord" refers to the presence of the seventh added on top of the triad (1–3–5–7).

3. *Ninth chord*, so called because the ninth is sounded above the seventh chord (1–3–5–7–9). It usually occurs as a *dominant ninth chord* (h).

4. *Diminished seventh chord* and its three inversions (i to l).

5. *Augmented sixth chord*, in three varieties, sometimes (although rather pointlessly) distinguished as *Italian* (m), *German* (n), and *French* (o) *sixth chords*.

6. *Added-sixth chord*, so called because it consists of a triad with the sixth added (1–3–5–6); see (p).

7. *Fourth chord*, consisting of

two intervals of a fourth (1–4–7); see (q).

8. *Tone cluster,* consisting of intervals of a second (r).

The triad and its inversions are *consonant* chords, all the others are *dissonant*. The chords described under (4) and (5) above are *altered* chords, because they have chromatically altered notes.

During the 20th century the principle of constructing chords by superimposing intervals of a third (*tertian harmony) has been abandoned by some composers. As a result, chords may be composed of such intervals as fourths (see *Quartal harmony*) or seconds (often called "tone clusters").

Chordal style. A composition or a passage is said to be in chordal style if its texture consists essentially of a series of chords. In strict chordal style there is a given number of parts, usually four, as in a harmonized hymn tune (Fig. 23); in free chordal style there is no such restriction, and a chord of, e.g., six notes may follow a chord of three notes.

Fig. 23

Chordophones. See under *Instruments.*

Choreography. The designing and planning of a ballet, somewhat comparable to the writing of a libretto for an opera.

Chôros (CHOR-os). A type of Brazilian popular music. Villa-Lobos has applied the term to fourteen of his compositions (varying from a guitar solo to a choral symphonic poem) in which his objective is a synthesis of all elements of Brazilian music.

Christmas Concerto. Corelli's Concerto Grosso in G minor, op. 6, no. 8, entitled "Fatto per la Notte di Natale" (Made for Christmas Night). The closing movement is a *pastorale.

Christmas Oratorio. (1) Composition for chorus, orchestra, and solo voices by J. S. Bach (1734), consisting of six cantatas to be performed on six different days: the three days of Christmas, New Year, Sunday after New Year, and Epiphany. The title Oratorio, although given by Bach, is somewhat misleading because the work is not based on a continuous, narrative text. Today it is usually performed in two parts, each including three cantatas (either complete on two days or, shortened, in a single performance). Particularly famous is the Sinfonia at the beginning of the second part (fourth cantata), written in the style of a *pastorale. — (2) An oratorio by Schütz, composed 1664 (original title: *Historia der freuden- und gnaden-reichen Geburt Gottes . . .*), for chorus, solo voices, and various instrumental combinations in the different movements.

Christ on the Mount of Olives (G., *Christus am Ölberg*). See *Mount of Olives.*

Christ lag in Todesbanden (KRIST lahg in TO-des-bahn-den: Christ Lay in Death's Bonds). Bach's Cantata no. 4 (1724), based upon a chorale by Martin Luther (composed 1524).

Christus. Oratorio by Liszt to words from the Scriptures and from the Roman Catholic liturgy, composed 1855–66. Also, an unfinished oratorio by Mendelssohn.

Chromatic, chromaticism (from Gr. *chroma*, color). The use of raised or lowered notes, instead of the normal degrees of the scale, e.g., in C major: c-d-d♯-e or c-d♯-e, instead of the *diatonic progression c-d-e. The *chromatic scale* is the scale including all of these altered degrees in addition to the normal ones (Fig. 24). It consists of twelve tones, each a half tone higher (ascending) or lower (descending). *Chromatic harmony* is characterized by the extensive use of altered chords, such as the diminished seventh chord and the augmented sixth chord (see under *Chords*), as well as of *appoggiaturas, chromatic passing tones, etc.

Fig. 24

Chromaticism often serves to heighten the emotional tension of music. In Baroque music chromatic-scale formations were used to express lament or grief, as, e.g., the chromatic ostinato bass in the "Crucifixus" of Bach's B-minor Mass (see under *Chaconne*). Bach's *Chromatic Fantasy is, for its time, a highly advanced example of chromaticism, especially noteworthy for its use of parallel diminished seventh chords. While chromaticism is comparatively rare in the works of Haydn and Mozart, it was fully exploited by the Romantic composers — Chopin, Schumann, Liszt, Wagner, Tchaikovsky, and others. After 1900 chromaticism lost its former meaning as a "color-modification" of the diatonic scale, and became established as a new tonal realm based on the equivalence of the twelve tones of the chromatic scale. This concept is realized in Debussy's *whole-tone scale and, much more completely, in Schönberg's *twelve-tone technique. About 1925, there began a reaction against excessive chromaticism. It found its most conspicuous expression in the *pandiatonicism of Stravinsky.

Chromatic Fantasy and Fugue. A composition for harpsichord by J. S. Bach, which uses extended chromatic harmonies in the fantasy and a chromatic progression in the theme of the fugue. The fantasy is in the character of a free improvisation, alternating between brilliant passage work, quiet arpeggios, and highly expressive recitatives. It is a relatively early work of Bach, displaying an exuberant and subjective spirit absent in his later works.

Chromatic harp. See under *Harp.*

Church modes. A medieval system of scales, each consisting of the tones of the basic diatonic scale (white keys of the piano), but starting on D, E, F, G, and limited to the range of one octave. On each of these four notes (called tonic, final, *finalis*) there are two modes distinguished by the different position of the octave range (*ambitus*), and called respectively *authentic* and *plagal*. In the authentic modes the range extends from the tonic to the upper limit, particularly in the cadential endings of the authentic modes. Furthermore, each mode has a so-called *dominant* (indicated by ⌢ in Fig. 25), that is, a secondary center tone which is of importance mainly in the *psalm tones. The three systems of designation for the eight modes are as follows:

Mode I	First authentic	Dorian
Mode II	First plagal	Hypodorian
Mode III	Second authentic	Phrygian
Mode IV	Second plagal	Hypophrygian
Mode V	Third authentic	Lydian
Mode VI	Third plagal	Hypolydian
Mode VII	Fourth authentic	Mixolydian
Mode VIII	Fourth plagal	Hypomixolydian

octave (Fig. 25a); in the plagal modes, from the fourth below the tonic to the fifth above it (Fig. 25b). The octave range can be slightly enlarged by the addition of the *subtonium*, i.e., the tone (indicated in Fig. 25 in parentheses) below its lower

In the 16th century (Glareanus, *Dodecachordon*, 1547) the system was enlarged to include the modes on A (Aeolian, Hypoaeolian) and C (Ionian, Hypoionian), thus increasing the number to twelve. Fig. 25c shows the tonic, the dominant, the range, and the subtonium of each mode.

Some modern theorists have enlarged this system to fourteen modes by adding two modes on B (Locrian, Hypolocrian). These, however, are entirely fictitious since they would have a diminished fifth above the tonic (b-f'), resulting in an impractical scale of only theoretical interest. Equally irrelevant and without historical foundation is the designation of the four authentic modes as "Ambrosian" and the four plagal ones as "Gregorian."

The church modes became obsolete during the 17th century, being replaced by the two modern modes, major and minor. For their revival in recent music, see *Modality*.

Fig. 25

Church sonata. *Sonata da chiesa;* see under *Sonata.*

Cimbalom. See under *Dulcimer.*

Cinelli (chi-NEL-lee: It.). Cymbals.

Cinquepace (SIN-ke-pays: from F. *cinque pas,* five steps). Name used by Shakespeare and other Elizabethan dramatists for the *galliard, which has five steps. It also occurs under the names *sinkpace* or *sincopas.*

Circle of fifths. The arrangement of the twelve keys in ascending fifths (C, G, D, A, etc.) and on a circle showing that after twelve such steps the initial key is reached again. It presents the keys in their natural order, that is, increasing by one the number of sharps or flats in the signatures. The sharp keys appear to the right side, the flat keys to the left side of the "neutral" key, C. The transition from the sharp to the flat keys, made at one of the bottom points of the circle (e.g., C-sharp = D-flat) is called *enharmonic change. The circle for the minor keys starts with A at the origin point, continuing similarly in ascending fifths (A, E, B, F-sharp, etc.). In this arrangement a major and a minor key having the same signature (relative keys) appear at the same place on the diagram. See Fig. 26.

Circular canon. Same as *round.

Cis (G.) C-sharp. See under *Pitch names.*

Cl. Abbreviation for clarinet or, in chamber music, cello. Also for clavier.

Clair de lune (clayr de LUIN: Light of the Moon). A very popular piano piece by Debussy, properly the third movement of his *Suite Bergamasque.* Written in 1890, it belongs to his early period before he began to experiment with such characteristic devices of his later style as parallel chords, whole-tone scale, etc.

Claquebois (clak-e-bwah: F.). Xylophone.

Clarinet. A wood-wind instrument consisting of an end-blown cylindrical pipe made of wood or ebonite (recently also of metal), with a characteristic mouthpiece, called beak, which has a single reed fixed to its back. See illustration on p. 59. At a distance the clarinet is easily confused with the similar-looking *oboe from which, however, it is distinguished mainly by the mouthpiece and by its larger size. While the oboe produces a "pastoral," slightly quaint and nasal sound of a rather consistent quality, the clarinet is not only

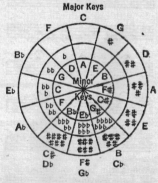

Circle of Fifths

Fig. 26

fuller and more "creamy" in timbre, but also shows a distinct variation of tone quality in its various ranges (registers).

The most common type is the *clarinet in Bb,* and next in importance is the *clarinet in A.* Both are notated as transposing instruments, with the written range shown in Fig. 27a, the sounding range of the Bb clarinet in Fig. 27b, and the sounding range of the A clarinet in Fig. 27c.

Fig. 27

The bass instrument of the clarinet family is the *bass clarinet,* whose range is an octave below that of the clarinet in Bb. Its lower end is curved upward in a metal bell, and the upper end, likewise of metal, is bent horizontally, thus bringing the mouthpiece within reach of the player's mouth. See illustration. Among the many other sizes and types of clarinets are the *alto clarinet in Eb* (sounding a fifth below the Bb clarinet) and the smaller instruments in D (Strauss, *Till Eulenspiegel*) and Eb (Berlioz, *Fantastic Symphony*). A member of the same family of instruments, the *basset horn,* is of special interest since it was used by Mozart (*Marriage of Figaro, Magic Flute,* etc.) as well as by recent composers, e.g., R. Strauss (*Salome, Electra*). It is a tenor size with an upturned bell, but without the bent mouthpiece of the bass clarinet. It is usually replaced today by the alto clarinet.

Clarin trumpet, clarino (clah-REEN, clah-REE-no). The natural (i.e., valveless) trumpet of the 17th and 18th centuries, an instrument pitched like the modern trumpet, but played by performers especially trained in the

Clarinet   *Bass clarinet*

art of producing the highest harmonics, from the third octave on, where they form a continuous scale (see under *Acoustics,* Fig. 2). This manner of playing, called *clarino,* enabled the trumpeters of Bach's day to perform those rapid passages (e.g., in the *Brandenburg Concerto* no. 2) which have baffled the most capable trumpet virtuosos of modern times. Today these passages are sometimes played on a specially constructed *Bach trumpet*, a short and straight instrument with three valves.

Classical, Classicism. In amateur parlance, "classical" music usually means everything outside the field of "popular" music. In musical terminology the term is used in a much more restricted sense; that is, it refers to the period represented by the Viennese Classics: Haydn, Mozart, the early works of Beethoven and, to some extent, Schubert. As opposed to the °Romantic style of the 19th century, Classical music is generally characterized by objectivity, emotional restraint, formalism, and simplicity. Since Haydn was born in 1732, and Beethoven and Schubert died in 1827 and 1828 respectively, the period extends from about 1750 to about 1820. It well deserves the name "classical" (properly, of high class or rank), because masterworks were produced at this time that to the present day have remained unsurpassed. Equally outstanding works have been created by other early masters, such as Bach and Palestrina, and the term "classical" is often applied to these composers as well. However, it is best to use the term not as a laudatory but as a strictly chronological one. See also *Neoclassicism*.

Classical Symphony. Prokofiev's First Symphony, op. 25, composed 1916–17, and so called because it is written in a "modernized" Mozart-Haydn idiom, with harmonic dissonances, unexpected rhythmic turns, etc. It is scored for a typical classical orchestra of strings and pairs of each wind instrument. The work is one of the earliest examples of 20th-century °Neoclassicism.

Clausula (CLAW-zoo-la). A form of early 13th-century music (see *Ars antiqua*), based on a short section of a Gregorian chant, usually a part of a gradual, alleluia, or responsory, to which one or two (rarely three) contrapuntal voices are added. The section is always one of the melismatic (vocalized) passages of the chant; therefore, a clausula has no full text, but carries only a word or a syllable, such as DO (from *Benedicamus DOmino*). The clausulae are of particular importance because they are the immediate ancestors of the medieval °motet.

Clavecin (CLAV-e-sanh: F.), **clavicembalo** (clav-i-CHEMbah-lo: It.). Harpsichord.

Claves (CLAHV-es). A Cuban percussion instrument consisting of two round sticks of hard wood (one held in each hand) which are beaten together.

Clavichord (CLAV-i-kord). The earliest type of stringed keyboard instrument. It originated in the 12th or 13th century, and was used commonly until the time of J. S. Bach and his son, C. P. E. Bach (d. 1788). It consists of an oblong wooden box, about four by two feet, with a keyboard of about three octaves, and with strings running parallel to the keyboard. The strings are made to vibrate by small T-shaped wedges made of brass, called *tangents*, which are fastened to the rear end of the pro-

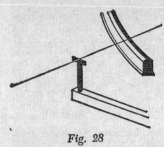

Fig. 28

longed keys and which strike the strings from below (see Fig. 28). The sound of the clavichord is very soft, ranging from pianissimo to piano, but of great delicacy and expressiveness. Unlike the harpsichord, it resembles the pianoforte in that gradations in volume can be obtained by modifying the touch. Certain compositions by Bach, e.g., the well-known C-major Prelude from the *Well-tempered Clavier* I, sound much better on the clavichord than on the harpsichord or the pianoforte. Bach's eldest son, Carl Philipp Emanuel, was particularly fond of the clavichord, and much of his keyboard music was written expressly for it.

Clavicymbal (clav-i-SIM-bal). Older English name (from *clavicembalo*) for the harpsichord.

Clavier (kla-VEER). Generic designation for the stringed keyboard instruments: harpsichord, clavichord, and pianoforte. In German usage of the Bach period the term also included the organ, as appears from Bach's *Clavierübung*. Later it denoted mainly the clavichord (C. P. E. Bach) and finally the pianoforte (19th century, usually spelled *Klavier*). In French the term means keyboard.

Clavier à lumières (clav-YAY ah luim-i-AYR: F., keyboard for light). A color organ (see *Color music*) prescribed in Scriabin's *Prometheus*.

Clavierübung (kla-VEER-ui-boong: G., keyboard practice). A collection of keyboard compositions, some for harpsichord, some for organ, by J. S. Bach, published in four parts: I (1731), Six *Partitas*; II (1735), *Italian Concerto and French Overture*; III (1739), chorale preludes (Catechism) preceded by the great Organ Prelude in E-flat and followed by the Fugue in E-flat (*St. Anne's Fugue*), also four Duets; IV (1742), the *Goldberg Variations*. The chorale preludes of Part III are partly related to the Lutheran catechism and partly to the Lutheran Mass; hence they are often referred to as *Catechism Chorales* or as *German Organ Mass*. Neither title, however, is wholly correct for the entire collection.

Clavilux. See under *Color music*.

Clefs. Signs written at the beginning of each staff which designate the pitches of the lines and spaces. There are three such signs, representing the tones g' (G clef), c' (C clef), and f (F clef). The G clef, also called *violin clef* (*treble clef*), is used on the second line of the staff and indicates that the note on that line is g' (Fig. 29a). The F clef, also called *bass clef*, is placed on the fourth line of the staff and indicates that the note on that line is f (Fig. 29b). The C clef is used in two positions, on the third line (*alto clef, viola* *clef*) or on the fourth line (*tenor clef*), and indicates re-

Fig. 29

spectively that the note on the third line (Fig. 29c) or that on the fourth line (Fig. 29d) is c'. The G clef is employed for the upper staff of piano music and for all high instruments (violin, flute, etc.); the bass clef for the lower staff of piano music and for low instruments (cello, double bass); the alto clef for the viola and other instruments of a similar range; the tenor clef for the high range of the cello, bassoon, etc. In choral compositions the tenor part is now often notated with a variation of the G clef (Fig. 29e) which indicates that the pitch is an octave below the normal one. In older scores (Bach, Handel) the soprano part is usually notated with the *soprano clef*, that is, a C clef placed on the lowest line of the staff.

Clemenza di Tito, La (cle-MENT-sa dee TEE-to: The Clemency of Titus). Opera by Mozart (libretto by Metastasio), produced in Prague in 1791, at the coronation of the Emperor Leopold II as King of Bohemia, for which occasion it was commissioned. While it contains much music fully worthy of Mozart's genius, it cannot compare with his master operas of the same period, *The Marriage of Figaro, Don Giovanni,* and *The Magic Flute.*

Cloches (closh: F.). Chimes.

Clock Symphony. Haydn's Symphony no. 101 (no. 11 of the *Salomon Symphonies), in D major, composed in London, 1794. The name refers to the steady pattern of the accompanying figure, which suggests the ticking of a clock, at the beginning of the slow movement.

Close harmony. See under *Position.*

C. o. Abbreviation for *coll' ottava,* i.e., playing the same notes at the upper octave. *C. o. b., coll' ottava bassa,* i.e., doubling at the lower octave.

Coda (It., tail). A concluding passage or section, falling outside the basic structure of a composition, and added in order to obtain or to heighten the impression of finality. Most compositions, even short ones, have a coda, a good example being Chopin's Nocturne in E-flat (see under *Binary form*). In the fully developed examples of *sonata form (first movements of sonatas, symphonies, etc., by Beethoven, Brahms, Bruckner) the coda often attains considerable proportions and importance, representing the final climax. In slow movements it often has the character of a pensive epilogue.

Codetta (It., little coda). Either a final coda of small dimension, or an intermediate coda, e.g., at the end of the exposition in sonata form.

Coffee Cantata. A secular cantata by Bach ("Schweigt stille, plaudert nicht," i.e., "Be quiet, don't prattle") for solo voices, chorus, and orchestra, composed *c.* 1732. It is a little dramatic scene between the father, Schlendrian, and his daughter, Lieschen, who, in spite of threat and persuasion, will not give up her beloved coffee until the father promises to get her a husband. In the end, however, she is going to have the coffee as well, declaring that there will be a clause to that effect in her marriage contract. The music conforms with this innocent jest to a degree hardly expected from the pen of Bach.

Col, coll', colla (It., with the). *Col arco,* with the bow (after *pizzicato*); *col basso,* with the bass; *col legno,* with the wood (indication to strike the violin strings with the stick of the bow); *coll' ottava* (abbreviated *c. o.*), play the same notes at the upper octave; *colla destra* (*sinistra*) with the right (left) hand (in piano playing); *colla parte, colla voce,* directions for the accompanist to follow the soloist in a passage to be performed in a free style.

Collegium musicum. A musical association, amateur in character and usually devoted to the revival of early music, which is usually connected with an institution of higher learning.

Color. See *Tone color.*

Coloratura (col-or-ah-TOO-rah: It.). In vocal compositions, the use of rapid scales, arpeggios, trills, and similar passage work of a virtuoso character. A coloratura soprano is a light soprano voice trained in the execution of such passages.

Color music. There have been various attempts to establish an association between the optical colors and music. One of these is the analogy of colors and tones of the scale (keys), externally supported by the fact that there are seven basic colors in the spectrum (rainbow) and seven basic tones (diatonic scale). Such associations are entirely subjective, as appears from a comparison of the schemes established by various interpreters. For instance, the keys of C, D, A, and F have been described by Rimski-Korsakov as white, yellow, rose, and green; by Scriabin as red, yellow, green, and red. In Arthur Bliss's *Colour Symphony* (1922) each movement represents a color.

Color organs are devices, operated from a keyboard, which project colors or optical patterns (circles, squares, spirals) on a screen, to accompany certain music, e.g., Scriabin's *Prometheus* (1910), Schönberg's *Die glückliche Hand* (1913). The *Clavilux,* built by T. Wilfrid in 1922, is designed for optical effects without music, or at least independent of it. It is used for "color recitals" in which colors or patterns are treated somewhat in the manner of a musical composition, with themes, motives, "allegro," "decrescendo," etc.

Combination tones. See *Resultant tones.*

Come (CO-may: It.). As, like. *Come prima* (as at first), *come sopra* (as above), indication that a passage should be played in the same manner as previously.

Comes (L.). See *Dux and Comes.*

Comic opera. An opera on a light or sentimental subject, with a happy ending, in which comedy usually plays a prominent part. The music is more "popular" in style than in serious opera, and the plot is apt to be taken from everyday life. Well-known examples are Mozart's *Così fan tutte* and *Abduction from the Seraglio*, Smetana's *Bartered Bride*, and the operettas of Gilbert and Sullivan.

As early as 1620, comic scenes were introduced into serious opera, one of the first instances being the light-hearted "Page duet" in Landi's *Il San Alessio* of 1632. An early example of a complete comic opera is *Chi soffre speri* by Mazzocchi and Marazzoli, produced in Rome in 1639. However, it was not until one hundred years later that comic opera became firmly established in Italy, under the name of *opera buffa*, owing to the tremendous success of Pergolesi's *La °Serva padrona* (1733) which, like some of its predecessors, was originally designed as an °intermezzo (see also under *War of the Buffoons*). Among Pergolesi's successors were Galuppi, Piccinni, Cimarosa, and finally Mozart. A characteristic peculiarity of the *opera buffa* is the use of spoken dialogue instead of the recitative of *opera seria*.

Parallel developments led to the French *opéra comique* (J. J. Rousseau, *Le Devin du village*, 1752; Grétry, *Richard Coeur-de-Lion*, 1784), the German *Singspiel* (Hiller, *Lisuart und Dariolette*, 1766; Dittersdorf, *Doktor und Apotheker*, 1786), and the English °ballad opera. The use of a spoken dialogue became so firmly established as an earmark of comic opera that even Bizet's serious and tragic °*Carmen* was designated as *opéra comique*, because it has spoken dialogue (the recitative used in modern performances is by E. Guiraut).

Common chord. The major (or minor) triad.

Common time. Designation sometimes used for 4/4 meter.

Communion. See under *Mass;* also *Service*.

Compass. The range of an instrument or voice, indicated by its lowest and highest notes.

Complement. See under *Interval*.

Compline. See under *Office*.

Compound interval. See under *Interval*.

Compound meter, time. See under *Meter*.

Compter (con-TAY: F.). Same as °*contano*.

Con (It.). With. *Con alcuna licenza*, with a little license or freedom, particularly in regard to tempo; *con brio*, with vigor; *con moto*, with motion, with animation; *con ottava, con 8va*, with the (higher) octave.

Concert. A performance of music, open to the public, usually by paid admission. Concerts in this sense are a fairly recent institution. In the earlier periods of music history, through the major part of the 18th century, musical performances took place mostly in the homes of noblemen, high dignitaries of the church, and wealthy people, or in closed circles such as Academies or Collegia Musica. The church was practically the only place where the majority of the people could hear well-prepared performances of good music. The first step toward public performance was made in opera, by the foundation of the *Teatro San Cassiano* in Venice, 1637. The first nonoperatic concerts were organized in London by the violinist John Banister (1672–78) and Thomas Britton (1678–1714). Later followed the Concerts of Ancient Music (1776–1848) and the Salomon Concerts (1791–95), for which Haydn wrote the °Salomon Symphonies. The earliest concerts in France were the *Concerts spirituels*, founded by Philidor in 1725; in Germany, the *Gewandhaus Conzerte* in Leipzig, founded by J. A. Hiller in 1781, which became internationally famous under Mendelssohn, Nikisch, Furtwängler, and Bruno Walter. In America the first concerts on record were held in Boston (1731), Charleston (1732), New York (1736), and Philadelphia (1757).

Concertant (conh-sayr-TAHNH: F.). The 18th-century name for symphonies (*Symphonie concertante*) with parts for several solo instruments, as, e.g., in Mozart's *Symphonie concertante* for violin, viola, and orchestra.

Concertgebouw (con-SAYRT-ghe-bow). Literally "concert hall" in Dutch, the word is most commonly known as the name of Holland's oldest and foremost orchestra. Subsidized by the state, the permanent home of the orchestra is the *Concertgebouw* in Amsterdam.

Concert grand. See under *Pianoforte*.

Concertina. See under *Accordion*.

Concertino (con-chayr-TEE-no: It., small concerto). (1) A short concerto, often in one movement. — (2) In Baroque music, the soloist group of the *concerto grosso* (see under *Concerto*).

Concertmaster. The first violinist of an orchestra; he sits closest to the conductor and occasionally substitutes for him.

Concerto (con-CHAYR-to). A composition for orchestra and a solo instrument, usually a pianoforte or violin. The form of a concerto is essentially that of the Classical sonata (see under *Sonata*, I) except for the following differences: (a) there are only three movements, the minuet or scherzo being omitted (Brahm's Piano Concerto, op. 83, is one of the few having a scherzo); (b) the first movement is in °sonata form, but with two expositions (instead of one exposition repeated) — the first for orchestra alone and in the tonic throughout, while the second is for orchestra-plus-soloist and modulates into the dominant; (c) the last movement is nearly always in °rondo form, while in sonatas, symphonies, string quartets, etc., it is often in sonata form; (d) the first movement includes an extended cadenza. The solo part of a concerto is usually written in a highly virtuosic style.

The history of the Classical and Romantic concerto starts

with Mozart, whose piano concertos include such masterworks as the D minor Concerto (K. 466; 1785), the A major Concerto (K. 488, 1786), and the *Coronation Concerto in D major (K. 537; 1788). Beethoven brought the Classical concerto to its culmination in his five piano concertos (see *Emperor Concerto*) and the Violin Concerto in D major, op. 61 (1806). Outstanding piano concertos of the Romantic period are those by Mendelssohn (G minor, op. 25, 1831; D minor, op. 40, 1837), Schumann (A minor, op. 54, 1841), and Brahms (D minor, op. 15, 1854; B-flat major, op. 83, 1881). Chopin's concertos (E minor, op. 11, 1830; F minor, op. 21, 1829) suffer from a scanty treatment of the orchestra. Other works often performed are Grieg's Concerto in A minor (op. 16, 1868), Tchaikovsky's in B-flat minor (op. 23, 1875), and Rachmaninoff's Second Concerto in C minor (op. 18, 1901).

The repertory of the violin concerto is smaller. The standard works are Beethoven's Concerto in D major, Mendelssohn's in E minor, several by Paganini, Brahms's in D major, Tchaikovsky's in D major, and Sibelius' in D minor.

Preceding the Classical concerto of Mozart is the Baroque concerto which flourished from about 1670 to 1750. Of particular importance in this period is the *concerto grosso*, a concerto employing a small group of soloists (the so-called *concertino*) against the full orchestra (*concerto, tutti, ripieno*). The concertino may consist of two violins, of violin and oboe, of violin and two flutes, or similar combinations, accompanied by the harpsichord and/or a small portion of the orchestra (see under *Ripieno*). Among the earliest concerti grossi are those by Corelli (probably composed *c.* 1680) and Torelli (*c.* 1690). Torelli created the standard form of the Baroque concerto in three movements, fast-slow-fast (the earlier concertos usually have four or five), and also wrote some of the first solo concertos, for one soloist only. Antonio Vivaldi introduced a novel style of rhythmic drive and brilliant precision, which was adopted by Bach in his *Brandenburg Concertos and by Handel in his eighteen organ concertos. The fast movements of the Baroque concerto are usually written in a free *ritornello form, in which an orchestral ritornello alternates with soloist episodes. The slow movement is usually in a continuous style (often in *binary form) with a soloist melody and an orchestral accompaniment.

Like so many other old forms and styles, the concerto grosso has attracted the interest of modern composers, in reaction against the excessive virtuosity and showiness of the late Romantic concerto (see *Neoclassical*). Compositions such as Bloch's Concerto Grosso for Strings and Pianoforte (1925), Hindemith's Konzert für Orchester (1925), Piston's Concerto for Orchestra (1933), Stravinsky's Dumbarton Oaks Concerto (1938), and Bartók's Concerto for Orchestra (1944) are generally modeled along the lines of the Baroque concerto, the emphasis being on inner musical vitality rather than on virtuoso display.

Concerto grosso. See under *Concerto.*

Concertstück (con-TSERT-shtuik: G., concert piece). Title for short pieces in the style of a concerto (orchestra with soloist), often in one movement or in short connected sections.

Concord. Practically the same as consonant chord (triad), emphasizing the aesthetic impression of "pleasantness" rather than the technical aspect.

Concord Sonata. The second of two piano sonatas by Charles Ives, composed 1909–15. Its complete title is "Concord, Mass., 1840–1860." Ives wrote that the sonata is "an attempt to present one person's impression of the spirit of transcendentalism that is associated in the minds of many with Concord, Mass., of over a half century ago," and he also provided a guide to the programmatic content of the four movements: *Emerson, Hawthorne, The Alcotts,* and *Thoreau.* Stylistically the sonata is representative of Ives's progressive techniques (extreme dissonance, complex rhythms, etc.) which mark him as a leading pioneer in 20th-century musical developments.

Concrete music. See under *Twentieth-century music.*

Conducting. The direction of an orchestra, chorus, opera, etc., by a leader (conductor) who employs motions of the hand and the body in order to bring about the coordination of all the players and singers. Its basic aspect is time beating, i.e., the clear indication of the metric pulse by motions of the right hand (usually with a baton), the main beats being marked by downward motions. Fig. 30 shows the basic diagrams of time beating. In addition, the conductor indicates the entrances of instruments or voices, as well as the shadings of dynamics, changes of mood, and numerous other details of performance. Modern conductors freely employ for these purposes suggestive motions of the hand, particularly the left, and of the whole body, as well as facial expressions.

Conductus (con-DOOK-tus). Latin songs of the 12th and 13th centuries, of varied forms and contents (religious, contemplative, lyrical, political, satirical), set to music monophonically or in two to four voice parts (see under *Ars antiqua*). They probably developed from songs accompanying the entrance of the priest (L. *conducere* means "to escort"), and were used for festive occasions of various kinds or for domestic performance. The polyphonic conductus are of spe-

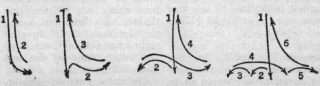

Fig. 30

cial interest because they are the earliest type of free composition, independent of Gregorian chant (see under *Cantus firmus*).

Conga. A Latin-American dancing song characterized by fast tempo in 4/4 time with a syncopated and accentuated fourth beat in each measure. The conga originated in Cuba and was introduced in the United States about 1940. It is usually accompanied by Latin-American rhythm instruments, e.g., maracas and claves, and by large tom-toms called conga drums.

Conjunct, disjunct. See under *Motion*.

Consecration of the House (G., *Weihe des Hauses*). Overture by Beethoven, op. 124 (1822), composed for the opening of the Josefstadt Theatre in Vienna.

Consecutive fifths, consecutive octaves. See *Parallel fifths, parallel octaves*.

Consequent. Antecedent and consequent (subject and answer). See under *Fugue*.

Conservatory. A school for music education. Originally, in Italy, a *conservatorio* was an orphanage where children were given general education and, particularly, musical instruction. The earliest institutions of this kind were founded in Naples (1537) and Venice.

Console. The desklike case that contains the playing mechanism (manuals, pedals, stops) of an organ.

Consonance and dissonance. Tones sounding simultaneously are said to be consonant or dissonant depending on whether they produce a pleasant or an unpleasant effect. Among intervals (the relation of two tones in regard to pitch), thirds, sixths, and octaves are generally felt to be consonant, while seconds and sevenths are dissonant. This explanation is rather unsatisfactory since it depends on the subjective impression of "pleasant" or "unpleasant." It is very difficult, however, to give an objective definition. Perhaps the most serviceable is the following: all the intervals existing between the tones of a triad in all of its inversions (c-e-g, e-g-c, g-c-e) are consonant, the others dissonant. This definition places not only the major and minor third (c-e, e-g) and the major and minor sixth (g-e', e-c') into the consonant category, but also the fifth (c-g) and the fourth (g-c') which technically must be considered as consonant intervals, although they are not necessarily "pleasant" to the ear, particularly of untrained listeners. It may also be noted that the ideas as to which intervals are consonant or dissonant have changed considerably during the history of music. Thus, in music of the 12th and 13th centuries the third and, especially, the sixth were considered dissonant, while in the so-called "Palestrina style" (late 16th century) the fourth is a dissonance. Among the combinations of three or more tones (chords), the major and minor triads are the only consonant ones.

Consonances provide stability and repose, while dissonances

produce tension and motion by "pulling" toward a resolution in a consonance. Prior to 1900, music was essentially consonant, with "disturbing" dissonances admixed to a smaller or larger degree. Developments in the 20th century, however, have led to the universal acceptance of dissonance for its own sake, with no functional relationship to consonance. In some contemporary music consonances are avoided completely. For those who are disturbed by this development, it may be reassuring to remember that enraged outcries of "unbearable dissonance" were raised, about 1850, against the music of Wagner and, about 1900, against that of Richard Strauss. Today many listeners have become completely adjusted to music which, twenty years ago, was generally felt to be ugly and incomprehensible.

Consul, The. Opera by Gian-Carlo Menotti (to his own libretto), produced in New York, 1950. The story details the tragic attempts of Magda Sorel (soprano) to obtain permission to join her husband, John (baritone), who has been forced to flee for political reasons. She and many others — a magician, an Italian woman, etc. — are hopelessly entangled in consular red tape, none of them ever succeeding in seeing the consul himself. In the course of her long wait, her baby son and her mother-in-law die. John, made imprudent by anxiety, returns and is caught by the police. Magda commits suicide. For the most part, dramatic considerations take precedence over musical ones, and the music is largely accompanied recitative with occasional arias and numerous ensembles and ballet scenes of considerable dramatic strength.

Contano (CON-tah-no: It., they count). Indication for players to count measures during a prolonged rest.

Contes d'Hoffmann, Les. See *Tales of Hoffman.*

Continuo (con-TEE-nwo: It.). Short for *basso continuo* (see *Thorough bass*).

Contrabass (CON-tra-bahs: G.), **contrabasso** (con-tra-BAHS-o: It.). Double bass (bass viol).

Contrabassoon. Same as double bassoon (see under *Oboe*).

Contrafagott (CON-tra-fag-OT: G.), **contrafagotto** (fag-OT-to: It.). Double bassoon.

Contralto. See under *Voices, Range of.*

Contrapuntal. In the style of *counterpoint.

Contrary motion. See under *Motion.*

Contratenor (CON-tra-TEN-er). In the 14th and 15th centuries, name for a third voice part, added to the basic two-voice texture of *superius* (descant) and *tenor*. It usually crosses the tenor, making frequent use of wide intervals (sevenths, octaves). During the last half of the 15th century, it was split into two separate parts, the *contratenor altus* and the *contratenor* *bassus*, the present-day alto and bass.

Contrebasse (conh-tre-BAHS: F.). Double bass (bass viol).

Contrebasson (conh-tre-bas-SONH: F.). Double bassoon.

Contredanse (conh-tre-DAHNS: F.). A French dance of the late 18th century, performed by two (or more) couples facing each other and executing a great variety of steps and motions. Probably it developed and took its name from the English °country dance. Beethoven wrote twelve Contredanses for orchestra (1802), one of which (no. 7) he used also in his ballet *Prometheus* (1801), in the so-called °Eroica Variations, op. 35 (1802), and in the last movement of the °Eroica Symphony (1804).

Convertible counterpoint. Same as °invertible counterpoint.

Coperto (co-PAYR-to: It.). Covered; used in *timpani coperti*, i.e., kettledrums muted by being covered with a cloth.

Coq d'or, Le (cok DAWR: The Golden Cockerel; original Russian, *Zolotoy Petushok*). Opera-ballet by Rimski-Korsakov (libretto by Bielsky, based on a fairy tale by Pushkin), produced in Moscow, 1909, one year after the composer's death. The story deals with the doddering King Dodon who depends on a golden cockerel, given him by his astrologer, for warning of imminent danger. When the cock signals alarm, the king discovers that his sons and their armies have been destroyed by the Queen of Shemakha, who, in a brilliant ballet, wins the king's heart. He wants to make her his bride, but the astrologer appears and, as a promised reward for the cockerel, demands the queen for himself. Dodon kills him and is in turn killed by the cockerel, who disappears with the intended bride in a moment of darkness. The people are left to bewail the death of their king.

The music is in the colorful style of most of the composer's works. A typical and well-known selection is the "Hymn to the Sun."

Cor (F.). Horn. *Cor à pistons*, valve horn, i.e., the modern (French) horn. *Cor anglais*, English horn.

Corda (It.), **corde** (F.). String. *Corda vuota, corde à jour* or *corde à vide*, open string.

Coriolan Overture (cor-i-o-LAHN). An orchestral composition by Beethoven (op. 62, 1807), written as an overture to a play by H. J. Collin, dealing with the same subject as Shakespeare's *Coriolanus*. It is one of the most concisely dramatic and masterful compositions of Beethoven, similar in spirit to the Fifth Symphony written two years earlier. See also under *Overture*.

Cornet. See *Brass instruments*, IIa.

Cornet-à-pistons (cor-NAYT-ah-pees-TONH: F.). Valve cornet, i.e., the modern orchestral cornet as opposed to valveless forms such as the bugle.

Cornetto (cor-NET-to: It., also *cornetta*). Cornet.

Corno (It.). Horn. *Corno a macchina* (*a pistoni, cromatico, ventile*), valve horn, i.e., the modern orchestral (French) horn. *Corno inglese*, English horn. *Corno di bassetto*, basset horn.

Coronach (COR-o-nakh: Gaelic, crying together). A funeral dirge of Scotland, sung by the bard on the death of a chief. Schubert wrote a *Coronach* for female chorus (op. 52, no. 4) based on a poem from Scott's *Lady of the Lake*.

Coronation Anthems. Four anthems by Handel, composed for the coronation of George II, in 1727: 1. "Zadok the Priest"; 2. "The King shall rejoice"; 3. "My heart is inditing"; 4. "Let thy hand be strengthened." Purcell also wrote a coronation anthem, "My heart is inditing," for the coronation of James II, in 1685.

Coronation Concerto. Mozart's Piano Concerto in D major (K. 537, 1788), so called because he played it (together with another concerto, K. 459) at the coronation of the Emperor Leopold at Frankfort in 1790.

Coronation Mass. Mozart's Mass in C major (K. 317, 1779), composed for the annual coronation of the statue of the Virgin at the shrine of Maria Plain, near Salzburg, Austria.

Corrente (It.). See under *Courante*.

Cortège (cor-TEZH: F.). A composition in the character of a solemn or triumphant procession.

Così fan tutte (co-ZEE fahn TOO-tay: Thus Do All [Women], or *La Scuola degli amanti* [The School of Lovers]). Comic opera in two acts by Mozart (libretto by da Ponte), produced in Vienna, 1790. The plot, set in 18th-century Naples, starts with a wager between the bachelor Don Alfonso (baritone) and two young officers, Ferrando (tenor) and Guglielmo (bass), to test the fidelity of their fiancées, Fiordiligi and Dorabella (sopranos). The officers, pretending to go on a trip, disguise themselves as rich Albanians and attempt to woo each other's sweetheart. The girls at first refuse them, but in the second act they give in and sign marriage contracts. At this moment the return of the officers is announced, whereupon the "Albanians" escape and reappear, undisguised, with the marriage contracts as evidence of the women's faithlessness. Finally, Alfonso, having won the bet, explains it all as a joke and reconciles the lovers. The maid, Despina (soprano), also plays the part of a doctor (when the "Albanians" take poison in order to convince the girls of their love) and of a notary (for the signing of the contracts).

Long neglected as an "inferior opera," *Così fan tutte* has recently been revived, and has proved itself highly attractive and amusing, no less a credit to

Mozart's genius than his great master operas.

Cotillion, cotilon. A 19th-century ballroom dance, consisting of a great number of figures and movements executed by a leading couple and imitated by all the others. Any suitable music (waltzes, mazurkas, polkas, etc.) was used. It usually formed the climax and close of an evening of dancing.

Council of Trent. A council of the Roman Catholic Church, held at Trent (Trento, in South Tyrol) in 1545–63, at which important decisions regarding church music were made, e.g., the abolishing of °tropes and of all but four °sequences. For a time, the abolishing of all polyphonic music was also considered, but this plan was not carried out. There is no truth in the story that Palestrina "saved church music" by performing his °Marcellus Mass at the Council.

Counter fugue. A fugue in which the answer is the inverted form of the theme, e.g., the fugues nos. 5, 6, and 7 of Bach's °Art of Fugue.

Counterpoint. Music consisting of two or more melodic lines sounding simultaneously. The term comes from the Latin *contrapunctus,* properly *punctus contra punctum,* meaning "note against note" or, by extension, "melody against melody." Counterpoint (contrapuntal) is practically synonymous with °polyphony (polyphonic), except for a difference of emphasis, the term polyphony being preferred

in connection with early music (medieval polyphony), the term counterpoint in connection with the 16th- to 18th-century period (Palestrina, Bach). The latter term is also used in the field of instruction as opposed to °harmony (see *Texture*). The simplest type of counterpoint is shown in Fig. 31a, with one note against each note of the given melody. Fig. 31b shows a more elaborate type of counterpoint.

cantus firmus

Fig. 31

Countersubject. In some fugues, a melody which is sounded as a counterpoint to the main subject each time that it appears after the initial statement. Examples are found in the fugues nos. 12, 14, and 17 of the *Well-tempered Clavier* I.

Country dance. A 17th- and 18th-century English dance in the character of a group dance, performed by men and women facing each other and moving in a great variety of intricate steps and gestures. The music consists of a number of gay tunes in phrases of eight measures, and the movements of the dancers change with every new phrase. The main source for the old country dances is Playford's *The English Dancing Master* (1651, reprinted 1933). Modern collections have been published by Cecil F. Sharp (*The Country Dance; Country Dance Tunes*). See *Contredanse*.

Coupler. See under *Organ*.

Courante (coo-RAHNHT: F., running). A French dance of the late 16th century which, in the 17th century, became one of the four standard movements of the *suite. Originally a very lively dance executed with running movements, it appears in the 17th century in two stylized varieties, the French *courante* and the Italian *corrente*. The courante is in moderate 6/4 or 3/2 meter, with frequent shifts from one to the other, that is, from the accents $\bar{1}$ 2 3 $\bar{4}$ 5 6 to $\bar{1}$ 2 $\bar{3}$ 4 $\bar{5}$ 6. The resulting instability of rhythm is a typical feature of the courante, as is also a subtle contrapuntal texture showing the two metric patterns in cross rhythm and with the melodic interest changing from the upper to the lower parts. The corrente is much faster, with continuous running figures and a chordal accompaniment. Most of the courantes in Bach's suites are of the French type. Especially remarkable for its rhythmic instability is that of the English Suite no. 2. The Italian type is found in the French Suites nos. 2, 4, 5, 6 and in the Partitas nos. 1, 3, 5, 6.

Crab canon (motion). See *Retrograde*.

Cracovienne. See *Krakowiak*.

Creation, The. An oratorio by Haydn, composed in 1797. It is based on a poem compiled by Lidley from Milton's *Paradise Lost,* which was suggested to Haydn by the concert-manager Salomon during his second stay in London (1794–95). Upon Haydn's return to Vienna the text was translated into German by his friend, the Baron von Swieten, and this translation (*Die Schöpfung*) became the basis of the oratorio, which was first performed in Vienna in 1798. Its fame soon spread everywhere, rivaling that of Handel's *Messiah*.

Creation Mass. Nickname of Haydn's Mass in B-flat (1801), so called because a theme from his oratorio, *The Creation,* is used in the "Qui tollis."

Creatures of Prometheus, The (G., *Die Geschöpfe des Prometheus*). Ballet by Beethoven (choreography by S. Vigano), produced in Vienna, 1801. It is remembered chiefly for its overture and for a theme in the finale which Beethoven used in three other compositions (see under *Eroica*).

Credo (L., I believe). The third item of the Ordinary of the *Mass.

Crescendo, decrescendo (cre-SHEN-do, day-cre-SHEN-do: It., growing, diminishing). The standard terms for increasing or decreasing loudness, abbreviated *cresc.* and *decresc.* (or *decr.*), or indicated by the signs $<$ and $>$. Another term for decrescendo is *diminuendo*.

Crescent, Turkish (also called Chinese crescent, Chinese pavilion, Jingling Johnny). A fanciful percussion instrument of Turkish origin (see *Janizary music*), consisting of a long pole with several crossbars, and frequently topped by a decoration in the shape of a crescent or a pavilion, all hung with numerous small bells and brass plates. It is shaken or pushed up and down while marching.

Croisez, croisement (crwah-zay, crwahz-mahnh: F.). Indication to cross the hands in piano playing.

Crook. A short piece of metal tube used formerly (rarely today) to change the tuning of a trumpet or a horn. It is inserted between the instrument and the mouthpiece. Before the invention of valves, it was generally used in order to obtain additional notes on the natural trumpet and horn.

Crooning. A style of singing popular ballads (soft and sentimental, with sliding and moaning effects) which was introduced about 1930 by American popular radio singers (e.g., Bing Crosby, Rudy Vallee).

Cross relation. A somewhat exceptional type of harmonic effect in which a tone and its chromatic alteration, for example, E and E-flat, appear successively in different voice parts (Fig. 32b, c), rather than in the same, as would be normal (Fig. 32a). In elementary counterpoint and harmony such progressions are considered inadmissible (as is implied in the alternative term, *false relation*), but examples are not infrequent in the works of great composers (Bach, Mozart, and others).

Cross rhythm. The simultaneous use of conflicting rhythmic patterns, e.g., two notes against three (triplets), or of conflicting accents, for example, 3/4 meter against 6/8 meter. See *Polyrhythm*.

Crotales (cro-TAL: F.). See under *Cymbals*.

Crotchet. See under *Notes*.

Crucifixus. A section of the "Credo" of the °Mass, often composed as a separate movement of sorrowful expression, as in Bach's B-minor Mass (see under *Chaconne and passacaglia*).

Crwth (crooth). A bowed string instrument of the ancient Celtic nations (see *Bard*), characterized by a rectangular body reminiscent of the ancient Greek °kithara. It was used in Wales as late as about 1820. See illustration.

C. s. Abbreviation for *colla sinistra* (with the left hand). See under *Col.*

Csárdás (CHAHR-dash). A Hungarian dance, usually consisting of a slow, rhapsodic introduction (*lassan* or *lassu*) followed by a rapid, wild dance (*friss* or *friska*). Liszt's Hun-

Fig. 32

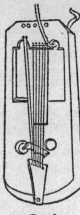

Crwth

garian Rhapsodies are written in this form.

Cue. In instrumental or vocal parts having a long rest, a short passage taken from another leading instrument or voice and printed in small notes, in order to warn the player of the entry of his part.

Cuivré (kwee-VRAY: F., brassy). In horn playing, indication for a loud, forced sound, as opposed to *bouché*, a soft, muted sound. Unfortunately, the two terms are often confused.

Cuivres (kweevr: F., copper). Brass instruments.

Cycle. In acoustics, term for the number of vibrations per second, for example, 440 cycles for a' (see *Acoustics*, 1).

Cycle of songs. See *Song cycle.*

Cyclic, cyclical. Symphonies, sonatas, etc., are said to be cyclic if some or all of the movements are internally related by the use of common thematic material. Cyclic treatment is most clearly indicated when the same initial theme recurs in every movement, with the necessary adjustments of rhythm and speed. The earliest example of this kind is Schubert's *Wanderer Fantasie, op. 15 (1822). Essentially the same method is used in Berlioz' *Fantastic Symphony (1830). In Schumann's Symphony no. 4, op. 120 (1841), all the movements are developed from ideas stated in the Introduction. Cyclic treatment was established as a principle of composition by César Franck and other French composers — d'Indy, Saint-Saëns, Fauré, Dukas. Statements to the effect that most of Beethoven's sonatas, etc., are cyclic should be accepted with great caution. A "germ motive" such as g-c'-d'-eb' is of such a general nature and is so frequent in many of his works that its presence in two movements of the Pathétique Sonata constitutes unconvincing evidence of this sonata's being conceived as a cyclic one. The cyclic principle as a deliberate means of unification was foreign to Beethoven except in those obvious cases where a movement shows the insertion (usually in the form of a reminiscence) of a short section from another movement as, e.g., in the Fifth Symphony (third movement quoted in the last movement), the Piano Sonata op. 101, and the Ninth Symphony.

Cymbals. A percussion instrument consisting of two large circular brass plates of equal size, with a strap attached at the middle of each plate, enabling the player to hold one in each hand. They are either clashed together, or a single cymbal is struck with a drum stick; occasionally it is struck with two sticks, in which case the cymbal is suspended. The cymbals have no definite pitch. There are, however, smaller cymbals of thicker metal which produce a fairly definite pitch, and these have been prescribed in French scores under the names *cymbales antiques* (Debussy) or *crotales* (Ravel, Stravinsky).

Czárdás. Incorrect spelling for °csárdás.

Czimbalom. Same as cimbalom (see under *Dulcimer*).

D

D. See under *Pitch names*.

Da capo (dah-KAH-po: It., *capo*, head). Indication (abbreviated D.C.) to repeat a composition from the beginning. *Da capo al fine*, to repeat from the beginning to the word *fine*. *Da capo al segno*, to repeat from the beginning to the sign :S:.

Da capo aria. See under *Aria*.

Dal segno. See under *Segno*.

Dame blanche, La (lah dahm blahnhsh: The White Lady). Opera by Boïeldieu (libretto by Scribe, after Scott's *Guy Mannering* and *The Monastery*), produced in Paris, 1825. The plot, laid in Scotland in 1759, deals with the imminent sale of a castle belonging to the unknown heir of the Count of Avenell, and guarded by the covetous Gaveston (bass). A young officer, George Brown (tenor), enters and meets a specter, the White Lady (soprano), who asks him to outbid all other bidders at the sale of the castle on the following morning. This he accomplishes after Gaveston has almost won the bidding. The White Lady is then revealed as being a young girl, Anna, who has safeguarded the old count's money, and George Brown as the young count and rightful heir who, of course, marries Anna.

Damnation de Faust, La (dahm-nah-SYONH de fost: The Damnation of Faust). Dramatic legend (cantata) for solo voices, chorus, and orchestra by Berlioz, op. 24 (1846), produced as an opera at Monte Carlo in 1893. Divided into four parts, it deals with the most important scenes from Goethe's *Faust I*. 1. Faust (tenor) wanders in the fields at sunrise, observing a crowd of dancing peasants and Hungarian troops approaching. 2. Faust in his study, ready to poison himself; appearance of Mephistopheles (baritone); scene in the wine cellar; Faust falling asleep in a garden and dreaming of Marguerite. 3. Faust and Mephistopheles concealed in Marguerite's room; Marguerite (soprano) enters; love scene between Faust and Marguerite interrupted by Mephistopheles who warns Faust of imminent danger and takes him away. 4. Marguerite, deserted, bewails her fate; Faust, back in his study, signs over his soul to Mephistopheles, who takes him on a wild ride through darkness and horror to his eternal damnation.

Some of the better-known numbers are *Rákóczi March, "Song of the Flea," "Dance of the Sylphes," "King of Thule," "Mock Serenade," and "Minuet of the Will-o'-the-wisps." The music is in the advanced harmonic and orchestral language that was already developed in Berlioz' early works. The cantata includes a number of ballet scenes, almost the only portions still performed frequently.

Damoiselle élue, La (F.). See *Blessed Damozel.*

Damper (F., *étouffoir;* G., *Dämpfer;* It., *sordino*). In pianofortes and harpsichords that part of the mechanism which terminates the vibration of the string — hence, the sound — at the moment when the key is released. The dampers of the pianoforte are small pieces of wood covered with felt which rest against the strings until removed by action of the keys or damper pedal mechanism (see *Pianoforte;* also *Mute*).

Damper pedal. See *Pianoforte;* also *Sordino.*

Dance music. It is very likely that music originated as a stimulus and accompaniment to dance movements. The dances of prehistoric men were ritual, serving to exert magic, to propitiate the gods, to heal illness, etc. The ancient Egyptians and Chinese (*c.* 1000 B.C.) had ceremonial dances of a highly stylized character, with strictly regulated movements of symbolic significance. In Greece, for the first time, the purpose of dancing became the expression of beauty and human feelings. In the early Christian era the Church strongly opposed dancing, although it was not able to suppress it.

The earliest extant examples of dance music date from the 13th and 14th centuries (see *Estampie*). The main dance of the 15th century was the *basse danse* of the Burgundian court. In the 16th century there appeared numerous dances, often in pairs, a slow walking dance being followed by a lively jumping dance in triple meter. The most important examples are the Spanish *pavane and *galliard and the Italian *passamezzo and *saltarello. They were superseded in the late 16th century by the *allemande, *courante, *sarabande, and *gigue, which became the standard movements of the 17th-century *suite. In the mid-17th century a great number of new dances, more refined and graceful in character, grew up at the court of Versailles in connection with the rise of the *ballet, e.g., the *anglaise, *bourrée, *gavotte, *minuet, *polonaise, *rigaudon. These were later incorporated into the suite as optional movements. The minuet is of special importance because it was the only dance that survived the decline of the suite (c. 1750) and was adopted into the sonata, symphony, string quartet, etc. A popular dance type of English origin was the *country dance. This is practically the only one of the early dances for which we have dance music in the literal sense of the word, as opposed to the more or less stylized and idealized music preserved in the dances of the ballets and suites.

Toward the end of the 18th century there appeared the *écossaise and the Austrian *Ländler which soon changed into the *waltz. The 19th century contributed, among others, the *polka, the *quadrille, and the *galop. Chopin brought the Polish *mazurka and *polonaise into prominence, and the rise of the national schools led to the cultivation of numerous other national dances, among them the Spanish *bolero and *fandango, the Cuban *habanera, the Argentine *tango, the Czech *dumka. In the early part of the 20th century America made its important contribution, *jazz, to dance music.

Danse macabre (dahns ma-CAHBR: F.). A symphonic poem by Saint-Saëns (op. 40, 1874) which depicts Death playing the violin and dancing in a graveyard at midnight. The gruesome effect is heightened by use of the plainsong *Dies Irae from the Requiem Mass.

Dante Sonata. A one-movement sonata (*Fantasia quasi sonata*) by Liszt, entitled "Après une lecture de Dante" and contained in vol. II of his *Années de pèlerinage* (1849).

Dante Symphony. A program symphony with choral ending by Liszt (1856) based on Dante's *Divina commedia*. It is in two movements, entitled "Inferno" (see also under *Dies Irae*) and "Purgatorio."

Daphnis and Chloë (DAF-nis and CLO-ay). Ballet by Ravel (choreography by M. Fokine), produced in Paris, 1912. It is based on a pastoral love story of Greek antiquity. Two suites from the ballet music, arranged by the composer, are played frequently in orchestral concerts.

Das. German for "the" (neuter singular). For titles beginning with *Das*, see entry under following word in the title.

Daughter of the Regiment, The (F., *La Fille du Régiment;* original It., *La Figlia del Regimento*). Opera in two acts by Donizetti (libretto by F. Bayard and J. H. Vernoy de Saint-Georges), produced in Paris, 1840. The central figure is Marie (soprano) who was found as a baby and "adopted" by Napoleon's 21st Regiment, with the old sergeant Sulpice (bass) as her special guardian. When the action begins in the Tyrol in 1815, Marie is a young woman and has fallen in love with a Tyrolean peasant, Tonio (tenor), who joins the regiment in order to be eligible to marry Marie. In the meanwhile, the Countess of Berkenfield (mezzo-soprano) claims Marie as her long-lost niece, takes her home to the castle, and arranges for her marriage to a nobleman. Lonely and despondent, Marie is ready to sign the marriage contract when the regiment arrives led by Tonio, now an officer. Marie declares that she will marry only Tonio, and the Countess, after revealing that she is actually Marie's mother, relents and gives her blessing.

Davidsbündler Tänze (dah-veets-BUIN-dler TENT-sa: Dances of the David-leaguers. Robert Schumann's cycle of eighteen *character pieces for piano, op. 6, composed in 1837. The title refers to an imaginary "League of David" frequently mentioned in Schumann's writings on music, to which he entrusted the task of fighting against the musical "Philistines" of his day, that is, against the mediocre drawingroom music which was then very much in vogue. Each piece is signed E. or F., letters which stand for the names Eusebius and Florestan. These are imaginary characters representing the pensive introvert and the impulsive extrovert side of Schumann's own personality. They also appear in his *Carnival together with a "March of the David-leaguers against the Philistines."

Db. Abbreviation for decibel (see *Bel*).

D. C. Abbreviation for *da capo.*

Death and the Maiden Quartet. Schubert's String Quartet no. 14 in D minor, composed 1826. The second movement consists of variations on his early song, "Death and the Maiden" (*Der Tod und das Mädchen*, 1817).

Death and Transfiguration (G., *Tod und Verklärung*). The second of R. Strauss's six famous tone poems, completed in 1889. The music depicts the fevered fantasies of an individual at the crisis of a fatal disease. The four sections are marked: I. Largo (Sleep, Illness, and Reverie); II. Allegro molto agitato (Fever and Struggle with Death); III. Meno mosso, ma sempre alla breve (Dreams, Childhood Memories, and Death); IV. Moderato (Transfiguration). The last portion of the work, by a gradual modification of one of the very agitated themes found in the earlier parts, suggests transfiguration.

Deceptive cadence. See under *Cadence.*

Decibel. See under *Bel.*

Decrescendo (It., decreasing). Abbreviated *decr.* or *decresc.* See under *Crescendo.*

Demisemiquaver. A thirty-second note. See under *Notes and rests.*

Der. German for "the" (masculine singular). For titles beginning with *Der*, see entry under the following word in the title.

Des (G.). D-flat. Also French and German genitive ("of the").

Descant. An old name for the highest voice in part music (soprano); hence, for high-pitched instruments (descant viol, descant recorder). In hymn singing, descant is a somewhat florid melody sung by a few sopranos as a decorative addition to the hymn (often wrongly called *fauxbourdon). See *Discant*.

Descriptive music. See *Program music; Word painting.*

Des Knaben Wunderhorn (G.). See *Youth's Magic Horn.*

Destro, destra (It.). Right (hand).

Détaché (F.). See *Bowing* (b).

Dettingen Te Deum. See under *Te Deum.*

Deutsche Tänze (DOY-che TENT-sa: G., German dances). See under *Ländler.*

Deutsches Requiem, Ein. See *German Requiem.*

Development. An important technique of composition consisting in the elaboration or working out of a theme or themes. This "unfolding" of thematic material is not in the nature of amplification and addition, but of fragmentation, modification, and combination of themes and motives. The technique occurs particularly in the *development section* of *sonata form. See also under *Motive.*

Devil's Trill Sonata. A violin sonata by Tartini, said to have been inspired by a dream in which the devil appeared to him. The long trill, from which its name derives, occurs in the last movement.

Diabelli Variations (dee-a-BEL-lee). Beethoven's op. 120 (1823) consisting of thirty-three variations on a waltz by Antonio

Diabelli (1781–1858), a Viennese publisher and amateur composer. Diabelli submitted his waltz to fifty-one composers (among them, Beethoven, Schubert, and Liszt, the latter then only eleven years old), asking each to contribute one variation to a collective work, which was published under the title *Vaterländischer Künstlerverein.* In a characteristic mood, Beethoven appropriated the theme for himself and wrote one of the greatest works in the field of variation.

Diabolus in musica (L., the devil in music). Old name for the *tritone which, in early music, was considered the most awkward melodic interval and therefore prohibited by theorists.

Diapente (deye-a-PEN-te: Gr., through five [steps]). Old name for the interval of the fifth. Hence, *canon in diapente,* canon at the upper fifth. The terms *diatessaron* (fourth), *epidiapente* (lower fifth), *epidiatessaron* (lower fourth) are used in a similar manner.

Diatessaron (deye-a-TESS-a-ron: Gr.). See under *Diapente.*

Diatonic (Gr., through the tones). Designation for the *major (also minor) scale as opposed to the chromatic *scale. Also applied to melodies and harmonies confined to the notes of these scales, to the exclusion of chromatic tones. For instance, in C major, c-d-e is diatonic; c-d-d#-e is chromatic.

Dichterliebe (DIKH-ter-LEE-ba: Poet's Love). A song cycle by Schumann, op. 48 (1840), consisting of sixteen songs to poems by Heine.

Dido and Aeneas. Opera by Purcell (libretto by Nahum Tate, after Virgil's poetic story), produced about 1689 at Josias Priest's boarding school for girls at Chelsea (London). It deals with the love of Dido (soprano), Queen of Carthage, and the Trojan prince Aeneas (baritone), who has come to her court after being shipwrecked. Their happiness is destroyed by a Witch (mezzo-soprano) who appears to Aeneas in the likeness of Jupiter's messenger Mercury (soprano or tenor), and commands him to return to Troy in order to restore the city from its ruins. Aeneas obeys and Dido, brokenhearted at his faithlessness, stabs herself.

The moving simplicity of the plot, together with Purcell's expressive music, make *Dido and Aeneas* a significant work of early opera, standing midway between Monteverdi and Gluck. Particularly famous is Dido's "Lament" before her death, a *chaconne based on a chromatic modification of the descending tetrachord, similar to the ground shown in Fig. 21b.

Die. German for "the" (plural or feminine singular). For titles beginning with *Die,* see entry under the following word in the title.

Dies Irae (L., day of wrath). A celebrated poem by Thomas Celano (died *c.* 1250) which is sung in the Roman Catholic Church at the Mass for the Dead (see *Requiem Mass; Sequence*). Its austere melody (Fig. 33a)

Fig. 33

has been used by several composers as a symbol of the horror attending death after a sinful life, e.g., in Berlioz' *Fantastic Symphony (Fig. 33b), in the "Inferno" movement of Liszt's *Dante Symphony, in Saint-Saëns' *Danse macabre,* and in Rachmaninoff's *Isle of the Dead.*

Dièse (dee-EZ: F.), **diesis** (dee-AY-sis: It.). Sharp; for example, fa-dièse is F-sharp.

Differential tones. See *Resultant tones.*

Diferencias (dif-er-EN-thi-as). Spanish 16th-century term for variations.

Diminished chords, diminished intervals. See under *Chords; Intervals.*

Diminuendo (dim-in-ew-EN-do: It., diminishing). Abbr. *dim.* or *dimin.* See under *Crescendo.*

Diminution. See *Augmentation and diminution.*

Di nuovo (dee NWO-vo: It.). Anew, once more.

Dis (G.). D-sharp (see under *Pitch names*). In older music (17th century) also E-flat. As late as 1805, Beethoven's

Eroica Symphony (in E-flat) was announced at the first performance as "in Dis."

Discant (from L. *discantus*, divergent song). (1) Originally, *discantus* meant music consisting of a "song" and a "divergent song," that is, polyphonic music in two (also three) parts, with all the parts proceeding according to the 13th-century principles of consonance and meter. The clausulae, motets, and conductus of the 13th century are in "discant style," as opposed to the "organal style," which is characterized by a metrically free upper part over a lower part in sustained notes (see *Organum*). — (2) See the various meanings of *descant*.

Discord. The opposite of °concord.

Disjoint, disjunct. See under *Motion*.

Disque (deesk: F.). Disc, record.

Dissonance. See *Consonance and dissonance*.

Dissonant (Dissonance) Quartet. Mozart's String Quartet no. 19 (K. 465) in C major, so called because of the unusual dissonances in the introduction to the first movement.

Distratto, Il (dees-TRAH-to: It., The Absent-Minded One). Nickname for Haydn's Symphony in C, no. 60. Hardly a symphony in the proper sense of the term, the six short movements were derived by Haydn from incidental music which he had composed in 1774 to a French comedy by Regnard (*Le Distrait*).

Divertimento (dee-vayr-tee-MEN-to: It.). An instrumental form of the period of Haydn and Mozart, which combines features of the sonata (symphony) with those of the suite. It consists of from four to ten short movements, some in the form and style of abstract sonata movements, interspersed with minuets or variations. Famous examples of this type are Mozart's *Eine* °*Kleine Nachtmusik* and *Ein Musikalischer Spass* (see under *Musical Joke*), Beethoven's Septet, op. 20, and Schubert's *Divertissement à l'Hongroise* (for piano, four hands).

Divertissement (dee-vayr-tees-MAHNH: F.). Same as °divertimento, also an operatic °potpourri.

Divisi (dee-VEE-zee: It.). In orchestral scores, *divisi* (abbr. *div.*) indicates that the players of a part (e.g., first violin) should be divided into two or more groups, each group playing a different part. See remark under *A due*.

Divisions. In English music of the 17th century, term for figuration or ornamentation such as results from the division of a note into smaller values. The term was also applied to improvised variations based on such figurations and played on a viol (*division viol*) or flute, to the accompaniment of a harpsichord.

Dixie. A song by Daniel D. Emmet (1815–1904), who wrote it in 1859 for his Negro minstrel shows. It was adopted, much against his intentions, by the Southern troops during the Civil War.

Djinns, Les (lay JIN: The Genii). Symphonic poem for piano and orchestra by Franck (1884), based on verses from Victor Hugo's poem, *Les Orientales*.

Do. See under *Pitch names; Solmization.*

Dodecaphonic (do-dek-a-FON-ik: from Gr. *dōdeka,* twelve). A term applied to *twelve-tone technique or compositions.

Dodecuple scale (from Gr. *dōdeka,* twelve). The chromatic scale in its modern interpretation, as used in the *twelve-tone technique.

Dolce (DOL-chay: It.). Sweet, soft; *dolcissimo,* very soft.

Domestic Symphony (*Symphonia Domestica*). A programmatic symphony (see *Program music*) by R. Strauss, op. 53, completed in 1904 and first heard in New York in the same year. It is an autobiographical work describing a husband, wife, and child. Structurally indistinguishable from a symphonic poem (tone poem), it is in one continuous movement divided into three sections: (a) Introduction and Scherzo: "Parents' Happiness — The Child at Play"; (b) Adagio: "Doing and Thinking — Love Scene — Dreams and Cares"; (c) Double Fugue and Finale: "Merry Argument — Happy Conclusion."

Dominant. The fifth degree of the scale (see *Scale degrees*), so called because of its "dominating" position in melody as well as in harmony. In the key of C, for example, the dominant is g and the dominant triad is the triad built on the fifth degree of the scale (g-b-d'). The dominant seventh chord adds a seventh degree to this triad (g-b-d'-f'). See *Chords; Cadence.*

Don Carlos. Opera by Verdi (libretto, in French, by F. J. Méry and C. DuLocle, after Schiller's drama), produced in Paris, 1867. The main characters are the 16th-century Spanish king, Philip II (bass), his son Don Carlos (tenor), the French princess Elizabeth of Valois (soprano), Carlos' friend Rodriguez, Marquis of Posa (baritone), and the Spanish Princess Eboli (mezzo-soprano). Don Carlos loves Elizabeth, but she is to marry his father for reasons of state. The marriage takes place and Carlos, still in love, goes to Flanders. Later he returns as the champion of the cause of Flemish freedom, and thus becomes also the political opponent of his father. Philip puts Carlos into prison and finally, on hearing (through the jealous Princess Eboli) of his secret meetings with Elizabeth, delivers him over to the Inquisition to be executed.

Don Giovanni (don jo-VAHN-ee). Opera in two acts by Mozart (libretto by da Ponte), produced in Prague, 1787. The action takes place in Seville during the 17th century and centers around the libertine of legendary fame, Don Giovanni (baritone), who is assisted in his amorous adventures by his servant Leporello (bass). Three women are involved in the plot: Donna Anna (soprano) — her father the Commandant (bass) is killed by Don Giovanni in the first scene — who, together with her betrothed, Don Ottavio (tenor), swears vengeance; Donna Elvira (soprano), the hero's deserted sweetheart who seeks to regain his love; and Zerlina (soprano), a pretty peasant girl about to be married to Masetto (bass). An especially dramatic touch is added to the action by the statue of the dead Commandant whom Giovanni mockingly invites to dinner and who, in the final scene, comes to deliver the unrepentant sinner to the demons of hell.

Don Giovanni is one of the greatest operas of all times. Particularly noteworthy are the overture, whose slow beginning anticipates the music accompanying the appearance of the statue in the final scene, the "Catalog Aria" by Leporello in which he relates to Donna Elvira the account of Don Giovanni's thousands of amorous adventures, Don Giovanni's "Deh vieni alla fenestra" (Come to the window), a serenade with mandolin accompaniment addressed to Zerlina, the "Ballroom Music" (end of Act I) which contains the famous minuet, and the "Dinner Music" near the end of the opera, with its quotations from Martin y Soler's °*Una cosa rara* and from Mozart's own *Figaro*.

Don Juan (Khwahn). (1) Symphonic poem by R. Strauss, op. 20 (1888), based on a dramatic poem by Lenau. — (2) For Mozart's opera, see *Don Giovanni*.

Don Pasquale (pas-KWAH-lay). Comic opera in three acts by Donizetti (libretto by the composer), produced in Paris, 1843. Don Pasquale (bass), an old bachelor, refuses to give permission for the marriage of his nephew, Ernesto (tenor), and the charming widow, Norina (soprano). His physician, Dr. Malatesta (baritone), proposes that Don Pasquale himself marry, and offers his "very beautiful sister" as the bride. Actually, the doctor is a friend of Ernesto, and has devised a scheme whereby the two young lovers may be married. Norina disguises herself as the "sister" and the marriage contract is signed. In order to force him into submission, she makes life so miserable for him that he is delighted upon discovering that he has been duped, and gladly gives permission for her marriage to Ernesto.

Don Quixote (kee-HO-tay). Symphonic poem by R. Strauss, op. 35 (1897), based on the famous novel of Cervantes, and composed in the form of an Introduction, Theme with Variations, and Finale. After the introduction, the variations proceed as follows: I. The Knight and his Squire (Sancho Panza) Start on Their Journey; II. The Victorious Battle against the Host of the Great Emperor Alifanfaron (actually a battle with a flock of sheep depicted by muted brass playing very dissonant harmonies); III. Colloquies of Knight and Squire; IV. The Adventure with the Penitents; V. The Knight's Vigil; VI. The Meeting with Dulcinea; VII. The Ride through the Air (during which a wind machine is used); VIII. The Journey in the

Enchanted Boat; IX. The Combat with Two Magicians; and X. The Defeat of Don Quixote. The finale depicts Don Quixote's death. In addition to the main "theme of a knightly character," there is a lyrical one portraying Don Quixote in love and a comic one for Sancho Panza. A notable feature is the employment throughout of a significant solo cello part.

Doppio movimento (DAWP-pyo mo-vee-MEN-to: It.). A direction indicating a speed exactly twice as fast as the preceding one.

Dorian. See under *Church modes; Greek music.*

Dorian Toccata and Fugue. A Toccata and Fugue in D minor by Bach for organ, written without the customary B-flat in the key signature, and thereby having the appearance of a composition in the Dorian mode. Actually, however, the accidentals for D minor are supplied throughout. The use of key signatures with one flat less than is used today (e.g., one flat for G minor, two flats for C minor) was a common practice in Bach's time.

Dot. A dot played above or below a note indicates °staccato. Placed after a note, it prolongs the note by one half of its value; see *Dotted note.*

Dotted note. A note having a dot at its right side, which adds to the note one half of its value. Thus, a dotted quarter note has the value of 1½ quarter notes or of 3 eighth notes. A double dot adds to the

note ½ plus ¼ of its value, resulting in a total of 1¾. Fig. 34a illustrates the use of dotted notes in duple meter. The rhythmic effect shown in (b) is called inverted dotting. It is also known as *Lombard rhythm* or *Scotch snap*, the latter name referring to its use in Scottish folksongs. In earlier music, for example, in Bach's time, dotted notes occasionally have to be played in a flexible manner, sometimes almost as double-dotted values (Fig. 34c), or as triplets (when they occur in conjunction with triplet figures, as in Fig. 34d).

Bach, Goldberg Variations, No. 16

Bach, French Suite No. 4, Courante

Fig. 34

Double (DOO-ble: F.). In the suites of Bach and other Baroque composers, name for an ornamented version of a dance movement, usually played immediately after the original version.

Double appoggiatura. See under *Nonharmonic tones.*

Double bass. The largest of the °stringed instruments, also known as *bass viol.* Both names are abbreviations of the original name, double-bass viol. This instrument has retained certain characteristics of the old °viols, especially the sloping shoulders at the top of the body (see illustration). Formerly equipped with three strings, it now usually

Double bass

has four strings tuned in fourths (E_1, A_1, D, G) to which occasionally a fifth string is added below, tuned to C_1. The music is notated an octave higher than it sounds.

Double bassoon. See under *Oboe.*

Double concerto. A concerto for two solo instruments, e.g., Bach's Concerto in D minor for two violins, or Mozart's for violin and viola (K. 364).

Double counterpoint. See under *Invertible counterpoint.*

Double dot. See under *Dotted note.*

Double flat. See under *Accidentals.*

Double fugue. A fugue based on two themes (I, II) which appear successively or simultaneously, one forming a counterpoint to the other. Bach's double fugues, such as the organ fugue in E-flat (*St. Anne's Fugue), usually consist of three sections: a fugue on I, a fugue on II, and a final fugue on I + II. A somewhat simpler scheme, including the sections I and I + II only, is found in the C-sharp minor fugue of the *Well-tempered Clavier* I. Fugues employing three or four themes in a similar manner are called *triple* or *quadruple fugues* (see *Art of Fugue*).

Double pedal. In organ playing, the simultaneous use of both feet for the rendering of two or more notes or parts.

Double pedal harp. See under *Harp.*

Double sharp. See under *Accidentals.*

Double stop. On violins, etc., the performance of two (also three or four) simultaneous notes, produced by stopping (and bowing) several strings at the same time.

Down-bow. See under *Bowing.*

Down beat. The downward motion of the conductor's baton, marking the first beat of the measure.

Dramma per musica (DRAHM-mah per MOO-zee-cah). Name for the earliest Italian operas, meaning musical drama. Bach used the term for some of his secular cantatas because they were designed for a modest stage performance.

Dream of Gerontius, The. An oratorio by Elgar, finished and first performed in 1900. The text is a poem by Cardinal Newman.

Dreigroschenoper, Die. See *Threepenny Opera*.

Drone. (1) The low-toned pipes of the *bagpipe used as accompaniment. — (2) In musical composition, a long sustained note, usually in the bass (drone bass); see *Pedal point*.

Drums. Percussion instruments having a skin stretched tightly over a frame or hollow vessel. They are among the oldest and most widespread of all instruments, existing in a great variety of shapes in all parts of the world. In the 12th century returning crusaders brought them from the Orient into Europe. The following types are used in the modern orchestra:

1. *Kettledrums* (*timpani*). These have a skin stretched over a hollow metal shell in the form of a half sphere. They are played by sticks consisting of a wooden handle and a globular head of felt or, for special purposes, of other material (leather, wood, sponge). They produce a sound of definite pitch which can be varied by means of screws placed around the rim or by a pedal attachment. At least two kettledrums are used in the orchestra, normally tuned to the tonic and dominant of the key of the composition. In modern compositions, change of tuning during a performance is frequently required. Twentieth-century composers often demand three or more kettledrums tuned according to specification. The kettledrums are important not only for rhythmic accentuation but also for special effects, such as extended drum rolls in increasing and decreasing loudness (thunderstorm scenes), etc.

2. *Snare drum*, also called *side drum* or *military drum*. This has a hollow cylindrical shell, with a skin stretched over either end. Catgut or metal strings, called snares, are stretched tightly over the lower skin and produce a rattling sound when the upper skin is struck by a pair of wooden drumsticks. This drum, as well as the ones subsequently listed, produces a sound of indefinite pitch.

3. *Tenor drum.* Similar in shape to the snare drum, but larger and deeper, and without snares.

4. *Bass drum.* Also of a similar shape and without snares, but very large and placed upright so that both skins can be played, one with each hand.

5. *Tambourine.* A shallow cylindrical frame covered with skin on one side, and with loose jingles (circular metal plates) affixed to the rim. It is struck by the hand or shaken. Not to be confused with the old *tambourin* (see *Tabor*).

Drum Mass. Nickname of Haydn's Mass in C major (1790), in which there is extended use of kettledrums.

Drum-Roll Symphony. Haydn's Symphony no. 103 in E-flat (*Salomon Symphonies no. 8), composed in 1795, so called because of the drum roll in the opening measure of the Introduction.

Drum-Stroke Symphony. See *Surprise Symphony*.

D. s. Abbreviation for *Dal *segno*.

Due corde (DOO-ay CAWR-day: It., two strings). In violin music, indication that for greater sonority the same tone should be sounded on two strings. In piano music, see under *Una corda*.

Duet. A composition, vocal or instrumental, in two parts or for two performers. Also called *duo*, *duetto*.

Dulcimer (DUL-si-mer). (1) A medieval stringed instrument having a flat soundboard, often triangular, with ten or more parallel strings which are struck by small hammers. It originated in the Middle Orient (Assyria, Persia), and appeared in Western Europe in the 12th century. Enlarged varieties are the *pantaleon*, constructed by Pantaleon Hebenstreit in the 18th century, and the Hungarian *cimbalom*. — (2) In early American usage, dulcimer designated homemade zithers plucked with the fingers.

Dulcitone (DUL-si-tone). A variety of the *celesta, with tuning forks instead of the steel bars.

Dumbarton Oaks. Concerto for fifteen instruments by Stravinsky (1938), written in the style of a modern concerto grosso. The name refers to the residence of R. W. Bliss near Washington, D. C.

Dumka (DOOM-ka: pl. *dumky*). A type of Slavic folk song, of a narrative character and with sudden changes from melancholy to exuberance. Dvořák's *Dumky Trio*, op. 90 (1891), consists of six movements each in the character of a dumka. He also wrote a *Dumka*, op. 35, and a *Furiant and Dumka*, op. 12, both for pianoforte.

Dump. An early type of English or Irish song, lamenting in character, although Shakespeare (*Romeo and Juliet*, IV, iv) mentions "merry dumps" as well as "doleful dumps."

Duo, duetto. Same as *duet.

Duodecuple. Same as dodecuple (see *Dodecuple scale*).

Duple meter (time). See under *Meter*.

Duplet. A group of two notes played in the place of three, hence the reverse of *triplet.

Dur (door: G.). Major key, for example, *Es dur*, E-flat major.

Dusk of the Gods, The. See under *Ring of the Nibelung*.

Dux and comes (L., leader and companion). Older terms for the leading and the imitating voice parts in fugues and canons.

Dynamic marks. Words or signs indicating degrees or changes of loudness, e.g., *piano, *forte, *crescendo, diminuendo.

Dynamism. A term sometimes used in reference to the style of Stravinsky about 1910. It is characterized by a large, brilliantly colorful orchestra, by strongly percussive rhythms in irregular metric patterns, and by harshly dissonant harmonies.

E

E. See under *Pitch names*.

Ear training. Elementary instruction designed to develop the sense of hearing as applied to music, e.g., recognition of pitch (absolute or relative), of intervals, chords, meter, rhythmic patterns, etc. See also under *Solfeggio*.

Ecclesiastical modes. Same as *Church modes*.

Échappée (F.). See under *Nonharmonic tones*.

Eclogue. Properly, a type of idyllic poetry by Vergil. Used as a title for compositions of an idyllic, pastoral character.

École d'Arcueil (ay-COL d'ahr-KEU-ee: School of Arcueil). A group of 20th-century French composers, organized in 1923 which included Henri Sauguet, Roger Désormière, Maxime Jacob, and Henri Cliquet-Pleyel. The name refers to the place of residence of Erik Satie, whom they considered their leader.

Écossaise (ay-co-SAYZ: F., Scottish [dance]). A dance which, in spite of its name, is not of Scottish origin, but belongs to the English country dances. It appeared about 1780 in England and France, and had a great vogue in the early 19th century.

Église (F.). See *Eclogue*.

Egmont. Incidental music, op. 84, composed by Beethoven in 1810 for Goethe's play. The overture is often played in concerts.

Eighteen Great Preludes. A group of eighteen chorale preludes by Bach, composed in the 1710's (Weimar period), but assembled and probably revised near the end of his life (autograph of *c*. 1748). It contains organ chorales of large dimensions and of varied treatment.

Eighteen-Twelve Overture. A festival overture by Tchaikovsky, op. 49, composed in 1882, in commemoration of the 70th anniversary of Napoleon's retreat from Moscow (1812).

Eight-foot. See under *Foot*.

Eighth note. See under *Notes and rests*.

Ein, eine. German for "a" or "an" (masculine, feminine). For titles beginning with *Ein* or *Eine*, see entry under the following word in the title.

Einleitung (EYEN-leye-toong: G.). Introduction.

Eisteddfod. See under *Bard*.

El Amor Brujo. See *Amor Brujo*.

Electra. Opera in one act by R. Strauss (libretto by Hofmannsthal, after Sophocles), produced in Dresden, 1909. The story takes place at the palace of Mycenae after the Trojan War. King Agamemnon has been murdered by his wife Clytemnestra (mezzo-soprano) and her lover Aegisthus (tenor). Electra (soprano), daughter of Agamemnon and Clytemnestra, desires revenge. She tries in vain to get help from her gentle sister Chrysothemis (soprano). Finally her brother Orestes (baritone), long believed dead, appears and kills the guilty pair with an axe, while Electra, rejoicing in the deed, dances herself to death.

To this story of hate and murder, Strauss has provided what is perhaps the most brutal and violent music ever written, an unrelenting piling up of intense orchestral effects from which there is only occasional relief, such as in the scene of recognition between Electra and Orestes.

Electrophonic (electronic) instruments. Instruments in which sounds are produced by electrical appliances such as vacuum tube oscillators, photoelectric cells, electromagnetic systems, etc. Perhaps the earliest of such instruments was the *Telharmonium*, invented early in the 20th century by Thaddeus Cahill. Among the instruments in current use are electronic organs (e.g. *Hammond organ), *Novachord, *Solovox, *Theremin, *Ondes musicales, *steel guitar.

Elegy. A plaintive poem; hence, a musical composition of a mournful character.

Elijah (Elias). Oratorio by Mendelssohn to words from the Old Testament, produced in the English version at the Birmingham Festival, 1846; in the German version at Hamburg, 1847.

Embellishment. Same as *ornament or ornamenting figure.

Embouchure ahm-boo-SHUIR: from F. *emboucher*, to put to the mouth; often misspelled *embrochure*). The position of the lips in the playing of wind instruments.

Emperor Concerto. Beethoven's Piano Concerto in E-flat, op. 73 (1809), the name suggested by the grandeur of the work. The first movement opens with an unusual improvisatory introduction played by the pianist and has a written-out *cadenza. Particularly noteworthy as a departure from traditional practice is a transitional passage linking the slow and the final movements.

Emperor Quartet. Haydn's String Quartet in C, op. 76, no. 3, so called because the slow movement consists of variations on the *Emperor's Hymn*, formerly the *national anthem of Austria, which was composed by Hadyn (as a four-part chorus) in 1797.

Encore (ahnh-CAWR: F., again). In public performance, the repetition of a piece, or an extra piece played in response to the applause of the audience. Another French term for this is *bis* (twice).

Enfance du Christ, L' (l'ahnh-fahnhs dui Kreest: The Childhood of Christ). Oratorio by Berlioz, op. 25 (1854), for solo voices, chorus, and orchestra.

Enfant et les sortilèges, L' (l'ahnh-fahnh ay lay sawr-tee-LEZH: The Child and the Sorceries; sometimes translated "The Bewitched Child"). Opera by Ravel (libretto by Colette) produced in Monte Carlo, 1925. The story is a fantasy which deals with a naughty boy who defaces the furnishings of his room and torments animals. The inanimate objects (chairs, clock, wallpaper, etc.) and the animals (squirrel, cats, etc.) turn on the child and repay his treatment in kind. Finally, as a result of the child's kindness to an injured squirrel, he is forgiven and peace is restored.

Enfant prodigue, L' (l'ahnh-fahnh prod-EEG: The Prodigal Son). (1) Cantata (lyric scene) by Debussy (libretto by E. Guinand), composed in 1884 for the *Prix de Rome;* produced as an opera in London, 1910. — (2) Ballet by Prokofiev, produced in Paris, 1929.

English flute. Old name for the *recorder, in distinction from the flute proper, then often called German flute.

English horn. See under *Oboe.*

English Suites. Six suites for the harpsichord by Bach composed in Köthen (1720?). Each opens with an extended prelude, often in the general style of the first movement of a concerto grosso. Possibly the name "English" (not applied by Bach) is explained by the fact that a manuscript in the possession of his son, Johann Christian Bach, had the rather mystifying inscription "fait pour les Anglais" (made for the English).

Enharmonic. (1) In ancient Greek music, a scale including quarter tones (see *Greek music*). — (2) In modern usage, the term refers to the two different "spellings" (enharmonic pairs) of one tone, for example, g♯ and a♭, c♯ and d♭, e♯ and f, etc. It is also applied to intervals and chords identical in sound, but written differently according to the context in which they appear (see Fig. 35a). Such ambivalent chords are frequently used for modulation, said to be effected by *enharmonic change* (see Fig. 35b, from Handel's *Samson*).

Fig. 35

While enharmonic tones are absolutely identical in pitch on pianofortes and organs, players of stringed instruments are aware that there is a minute difference between, for example, g♯ and a♭, the former being higher than the latter. In this respect it is interesting to note that in *just intonation the sharp variety is lower than the flat one. See also Circle of fifths.

Enigmatic canon. A *canon notated in a deliberately enigmatic manner, for instance, without indication as to where (or at what interval) the imitating voice should start.

Enigmatic scale. A curious scale, c-d♭-e-f♯-g♯-a♯-b-c', used by Verdi in his Ave Maria (1898).

Enigma (Variations). Theme with variations for orchestra by Elgar, op. 36 (1899), so called because each variation depicts one of his friends, who are enigmatically indicated by their initials or by a nickname. According to another explanation, the name refers to the presence of a "mysterious, unheard theme."

En Saga. See Saga, En.

Ensemble (F., together). (1) A group of performers. — (2) General name for concerted music, particularly in terms such as "good ensemble" or "bad ensemble," referring to the degree of unification and balance achieved in performance.

Entführung aus dem Serail, Die. See Abduction from the Seraglio.

Entr'acte (ahn-TRAHCT: F.). An instrumental piece or a dance performed between the acts of a play or an opera. See Interlude; Intermezzo.

Entry. The entering of the theme (first, second entry) in the different voice parts of a fugue.

Éolides, Les (lays ay-o-LEED: F., from Aeolus, god of the winds). Symphonic poem by Franck, composed in 1876. It is based on a poem by Leconte de Lisle, an evocation of the winds in Southern lands.

Epidiapente, epidiatessaron. See under Diapente.

Epilogue. Same as *coda (a concluding section or movement).

Episode. A secondary passage or section of a composition, forming a digression from the main theme. The term is used mainly in connection with the *fugue and sometimes with the *rondo, the latter sometimes being called episodic form. However, the latter term is also used for loosely constructed pieces consisting "only of episodes," such as the third movement of Franck's Violin Sonata.

Epistle sonata. A term associated chiefly with Mozart's seventeen brief sonatas for organ and strings (a few include wind instruments), to be used during the service following the reading from the Epistles during the Mass. They were all composed in Salzburg.

Equale (ay-KWAH-lay: It.). A composition for equal voices, i.e., all male or all female; also for equal instruments, e.g., Beethoven's three Equale for four trombones (1812) which, arranged for male chorus, were performed at his funeral.

Equal temperament. Name for the present-day system of tuning (especially pianofortes and organs), based on the division of the octave into twelve equal parts, each part representing a half tone. The great advantage of this system over earlier methods of tuning (see under *Temperament*) is that it makes playing in all keys possible. In the older systems it was possible to tune the simple keys (C, G, F, etc.) more correctly, but the keys with five or more sharps or flats could hardly be used.

Equal temperament is usually said to have been invented about 1690 by Andreas Werkmeister (1645–1706), and brought into practical use by Bach's *Well-tempered Clavier*. Actually, the theory behind it was known as early as the 16th century; on the other hand, it was not generally accepted until about 1800.

Equal voices. The term is used to designate compositions for voices of the same pitch level (e.g., alto voices only). See *Equale*.

Erl King, The. A celebrated song from Schubert's earliest period, composed in 1815 (at the age of 18) and published in 1821 as op. 1. It is set to Goethe's ballad, *Der Erlkönig*. Karl Loewe (1796–1869) also composed a musical setting of the poem.

Ernste Gesänge. See *Vier ernste Gesänge*.

Eroica (It., heroic). Beethoven's Third Symphony in E-flat, op. 55, composed in 1804. It was written in homage to Napoleon, but Beethoven withdrew the planned dedication when Napoleon assumed the title of Emperor, changing the title from "Sinfonia grande: Buonaparte" to "Sinfonia eroica composta per festeggiar il sovvenire d'un gran uomo" (Heroic Symphony Composed to Celebrate the Memory of a Great Man).

The programmatic idea suggested by the title and the original dedication is realized only in the most general way, except for the slow movement, called *Marcia funebre* (Funeral March), in which the dead of the Napoleonic wars (and, symbolically, the dead of all wars) are commemorated. The last movement is a series of free variations, also including fugal sections, all based on a dancelike (entirely unheroic) theme which Beethoven had used in three other compositions: in the ballet, *The *Creatures of Prometheus* (1801); in the *Contredanses* (1802); and in the *Eroica Variations* (1802). Extensive use is also made of the bass of this theme in the initial variations as well as in the fugal sections.

Eroica Variations. Variations for pianoforte by Beethoven, in E-flat major, op. 35 (1802), so called because the theme is the same as the one he employed later in the last movement of the *Eroica Symphony. Another name is *Prometheus Variations*, after the ballet, *The *Creatures of Prometheus*, in which the theme occurred for the first time.

Eroticon. A love song, or an instrumental piece portraying passionate love.

Erwartung (ayr-VAHR-toong: Expectation). A monodrama by Schönberg (text by Marie Pappenheim), completed in 1909. Lasting about half an hour, the opera has only one character, a woman (soprano) seeking, in a dimly moonlit forest, her lover who has been taken from her by another woman. She comes upon his corpse, but refuses to believe that he is dead, even in the broad daylight that finally floods the scene. This intense psychopathological drama is played out to an orchestral accompaniment in the near-atonal style which the composer had developed in that period.

Es (G.). E-flat (see *Pitch names*).

Esercizio (ez-ayr-CHEE-tsyo: It.). Exercise, etude. Also the original designation of D. Scarlatti's sonatas.

España. A rhapsody for orchestra by Emmanuel Chabrier, composed in 1883. The work is a rhapsodic treatment of several Spanish dance tunes, and is a sparkling portrayal of the festive native spirit.

Estampes (es-TAHNHP: F., engravings). A set of three piano pieces by Debussy (1903): "Pagodes" (Pagodas); "La Soirée dans Granade" (Evening in Granada); "Jardins sous la pluie" (Gardens in the Rain).

Estampie (es-tahnh-PEE). A dance type or form of the 12th to 14th centuries, known to us through one troubadour song, *Kalenda maya* (In the month of May), by Raimbaut de Vaquei-

ras (fl. 1180–1207), and through a considerable number of instrumental pieces, monophonic or in two parts. Common to all of them is a musical form consisting of a number (up to seven) of sections, each of which is repeated: a a, b b, c c, etc.

Estey organ. See under *Harmonium*.

Étouffé (ay-too-FAY: F.). Damped, muted; a direction to deaden the sound of instruments such as the harp and the kettle-drums.

Etude (AY-tood: from F. *étude*, study). A composition designed to aid the student of an instrument in the development of his technical ability. An etude is usually devoted entirely to one of the special problems of instrumental technique, such as scales, arpeggios, octaves, double stops (for violin), trills, etc. Important collections of etudes for the piano were written by Clementi, Czerny, Cramer, Moscheles, Heller, Bertini; for the violin by Kreutzer, Rode, Paganini, d'Alard, and Bériot. Apart from these stand the etudes by Chopin, designed not only for study but also for public performance, and combining technical difficulty with high artistic quality. Other etudes of the same type are those by Liszt, Scriabin, and Debussy.

Études symphoniques (F.). See *Symphonic Studies*.

Eugen Onegin (OY-gayn on-YAY-gin). Opera in three acts by Tchaikovsky (libretto by Shilovsky and Tchaikovsky after a poem by Pushkin), produced in Moscow, 1879. The main plot is the love of the young Tatiana (soprano) and Onegin (baritone). Tatiana declares her love by writing a letter, but Onegin politely refuses her. Six years later (Act III) she is married to the Prince Gremin (bass) and, although still in love with Onegin, firmly rejects the latter's ardent vows, asking him never to return. Another pair of lovers is Tatiana's lively sister, Olga (contralto), and Onegin's friend, Lensky (tenor), who is killed by Onegin in a duel.

Eunuch singer. See *Castrato*.

Euphonium. See *Brass instruments,* IId.

Eurhythmics. The coordination of simple, improvised bodily movements with musical rhythms as a means of self-expression. Most notable in the development of the theory and practice of eurhythmics in music education was Émile Jacques-Dalcroze (1865–1950). Schools which perpetuate his system are functioning in most metropolitan centers of Europe and America.

Euridice, L' (le-oo-ri-DEE-che: It.). Title of the two earliest (produced 1600) extant operas, one by Peri, the other by Caccini, both produced at Florence and based on the same libretto (by Rinuccini) which relates the story of Orpheus and Euridice (see *Orfeo*). The music consists almost entirely of recitative which, although not free from monotony, is remarkable for its austere expressiveness, particularly in the opera by Peri.

Evensong. Same as °Vespers.

Exposition. The initial presentation of thematic material, particularly in the °sonata form and in the °fugue.

Expression. Expression in musical performance may be said to be that part of music which cannot be indicated by notes, or, in its highest manifestation, by any sign or symbol whatever. It includes all the nuances of tempo, dynamics, phrasing, accent, touch, bowing, etc., by which the combination and succession of sounds is transformed into a vital communication. Compositions of the 19th century are generously provided with signs indicating such nuances, as well as with expression marks such as *dolce, cantabile, passionato,* etc., all indicating the general feeling and mood of the music. However detailed and subtle these indications are, they still leave ample room for individual interpretation. The ideal performer is the one who succeeds in bestowing upon the composition a personal and original expression within the stylistic idiom of the work and in full compliance with the composer's intentions. Interpreters of this stature are rare, since there is a general tendency to overemphasize the "personal" factor and to disregard the composer's intentions. Particularly the works of Bach (also Mozart) are often distorted by performing them with a multitude of nuances and subtle shadings, as if they were by Schumann or Chopin, for example. Early music requires self-subordination and reserve on the part of the performer rather than subjective interpretation. Expression marks in Bach's music are practically limited to a few instances of f, p, and pp. In view of the excessive amount of expression marks found in the modern editions of his works, it should be recognized that Bach's entire manuscript of the *Well-tempered Clavier* contains nothing but the notes and signs of ornamentation.

Expressionism. A term denoting a certain trend in music beginning during the second decade of the 20th century, particularly in Austria and Germany. Like the term *Impressionism, it was taken over from the graphic arts in which it designated a group of German painters (Nolde, Kirchner, Schmidt-Rotluff) who cultivated a style of vehement emotionalism and deeply probing self-expression, in reaction against the highly refined suggestiveness of the impressionistic school. Transforming "impressions gained from the outer world" to "expression of the inner self" found a reflection in music, leading (about 1910) from the sensuous and highly coloristic program music of Debussy to a deeply introspective and entirely nonprogrammatic type of music in which distorted melodies, discordant harmonies, *atonality, and disintegrated lines are used to convey a typically "expressionistic" expression of tortuous emotions and psychoanalytical complexes. The main representatives of the expressionistic school are Schönberg and his followers, Anton von Webern, Alban Berg, and Ernst Křenek.

F

F. (1) See *Pitch names.* — (2) Abbreviation for *forte* (*ff* for *fortissimo*). Also *F clef,* see under *Clefs. F holes,* see *Sound holes.*

Fa. See under *Pitch names; Solmization; Tonic Sol-fa.*

Faburden. See under *Fauxbourdon.*

Façade. An "entertainment" for reciter and chamber ensemble composed in 1922 by Walton. It consists of twenty-one poems by Dame Edith Sitwell which are recited in strict meter to instrumental accompaniment. A popular ballet of the same title has been produced using several selections without the reciter.

Fado, fadinho (FAH-do, fah-DEEN-o). The popular music of the cities of Portugal, frequently heard in the cafes and on the streets. It consists of song and dance to the accompaniment of a guitar.

Fagott (fa-GOT: G.), **fagotto** (fa-GOT-to: It.). Bassoon.

Fair at Sorochinsk. Unfinished opera by Moussorgsky, to his own libretto, based on a short story by Gogol. Revised and completed by several composers, it is occasionally performed in the version of Nicolas Tcherepnin.

Fair Maid of the Mill. See *Schöne Müllerin.*

Fa-la, fa-la-la. A special type of late 16th-century song (light madrigals) in which the syllables "fa la la" or similar ones are sung as a refrain. Numerous examples exist by Italian, English, and German composers (Gastoldi, Lasso, Morley, Weelkes, Hassler).

False. *False cadence,* same as deceptive *cadence. False fifth* (*triad*), old term for the diminished fifth (triad). *False relation,* see *Cross relation.*

Falsetto (fahl-SET-to: It.). An artificial method of singing used by male singers, particularly tenors, to obtain notes above the normal range of their voices. These tones, being nasal and somewhat weak, are little used today other than for comical effects. In early music prior to 1600, singers especially trained in falsetto were normally required for the high parts of Masses and motets. Today this use of falsetto survives only in some English glee clubs and church choirs (see *Alto*).

Falsobordone. See *Fauxbourdon.*

Falstaff. Opera in three acts by Verdi (libretto by Boito, after Shakespeare's *The Merry Wives of Windsor*) composed in 1893. The libretto relates, with slight alterations, the well-known episodes from Shakespeare's play. The "merry wives," Mistress Ford (Ford's wife, called Alice in the opera; soprano), Mistress Page (soprano), and Mistress Quickly (contralto) plot against Sir John Falstaff (baritone) and at the same time succeed in marrying Ford's daughter Anne (called Nanetta; soprano) to the young Fenton (tenor), instead of to Ford's protégé, Dr. Caius (tenor).

In every measure *Falstaff* displays a consummate craftsmanship (e.g., the final fugue, "Tutto nel mondo") and a lucid plasticity, such as only lifelong experience can produce. Together with the earlier *Otello* (1886), it represents the climax of Verdi's operatic work. Influenced by Wagner's music drama, Verdi largely abandoned in these two the "number style" of his earlier operas (see *Number opera*) and adopted a greater continuity of music and action. However, Wagner's symbolization and chromatic harmonies are conspicuously absent in *Falstaff.*

Familiar style. A style of vocal music in which all the voices move along simultaneously, in note values as well as in the underlaying of the text, normally with one note to each syllable. This style is regularly used in church hymns, but the term is applied chiefly to the purely chordal sections in the polyphonic Masses and motets of the 16th century.

Fanciulla del West, La. See *Girl of the Golden West*.

Fancy. An important type of English 17th-century instrumental music, chiefly for three, four, or five viols. The fancy derived from the Italian *fantasia* of the 16th century and, like this, was written in a contrapuntal and imitative style, with frequent change of themes, meter, or tempo, occasionally also with dancelike sections inserted. The free, improvisatory element of the modern *fantasy is completely absent. Purcell (1659-95) was the last composer of fancies.

Fandango (fan-DANG-go). A Spanish dance in fast triple time, danced by a couple to instrumental accompaniment including guitar and castanets, in alternation with sung couplets. The instruments play characteristic rhythmic patterns such as shown in Fig. 36a. An older type, current in the 18th century, was in slower tempo and lacked the exciting rhythms of the modern fandango. An example of this exists in a popular melody used by Gluck in his ballet *Don Juan* (1761) as well as by Mozart in his *Figaro* (1786; see Fig. 36b, the finale of Act III). Local

varieties of the fandango are the *Malagueña* (from Malaga), the *Granadina* (Granada), the *Murciana* (Murcia), and the *Rondeña* (Ronda).

Fanfare. A short tune or motive for trumpets, used as a signal for ceremonial, military, or similar purposes. Since they were originally played on natural instruments (see *Natural horn*), they consist normally of the tones of the triad. Fanfare motives have often been used effectively in art music, particularly in operas, e.g., in Beethoven's *Fidelio* (Act II, arrival of the Governor; also in the *Leonore Overture*) and in Wagner's *Tristan* (introduction to Act II, portraying the departure of King Mark with the hunting party).

Fantaisie (F.), **Fantasia** (It.), **Fantasie** (G.). See *Fantasy*.

Fantasiestücke (fahn-tah-ZEE-shtuik-a: G., fantasy pieces). An ambiguous title used by Schumann for several short compositions: op. 12 and op. 111 for piano, op. 73 for violin (or clarinet or cello) and piano, op. 88 for violin, cello, and piano. All belong to the general category of *character piece.

Fantastic Symphony (F., *Symphonie fantastique*). A program symphony, subtitled "Episode de la vie d'un artiste," by Berlioz, op. 14, composed in 1830. Temporarily disappointed in his suit for the Irish actress Henrietta Smithson, the 27-year-old Berlioz expressed his agonized feelings as the narcotic dreams of a young musician ending in the horrors of hell. The sym-

Fig. 36

phony has five movements: "Dreams and Passions," "A Ball," "Scenes in the Country," "March to the Scaffold," and "Dream of a Witches' Sabbath." The movements are unified by a recurring theme, called *idée fixe*, which, ingeniously modified, represents the beloved one in the various episodes of the dream (see under *Cyclic; Transformation of themes*). In the "Witches' Sabbath" the melody of *Dies Irae* is heard repeatedly as a grim foreboding of impending death.

The *Fantastic Symphony* holds an outstanding place in symphonic literature, not only because it established a new ideal of descriptive orchestral music, but also because of the vivid musical imagination pervading every page of the score, manifesting itself in a fascinating variety of ideas which, although often distinctly unpleasant and against the rules, are always inspired and colorful. In many of its aspects, particularly orchestration and harmonic language, it is decades ahead of the time it was written, which was only three years after Beethoven's death.

Fantasy. An instrumental composition in which "free flight of fancy" manifests itself in one way or another. The term covers a great variety of types: (1) Compositions suggesting free improvisation (Bach's Chromatic Fantasy; Mozart's Fantasy in D minor; Beethoven's Fantasy, op. 77); — (2) Romantic character pieces in rather strict form and style, but expressing a fanciful or dreamlike mood (Brahms' Fantasien, op. 116; Schumann's

Fantasiestücke; — (3) Sonatas in a freer form, or of a special character (Beethoven's *Moonlight* Sonata; Schumann's Fantasie, op. 17, a free, romantic sonata in three movements; — (4) Operatic potpourris of a free and somewhat improvisatory character (Liszt's Don Juan Fantasy). For the *fantasias* of the 16th to 17th centuries, see under *Fancy*.

Farandole (far-an-DOL: F.). A dance of Provence (southern France), performed by a long chain of men and women holding hands and following the leader through a variety of complicated motions, as in the *cotillion*. The music is usually in 6/8 meter, played on the *pipe* and tabor.

Farce (from L. *farcire*, to stuff). (1) Originally, a term for certain methods of interpolation ("stuffing"), particularly for inserting new texts between two words of a liturgical text. Today this is commonly referred to as *troping*. Hence, a farced Kyrie is the same as a troped Kyrie. — (2) In plays and operas, chiefly of the 18th century, farcing means the introduction of alien elements (e.g., popular songs, themes from other operas), usually of a humorous, comical, or even lascivious nature. This led to the present-day meaning of the word farce, i.e., a light and sometimes vulgar comedy.

Farewell Sonata. Beethoven's Sonata for pianoforte, op. 81a, in E-flat (1809), entitled *Les Adieux, l'absence, et le retour* (Farewell, Absence, and Return). It was inspired by the departure of the Archduke Rudolf from Vienna.

Farewell Symphony. Haydn's Symphony no. 45, in F-sharp minor, composed in 1772. The name refers to the last movement, the closing section of which is so designed that the players can leave one by one, the last measures being played by only two violins. This charming jest was meant to convey to the Prince of Esterhazy, whom Haydn served as a conductor, the desire of the orchestra to leave the summer palace in the country and return to Vienna.

Faschingsschwank aus Wien (FAHSH-ings-shvank ows veen: Carnival Prank from Vienna). A composition for piano by Schumann, op. 26 (1839), written as a result of a visit to Vienna during carnival time. It is in the general form of a suite in five movements: Allegro, Romanze, Scherzino, Intermezzo, and Finale.

Fasola (fah-so-lah). A 17th- and 18th-century American (and English) system of indicating the tones of the scale chiefly by the syllables fa, sol, and la (derived from the ancient system of *Solmization), as follows:

c   d   e   f   g   a   b   c'
fa sol   la fa sol   la   mi fa

In early American song books this system was used by placing the letters F, S, L, M on a staff,

fa sol   la fa sol   la   mi fa

Fig. 37

instead of notes. In 1802, William Little (*The Easy Instructor*) further clarified the meaning of the four syllables by using four different shapes of notes. These are known as *buckwheat notes, four-shape notes,* or simply *shape notes* (see Fig. 37).

Fate Symphony. Nickname sometimes applied to Beethoven's Symphony no. 5 in C minor, op. 67 (1807). It owes its origin to the story that Beethoven characterized the four opening notes by saying, "Thus knocks fate at the door." Expanding this idea, program annotators have seen the symphony as a musical representation of the struggle and final victory of Beethoven (or of mankind) over the adverse forces of fate. Among Beethoven's symphonies it is the finest realization of his incomparable powers of unfolding an idealistic drama in the most concise and convincing language. A remarkable aspect of the symphony is the unification of the scherzo and the last movement. The scherzo, after an ominous passage of slow kettledrum beats played *pp,* leads in a sudden crescendo directly into the triumphant finale; the same scherzo passage occurs once more within this finale, preparing in a similar manner the recapitulation of the triumphant theme. Also called *Victory Symphony.*

Faust. Opera by Gounod (libretto by Jules Barbier and Michel Carré, based on Goethe's poem), produced in Paris, 1859. The story deals with the love of the aged philosopher Faust (tenor) and the young Marguerite (soprano). Through a pact with the devil, Mephistopheles (bass), Faust regains his youth and succeeds in seducing Marguerite despite the efforts of her devoted admirer, Siebel (mezzo-soprano; sometimes sung by a tenor), to protect her from the dark powers of evil. Her brother Valentine (baritone) engages Faust in a duel to avenge her honor, but is killed by Faust who then deserts Marguerite to enjoy the revelries of the Walpurgis Night. In the final scene he comes to rescue her from the prison to which she has been committed after killing their child. Insane and uncomprehending, Marguerite repulses Faust and dies, being transported by angels into heavenly rest.

Faust Overture. An orchestral composition by Wagner (1840, revised 1855) suggested by Goethe's *Faust.*

Faust Symphony. A *program symphony by Liszt (1857, revised 1880), in three movements ("character pictures") representing (1) Faust, (2) Marguerite, and (3) Mephistopheles. It ends with a chorus in the nature of an apotheosis, set to the closing words of Goethe's drama, "Alles Vergängliche ist nur ein Gleichnis" (Everything transitory is only a simile).

Fauxbourdon (fo-boor-DAWNH: F.). Properly, an early 15th-century term (Dufay, Binchois) for music composed in two voice parts with a third voice part (not notated) following the melody of the upper part strictly at the interval of a fourth below. This results in a successsion of parallel

Fig. 38

sixth chords interspersed with open triads (Fig. 38a: Dufay). Today the term is used as a general denomination for progressions in parallel sixth chords, such as shown in Fig. 38b (Bach, Cantata *Ach wie flüchtig*). In the 16th century the terms *falso bordone* (It.) and *fabordone* (Sp.) were used for four-voice harmonizations of psalm tones, obviously because such harmonies were considered as a kind of three-voice fauxbourdon with a bass added.

In present-day English usage fauxbourdon (faburden) denotes what is correctly termed "descant," i.e., a somewhat florid high soprano part sung as an embellishment of a congregational hymn.

F clef. See under *Clefs.*

Feldmusik, Feldpartita (G., *feld,* field). A term used by Haydn and others for compositions similar to a divertimento, to be played in the open air by wind instruments or a military band.

Feminine cadence. See *Masculine and feminine cadence.*

Fermata (fayr-MAH-ta: It.). Pause.

Feste Romane (It.). See *Roman Festivals.*

Festivals (F., *Fêtes*). One of Debussy's three *Nocturnes for orchestra, this impressionistic tone poem was completed in 1898 and first performed in Paris in 1900. According to the composer, the music is designed to convey the vibrating, dancing rhythm of a festival with sudden flashes of light while a procession passes through and merges with the festive scene.

Fêtes. See *Festivals*.

Feuille d'album (feu-ye dal-BUIM: F.). Album leaf.

Ff. *Fortissimo*, very loud. Sometimes *fff* or *ffff* is used to indicate extreme loudness.

Fg. Abbreviation for *Fagott* (G.) or *fagotto* (It.) meaning bassoon.

F holes. See *Sound holes*.

Fiato (fee-AHT-o: It.). Breath. *Fiati* or *stromenti da fiato*, wind instruments.

Fiddle. Colloquial for violin and the like, particularly the American homemade varieties. Also used to designate the primitive ancestors, oriental or medieval, of the violin.

Fidelio (or *Die eheliche Liebe*, Conjugal Love). Opera by Beethoven (libretto by Sonnleithner and Treitschke), produced in Vienna, 1805 (revised 1806, 1814). The scene is 18th-century Spain in a prison near Seville where the nobleman Florestan (tenor) is held captive by the tyrannic warden Pizarro (baritone). Florestan's wife Leonore (soprano), disguised as a boy and using the name "Fidelio," enters the service of the jailer Rocco (bass) and, in the second act, helps him to dig a grave for Florestan whom Pizarro is determined to kill. He is delayed by Fidelio until trumpet calls are heard heralding the arrival of the minister of state Don Fernando (baritone), who frees Florestan and arrests Pizarro.

In spite of moments of great emotional tension (grave-digging scene, trumpet calls) the opera lacks, on the whole, that dramatic impact which Beethoven commanded in his symphonies and his other instrumental works. His note to Treitschke — "The whole business of opera is the most distressing thing in the world" — reveals his reactions to opera writing as well as the adverse circumstances that accompanied the production of *Fidelio*. See also *Leonora Overtures* and reference under *Melodrama*.

Fife. A small transverse flute with from six to eight finger holes and several keys, used in military bands.

Fifth. See under *Intervals*.

Fifth Symphony. For Beethoven's, see *Fate Symphony*.

Fifths Quartet. See *Quinten Quartet*.

Figaro, Figaro's Marriage. See *Marriage of Figaro*.

Figlia del Regimento, La. See *Daughter of the Regiment*.

Figured bass. A bass part provided with figures (numerals) which indicate harmonies. See *Thorough bass*.

Fille du Régiment, La. See *Daughter of the Regiment.*

Final, finalis (L.). See under *Church modes.*

Finale (fee-NAH-lay: It.). The last movement of a sonata, symphony, string quartet, concerto, etc. Also the last scene of an operatic act, if it is on an extended scale, including several numbers and involving some quick dramatic action.

Fin' al segno (It.). See under *Segno.*

Fine (FEE-nay: It.). End, close.

Fingal's Cave. See *Hebrides.*

Finger board. On stringed instruments, a long strip of black wood fixed to the neck, over which the strings are stretched and against which the strings are pressed by the fingers according to the sound desired.

Finger holes. On wood-wind instruments, the holes bored at different places in the side of the tube which, if covered or uncovered by means of the keys (formerly by the fingers), produce different tones.

Fingering. The methodical use of the fingers in the playing of instruments, and their indication by numbers 1 to 5. More than any other instrument, the pianoforte has a "natural system of fingering" owing to the conformity between the fingers and the keys. Three chief types of fingering may be distinguished: (1) normal fingering, where the hand and each finger stay in the same position, e.g.,

$$\begin{matrix} c & e & g & d & f \\ 1 & 3 & 5 & 2 & 4 \end{matrix}$$

$$\begin{matrix} e & c \\ 3 & 1 \end{matrix};$$ (2) contracted or expanded fingering, leading to shifted positions of the hand, e.g.,

$$\begin{matrix} g' & g & a \\ 5 & 1 & 3 \end{matrix}$$

$$\begin{matrix} b & c' & a & f & g & c \\ 4 & 5 & 4 & 2 & 3 & 1 \end{matrix};$$ and (3) passing fingering, when the thumb passes under the second, third, or fourth finger or any of these fingers passes over the thumb. This fingering is used particularly for scales, e.g.,

$$\begin{matrix} c & d & e & f & g \\ 1 & 2 & 3 & 1 & 2 \end{matrix}$$

$$\begin{matrix} a & b & c' & d' & e' & f' \\ 3 & 4 & 1 & 2 & 3 & 1 \end{matrix} \cdots$$ The basic fingering for all scales is a group of three fingers (1 2 3) alternating with one of four (1 2 3 4). However, in some scales extra fingers must be used at the beginning in order to avoid the thumb's falling on a black key. Thus the fingering for the B-flat major scale is 2 1 2 3 1 2 3 | 4 1 2 3 . . . , and that for C-sharp major is 2 3 1 2 3 4 1 | 2 3 1 2 . . . (the vertical line indicates the beginning of a new octave). For the principle of fingering on stringed instruments, see *Position.*

Finlandia. A symphonic poem by Sibelius, op. 26, which has become for most people the epitome of the Finnish character expressed in music. Composed in 1899, its melodies are in the character of Finnish folk songs, but were invented by the composer.

Fipple flute. Generic designation for instruments of the *recorder or *flageolet type. Fipple is an old name for the plug inserted at the mouth of these instruments.

Firebird, The (F., *L'Oiseau de feu*). Ballet by Stravinsky, produced by the Russian Ballet (Diaghilev and Fokine) in Paris in 1910. The story, taken from Russian legend, deals with Prince Ivan who captures the fabulous Firebird, from whom he receives a magic feather. Forest maidens (a Princess and her companions) warn the Prince that the wicked wizard Kastchey turns people to stone. Kastchey appears and is dazed in a frenzied dance led by the Firebird. The Prince finds the huge egg which contains the secret of the power of Kastchey and smashes it, whereupon Kastchey and his hordes disappear in a flash. The Prince marries the Princess.

The Firebird is an outstanding product of Stravinsky's early period when the composer was following the nationalistic tradition of his teacher, Rimski-Korsakov. Three versions of a suite taken from the ballet have been made by the composer. The first (1919) consisted of seven selections: Introduction and Dance of the Firebird, Adagio, Scherzo, Round Dance of the Princesses, Infernal Dance of King Kastchey, Berceuse, and Finale. The second version reduced the size of the orchestra and omitted the Adagio and Scherzo. In 1945, Stravinsky restored the two movements, retaining the smaller orchestra of the second version.

Fireworks. (1) A symphonic poem by Stravinsky, his first attempt at a large orchestral score, composed (1908) as a wedding gift for the daughter of his teacher, Rimski-Korsakov. The work shows clearly the mark of his apprenticeship under the Russian master. — (2) One of Debussy's twenty-four preludes (F., *Feux d'artifice*).

First-movement form. Same as *sonata form.

Fis (G.). F-sharp (see under *Pitch names*).

Five, The. Designation for a group of five Russian composers, Balakirev, Borodin, Cui, Moussorgsky, and Rimski-Korsakov, who were united (from the 1860's on) in the objective of establishing a truly national school of Russian music as distinguished from the more cosmopolitan style of Anton and Nicolas Rubinstein and Tchaikovsky. They are also known as "The Mighty Five" (*mogutchaya kutchka*, literally, "the mighty handful").

Five-part form. Term for formal schemes such as A B A B A or A B A C A. They are enlargements of the *ternary form, A B A.

Five-three chord. The triad, so called because, in figured bass, it is indicated by the figure $\frac{5}{3}$ (third and fifth to be sounded above the written root).

Fixed-do(h). See under *Solmization*.

Fl. Short for flute, *flauto, Flöte*.

Flageolet (flaj-o-LET). A small wind instrument similar to the *recorder (see also under *Fipple flute*), with four finger holes in front and two thumb holes on the under side.

Flageolet tones. A term (from French and German terminology, rarely used in English) for the *harmonics of the violin and other instruments.

Flam. A single stroke on the snare drum, as distinct from a roll.

Flamenco. The dance and dance music of the Spanish gypsies, characterized by fanciful and colorful costumes, alluring erotic movements, stamping of the feet (*zapateado*), clapping of the hands (*palmada*), the skillful use of the castanets, etc. The flamenco style is well represented in Bizet's *Carmen*. It is not, however, a typical example of genuine Spanish dancing, which is much less showy and provocative. The original meaning of the term flamenco is obscure.

Flat. See under *Accidentals.*

Flatterzunge (FLAHT-tertzoong-a: G.). Flutter *tonguing.

Flautando, flautato. In violin playing, the use of the bow near the finger board, producing tones of a flutelike character. The term is also used as an indication for the *harmonics.

Flauto (It.). Flute. *Flauto piccolo,* piccolo. In older scores (Bach, Handel) *flauto* always means the recorder, the flute being indicated as *flauto traverso* (transverse flute). Similarly, *flauto piccolo* is a small recorder, not the piccolo of the modern orchestra.

Fledermaus, Die (dee FLAY-der-mows: The Bat). Operetta by Johann Strauss, Jr. (libretto by Haffner and Genée, derived from a French farce, *Le Reveillon,* by Meilhac and Halévy), produced in Vienna, 1874. The action takes place in "gay Vienna" of the 1870's. The notary Falke (baritone) decides to play a joke on his friend, the Baron von Eisenstein (tenor) who, at a masked ball the previous year, had compelled him to wear his bat costume in broad daylight. Eisenstein is supposed to start a term in jail for a minor offense, but Falke persuades him to go instead to a splendid ball, which Eisenstein agrees to do without telling his wife Rosalinda (soprano). Falke also invites to the ball the warden of the jail, Frank (bass), the maid Adèle (mezzo-soprano), and Rosalinda who, disguised as a Hungarian countess, flirts with her husband. After a night of reveling, they all find themselves the next morning at the prison, along with the drunken jailer Frosch. Finally Falke arrives with the guests from the ball and explains the whole affair.

Flemish School. The leading school of the Renaissance following after the *Burgundian School (see also *History of music*), represented by a great number of composers born in Flanders (part of present-day Belgium) and northern France. The name *Netherlands Schools is sometimes used for both the Burgundian and the Flemish masters. Some of the most important Flemish composers are: Johannes Ockeghem (*c.* 1430–95); Jacob Obrecht (*c.* 1453–1505); Hendrik Isaac (*c.* 1450–1517); Josquin des Prez (*c.*

1450–1521); Adrian Willaert (c. 1480–1562); Nicolaus Gombert (c. 1490–c. 1560); Jacob Arcadelt (c. 1505–after 1557); Clemens non Papa (c. 1510–after 1557); Cypriano de Rore (1521-1603); Orlando di Lasso (1532-1594); Jan Pieterszoon Sweelinck (1562–1621). Most of them emigrated to other countries (Italy, Spain, Germany, France, England) where they held high positions in church choirs and princely chapels, and where, in the first half of the 16th century, they brought about the rise of various national schools. The second half of the 16th century presents an interesting picture of artistic rivalry between the Flemish teachers and their native pupils, e.g., Palestrina (Italy), Vittoria (Spain), Hassler (Germany), Byrd (England).

The great contribution of the Flemish masters was the establishment of a highly developed polyphonic style characterized by the (ideal) equivalence of all the voice parts and, beginning with Josquin, the consistent use of imitation. Their compositions are chiefly motets and Masses. To these were gradually added the various "national" types of secular music, the French chanson, the Italian madrigal, the German Lied, etc.

Flicorno (flee-COR-no: It.). An Italian instrument similar to the Flügelhorn (see Brass instruments, IIb).

Fliegende Holländer, Der (G.). See *Flying Dutchman*.

Flöte (FLEU-ta: G.). Flute, also called *Grosse Flöte* in dis-

tinction from *Kleine Flöte*, i.e., the piccolo.

Flötenuhr (G.). See under *Mechanical instruments*.

Flourish. In old English (Shakespeare), a trumpet call or fanfare. Nowadays, a decorative passage of a somewhat showy character.

Flue pipes (stops, work). See under *Organ*.

Flügel (G., wing). The grand pianoforte, so called because of its wing-shaped form.

Flügelhorn (G.). See *Brass instruments*, IIb.

Flute. A wood-wind instrument in the form of a straight pipe, held horizontally and played through a mouth hole located near one end of the pipe. Toward the other end there are a number of finger holes covered by keys according to the *Boehm system. The flute has a compass of three octaves, from c' (middle C) up. The lowest tones are thick and mellow, the higher ones becoming increasingly thin and bright. Because the instrument is capable of great agility, parts written for it often include rapid scales and numerous trills. Flutes were formerly made of wood, and are therefore still classified as wood winds, although they are now generally made of silver.

The *piccolo* (from It. *flauto piccolo*, i.e., small flute) is a small flute pitched an octave higher. In spite of its smallness, it is one of the brightest and most penetrating instruments of the orchestra. See illustrations.

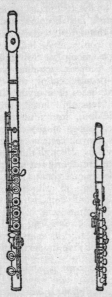

Flute   *Piccolo*

Flûte (fluit: F.). Flute. Prior to about 1750, *flûte* (also *flûte douce, flûte à bec,* i.e., beak flute) meant the recorder, the flute being called *flûte traversière* (transverse flute).

Flutter tonguing. See under *Tonguing.*

Flying Dutchman, The (G., Der Fliegende Holländer). Opera by Wagner, to his own libretto (based on Heine's *Memoiren des Herrn von Schnabelewopski*), produced in Dresden, 1843. The opera centers around the legendary Flying Dutchman (baritone) who is condemned to range the seas forever unless he can be redeemed by the love of a woman. Senta (soprano), daughter of the Norwegian sea-captain Daland (bass), deserts the young huntsman Erik (tenor) and follows the Flying Dutchman to death — and final salvation.

The Flying Dutchman, one of Wagner's early works, with its supernatural element approximates the Romantic opera established by Weber (*°Freischütz*) and Marschner. The musical style also is descended from these precursors, both in the long, flowing melodic line and in the rich and colorful orchestration. Such typically Wagnerian features as the use of leitmotivs, continuous recitative melody, and symphonic treatment of the orchestra had not yet been developed.

Folia, follia (fo-LEE-a: It.), **Folies d'Espagne** (faw-lee des PAHN-ye: F.). A famous melody of the 17th century which has been used by a great number of composers as a theme for continuous variations, similar in form and treatment to the *°chaconne and passacaglia.* Particularly well known are those by Corelli, published in 1700. Others are by M. Farinelli (for violin, 1649), d'Anglebert (for harpsichord, 1689), A. Scarlatti (for harpsichord, *c.* 1700), Liszt (*Rhapsodie Espagnole,* 1863), and Rachmaninoff (*Variations on a Theme by Corelli,* op. 42, 1932). The tune itself, without variations, appears in Bach's *°Peasant Cantata,* in Cherubini's opera *L'Hôtellerie Portugaise,* and in several other operas. The name *folia* (i.e., folly) suggests a connection with the ancient tradition of the Fool's Dance.

Folk song. A folk song may be defined as a song of some an-

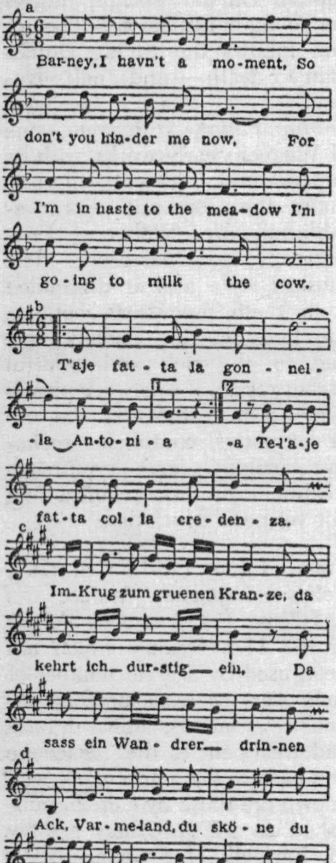

a.

Bar-ney, I havn't a mo-ment, So

don't you hin-der me now, For

I'm in haste to the mea-dow I'm

go-ing to milk the cow.

b.

T'aje fat-ta la gon-nel-

-la Anto-ni-a -a Te-l'a-je

fat-ta col-la cre-den-za.

c.

Im Krug zum gruenen Kran-ze, da

kehrt ich— dur-stig— ein, Da

d.

sass ein Wan-drer— drin-nen

Ack, Var-me-land, du skö-ne du

här-li-ge-land du Kro-na bland

Sve-a-ri-kes län-der.—

e.

Fig. 39

tiquity and of unknown authorship, which has been handed down orally for many generations and has become widely known throughout a nation or a smaller community. Folk song develops among the less sophisticated peoples, together with artless poems dealing with the various phases of everyday life: work, dancing, love, drinking, children, festivities, death, etc. Folk songs of the different nations have certain national traits which, although difficult to describe, are clearly felt to represent the general character of the people. Fig. 39, showing five examples, will demonstrate this point (a. American; b. Italian; c. German; d. Swedish; e. Hungarian). Many listeners would probably be able to identify their nationalities or at least to match them correctly with the five countries.

Although folk songs are obviously old, their age is usually exaggerated. In few fields of musical study have pure fancy and wishful thinking been given rein to such a degree as in the field of folk music, where melodies showing unmistakable traits of having originated in the 17th and 18th centuries are said to date back to pre-Christian eras. For instance, practically all the folk songs currently used in Germany date from the period about 1800. Those of Italy are even more recent, while the English ones frequently show evidence of an earlier origin (16th century). Equally unfounded is the claim, often made on behalf of folk song, of its being the root and foundation of art music. Such a statement is valid only in the sense that folk song, as a general phenomenon, existed long before the earliest development of art music. It is not, however, correct with regard to the historical evolution of Western music, which sprang from entirely different sources and has received only sporadic impulses from folk music. In fact, art music has probably exercised a greater influence on folk music than the other way around. The folk songs of America, England, France, etc., are all "civilized" folk songs, which show the influence of art music in such features as strict meter, clear and regular phrases (usually of four measures), well-defined tonality with emphasis on tonic and dominant. This becomes immediately clear if they are compared with a truly "aboriginal" folk song, such as are found in primitive cultures, e.g., among the American Indians (see Fig. 40, Hopi Indians). Thus, in the

Fig. 40

case of American folk song, a clear line of demarcation must be drawn between the aboriginal melodies of the Indians and the civilized folk songs of the white settlers and the Negroes. For American folk song, see also under *Ballads*.

Follia. See *Folia*.

Fontane di Roma. See *Fountains of Rome*.

Foot. In organ building, foot is the unit for the measurement of pipes. An open pipe sounding C is (approximately) 8 ft. in length, that for the higher octave (c) is 4 ft., for the lower octave (C₁) is 16 ft., etc. Hence the terms 8 ft. (8'), 4 ft. (4'), etc., are used to indicate the pitch level of entire ranks of pipes (stops), 8 ft. being the normal range (in which the pitch sounded corresponds to the key pressed), 4 ft. the higher octave, 16 ft. the lower octave, etc. This terminology is also sometimes used for high- and low-sounding instruments. For example, the piccolo is called a 4-ft. instrument, the bassoon a 16-ft. instrument.

Forlana (for-LAH-na: It.). A dance from Friuli, a district of northern Italy. It is usually in fast triple meter with dotted rhythms, similar to the gigue. Two well-known examples are by Bach (Orchestral Suite in C) and Ravel (*Tombeau de Couperin*).

Form. (1) In the most general sense, form includes all the elements and relationships that distinguish music from a haphazard combination of sounds such as street noises. Even the simplest melody shows relationships of pitch (intervals) and time values (rhythm); thus, it has "form." All of the basic elements of music, e.g., meter, rhythm, melody, harmony, tonality, texture, etc., contribute to musical coherence, and may be designated as components of form *in* (*within*) music. — (2) More specifically and properly, form is the scheme of organization that determines the basic structure of a composition, comparable to an architect's ground plan. There exist a considerable number of such schemes or "plans" which may collectively be designated as forms *of* music or musical forms. The most important of these musical forms are the following:

I. Single forms (individual pieces or movements)
  A. Sectional forms
     1. *Strophic form:
        a a a a . . .
     2. *Variation form:
        a a' a" a"' . . .
     3. *Binary form:
        ||:a:||:b:||
     4. Rounded b i n a r y
        form:
        ||:a:||:b a:||
     5. *Ternary form: a b a
     6. *Sonata (or sonata-allegro) form: Exposition — Development — Recapitulation
     7. Four-part form:
        a b a b
     8. Five-part form:
        a b a b a
     9. * R o n d o   f o r m
        (short) a b a c a;
        (long) a b a c a
        b a
  B. Continuation forms
     1. Through - composed forms (no repetition of materials), e.g., organum, medieval motet, recitative.
     2. I m i t a t i v e forms (continuous treatment of material involving *imitation in *polyphonic texture), e.g., fugue, ricercar, Renaissance motet.

II. Composite forms (two or more movements)
  A. Instrumental: *sonata, *symphony, *string quartet, *concerto, *suite, etc.
  B. Vocal: *cantata, *Mass, *oratorio, * o p e r a, *Passion, etc.

The foregoing list is not exhaustive, and should be considered only as a general indication of the variety and the structural principles of musical forms. The schemes indicated are by no means inflexible; composers can and do deviate considerably from the patterns while still maintaining the identity of the form.

History shows that in almost every period certain forms become traditionally established and are used by composers as basic molds. For example, during the last half of the 18th century, the sonata (in its various manifestations as symphony, concerto, string quartet, etc.) was the prevailing form of instrumental music. During the late 19th century and early 20th century there was a tendency to minimize the importance of musical form, and in numerous examples of program music (Strauss) and many symphonies (Mahler, Sibelius) of the period the traditional schemes are greatly modified if not entirely abandoned. Since about 1920, however, composers have generally returned to traditional formal principles.

Forte (It.). Loud, abbreviated *f*; *fortissimo* (*ff*), very loud; *fortississimo* (*fff*), extremely loud; *forte-piano* (*fp*), loud followed by soft.

Fortepiano (It.). Older name for the pianoforte.

Forty-eight, The. Popular name for Bach's °*Well-tempered Clavier,* consisting of forty-eight preludes and fugues.

Forza del Destino, La (FOR-tsa del des-TEE-no: The Force of Destiny). Opera by Verdi (libretto by F. M. Piave), produced in St. Petersburg, 1862. The plot, taking place in 18th-century Spain, involves the Marquis of Calatrava (bass), his son Don Carlo (baritone), his daughter Leonora (soprano), and a young nobleman, Don Alvaro, who is in love with Leonora. Alvaro accidentally kills the Marquis, and thus becomes the object of revenge on the part of Don Carlo. While Alvaro and Carlo are serving side by side in the Spanish army under assumed names, Alvaro is severely wounded in battle, and before leaving confides to Carlo a bundle of letters in which Carlo finds a picture of his sister, thereby recognizing Alvaro. Carlo discovers Alvaro in a monastery (near a cave where Leonora has determined to spend the rest of her life) and they duel. Carlo is mortally wounded, stabs Leonora who has rushed out in order to help him, and Don Alvaro, to complete the tragedy, flings himself off a cliff.

Foundation stops. See under *Organ.*

Fountains of Rome (It., *Fontane di Roma*). The first of three large symphonic poems by Respighi depicting scenes from Rome (see *Pines of Rome; Roman Festivals*), composed in 1924. The work, in the Italian impressionistic style, is in four parts, each portraying a fountain of the city: "Valle Giulia at Dawn," "Triton in the Morning," "Trevi at Midday," "Villa Medici at Sunset."

Four-part form. A form consisting of the alternation of two contrasting sections, A B A B, occasionally found in slow movements of sonatas.

Four Saints in Three Acts. Opera by Virgil Thomson, based on a play by Gertrude Stein, produced in Hartford, Conn., 1934. There being more than a dozen saints and four acts, the title is a bit of whimsy. The principal figures are the historical characters of St. Teresa of Avila and St. Ignatius Loyola. Act I is a pageant in which St. Teresa enacts some of her own life to instruct other saints and visitors. In Act II two lesser figures, with the blessing of the saints, fall in love and are married. In Act III St. Ignatius describes his vision of the Holy Ghost. Act IV is a closing tableau revealing the saints in heaven.

The text, in the stream-of-consciousness style of Miss Stein, is often meaningless, the juxtaposition of interesting word sounds being the primary objective. The music, which includes a number of ballet scenes, is in a clear, crisp, rhythmic style somewhat reminiscent of 1920 jazz, with the simplest harmonies and a great deal of monotone recitation of the text.

Four Serious Songs. See *Vier ernste Gesänge.*

Four-shape notes. See under *Fasola.*

Fourth. See under *Intervals*.

Fourth chord. Any of various chords consisting of superimposed fourths, for example, c-f-b♭, c-f♯-b-e, or of fourths in dissonant combinations with other intervals. These chords are important in the harmonic idiom of modern composers (Scriabin, Bartok, Hindemith), sometimes replacing the traditional harmonies resulting from the superposition of thirds (triad, seventh chord, ninth chord). Several of Scriabin's compositions are based on a single fourth-chord formation, the so-called *mystic chord* c-f♯-b♭-e'-a'-d'' (used in *Prometheus* and in the Seventh Piano Sonata, op. 64). See *Quartal harmony; Chords*.

Fox trot. An American ballroom dance dating from about 1910 which became the basis for most subsequent dance steps in duple meter with the exception of such foreign importations as the rhumba, tango, etc. The term dropped out of usage about 1930.

Fp. *Forte-piano*, i.e., loud followed by soft.

Française (frahnh-SEZ). A type of °contredanse in 6/8 meter, popular in the 18th and early 19th centuries.

Francesca da Rimini (frahn-CHES-ka dah REE-mee-nee). Symphonic poem (fantasy) by Tchaikovsky, op. 32 (1876), based on Dante's poem relating the story of the Italian noblewoman who, married to the ugly Count Malatesta, betrayed him with his stepbrother Paolo and was put to death in 1284.

Frauenliebe und Leben (FROW-en-leeb-a oont LAY-ben: Woman's Love and Life). A cycle of eight songs by Schumann, op. 42 (1840), based on a group of poems by Adalbert von Chamisso (published under the same title). It was composed in his "song year," shortly after he had married Clara Wieck.

Freischütz, Der (FREYE-shuits: The Freeshooter, The Marksman). Opera in three acts by Weber (libretto by F. Kind), produced in Berlin, 1821. The plot is based on the legend of "magic bullets" which never miss their mark and which can be obtained through a pact with the spirits of hell. The hunter Max (tenor), on the advice of his sinister companion Caspar (bass), resorts to this scheme in order to win Agathe (soprano), who is to be given as a prize to the winner in the marksmen's competition. Six of the seven bullets reach their goal, but the seventh, under the control of the hellish spirit Samiel (speaking part), is directed against Agathe. She is protected by the Hermit (bass) and by her bridal wreath, however, and Samiel, failing in his scheme, seizes his agent Caspar, who dies.

Der Freischütz marks the beginning as well as the artistic peak of the German Romantic opera. Folklore, awe of nature, and superstition are the roots out of which this opera grows, admirable for the charm of its folklike melodies and dance tunes as well as for its touches of dramatic tension and Romantic excitement. Particularly remarkable is the bold use of wind instruments: the horns which capture the atmosphere of the "German forest"; the trombones which accompany the hermit; the clarinet which characterizes Agathe; and the low registers of the flute which portray Samiel. See reference under *Melodrama*.

French horn. The orchestral *horn, so called in order to distinguish it from the English horn.

French overture. See under *Overture*. Bach's French Overture, published in the *Clavierübung II, is a suite with an introductory movement in the style of the French overture.

French sixth. See under *Chords* (5).

French Suites. Six suites for harpsichord by Bach, composed around 1720 (in Koethen). The name French (not by Bach) has little significance since French elements are present here to the same extent as in all the suites of Bach and his German predecessors (Pachelbel, Froberger). See under *Suite*.

Frets. Narrow strips of metal or wood fixed across the finger board of certain stringed instruments (lute, guitar, viol, balalaika, banjo) to mark the correct place for stopping, thus facilitating playing in correct pitch and making the stopped notes sound like the open ones.

Frog. The part of the violin bow held in the player's hand.

Frog Quartet. Nickname of Haydn's String Quartet in D (no. 49, or op. 50, no. 6), so called because the main theme of the last movement is vaguely suggestive of "croaking."

From Bohemia's Meadows and Forests. The fourth of the six symphonic poems by Smetana forming the cycle *Má Vlast.

From My Life. Smetana's name for each of his two String Quartets, in E minor (1876) and in C minor (1882), both of them autobiographical. Today the name attaches particularly to the E-minor Quartet which describes the happy experiences of his youthful life, but contains in the finale a long-drawn high note which he heard for many years before he became deaf.

From the New World. Dvořák's Ninth Symphony (usually called no. 5), in E minor, op. 95 (1893). It was written during Dvořák's residence in the United States, and incorporates themes modeled after the songs of the American Negroes and Indians. Some of this material, however, sounds Bohemian rather than American.

Frottola (FRAW-to-la: It.). A type of north-Italian poetry and music that flourished about 1500, preceding the madrigal. The music is in three or four voices, mostly homophonic, and with frequent chord progressions from the dominant (V) to the tonic (I), which are relatively rare in the main repertory of this period (Masses, motets). The frottola was cultivated in courtly circles, particularly at Mantua where the two most important composers of frottolas, Marco Cara and Bartolomeo Tromboncino, lived.

Fugato (foo-GAH-to: It.). A passage in the general style of a fugue, forming a part of a non-

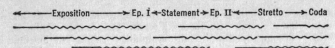

Fig. 41

fugal composition, e.g., of a movement from a sonata, symphony, or string quartet. A fugato is nearly always designed in such a way as to build up a strong dynamic climax, beginning with one instrument and gradually bringing in the others until a full *fortissimo* is reached.

Fughetta (foo-GET-ta: It.). A short fugue.

Fugue (from L. *fuga*, flight). A polyphonic composition based on a theme (subject) which is stated at the beginning in one voice part alone, being taken up (imitated) by the other voice or voices in close succession, and reappearing throughout the piece at various places in one voice part or another (see under *Imitation*). The initial section, up to the point where the theme has been stated in each voice, is called the *exposition*. The subsequent statements of the theme are often also grouped together in a similar manner, such groups being sometimes called second (third) exposition. Each fugue also contains *episodes*, that is, relatively short sections where the subject is not being stated in any voice part. Fig. 41 is an abridged schematic representation of a fugue, the theme being represented by a straight line, other melodic materials by wavy lines. Short empty spaces are meant to illustrate the fact that often one of the voice parts has

a rest, particularly before a new entrance of the theme.

In the exposition (often also in the later course of the fugue) the statements of the theme alternate between tonic and dominant, the first being in the tonic (e.g., beginning on C), the second in the dominant (e.g., beginning on G), the third reverting to the tonic, and the fourth again in the dominant. Hence they are called *subject* and *answer*, or *antecedent* and *consequent*, or *dux* and *comes* (L., leader and follower), the first in each pair of names referring to the tonic statements, the second to those in the dominant. If the

Fig. 42

answer is in exact imitation of the subject, it is called a *real answer*, but when the answer is slightly altered because of tonal restrictions, it is called a *tonal answer* (see *Tonal and real*). Fig. 42 shows a full fugal exposition (Bach, *Well-tempered Clavier* II, Fugue 9).

In the middle of a fugue, modulation into other keys usually takes place, with a return to the main key near the end. As a result, the fugue is often said to be a three-part form. This statement is somewhat misleading, however, since the fugues of Bach and others show great variety in this matter as well as in other details. It is interesting to observe that structurally the fugue is much more flexible than, e.g., the sonata of the Classical period, and thus may be more properly considered a "procedure" than a "form."

In fugues of a more elaborate character the theme is often presented in *inversion *augmentation or diminution, *stretto, or in combination with other themes (double, triple, quadruple fugue). See *Art of Fugue.*

Fuguing tune, fugue-tune. A type of hymn tune, current in Eng-

land and America during the 18th and early 19th centuries, which makes some use of successive entry of voices in the manner of a *fugue). A number of such tunes were written by William Billings (1746–1800), who declared them to be "more than twenty times as powerful as the old slow tunes." Henry Cowell has used the term in the titles of several short works for various media.

Furiant. A lively Bohemian (Czech) dance in 3/4 meter with frequently shifting accents. It has been repeatedly used by Dvořák, Smetana, and others. See under *Dumka.*

Furlana. See *Forlana.*

Futurism. A movement of the 1910's, instigated by Marinetti, aiming at extreme radicalism in literature and in all the arts. In music it remained largely theoretical (orchestras consisting of machine guns, sirens, steam whistles, etc.).

Fz. Abbreviation of *forzando, forzato*, same as *sforzando* (*sf, sfz*).

G

G. See *Pitch names.*

Gagliarda (It.). See *Galliard.*

Galanterien (gah-lahn-ter-EE-en: G.). An 18th-century name for short, entertaining pieces, particularly dances such as minuets, gavottes, etc. Also applied to ornaments used in the harpsichord music of that period.

Gallant style (from F. *style galant*). The elegant and delicate style of the *Rococo.

Galliard (gal-yard: from F. *gaillarde*, gay, rollicking). A 16th-century dance – in moderately quick triple time. It was executed with exaggerated leaps which often took on features of wantonness. In art music the galliard was often combined with the *pavane, particularly in England. See also *Cinque-pace*.

Galop. A dance of the mid-19th century in lively duple time, with a characteristic rhythmic pattern (see Fig. 43) executed with hopping movements and frequently changing steps.

$$\frac{2}{4} \; \flat \,|\, \sqcup \sqcup \, . \; \flat \,|\, \sqcup \sqcup \, .$$

Fig. 43

Gamba (It.), **Gambe** (G.). Abbr. for *viola da gamba.

Gamelan (GUM-e-lan). A native orchestra of the Siamese and Javanese, consisting mainly of a variety of percussion instruments, somewhat like xylophones, glockenspiels, chimes, gongs, and drums. All instruments play essentially the same melody though individual parts may vary slightly.

Game of Cards (Stravinsky). See *Jeu de cartes*.

Gamut. Originally *gamma ut*, the medieval name for G, then the lowest tone of the scale (see under *Hexachord*). The term later acquired the meaning of "all the tones above *gamma ut*," i.e., the whole scale. Hence the French term *gamme* for scale, and the English "gamut" for compass or range.

Gapped scale. A scale resulting from the omission of certain tones, e.g., the pentatonic scale (as compared to the diatonic), or the whole-tone scale (as compared to the chromatic).

Gaspard de la nuit (gas-pahr de la NWEE: F.). A set of three piano pieces by Ravel (1908) inspired by the collected poems of Bertrand, which were published under the same title (literally: Caspar of the Night, a nickname for Satan): (1) *Ondine*, a water nymph attempting in vain to win a mortal for a spouse; (2) *Le Gibet*, a grisly monotone composition describing the swinging of a corpse from a gibet — a gallows; (3) *Scarbo*, a character sketch of the traditional clown in the Punch and Judy show.

Gavotte. A French dance of the 17th and 18th centuries, in moderate 4/4 time, usually starting on the third beat of the measure: 3 4 | 1 2 3 4 | 1 2 . . . . It often occurs in the optional group of the *suite.

G clef. See under *Clefs*.

Gebrauchsmusik (ge-BROWKHS-moo-ZEEK: G.). A term originating in the 1920's, roughly translated as "utility music" or "workaday music," i.e., music designed for informal use by amateurs, as distinguished from music intended for concert performance by professionals. Because of its purpose, *Gebrauchsmusik* avoids technical difficulties so that it may be performed by amateurs and is simple and attractive in form and content so that it may be readily understood and appreciated by unsophisticated listeners.

In another connotation, the term is applied to pieces composed for one specific occasion, e.g., the dedication of a school or a birthday celebration.

Hindemith, who has been closely identified with this type of music, has furnished some informative remarks on *Gebrauchsmusik* in the introductory notes to his *Plöner Musiktag* (1932) and *Wir bauen eine Stadt* (1931).

Geige (GEYE-ga: G.). Violin.

Geistertrio (G.). See *Ghost Trio*.

Generalbass (gen-e-RAHL-bahs: G.). *Thorough bass.

German flute. An 18th-century name for the transverse flute, as distinguished from the recorder, then called the English flute.

German Organ Mass. See under *Clavierübung*.

German Requiem, A (G., *Ein deutsches Requiem*). An extended work for solo voices, chorus, and orchestra by Brahms, op. 45, composed 1857–1869, partly motivated by the death of his mother in 1865. Like the *requiem of the Roman Catholic Church, it is in commemoration of the dead, but with the traditional Latin texts replaced by Brahms' own selections from German Scriptures. It is one of the most outstanding examples of religious music after Beethoven's *Missa solemnis*.

German sixth. See under *Chords* (5).

German Suites. A name sometimes applied, without justification, to Bach's *Partitas*.

Ges (G.). G-flat. See under *Pitch names*.

Geschöpfe des Prometheus, Die (Beethoven). See *Creatures of Prometheus*.

Gestopft (ge-SHTOPFT: G.). Stopped, in horn playing.

Gewandhaus Concerts (ge-VAHNT-hows). Concerts named after an ancient guild hall (Cloth Hall) in Leipzig in which they were given, starting in 1781. On the roster of celebrated conductors of the Gewandhaus orchestra are Mendelssohn (1835–1843) and Wilhelm Furtwängler (1922–1928).

Ghost Trio. Nickname of Beethoven's Pianoforte Trio in D, op. 70, no. 1, so called because of the ghostlike character of the slow movement.

Gianni Schicchi (JAHN-ee SKEE-kee: It.). See under *Trittico*.

Giant Fugue. A nickname occasionally applied to Bach's chorale prelude "Wir glauben all' an einen Gott" (We all believe in one God) from the *Clavierübung* III (ed. Peters, vol. VII, no. 60), because of the striding figure in the pedal part. The name is rather inappropriate since the figure is only vaguely suggestive of "giant steps" and, furthermore, is used as an ostinato, not as a theme for a fugue. The term is also sometimes used for the Dorian Fugue (see *Dorian Toccata and Fugue*) and for the fugue of the D-minor Toccata and Fugue (ed. Peters, vol. IV, no. 4), both of which have themes that might be called "giantlike."

Gigue (zheeg: F.; It., *giga*). A dance in lively triple meter (usually 6/8) which forms the last movement of Baroque °suites. It is in binary form, usually with a fugal opening for each section, the second section often using the inversion of the initial theme, as in the accompanying example (Fig. 44) from Bach's French Suite, no. 4. The gigue developed from the °jig, an Irish, English, or Scottish dance of the late 16th century.

Fig. 44

Gigue Fugue. Nickname of an organ fugue in G major by Bach (ed. Peters, vol. IX, no. 4) which, in its meter (12/8) and character, is similar to a gigue.

Gimel. See *Gymel*.

Girl of the Golden West, The (It., *La Fanciulla del West*). Opera in three acts by Puccini (libretto after a drama by D. Belasco), produced in New York, 1910. The plot is laid in a California goldmining town about 1850, and the central figures are Minnie (soprano), Dick Johnson (tenor), an outlaw in disguise, and the sheriff, Jack Rance (baritone). Dick plans to rob Minnie's saloon, but changes his mind when he and Minnie fall in love. He is wounded by the sheriff (a disappointed suitor of Minnie's). After nursing Dick, Minnie wins his freedom in a poker game with Rance, whereupon the lovers leave the West to start life together elsewhere.

Giselle (ji-ZEL). Ballet by Adolphe Adam (choreography by Jean Corali, based on a story by Heine), produced in Paris, 1841.

Gitana, Alla (gee-TAH-na: It.). In the gypsy style.

Giusto (JOOS-to: It.). Just, proper; used in connection with tempo marks, e.g., *allegro giusto*, *tempo giusto*, to indicate a tempo "just right" and strict.

Glass harmonica. An instrument invented (or perhaps only improved) by Benjamin Franklin in 1763, in which a series of graded glass disks, shaped like saucers, are fixed on a horizontal spindle which is made to revolve by foot action. The sound is produced by a delicate friction of the fingers against the glass rims, which are kept wet. The instrument had a great vogue, particularly in Germany and Austria.

Mozart wrote for it (Adagio in C, K. 356, new ed. K. 617a; Quintet in C, K. 617, both composed in 1791), and Beethoven used it in his melodrama, *Leonora Prohaska* (1814). Beethoven's instrument probably had a keyboard mechanism replacing the direct finger action of the earlier instruments.

Glee (probably from Anglo-Saxon *glēo* or *gliw*, meaning music or entertainment). An 18th-century type of unaccompanied choral composition for three or more men's voices. It replaced the °madrigal as the most popular form for recreational singing. Glees are rather short, sectional pieces, basically chordal, but not without polyphonic interest. They were extensively cultivated in England until their vogue was replaced by the °part song during the 19th century. However, there are glee clubs in both England and America which perpetuate the tradition, although their repertories are not limited to glees. Among the most celebrated glee writers were Benjamin Cooke (1734–1793), Stephen Paxton (1735–1787), Samuel Webbe (1740–1816), and John Calcott (1766–1821). Webbe's famous glee, "Glorious Apollo," has long been the traditional opening number on programs of glee clubs. Novello's *Standard Glee Book* contains the most popular pieces.

Gli Scherzi (Haydn). See *Scherzi, Gli.*

Glissando (glis-SAHN-do: from F. *glisser*, to glide). A rapid scale executed by a sliding move-

ment. Particularly suited to the harp, it is produced by drawing a finger swiftly across the strings; on the piano it is executed by drawing the nail of the thumb (or another finger) over the keys. On the violin a true glissando scale is a very difficult virtuoso effect. A simple sliding of the hand produces, not a rapid scale, but a continuous change of pitch, properly called °portamento. This portamento effect is also frequently produced by singers and trombone players.

Glocken (G.). (1) Bells. — (2) Orchestral chimes.

Glockenspiel (GLOK-en-shpeel: G., set of bells). A percussion instrument which has a series of steel bars of varying length fixed to a horizontal frame, and arranged somewhat in the manner of a keyboard, i.e., with the plates for the "black keys" being set further back than the others. It is played with two hammers. In the 18th century the name *glockenspiel* was used for small instruments of the °celesta type, having a real keyboard with hammers which sounded steel bars inside a box (this is probably the instrument called for in Mozart's *Magic Flute* under the name *strumento d'acciaio* [steel instrument]). The portable glockenspiel employed in bands is known as the *bell-lyra* from its U-shaped frame reminiscent of the ancient Greek lyre.

Gloria. The second item of the Ordinary of the °Mass.

Glückliche Hand, Die (GLUIK-likh-a hahnt: The Lucky Hand).

Monodrama by Schönberg (to his own libretto), composed in 1913, first performed in Vienna, 1924. The only singing character (baritone) is a disillusioned man whose somewhat surrealistic stream of consciousness centers around two pantomimic characters, allegorical male and female, who represent various kinds of love. In addition, there is a chorus of six men and women whose heads appear through holes in a backdrop, and who comment on the action in a *speech-song style.

G. O. In French organ music, *grande orgue*, i.e., great organ.

God's Time is Best (Bach). See *Actus Tragicus*.

Goldberg Variations. Thirty variations by J. S. Bach on a theme of his own, published in 1742 as Part IV of the *Clavierübung. The work, commissioned by the Russian Count Kayserling, was named after Bach's pupil, Johann Gottlieb Goldberg (1727–1756), a harpsichordist in the employ of the count. It is written for a two-manual harpsichord according to a special plan: two variations in a free, often highly virtuoso style are followed by a single variation in the form of a canon (nos. 3, 6, 9, . . .) and so on. The final variation is a *quodlibet.

Golden Age, The. Ballet by Shostakovich, produced in Moscow, 1931. The best known excerpt is the "Polka" from Act III.

Golden Cockerel, The. See *Coq d'or*.

Golden sequence. See under *Sequence* (2).

Golden Sonata. Popular name for Purcell's Sonata in G minor (no. 9 of the Ten Sonatas in Four Parts) for two violins, cello, and continuo.

Gondoliera (It.). Gondola song, *barcarole.

Gondoliers, The, or **The King of Barataria.** Operetta by Sullivan (libretto by Gilbert), produced in London, 1889.

Gong. An orchestral percussion instrument, of Chinese origin, consisting of a large circular bronze disk with the edge turned, thus resembling a shallow plate. It is suspended in a frame so as to hang freely, and is struck with a heavy bass-drum beater. It is also called a tamtam.

Gopak. See *Hopak*.

Gorgheggio (gorg-EJ-yo: It., from *gorgia*, throat). Vocal passages of a virtuoso character, such as trills, rapid ornamentations, or *coloraturas.

Gothic music. A term used by some music historians to denote the music of the period c. 1200 (Perotinus) to c. 1450 (Dufay), coeval with the Gothic era in architecture and painting. See *History of music.*

Götterdämmerung, Die (GEUT-ter-DEM-er-oong: The Twilight of the Gods). See *Ring of the Nibelung.*

Goyescas. Two sets of piano pieces by Enrique Granados

(1914), inspired by etchings of the Spanish painter Francisco Goya (1746–1828). Translated, the titles of the individual pieces are: I. The Compliments; Colloquy at the Grilled Window; The Fandango of the Lantern; Plaints, or The Maja and the Nightingale; II. Love and Death; Epilogue; Serenade of the Specter. Granados also wrote an opera *Goyescas* (1916) which includes material from the piano pieces.

G. P. (1) In orchestral scores, general pause, i.e., a rest for the whole orchestra. — (2) In French organ music, *grand positif*, i.e., great and choir organs coupled.

G. R. In French organ music, *grand récit*, i.e., great and swell organs coupled.

Grace. A 17th-century English term for ornament.

Grace note. A note printed in small type to indicate that its time value is not counted in the general rhythm and must be subtracted from that of the preceding or following normal note. Fig. 45 illustrates the two possibilities, (a) representing the earlier practice (Bach, Mozart, Beethoven), (b) representing the later practice (Chopin). See

Fig. 45

Ornaments. Large groups of grace notes, such as found in Chopin and Liszt, are in free rhythm, not subject to regular beat.

Gradual. (1) The second item of the Proper of the °Mass. — (2) The liturgical book of the Roman Catholic Church containing the chants for the Mass (see *Gregorian chant*).

Gradus ad Parnassum (L., Steps to Parnassus, the abode of the Muses; hence, steps to highest perfection). (1) A treatise on counterpoint by J. J. Fux (1725). — (2) A collection of piano etudes by Clementi (1817).

Granadina. See under *Fandango*.

Gran cassa, gran tamburo (It.). Bass drum.

Grand (grahnh: F., great). *Grand jeu, grand orgue,* full organ; *grand opéra,* opera (usually serious) with fully composed text, as distinct from *opéra comique,* which has some spoken dialog (see *Comic opera*).

Grand Fugue. See *Grosse Fuge*.

Gran Mass (G., *Graner Messe*). A Mass by Liszt, composed in 1855 for the consecration of the cathedral in Gran (Hungary).

Grand piano. A wing-shaped °pianoforte in which the strings and soundboard are placed horizontally, as distinguished from an *upright piano* in which the strings and soundboard are in a vertical position.

Grave (GRAH-vay: It.). Slow, solemn.

Great Fugue. See *Grosse Fuge*.

Great organ. See under *Organ*.

Greek music. The music of the ancient Greeks is of interest primarily for its theory, which influenced in several ways the theory of early Western music. The basis of this music is the *tetrachord* (four strings), i.e., a succession of four descending notes forming successively a whole tone, whole tone, and half tone: a-g-f-e, or e-d-c-B. By repeating the same process at the higher octave, a two-octave descending scale (all Greek scales are descending) from a' to B was formed, which was completed by the addition of the low A. Its middle note, a, was called *mese*, and the entire scale is referred to as the *Greater Perfect System*. There also existed a *Lesser Perfect System*, ranging from d' down to A:

Greater Perfect System   a' g' f' e' d' c' b   a g f e d c B A

Lesser Perfect System   d' c' bb a g f e d c B A

In addition to the normal or *diatonic* tetrachord, there existed two varieties, called *chromatic* and *enharmonic*. The chromatic tetrachord is a-gb-f-e, while the enharmonic is a-f-x-e (x stands for the quarter tone between f and e). Either of these tetrachords might replace the diatonic tetrachords in the Greater

Perfect or Lesser Perfect Systems, for example, a'-gb'-f'-e'-db'-c'-b-a . . . .

This basic tonal material was divided into *octave species*, that is, segments of eight (descending) tones starting at different points of the complete system and named as shown below:

a'-a: Hypodorian	e'-e: Dorian
g'-g: Hypophrygian	d'-d: Phrygian
f'-f: Hypolydian	c'-c: Lydian
b-B: Mixolydian	

The octave species are often called "Greek modes," since they show a certain similarity to the *church modes. It should be noted that the same names are used differently in the two systems. For instance, the Greek Dorian starts from e, the medieval Dorian from d.

Only a few — and relatively late — documents of Greek music survive, among them two Delphic Hymns (*c.* 130 B.C.), the Hymn to the Sun by Mesomedes (*c.* 130 A.D.), and the Seikilos Song (*c.* 1st century A.D.).

Gregorian chant. The liturgical music of the Roman Catholic Church, named after Pope Gregory I (590–604) although it is very likely of post-Gregorian origin. The music is entirely *monophonic and in free rhythm, lacking regular meter and measure. It is sung partly by the choir, partly by soloists. Chants sung in alternation by a soloist and the choir are called *responsorial*, while those sung by alternating half choruses are called *antiphonal*. From the liturgical point of view the chants fall into two main categories, those for the °Mass and those for the °Office (all the services other than the Mass, held at the various Office Hours). The music for the latter consists mostly of psalms, sung to one of the °psalm tones, and of °hymns. One of the Offices, the service of Vespers, also includes the Magnificat (see under *Canticles*), and that of Compline includes the four Antiphons of the Blessed Virgin Mary (see under *Antiphon*). The chants for the Mass are collected in a book called the *Gradual*, those of the Office in the *Antiphonal*. Both are conveniently combined in the modern *Liber usualis*.

Stylistically, a distinction can be made on the basis of text setting between three types of chants (see Fig. 46). The *syl-*

Fig. 46

labic chant has only one note to each syllable; the *neumatic* includes occasional groups (neumes) of from two to four notes for a single syllable; the *melismatic* shows extended groupings (melismas), often of

twenty or more notes for a single syllable. The chants of the Mass are, on the whole, more elaborate than those of the Office, and those of the Proper of the Mass more elaborate than those of the Ordinary.

The tonal basis of Gregorian chant is the eight °church modes. The rhythmic interpretation is still problematic. In the past forty years the °Solesmes method of performance has gained universal acceptance wherever Gregorian chant is sung. The basic principle of this method is that all the notes of a chant are equally long (e.g., eighth notes), except for longer values at the end of a phrase. The melodic line is divided into elementary groups of two or three notes, often marked by an *ictus* (') , which calls for a subtle stress (see Fig. 47). Present-

Fig. 47

day musicologists, however, are almost universally agreed that this method of performance is not historically correct, and that in Gregorian chant there existed two, possibly three, time values, such as the eighth, the quarter, and the dotted quarter note.

Gregorian modes. See under *Church modes*.

Gr. Fl. In German orchestral scores, *Grosse Flöte*, i.e., the flute, in distinction from *Kl. Fl.* (*Kleine Flöte*), i.e., piccolo.

Gross (G., great, large). *Grosse Flöte*, flute (see under *Gr. Fl.*). — *Grosses Orchester*, full orchestra. — *Grosse Trommel*, bass drum.

Grosse Caisse (F.). Bass drum.

Grosse Fuge (GRO-sa FOO-ga: G., great fugue). Beethoven's very extended and complex fugue for string quartet, op. 133. It was composed in 1825 as the last movement of his String Quartet op. 130, but later published as a separate composition. It is highly remarkable for the boldness of the theme as well as the boldness of its treatment, which is "tantôt libre, tantôt recherchée" (partly free, partly studied).

Ground, ground bass. A melodic phrase (normally from four to eight measures in length) which is repeated over and over again as a bass line, while the upper parts are varied. The resulting composition is also called a "ground." The contrast between the fixed framework of the bass and the free display of imagination in the upper part or parts constitutes the peculiar charm of this form. The ground bass, also called *basso ostinato* (It.), may range from such simple formations as the descending tetrachord, a-g-f-e (one note to the measure; see under *Chaconne*), to full-length melodies, as in Fig. 48 (Purcell). The ground belongs to the general category of "continuous variations" (see under *Variations*). It is a characteristic form of Baroque music.

Gr. Tr. In German orchestral scores, *Grosse Trommel*, i.e., bass drum.

Gsp. Short for *glockenspiel.

Guerre des bouffons (F.). See *War of the Buffoons*.

Guidonian hand (gwee-DO-nee-an). A device of medieval music instruction (named after Guido of Arezzo, *c*.995–*c*.1050, but invented later), making use of the human hand as an aid in memorizing the scale, each part of the hand being identified with one of the tones from G to e" (the e" is placed above the hand).

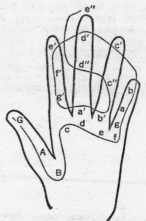

Fig. 49

Guillaume Tell (Rossini). See *William Tell*.

Guitar. A plucked stringed instrument somewhat in the shape

Fig. 48

of a violin, but with entirely flat upper and lower surfaces and with a rounded waist instead of corners. It has six strings, now normally tuned E A d g b e', and a fretted fingerboard. The instrument was much in vogue during the 17th century, superseding the earlier lute. During the 20th century it has been used chiefly to furnish accompaniment to folk, Western, and hillbilly music. It is also used in the rhythm sections of dance bands, sometimes replaced by the Hawaiian guitar.

Gurre Lieder (GUR-ra LEE-der: Songs of Gurra). A song cycle ("Great Cantata") by Schönberg, to poems (originally in Danish) by J. P. Jacobsen, for 5 solo voices, 3 four-part male choruses, 1 eight-part mixed chorus, narrator, and large orchestra, started by the composer in 1901–1902 but not finished until 1911. The poems are based on the Danish legend of King Waldemar IV and his love for the Princess Tove, who dwells in the castle of Gurra. The jealous queen plans and accomplishes Tove's death, which is announced in a song of the Forest Dove (Part I). Part II contains Waldemar's plaint and rebellion against God. For this he is sentenced to hunt nightly with ghostly companions (Part III: The Wild Chase). The musical style represents the climax of late Romanticism. An arrangement for smaller orchestra has been made by E. Stein.

Gymel (GIM-el: from L. *cantus gemellus,* twin song). Medieval term for music in two parts connected by the interval of the third, either in parallel thirds, or with the parts crossing. See Fig. 50.

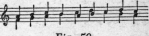

Fig. 50

Gypsy scale. A scale characterized by the inclusion of two augmented seconds: c d♭ e f g a♭ b c'. It is often employed in the music of the Hungarian gypsies, who probably adopted it from Hindu or Turkish music.

H

H. The German name (pronounced hah) for B natural, e.g., *H moll,* B minor. See under *B A C H; Carnival; Pitch names.*

Habanera (ah-bah-NAY-ra). A dance from Havana, Cuba, in slow to moderate duple time, with dotted or syncopated patterns as shown in Fig. 51. It

$$\frac{2}{4}\ \text{♪♪♪ ♩♪♪♪}\ |$$

Fig. 51

appeared in Spain about 1850 and soon became associated with the *flamenco style of dancing. Sebastian Yradier (1809–1869), who lived in Cuba for some time, wrote the most famous haban-eras, *La Paloma* and *El Arreglito*. The latter became known universally through a composition of Bizet, who used it in the first act of *Carmen*.

Haffner Serenade and **Haffner Symphony.** Two orchestral works by Mozart (K. 250, K. 385), composed in 1776 and 1782, for celebrations in the family of Sigmund Haffner, burgomaster of Salzburg.

Half cadence, half close. See under *Cadence*.

Half note. See under *Notes and rests*.

Half tone, half step. The smallest interval commonly used in music, e.g., from C to C-sharp. See under *Intervals*.

Hallelujah, Halleluiah (Hebrew, *Halleluyah*, Praise ye the Lord). An exclamation of praise to God, often used as the text for concluding choruses in cantatas and oratorios, e.g., at the end of the first movement of Bach's cantata *Christ lag in Todesbanden*, or of Part II of Handel's *Messiah*. In Gregorian chant the Latinized spelling *alleluia* is used.

Halling. A Norwegian dance from the Hallingdal, executed with a great variety of motions ranging from the intentionally awkward to the violent. It is usually in moderate 2/4 time.

Hammerklavier (HAHM-er-klah-VEER: G.). Early German name for the pianoforte. Beetho-ven used the designation "für das Hammerklavier" in his sonatas, op. 101 and 106, because at that time he generally preferred German instead of Italian terms (also in the expression marks). The name *Hammerklavier Sonata* has been associated only with his Sonata in B-flat, op. 106, composed in 1818, which is by far the most extended and most complex of all the Beethoven sonatas.

Hammond organ. An *electrophonic instrument invented by L. Hammond in Chicago. Designed to replace the organ in smaller churches, it frequently has been found to be an acceptable substitute. In addition, it has been used to provide dance music, dinner music, background music, etc.

Handel Variations. Twenty variations (and a fugue) for pianoforte by Brahms, op. 24 (1861), based on a theme by Handel (the "Air" from his harpsichord suite in B-flat). The fugue is based on a theme freely derived from the initial notes of the tune.

Hänsel und Gretel. Opera by Humperdinck, produced in Weimar, 1893. The libretto, written by his sister, Adelheid Wette, is based on the well-known story from Grimm's *Fairy Tales*. Although lacking in originality, the music provides a suitable background for the plot through its folklike simplicity and its warmth of feeling.

Harfe (G.). Harp.

Harmonica. (1) Mouth harmonica or mouth organ, a small

wind instrument in the form of a rectangular box with a number of openings on one oblong side, each of which is a channel leading to a metal reed inside the box. Different tones are obtained by moving the instrument across the lips according to the notes desired, and by alternating between exhaling and inhaling in producing the sound. A number of harmonica bands exist in the United States and elsewhere, and a remarkable degree of virtuosity has been achieved by performers, some of them playing on diminutive as well as on giant sizes of the instrument. The invention of the instrument is variously credited to F. Buschmann (Vienna, 1821) or to Sir Charles Wheatstone (London, 1829).— (2) See *Glass harmonica.*

Harmonic analysis. The analysis of a composition from the point of view of its harmonies and their tonal functions. The basic method is to identify each chord as to its structure, whether triad, seventh chord, sixth chord, etc. (see under *Chords*), and also as to its *scale degree. According to the most widely accepted practice, triads are indicated by Roman numerals (I, II, . . . V, . . .); additional tones and inversions are indicated by Arabic numerals: e.g., sixth chords by I_6, . . . , seventh chords by I_7 . . . , six-four chords by I_4^6 . . . , etc. (see *Thorough bass*). The Roman numerals invariably indicate the scale degree of the *root (not necessarily the bass tone) of the chord. Fig. 52 serves to illustrate this method.

Various systems have been devised for the analysis of some

I I_6 IV II_6 V_2^4 I_6 I_4^6 V   I

Fig. 52

20th-century music to which the foregoing system is not applicable. Some of the best-known books on harmonic analysis are: W. Piston, *Harmony* (1941); A. McHose, *The Contrapuntal Harmonic Technique of the 18th Century* (1947); R. Sessions, *Harmonic Practice* (1951); Murphy and Stringham, *Creative Harmony* (1951).

Harmonic inversion. See under *Inversion.*

Harmonic minor (scale). See under *Scale.*

Harmonics. (1) Secondary tones which form a component of every musical sound, though they are not heard distinctly. See *Acoustics* (4).— (2) Highpitched tones of a flutelike quality which are produced on stringed instruments by lightly touching the string at a certain point instead of pressing it down firmly against the fingerboard (stopping). In Fig. 53 the diamond shapes indicate the point of touch (on the G string), while the black notes indicate the resultant pitches. In musical notation the harmonics are indicated by small circles. In addition to the "natural harmonics" just described, which are obtained from an open string, there are also "artificial harmonics" obtained from a stopped string. Fig. 53b illustrates their notation

Fig. 53

(lower staff) and actual sound (upper staff). The introduction of the harmonics into concert music is variously ascribed to Tartini's pupil, Domenico Ferrari (1722–1780), and to Jean de Mondonville (1711–1772). Harmonics are also used on the harp. See also *Tromba marina*.

Harmonic scale. Harmonic minor scale. See under *Scale*.

Harmonic series. The series of the acoustical harmonics (overtones, partials). See *Acoustics* (4).

Harmonie der Welt (har-mo-NEE dayr VELT: Harmony of the World). A symphony by Hindemith, composed in 1951. As in the case of °*Mathis der Maler,* the three movements were derived from the composer's opera of the same title before the opera was finished and performed. The titles of the movements are "Musica Instrumentalis," "Musica Humana," and "Musica Mundana."

Harmonious Blacksmith, The. Popular name for the "Air" with variations from Handel's harpsichord suite no. 5, in E (1720). The name appears (for the first

time?) in an edition published about 1780 by J. and W. Lintern, one of whom had been a blacksmith in his youth.

Harmonium. A keyboard instrument, also called "reed organ," whose tones are produced by thin metal tongues or reeds, which are set in vibration by wind from bellows operated by the feet of the player. The instrument is used as a substitute for the organ, which it resembles particularly in having a number of stops which produce a variety of tone colors. An "expression stop" enables the player to produce gradations of intensity of sound, not by finger touch (as in the pianoforte) but by foot control (regulation of the pressure in the bellows). The harmonium developed in the 19th century from Grenié's *Orgue expressif* (1810; suggested by the Chinese mouth organ, *sheng*). Experimental forms such as the *Aeoline* (1816), *Physharmonica* (1818), *Aerophone* (1829), *Séraphine* (1833), and *Mélophone* (1837) led to the first real harmonium, constructed by 1840 by A. Débain. The expression stop was invented by Mustel in 1854 (*Mustel Organ*). The *American Organ* is a variety in which the wind is not forced outward, but is drawn inward by evacuation of the air in the bellows. It has a softer and more organlike tone, but lacks the expressive device of the harmonium. The principle of the American instrument was invented about 1835 in Paris, and developed by Estey in Brattleboro, Mass. (*Estey Organ,* 1856), and by Mason and Hamlin, Boston (1861).

Harmony. The simultaneous occurrence of musical tones, as opposed to *melody (i.e., succession of tones). Although the term suggests "pleasantness" of sound, it is properly applied to any combination of tones, whether consonant or dissonant. Such combinations, considered singly, are usually termed *chords, while harmony denotes the "chordal aspect" of music, i.e., the succession and relationship of chords as they occur in a composition. Thus, harmony refers to the vertical structure of music, while melody (and counterpoint) pertain to its horizontal element (see under *Texture*). See also *Harmonic analysis*.

Harold in Italy. A program symphony by Berlioz, op. 16, written in 1834 at the request of Paganini, who wanted a work in which he could feature an exceptional viola he had just acquired. The symphony, which has a prominent viola part, is in four movements after portions from Byron's *Childe Harold:* (1) Harold in the Mountains, (2) Pilgrim's March and Prayer, (3) Serenade of an Abruzzi Mountaineer, and (4) Orgy of the Brigands.

Harp. A stringed instrument of the modern orchestra, having a large triangular frame in which are stretched about forty-five parallel strings, decreasing in length, and tuned diatonically (seven strings to the octave) in the key of C-flat, through six octaves and a fifth, i.e., from Cb_1 to gb''''. At the foot of the instrument (front pillar) are seven pedals, one controlling all the C-strings, one all the D-

strings, etc. Each pedal can be depressed to two notches (hence the name *Double Pedal Harp* or *Double Action Harp*), and by each action the corresponding strings are shortened to sound a half tone higher. Thus, the C-pedal in high position gives the tone Cb, in the first notch, C, and in the second, $C\sharp$. Operation of the various pedals makes all the major and minor keys available. The double-pedal harp was invented about 1810 by Sébastien Érard in Paris. In 1897 the Parisian firm of Pleyel introduced the *chromatic harp*, in which the pedal mechanism is abandoned, separate strings being provided for all the chromatic tones. These strings are stretched in two intersecting planes, one for all the "white keys," the other for all the "black keys." It has been used mainly by French composers.

Harps are among the oldest of all instruments, second only to drums. In Mesopotamia they are documented as far back as 3000 B.C., and they were widely used in ancient Egypt. The biblical "harp of King David," however, was probably a *lyre, similar to the Greek *kithara. In Europe, harps appeared first in Ireland (8th or 9th century).

Harp Quartet. Popular name for Beethoven's String Quartet, op. 74, in E-flat (1809), so called because of some pizzicato arpeggios which occur in the first movement.

Harpsichord. The most common stringed keyboard instrument of the 16th to 18th centuries, similar in shape to the grand piano but differing from it chiefly in the means used to produce sound. Harpsichord strings are plucked by short tongues (*plectra*) made from crow quills or from leather, rather than being struck, as they are in the piano. The tongues in the harpsichord are attached to the upper part of long, rectangular pieces of wood called *jacks,* which rise when the key is depressed, thus bringing the tongue in contact with the string. Larger instruments usually have two or three sets of jacks with harder or softer quills, and also different sets of strings producing higher and lower octaves (4 ft., 8 ft., 16 ft.). Thus, the instrument can produce a variety of tone colors by means of two manuals and a number of stops. The old instrument had hand stops, while on modern harpsichords the stops are usually operated by pedals. This tonal variety, similar to that of the organ, compensates for the main deficiency of the instrument, i.e., the impossibility of varying the sound by means of finger touch (as on the pianoforte and clavichord).

The harpsichord produces a sharp, silvery sound of great charm. Although lacking the dramatic and expressive qualities of the pianoforte, it is an excellent medium for contrapuntal music, since it enables the inner and lower parts of a composition to stand out clearly. It also combines very well — better than the pianoforte in some music — with the violin or flute.

Hauptwerk (HOWPT-vayrk: G.). Great organ.

Hautbois, hautboy (o-BWAH: F.; HO-boy: Eng.). Oboe.

Haydn Quartets. Familiar name of six string quartets by Mozart (K. 387, 421, 428, 458, 464, 465), composed between 1782 and 1785, and all dedicated to Haydn. They are listed as nos. 14 to 19 in the total series of Mozart's string quartets.

Haydn Variations. A set of variations by Brahms, based on a theme called "St. Anthony's Chorale" which was used by Haydn in one of his divertimentos (as yet unpublished) for wind instruments (*Feldmusik* in B-flat). Very likely the theme was a hymn popular in Haydn's time. Brahms' work, published simultaneously (1873) for orchestra (op. 56a) and for two pianos (op. 56b), consists of eight variations and a finale in the form of a passacaglia.

Hb. Short for F. *hautbois,* oboe.

Head voice. See under *Register* (2).

Hebrides, The or **Fingal's Cave.** Concert Overture by Mendelssohn, op. 26 (1830), inspired by his visit in 1829 to the Hebrides west of Scotland.

Heckelclarina (HEK-el-clar-EE-nah: erroneously spelled Heckelclarind). A special instrument with a single reed and a markedly conical metal pipe, constructed by Heckel for the "shepherd's pipe" in Act III of Wagner's *Tristan.* The part is now generally played on the English horn.

Heckelphone. See under *Oboe.*

Heldenleben, Ein (G.). See *Hero's Life.*

Heldentenor (HEL-den-ten-AWR: G., heroic tenor). A tenor voice of great brilliancy and volume, suited for parts such as Siegfried in Wagner's *Ring of the Nibelung*.

Helicon. See *Brass instruments,* IIe.

Hemidemisemiquaver. See under *Notes and rests*.

Hemiola, hemiolia, hemiole (hem-ee-O-la, hem-ee-O-lee-a, HEM-ee-ole: Gr., one and one half). In 15th- and 16th-century theory, term for note values standing in the relationship of 3 to 2, as in the modern triplets or, especially, in rhythmic patterns such as shown in Fig. 54a, where two dotted notes are replaced by three simple ones, resulting in a change from 6/4 to 3/2 or vice versa. This device is

Fig. 54

frequently used in the courantes and sarabandes of Baroque suites. Among 19th-century composers, Brahms is known for his frequent use of hemiola rhythms (see Fig. 54b, from his Second Symphony).

Hen, The (Symphony). See *Poule, La.*

Hero's Life, A (G., *Ein Heldenleben*). Symphonic poem by R. Strauss, op. 40, completed in 1898. The work describes the composer's own struggles to achieve recognition, depicting the jibes of the critics (by a dissonant "adversaries section" and a noisy "battle scene"), and the unceasing devotion of his wife (by an extended violin cadenza). Of special interest are the easily recognizable quotations from his earlier tone poems.

Heterophony (Gr., other sound). A term used by Plato and adopted by modern musicologists to describe a primitive type of polyphony in which two (or more) performers produce essentially the same melody with slight modifications in one part, mainly that of omission or addition of some notes. This style is frequently found in Chinese, Japanese, Javanese, African, etc., music.

Heure espagnole, L' (leur espah-NYOL: The Spanish Hour). One-act musical comedy by Ravel (libretto by Franc-Nohain), produced in Paris, 1911. The story centers around Torquemada (tenor), a clockmaker in 18th-century Toledo, who leaves a waiting customer, Ramiro (baritone), in his shop while he attends to business in the town. Torquemada's wife, Concepción (soprano), has secret lovers (Gonzalve and Inigo) whom she has hidden in grandfather clocks which the brawny Ramiro carries upstairs. Attracted by the strength of the guileless Ramiro, Concepción starts flirting with him, forgetting that her lovers are close at hand. The husband returns and discovers the lovers, but accepts the situation and joins in a merry closing ensemble. The music is in a delicate impressionistic style.

Hexachord (Gr., six strings). In medieval theory, a group of six consecutive tones of the scale, with a half tone in the middle, for example, c d e f g a (a segment such as d e f g a b is not properly a hexachord, although the term is often loosely used in modern writings to denote any group of six tones; see *Tetrachord*). The hexachord is the basis of a theoretical system initiated by Guido of Arezzo (*c.* 995–*c.* 1050) and based on the fact that in the diatonic scale, adding the tone bb, there are three hexachords, one starting on c (*hexachordum naturale*), one on g (*h. durum:* g a b c' d' e') and one on f (*h. molle:* f g a bb c' d'). In each group the tones were named ut, re, mi, fa, sol, la (see *Solmization*), so that mi-fa always denoted the half tone. By repeating these three hexachords in various octaves, the entire medieval scale from G to e" (see *Guidonian hand*) was constructed out of seven overlapping hexachords, as shown in Fig. 55. The transition from one hexachord to another, necessary for melodies of greater range, was known as mutation.

When applied to 20th-century music, the term hexachord is sometimes used for groups of six tones resulting from the halving of a twelve-tone row.

Hexentanz (HEX-en-tahns: G.). Witches' dance.

Hidden fifths, octaves. See under *Parallel fifths, octaves*.

High fidelity. Often abbreviated as *hi-fi*, high fidelity pertains to a standard of excellence in the reproduction of sound on discs, tape, wire, and film. The more closely a recording reproduces the original sound (under ideal acoustical conditions), the higher the fidelity. Recording companies and manufacturers of reproducing equipment have made tremendous progress since about 1945 in achieving clarity, sonority, and brilliance in recorded music.

Histoire du soldat, L' (lees-TWAHR dui sol-DAH: The Soldier's Tale). A stage work by Stravinsky (libretto by Ramuz), produced in Lausanne, 1918. It is somewhat in the character of a *ballet d'action*, combining ballet performance with a story told in dialogue by the characters and by a narrator. The Soldier, homeward bound, trades his fiddle for a magic book which the Devil, disguised as an old man, offers him. After a series of disillusioning experiences, he wanders to a city where the Princess is ill,

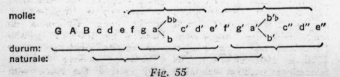

Fig. 55

regains his fiddle from the Devil by a ruse, cures the Princess with his playing, and marries her. The Devil vows to have the Soldier if he ever leaves his new kingdom and finally seizes him when, overcome with homesickness, he departs. The music, in acrid dissonances and pungent rhythms, consists of a number of °character pieces such as March, Tango, Waltz, Ragtime, and Chorale, composed for a chamber orchestra of six instruments and percussion.

History of music. The development of Western music (disregarding the music of the Orient, the Near East, etc.) may be divided into three epochs: °monophonic (from the beginnings until c. 1300), °polyphonic (from c. 800 until c. 1750), and °homophonic (from c. 1600 to the present).

A. *The Monophonic Period.* The pre-Christian development was carried mainly by the Greeks, who developed an important theoretical system (see *Greek music*), and by the Jews, about whose singing and playing of instruments there is meager information in the Scriptures. The rise and spread of Christianity brought with it a magnificent development of liturgical music known as °Gregorian chant. A parallel development, confined mostly to the city of Milan, is the °Ambrosian chant. Later additions to Gregorian chant are the °sequences and °tropes (9th to 12th centuries). There followed a splendid flowering of secular song under the °troubadours, °trouvères, and °minnesingers (12th to 14th centuries). The minnesinger tradition was taken up by the °mastersingers in the early 15th century. An impressive repertory of devotional songs is formed by the Italian °laude and the Spanish °cantigas, both from the late 13th century.

B. *The Polyphonic Period.* For the purpose of a survey, it is interesting and helpful to note that three times, at an interval of 300 years, the evolution of music has led to innovations so striking that contemporary writers described them as something "new": the °*Ars nova* of 1300, the °*Nuove musiche* of 1600, and the °*New Music* of 1900. These landmarks, together with others occurring almost exactly at the middle of the 300-year periods (e.g., 1750, death of Bach and Handel), serve as the basis of the following survey:

I. 800–1300. The earliest polyphonic music was called °organum. It developed out of primitive beginnings (parallel organum) into highly remarkable art forms (*organa dupla* of the School of °St. Martial), culminating in the *organa tripla* and *quadrupla* of Perotinus (c. 1160–1220). The 13th-century development, known as °Ars antiqua, brought with it the rise of the polyphonic °conductus, the °clausula, and the °motet.

II. 1300–1450. Novel concepts of rhythm and meter are the main characteristic of the Ars nova (Philippe de Vitry). The motet adopted large dimensions and complex structural features, mainly under Guillaume de Machaut (c. 1300–1377), who also cultivated secular polyphony (°ballade, °rondeau, °virelai). Italy entered the scene with

Francesco Landini (c. 1325–1397), composer of °madrigals and °ballatas (see also Caccia). In the early 15th century the English master, John Dunstable (c. 1375–1453), instigated a new trend toward euphony and fullness of sound, a trend which was continued by the °Burgundian composers Dufay (c. 1400–1474) and Binchois (c. 1400–1460). An important new form was the polyphonic °Mass.

III. 1450–1600. This period brought about a renewed emphasis on sacred music (Mass, motet) under the numerous masters of the °Flemish School (Ockeghem, Obrecht, Isaac, Josquin, Gombert, Lassus, and many others), and their followers in Italy (Palestrina, Gabrieli), England (Tallis, Byrd), Spain (Morales, Victoria), and Germany (Stoltzer, Hassler). The 16th century witnessed the rise of secular vocal forms (°frottola, °madrigal, °chanson, °lied) and of instrumental music (°ricercar, °toccata, °canzona, °variations). The Renaissance came to an impressive close in the °polychoral works of the °Venetian School (G. Gabrieli).

IV. 1600–1750. The years around 1600 constitute one of the most fundamental landmarks in the history of music (see Nuove musiche), leading to the waning (at least temporarily) of the polyphonic ideal of the 16th century, and to the cultivation of the monodic style (see Monody) in connection with such novel forms as °opera, °oratorio, and °cantata. Of equal importance is the development of larger instrumental forms, the °suite, the °sonata, and the °concerto. For more details see

under Baroque music. For a continuation of the 16th-century tradition, see under Roman School.

C. The Homophonic Period.

I. 1750–1900. Even while Bach and Handel wrote their great masterworks, new trends appeared leading away from the dignified grandeur of late-Baroque music to the light-minded elegance of the °Rococo (Couperin, Pergolesi). In France the contest between the old and the new art found an interesting expression in the °War of the Buffoons. About 1740, the members of the °Mannheim School (Stamitz, Richter) laid the foundation for the development of the °symphony, with parallel movements leading to the classical sonata and the °string quartet. Vienna became the center of the musical world under Haydn, Mozart, Beethoven, and Schubert (see Classicism). The °Romanticists, Schumann, Mendelssohn, and Chopin (all born about 1810), cultivated particularly the °character piece for pianoforte in which they achieved more perfect results than in the large forms of the classical period. It was not until the 1870's that the symphonic tradition was significantly revived, under Bruckner, Brahms, Franck, and finally Mahler. About 1850 the °symphonic poem developed as a new type of orchestral music, and operatic productivity attained renewed importance under Verdi and his German rival, Wagner. Against the dominant position of German music there arose, about 1860, the movement known as °Nationalism, which brought the musically dominated nations

(Bohemia, Norway, Russia, Spain, etc.) into the limelight under composers such as Dvořák, Smetana, Grieg, Moussorgsky, Rimski-Korsakov, and Albeniz. The 1890's saw the rise of °impressionistic music under Debussy.

II. Since 1900. Impressionism was the first indication of a quickly growing reaction against the Romanticism of the 19th century. There followed, in the first two decades of the 20th century, a period of revolutionary experiments, well deserving of the name New Music by which it is often referred to. Its most influential leaders were Schönberg (°twelve-tone technique) and Stravinsky (°dynamism). Since the 1920's the major trend has been °neoclassicism. For more details see under *Twentieth-century music.*

Hoboe. Older spelling for oboe, derived from F. *hautbois.*

Hochzeitsmarsch(HOKH-zeyets-marsh: G.). Wedding march.

Hocket, hoketus (L.). In medieval music (*c.* 1275–1350), a peculiar technique of composition characterized by the quick alternation of two (rarely three)

voice parts with single notes or short group of notes, one part having a rest where the other has notes. See Fig. 56. Numerous motets of the period (Petrus de Cruce, Philippe de Vitry, Machaut) include passages in hocket style.

Holberg Suite. A suite by Grieg, op. 40 (for piano solo or for string orchestra), consisting of a Prelude, Sarabande, Gavotte, Air, and Rigaudon. Entitled "From Holberg's time," it was written in commemoration of the Danish playwright Ludwig Holberg (1684–1754), a contemporary of Bach.

Holzharmonika (G.). Xylophone.

Homme armé, L'. See *L'homme armé.*

Homophonic, polyphonic (Gr., joint sounds, many sounds). Music is said to be homophonic if it consists of a single melodic line supported by chords or other subordinate material; polyphonic (or °contrapuntal) if it consists of several (two or more) melodic lines, each having individual significance and independence. Fig. 57 shows a melody treated (a) in homophonic and (b) in polyphonic texture. If sounded alone, the melody would fall under the category of °monophonic texture. The homophonic style is the one most familiar to present-day listeners. Practically all music from Haydn to Debussy is essentially homophonic, although it occasionally employs some polyphonic elaboration (as in late Beethoven,

Bethle-e—   e—   e—

o - li - ve—

e—   e—

Fig. 56

Fig. 57

Brahms) or includes some truly polyphonic sections, e.g., *fugatos* or *canons*. Since about 1920 there has been a notable renewal of interest in polyphonic style by most major composers. Polyphonic music makes greater demands on the hearing faculty of the listener, but offers rewarding satisfaction through its inner fullness and animation. See under *History of music; Texture.*

Hopak (also *gopak*). A lively Russian dance in duple meter.

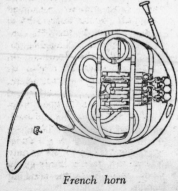

French horn

Horizontal writing. See under *Texture.*

Horn. An orchestral *brass instrument (often called *French horn* in order to distinguish it from the *English horn* — see illustration below and on p. 197) consisting of a narrow conical tube about 12 ft. long and wound twice in a circle, with a large flaring bell and a funnel-shaped mouthpiece. Inside the circle there are three valves, and the additional length of tubing required for them. It is normally pitched in F, and has a range from B_1 to f''. Of all the orchestral instruments, the horn, probably the most difficult to play, is one of the most useful. Played softly, it blends beautifully with the strings and wood winds, and its loud tones are clearly audible without ever being harsh. Special effects are *stopping* (blocking the bell with the hand), *mute* (insertion into the bell of a pear-shaped piece of metal or wood), and *cuivré* (a "brassy" tone obtained by an increased tension of the lips). Early symphonies (Haydn, Mozart) require two horns; modern scores normally call for four. See also *Natural horn.*

Horn fifths. See under *Parallel fifths.*

Hornpipe. A dance popular in England during the 16th to 19th centuries which, in its later development, was performed as a solo dance by sailors. It took its name from an obsolete wind instrument (also called *pibgorn*) which was used to accompany the dance. Various English composers have written hornpipes, e.g., Purcell and Handel (Concerto Grosso no. 7). A prominent feature is the use of dotted and inverted (Scotch snap) rhythms.

Horn Signal, Symphony with the. Haydn's Symphony no. 31 in D (1765), so called because of the frequent use of horn fanfares in the first movement. It is one of the most notable among the earlier Haydn symphonies.

Horn Trio. A celebrated trio by Brahms, op. 40 (1865), for horn, violin, and piano.

Horseman Quartet. Haydn's String Quartet no. 74 (op. 74, no. 3), in G major, so called because of the rhythmic patterns in the first movement which suggest the galloping of horses.

Hptw. In German organ scores, abbreviation for *Hauptwerk*, great organ (see under *Organ*).

Humoresque (F.), **Humoreske** (G.). A 19th-century name for instrumental compositions of a humorous or, more often, capricious character. In Schumann's Humoreske, op. 20, an extended composition in a number of sections, the name seems to refer to the frequent "change of humor."

Hungarian Dances (G., Ungarische Tänze). A collection of twenty-one dances by Brahms, for piano, four-hands, published in four volumes (1852–69). Some of them employ genuine Hungarian melodies, while others are freely invented in the Hungarian gypsy style.

Hungarian Rhapsodies. A group of about twenty piano composi-

tions by Liszt, in the character of free fantasies based on Hungarian themes. Each of them opens with a slow introduction and continues with a fast, dancelike movement in imitation of the Hungarian °csárdás.

Hunt Quartet. (1) Nickname of Mozart's String Quartet in B-flat, K. 458 (no. 4 of the °Haydn Quartets), also called *La Chasse,* with reference to the hunting-horn motif in the opening theme. — (2) Nickname of Haydn's String Quartet in B-flat, op. 1, no. 1, composed in 1755.

Hunt Symphony. Haydn's Symphony in D, no. 73 (1781), also called *La Chasse,* with reference to the last movement which was originally composed to depict a hunting scene in his opera *La Fedeltà premiata* (1780).

Hurdy-Gurdy. (1) The name for a medieval fiddle in which the strings are made to vibrate, not by a bow, but by a rotating rosined wheel inserted into an opening in the table (at the place occupied by the bridge on a violin) and operated by a handle at the lower end of the body. This curious instrument was quite popular in the 10th to 14th centuries. In the 18th century it became fashionable, together with the °musette, in French aristocratic circles as a mock-shepherd instrument. Haydn wrote five concertos and seven °notturnos for two hurdy-gurdies called, rather misleadingly, *lyra* or *lira organizzata.* — (2) Popular name for the street organ (barrel organ) whose only resemblance to the hurdy-gurdy would seem to be the cranking handle.

H. W. In German organ music, the abbreviation of *Hauptwerk*, great organ (see under *Organ*).

Hydraulis (Gr., water pipe). The organ of the ancient Greeks, invented by Ktesibius of Alexandria (*c.* 300–250 B.C.). Instead of bellows it had a metal container filled with water which served as a means of communicating and regulating air pressure provided by hand pumps and carried into a diving bell surrounded by the water. The hydraulis was in use until the 4th century after Christ and later.

Hymn. A song of praise or adoration of God (originally in honor of Apollo, the Greek god of the Muses). In the Christian churches (Roman, Anglican, Lutheran, etc.) it denotes non-Scriptural songs of praise, as distinguished from Psalms and canticles taken from the Bible. The hymns of the Roman Catholic Church are Latin poems consisting of various stanzas sung to the same melody, in the manner of strophic songs. Among the oldest Christian hymns preserved with music are those by St. Ambrose (*d.* 397), known as *Ambrosian hymns. Most of the hymns were written in the 5th to 10th centuries. A new

development started in the 16th century, when Luther introduced hymns in the German tongue into the service of the German Protestant Church (see *Chorale*). These are also strophic songs, usually sung in four-part harmony. The other reformed churches (Anglican, Calvinist, etc.) did not originally admit hymns, because their texts were "man-made," that is, not taken from the Scriptures. Here the *psalter was the only source for congregational singing. It was not until after 1700 that hymns were gradually admitted in the English-speaking countries. The American Methodists, under the leadership of John Wesley (whose first hymnal was printed in 1737 in Georgia), played a leading role in this development. The most important collections of English hymns are *The English Hymnal, The Oxford Hymn Book,* and *Hymns Ancient and Modern*.

Hyper-, hypo- (Gr., above, below). Prefixes denoting higher and lower pitches. *Hyperdiatessaron* is the upper fourth, *hypodiatessaron,* the lower fourth; *hyperdiapente, hypodiapente* are the upper or lower fifths. For *hypodorian,* etc., see under *Church modes* and *Greek music*.

I

Iberia (Latin name of the Spanish peninsula). Twelve piano pieces, in four sets of three each, by Albeniz, composed *c.* 1906–09. Each is based on a Spanish theme or locale. For Debussy's *Ibéria* see under *Images*.

Ictus (L.). See under *Gregorian chant*.

Idée fixe (ee-DAY feeks: F.). See under *Fantastic Symphony*.

Idiophones. See under *Instruments*.

Idomeneo Re di Creta (ee-do-me-NAY-o ray dee CRAY-ta: Idomeneus, King of Crete). Opera by Mozart (libretto by G. B. Varesco), produced in Munich, 1781. The story takes place after the Trojan War and tells of King Idomeneo (tenor) who, to placate the god Neptune, promises to sacrifice the first person he meets upon his return to Crete. This turns out to be his son Idamante (male soprano; sung by a tenor in modern performances). Unwilling to sacrifice him, Idomeneo brings down even greater wrath on his people until the god agrees to a milder judgment — Idomeneo must abdicate in favor of his son. There is a subplot involving the lovers Idamante and Ilia (soprano) and Electra (soprano).

Images (ee-MAHZH: F., pictures). Title used by Debussy for two cycles of compositions. (1) Six piano pieces in two sets of three each: I (1905), *Reflets dans l'eau* (Reflections in the Water), *Hommage à Rameau*, and *Mouvement*; II (1907), *Cloches à travers les feuilles* (Bells Sounding through the Leaves), *Et la lune descend sur le temple qui fut* (And the Moon Descends on the Temple of Yore), *Poissons d'or* (Goldfish). — (2) Three symphonic poems (*Images pour orchestre*, 1909–11): *Rondes de printemps*

(Dances of Spring), *Ibéria* (Spain), *Gigues.* The second, *Ibéria*, consists of three movements: *Par les rues et par les chemins* (On Streets and Alleys), *Les parfums de la nuit* (Perfumes of the Night), and *Le Matin d'un jour de fête* (The Morning of a Feast Day).

Imbroglio (It., confusion). An operatic scene in which the idea of intricate complication is artfully carried out by the simultaneous use of seemingly incongruous melodies, conflicting rhythms, etc. Famous examples are the ballroom scene in Mozart's *Don Giovanni* (end of Act II) and the street scene in Wagner's *Meistersinger* (end of Act II).

Imitation. The restatement in close succession of a musical idea (theme, subject, motive, or figure) in different voice parts of a contrapuntal texture. Compositions based on this device, such as the °canon and the °fugue, are said to be in imitative counterpoint. Among other compositions using imitation are Bach's °Inventions and 16th-century motets (see *Point of imitation*). Imitation may involve certain modifications of the musical idea, e.g., °inversion, °augmentation, diminution, etc.

Impériale, L' (lamh-pay-ree-AHL). Nickname (for no known reason) of Haydn's Symphony no. 53, in D major (*c.* 1775).

Imperfect. See under *Cadence*.

Impresario, The (G., *Der Schauspieldirektor*). A comedy with incidental music by Mozart (libretto by G. Stephanie), produced in Vienna, 1786. The story revolves around two rivaling sopranos, Madame Herz and Mademoiselle Silberklang, and a tenor, Monsieur Vogelsang.

Impressionism. An artistic movement of the late 19th and early 20th centuries represented in music chiefly by Claude Debussy (1862–1918). The term is borrowed from painting, and properly indicates the close relationship of contemporary trends in the various fields of art. The paintings of the French impressionists (e.g., Monet, Manet, and Renoir) and the refined poetry of Verlaine, Baudelaire, and Mallarmé suggested to Debussy a new type of music. Eminently French in character, it is a music which seems to hint rather than to state; in which suggestions of tonal colors take the place of logical development; a music which is as vague and intangible as the changing lights of the day and the subtle noises of the rain and the wind.

Foreshadowed in the works of Edouard Lalo and Alexis Chabrier (also in the late compositions of Liszt), impressionism was first fully realized in Debussy's °*Afternoon of a Faun* (1892) and later in his °*Nocturnes for Orchestra* (1893–99), the orchestral suite *La* °*Mer* (1903–05), the opera °*Pelléas et Mélisande* (1902), and the collections for pianoforte, °*Images* (1905, 1907), *Préludes* (1910–13), and *Études* (1915). Although Debussy was the originator and only full-fledged representative of impressionism, many other composers were strongly influenced by his innovations,

e.g., Ravel, Dukas, Roussel, de Séverac in France; Gräner, Schreker, Niemann in Germany; Loeffler, Carpenter, Griffes in America; Delius, Bax, Scott in England; Respighi in Italy; Falla in Spain; Scriabin in Russia; and Schönberg and Stravinsky in their early works.

Important technical devices of impressionistic style are °parallel chords and the °whole-tone scale.

Impromptu (F.). Properly, an improvisation, or a composition suggestive of improvisation. This element, however, is hardly present in the impromptus of Schubert, Chopin, and other Romantic composers who obviously used the title in order to indicate the somewhat casual origin of the composition (see under *Character piece*).

Improperia (L., reproaches). In the Roman Catholic service, chants assigned to Good Friday morning. They are based on admonishing texts from the Prophets. Palestrina, Vittoria, and others set these texts to simple four-part harmonizations, which are annually sung on Good Friday in the Sistine Chapel.

Improvisation. The art of spontaneously creating music (extempore) while playing, rather than performing a composition already written. Many of the older masters such as Bach, Handel, and Beethoven were as famous for their skill in improvising as for their written compositions. After Beethoven, the art of improvisation declined. Today it is practiced only by a few organists and pianists who improvise on themes given them by members of the audience.

More common is the art of introducing improvised details into a written composition. The three outstanding examples of this are the °thorough-bass accompaniment, the improvised ornamentations of the Baroque period, and the °cadenzas of the Classical concerto. There has been an interesting revival of improvisation technique in the development of jazz (see *Jam*).

Incidental music. Music used in connection with stage plays. It may consist of occasional songs, marches, dances, and fanfares; background music to monologues and dialogues; or instrumental music before and after the acts. Nearly all of Purcell's dramatic music is incidental music. More recent examples are Beethoven's *Egmont* (play by Goethe), Mendelssohn's *Midsummer Night's Dream* (Shakespeare), Bizet's *L'Arlésienne* (Daudet), and Grieg's *Peer Gynt* (Ibsen).

Incoronazione di Poppea, L' (leen-cor-o-na-tsi-O-nay dee pop-PAY-a: The Coronation of Poppaea). Opera by Monteverdi (libretto by G. F. Busenello), produced in Venice, 1642. Monteverdi's last opera, and the first opera to deal with a historical (rather than Biblical or mythological) subject, *L'Incoronazione* tells of the love of the Emperor Nero and the Roman matron Poppaea, and of the intrigues into which they enter to rid themselves of their respective mates. With the help of the gods they are successful, and Poppaea is crowned empress.

Incredible Flutist, The. Ballet by Walter Piston, composed in 1938. A suite derived from the score is played in orchestral concerts.

Instrumentation. See *Orchestration*.

Instruments. The generic name for all contrivances producing musical sounds, with the exception of the human voice. Instruments are usually classified into four categories: stringed, wood wind, brass, and percussion.

Interlude. Music designed to be played between the sections or movements of a composition or, more frequently, between the acts of an opera or play (see *Entr'acte; Intermezzo*). It may also be played between two parts of a liturgical service.

Intermezzo (in-ter-MED-zo: It.). (1) A 19th-century °character piece (Schumann, Brahms). The term suggests the casual origin of the composition, as if it were written between works of greater importance. — (2) Same as °interlude, °entr'acte. — (3) An 18th-century short comic opera in two scenes for two or three characters, so called because the scenes were performed during the two intermissions of a serious opera. The most famous example is Pergolesi's *La °Serva padrona*, originally performed in connection with his *Il prigioniero superbo* (1733), and usually considered the beginning of °comic opera. Throughout the 17th century, intermezzos (*intermedio, intermède*) consisting of madrigals, ballets, or little operatic scenes were performed between the acts of a masque, a grand ballet, or an opera.

Internationale, L' (F). See under *National anthems* (7).

Intervals. An interval is the distance in pitch between two notes. If the notes are sounded successively, it is a *melodic interval;* if sounded simultaneously, a *harmonic interval.* The smallest interval of our musical system is the *half tone* or *semitone* (ab-a, c-c♯ or e-f), of which there are twelve to the octave. The distance of two half tones is called a *whole tone* or simply *tone* (ab-bb, c-d or e-f♯), of which there are six to the octave, for example, c-d, d-e, e-f♯, f♯-g♯, g♯-a♯, a♯-c. The major scale consists of five whole tones (w) and two half tones (h) in the arrangement of w w h w w w h (see under *Scale*). For example, in the scale of C,

```
      w w h w w w  h
      c d e f g a b c'
```

The names for intervals refer to the number of scale steps from the lower to the higher note, as follows:

c-c unison (prime)	c-d second	c-e third	c-f fourth
c-g fifth	c-a sixth	c-b seventh	c-c' octave
c-d' ninth	c-e' tenth	c-f' eleventh	c-g' twelfth

The intervals larger than an octave are called *compound intervals,* in contradistinction to *simple intervals* which do not exceed an octave in range, e.g., a ninth (compound) is made up of an octave and a second (simple).

Intervals leading downward are called "lower," e.g., the lower fifth of c is F. If two intervals sum up to an octave (c-g and g-c'), each of them is said to be the *complement* or the *inversion* of the other. Thus the fourth is the complement (or inversion) of the fifth, the third that of the sixth, and the second that of the seventh.

The same names are applied to intervals starting on notes other than c. Thus, the intervals d-f, e-g, f-a, g-b are all thirds. Since, however, they are not all alike (d-f and e-g are w h, the others, w w), it is necessary to distinguish between various types of thirds, fourths, etc., according to the number of half tones found between the outer notes. The fourth, fifth, and octave exist in three varieties, *diminished, perfect,* and *augmented,* while each of the other intervals has four varieties, *diminished, minor, major,* and *augmented.* In the table on p. 143, the figures in parentheses indicate the number of half tones contained in each interval.

In the Steppes of Central Asia. A symphonic poem by Alexander Borodin (1880) which depicts the passage of an Oriental caravan across the Russian desert.

Intonation. (1) Degree of adherence to correct pitch. Good intonation implies close approxi-

	Diminished	Minor	Major	Augmented
Second	c#-db (0)	c-db (1)	c-d (2)	c-d# (3)
Third	c#-eb (2)	c-eb (3)	c-e (4)	c-e# (5)
Sixth	c#-ab (7)	c-ab (8)	c-a (9)	c-a# (10)
Seventh	c#-bb (9)	c-bb (10)	c-b (11)	c-b# (12)
		Perfect		
Fourth	c#-f (4)	c-f (5)		c-f# (6)
Fifth	c#-g (6)	c-g (7)		c-g# (8)
Octave	c#-c' (11)	c-c' (12)		c-c#' (13)

Table of Intervals

mation of the pitch; poor intonation implies deviation from pitch. — (2) In Gregorian chant, the opening notes of a °psalm tone.

Intrada (in-TRAH-da). An introductory piece of a festive or marchlike character, current around 1600, often found at the beginning of a suite. Mozart and Beethoven used the name occasionally for short overtures.

Introduction. An opening section frequently found at the beginning of musical compositions. Introductions of symphonies, string quartets, sonatas, etc., are usually in a slow tempo. See *Sonata*.

Introit (IN-troyt). The first item of the Proper of the °Mass.

Inventions. Collective name for two sets of keyboard pieces composed about 1723 by Bach, 15 in two parts and 15 in three, distinguished as *Two-Part* and *Three-Part Inventions*. Bach's original title for the first set was *Inventiones* (L.) and for the second, *Sinfoniae*. They are masterful studies in a special type of imitative counterpoint.

Inversion. A term applied to various procedures involving the substitution of higher for lower tones and vice versa. In connection with intervals, chords, and contrapuntal voice parts, inversion is effected by transposing one or more of the constituents into a higher (or lower) octave. An interval is inverted by transferring its lower tone into the higher octave, e.g., changing c to c', thus changing the interval from c-g to g-c' (Fig. 58a; see also under *Intervals*). A chord is inverted in the same way, for example, c-e-g becomes e-g-c' or g-c'-e' (Fig. 58b; see also under *Chords*). Counterpoint is inverted by transferring the upper part down an octave so that it becomes the lower part, or the lower part into a higher octave (see *Invertible counterpoint*). Basically the same thing occurs in an inverted pedal, a °pedal point occurring, not in the bass, but in a higher part.

All of the foregoing types of inversion are collectively called *harmonic inversion*. Essentially different is the inversion of a single melody (e.g., a fugal sub-

original   inversion

Fig. 58

ject or a theme of a sonata movement), known as *melodic inversion.* This means that each ascending interval of an entire melody is changed into its opposite descending interval and vice versa. Thus, the progression c'-f' becomes c'-g, and c'-d'-a becomes c'-b-e'. The result is a mirrorlike exchange of upward and downward motions, comparable to the contours of a forest and its reflection in a lake (Fig. 58c). Melodic inversion plays an important role in fugues and in the development section of sonatas. It also forms an essential ingredient of the °twelve-tone technique.

Inverted mordent, turn. See under *Mordent; Turn.*

Invertible counterpoint. A passage in contrapuntal texture is said to be invertible (convertible) if it is so designed that, by some means of transposition — usually of an octave — the lower part may become the higher one and the higher, the lower (Fig. 59a). The device, if applied to two parts, is called double counterpoint; if applied to three (or four) parts, triple (or quadruple) counterpoint. In double counterpoint of the fifth (tenth, twelfth), one part is transposed up a fifth (tenth, twelfth), instead of an octave, while the other appears unchanged or in octave transposition. Fig. 59b shows an example from Bach's *Five Canonic Variations.*

Invitation to the Dance (G., *Aufforderung zum Tanz*). A piano composition by Weber, op. 65 (1819), in the character of a waltz, preceded by an introduction (the "invitation") and concluded by an epilogue. It is the first example of a real waltz in art music.

Ionian. See under *Church modes.*

Iphigenia (if-i-je-NEE-a). Two operas by Gluck, *Iphigenia in Aulis* (*Iphigénie en Aulide*), produced in Paris, 1774, and *Iphigenia in Tauris* (*Iphigénie en Tauride*), produced in Paris, 1779. Both are based on dramas by Euripides.

Isle of the Dead, The. A symphonic poem by Rachmaninoff (op. 29, 1907), inspired by A. Boecklin's painting of the legendary destination of departed souls. The plainsong °*Dies Irae* is used effectively.

Isorhythm (EYE-so-rithm: Gr., equal rhythm). An important device of 14th-century composition, found in the motets of Vitry, Machaut, and their successors, Dunstable and Dufay. It denotes employment of a fixed pattern of time values for the liturgical melody (°*cantus firmus*) of the

Fig. 59

tenor, this rhythmic pattern being restated several times during the course of the melody. The rhythmic pattern is called *talea*, the melody, *color*. Fig. 60 shows

Fig. 60

an example of *color* divided into three *taleae* (a, b, and c). Usually the entire tenor consists of two *colores* (I, II), the second being a diminution (halved note values) of the first.

Israel in Egypt. Oratorio by Handel (to a Scriptural text), composed in 1738.

Istar Variations (IS-tahr). Seven orchestral variations by d'Indy, op. 42 (1896), which are a unique example of "variation in the reverse," starting with the most complex variation and ending with the theme in octaves. This process of "disrobing" is implied in the title, Istar being the Babylonian goddess of passion.

Istesso tempo, L' (lis-TES-so TEM-po: It., *stesso*, the same). Indication that, though the me-

ter changes (e.g., from 3/4 to 4/4), the beat remains the same (i.e., the duration of the quarter notes does not change).

Italian Concerto. A composition for harpsichord by Bach, published in 1735 (see under *Clavierübung*). It is written in the form and style of the orchestral concertos of Italian composers such as Vivaldi. The contrast between *solo* and *tutti* is imitated by the use of dynamic contrasts, *forte* and *piano,* on the two manuals of the harpsichord. It consists of three movements (fast-slow-fast) the first and third in °ritornello form, the second a continuous melody over an accompaniment based on a one-measure rhythmic and textural pattern.

Italian overture. See under *Overture.*

Italian Serenade. (G., *Italienische Serenade*). A short piece for string quartet (1887) by Hugo Wolf. It was transcribed (1892) for small orchestra by the composer and is most frequently heard in this later arrangement.

Italian sixth. See under *Chords* (5).

Italian Symphony. Mendelssohn's Symphony no. 4 in A major, op. 90 (1831–33), begun in Italy and containing allusions to Italian folk music, particularly in the last movement, entitled "Saltarello." The slow movement is sometimes called the "Pilgrim's March."

J

Jack. See under *Harpsichord*.

Jahreszeiten, Die. See *Seasons*.

Jalousieschweller (zha-loo-ZEE-shvel-ler: G.). The °swell pedal of the organ.

Jam. Jazz musicians' term for improvisation. At a *jam session*, a group of musicians choose a familiar popular tune (e.g., "Tea for Two," "The Sheik") and improvise both in ensemble and as soloists. Jamming is thus distinguished from the "hot chorus" or "take off," in which an improvised solo is played against a written or memorized accompaniment performed by the ensemble players.

Janizary music. Music of the military bodyguard of the Turkish sultans (from about 1400 to 1826, when they were dethroned) which employed big drums, cymbals, triangles, and the Turkish °crescent. This noisy and strongly rhythmic type of music became very popular in Europe toward the end of the 18th century. Haydn imitated it in his °Military Symphony, Mozart in both the *Abduction from the Seraglio* and the last movement of his Piano Sonata in A (K. 331: *Alla turca*), and Beethoven in the °*Ruins of Athens*.

Jazz. General term for the 20th-century development of American popular music. Growing out of °ragtime (most features of which were taken over into jazz), jazz embraces the °blues, °swing, °jive, and °bebop. It is primarily dance music in duple meter, characterized by the frequent use of syncopation and other rhythmic complexities. The instruments normally used in jazz are trumpets, trombones, clarinets, saxophones, and the rhythm instruments — piano, guitar, bass, and drums (°traps). Most of the various types of jazz developed in the Negro districts of the large cities of the South (New Orleans, St. Louis) and spread to Chicago and New York, where they were commercialized (°Tin Pan Alley). The word jazz, of uncertain origin, first appeared in print in 1916. The attribute "hot" was introduced in the 1920's to express approval of jazz improvisation (Dixieland). "Hot" playing by a soloist is marked by ingenuity, technical brilliance, and speed, in contrast to "sweet" music, which is played or sung without strict regard for time (*rubato*), at medium or slow tempo, and with less improvisation. Illustrative of the transitory nature of jazz terminology is the fact that excellence is now referred to as "cool," not "hot," although the meaning of the newer term is close to that of the older one.

Jeanne d'Arc au Bûcher (zhan DARK o bui-SHAY: Joan of

Arc at the Stake). An oratorio by Honegger (libretto by Paul Claudel) produced in Basel, 1938. Although it is usually performed in concert form, i.e., without staging and costuming, it may be performed as an opera.

Jena Symphony (YAY-na). A symphony which was discovered at Jena, Germany, in 1910. Although it was acclaimed as an early work of Beethoven, it has not been generally accepted as such.

Jephtha. (1) Handel's last oratorio (English text by Thomas Morell), produced in London, 1752. — (2) Oratorio by Carissimi (Latin text from the Scriptures) composed about 1650.

Jeu (zheu: F., plur. *jeux,* play). *Jeu de timbre* and *jeu de clochettes* mean glockenspiel. In organ music, *jeux* means stops, e.g., *jeux de fonds,* foundation stops; *jeux à bouche,* flue stops; *jeux d'anche,* reed stops.

Jeu de Cartes, Le (zheu de CART: The Card Game). Ballet "in Three Deals" by Stravinsky, produced in New York, 1937. The dancers represent the chief cards in a poker game which proceeds through three deals, each deal being successively more complex.

Jeune France, La (zheun frahnhs). A group of French composers, formed in 1936, consisting of Yves Baudrier (b. 1906), André Jolivet (b. 1905), Daniel-Lesur (b. 1908), and Olivier Messiaen (b. 1908). These men presented concerts of their (and other French) music,

and were unified in the common objective of "sincerity, generosity and artistic good faith."

Jew's harp (or **trump**). A primitive instrument consisting of an elastic strip of metal fixed in a small horseshoe-shaped iron frame. The frame is held between the teeth (possibly "Jew" is a perversion of "jaw"), and the protruding strip is made to vibrate by a stroke of the finger. Different tones can be obtained by varying the cavity of the mouth.

Jig. In the 16th century, an English popular dancing song of a lively and comic character. In the 17th century it was used by and associated with famous clowns in English comedies (Kemp's Jig, Slaggin's Jig). Another 17th-century development was the °gigue, one of the standard dances of the Baroque suite. According to a recent theory, the jig is also the ancestor of the grotesque dances of the early American minstrel shows, and thus eventually of jazz.

Jig Fugue. See *Gigue Fugue.*

Jive. A general term — no longer current in jazz terminology — used both as a noun and as a verb to describe improvised jazz which is usually played at a fast tempo.

Jodel. See *Yodel.*

Jongleurs (zhonh-GLEUR: F.). French °minstrels (professional musicians, entertainers) of the 12th and 13th centuries, often in the service of the °troubadours and °trouvères whose songs they sang and may have accompanied on instruments.

Joshua. Oratorio by Handel (libretto by T. Morell), produced in London, 1748.

Jota (KHO-ta: Sp.). A dance of Aragon (a province in northeastern Spain) in rapid triple time, performed by one or more couples to music played on guitars and castanets. One of the most popular melodies has been used by Liszt in his Spanish Rhapsody (*Folies d'Espagne et Jota Aragonese*) and by Glinka in his orchestral overture, *Jota Aragonese*.

Jubel-Ouvertüre, Jubilee Overture. An orchestral overture by Weber, op. 59 (1818), composed (together with a *Jubel-Cantate*) for the fiftieth anniversary of the accession of Frederick August, King of Saxony. It closes with the melody of "God Save the King."

Jubilus. In Gregorian chant, the long *melisma sung to the final vowel of the *Alleluia.

Judas Maccabaeus. Oratorio by Handel (libretto by T. Morell), produced in London, 1747.

Jupiter Symphony. Nickname of Mozart's last symphony, in C major, no. 41 (K. 551), composed in 1788. The name would seem to refer mainly to the "majestic" opening of the first movement. The last movement is in sonata form, but makes extended use of fugal writing.

Just intonation. A theoretical system of tuning in which the third as well as the fifth are "pure," i.e., acoustically correct (see *Acoustics*, 2), and in which all the other intervals are derived from these two, e.g., the second as a double fifth (c-g, g-d'), the sixth as a lower third, etc. The system has great theoretical interest, but cannot be used as a basis for practical music because of several serious disadvantages: (a) The tones of the C-major scale include one dissonant fifth, namely d-a. (b) The C-major scale has two different sizes of whole tones, c-d being slightly larger and d-e considerably smaller than the whole tone in *equal temperament. (c) Modulation is impossible; the first three tones of the G-major scale (g-a-b) have different intervals from those of the C-major scale (c-d-e). Hence, two different tones *a* would be necessary, one for the sixth of c, the other for the second of g.

Modern singers and violinists often refer to just intonation in order to justify their practice of using certain pitches slightly different from those of equal temperament, e.g., sharp thirds and leading tones, or, in *enharmonic pairs, a higher pitch for the sharps (e.g., g♯) than for the flats (e.g., a♭). Actually, none of these deviations has anything to do with just intonation, in which all the above-mentioned pitches differ from equal temperament in exactly the opposite direction (e.g., g♯ is lower than a♭, and the third is lower than that of equal temperament).

K

K. In connection with works of Mozart, abbreviation for Ludwig von Köchel who, in 1862, published a chronological list of all the compositions by Mozart, known as Köchel Catalogue (G., *Köchel-Verzeichnis, K. V.*). Mozart's works are identified by the numbers of this Catalogue (recently revised by A. Einstein), e.g., K. 357 or K. V. 357.

Kaffeekantate (G.). See *Coffee Cantata.*

Kalevala (kahl-ay-VAHL-a). The national epic of the Finns, dating from the 13th and 14th centuries. Several symphonic poems by Sibelius (and other Finnish composers) are based on legends from this epic, e.g., *°Lemminkainen's Homecoming, °Pohjola's Daughter, °Swan of Tuonela, °Tapiola.*

Kammer (G.). Chamber, e.g., *Kammermusik,* chamber music.

Karelia (kah-RAY-li-a). Orchestral Overture (op. 10) and Suite (op. 11) by Sibelius, composed in 1893. Karelia is the southern province of Finland where the composer lived at that time.

Kastagnetten (G.). Castanets.

Kazoo (ka-ZOO). A toy instrument into which the performer hums, a membrane changing the timbre of the voice. Today it is usually made in the approximate shape and size of a cigar. Older specimens, known as onion flute or mirliton, were in the shape of a flute.

Kb. Abbreviation for G. *Kontrabass,* i.e., double bass.

Kesselpauke (G.). Kettledrum.

Kettledrum. See under *Drums* (1).

Key. (1) On pianos, organs, etc., the levers which are depressed by the fingers; collectively called keyboard. — (2) On wood-wind instruments, metal levers covering the finger holes which cannot conveniently be covered directly by the fingers. They greatly facilitate the playing of the instruments (see *Boehm system*). — (3) In connection with tonality, key means something like "tonal center" or "main note" of a composition and, by extension, all of the notes related to this central note and forming the tonal material for the composition. To a certain extent, key is identical with scale. To each scale there is a corresponding key, e.g., C major, C minor, C-sharp major, C-sharp minor, etc., resulting in a complete system of 24 keys (or more, if enharmonic equivalents are added, e.g., D-flat in addition to C-sharp). Actually, however, key has a considerably wider meaning than scale, admitting not only chromatic variants of the notes of the basic scale but also *modulation into other keys. In the case of compositions consisting of several movements, the key designation (e.g., Concerto in E-flat, Symphony in B minor) means only that the first and last movements are in this key, some of the middle movements usually being in different keys. In the Baroque suite (Bach), however, all the movements are in the same key. See also *Tonality; Key signature.*

Keyboard. The whole set of keys (see *Key*, 1) as found in pianofortes, organs, and other keyboard instruments. Modern pianos have a keyboard of seven octaves, from C_1 to c'''', plus three keys below. In each octave there are seven white and five black keys, arranged as shown in Fig. 61.

Fig. 61

Keyboard instruments. Generic name for instruments having a keyboard, e.g., the pianoforte, organ, harmonium, harpsichord, clavichord, etc. The term is used mainly with reference to early music (16th, 17th centuries) in which there is often no clear distinction between music for the organ, the harpsichord, and the clavichord. Other instruments having a (small) keyboard are the *accordion and the *hurdy-gurdy.

Keynote. Same as *tonic.

Key relationship. Generic term to indicate the various degrees of relationship between two keys (see *Key*, 3), particularly between the main key of a composition and others appearing by way of modulation, or of change of key from one movement to the next. All keys are related, but in different degrees. Closest to a given key (e.g., C major) are the keys of the dominant (a fifth higher, G major) and of the subdominant (a fourth higher, F major). Other important relationships are: (a) *parallel key*, i.e., major and minor with the same tonic but with different signatures (C major and C minor); (b) *relative key*, i.e., major and minor with the same key signature (C major and A minor; C minor and E-flat major); (c) *closely related keys*, i.e., those whose signatures differ by no more than one sharp or flat from that of the main key (for C major: A minor, G major, E minor, F major, D minor).

Key signature. The sharps or flats appearing at the beginning of each staff, indicating the scale and the key of the composition. This indication, however, is not unequivocal, since there are always two keys, one major and one minor, having the same key signature (relative keys). For instance, a signature of three flats shows that the key is either E-flat major or C minor. The decision between these two possibilities has to be made from the music itself, either its beginning or, most clearly, the bass note of the final chord. Following is a table showing all the key signatures.

Sharps	Major Key	Minor Key		Flats	Major Key	Minor Key
–	C	A				
1	G	E				
2	D	B				
3	A	F-sharp				
4	E	C-sharp				
5	B	G-sharp	=	7	[C-flat]	A-flat
6	F-sharp	[D-sharp]	=	6	G-flat	E-flat
7	C-sharp	[A-sharp]	=	5	D-flat	B-flat
				4	A-flat	F
				3	E-flat	C
				2	B-flat	G
				1	F	D
				–	C	A

The sharp and flat keys appearing on the three middle lines (5,6,7) are *enharmonic equivalents. The alternatives in brackets are rarely used. Fig. 62 shows the key signatures up to seven sharps and five flats, with a white note indicating the major key, a black one the minor key for each signature. The following is a memorizing rule for the major keys: For a major key using sharps, the keynote is one tone above the last sharp in the signature; for a major key using flats, the keynote is on the pitch of the next-to-last flat in the

Fig. 62

signature. The keynote for a minor key is a minor third lower than for the corresponding major.

Kfg. In German orchestral scores, short for *Kontrafagott*, i.e., contrabassoon.

Kinderscenen (KIN-der-stsaynen: Scenes from Childhood). A

composition by Schumann, op. 15 (1838), consisting of thirteen short and simple *character pieces for piano. The familiar "Träumerei" (Dreams) is no. 7 in the group.

Kindertotenlieder (KIN-der-toten-LEE-der: Children's Death Songs). A cycle of five songs with orchestra or pianoforte by Mahler (poems by Rückert), composed in 1902. The poems are an elegy on the death of Rückert's child. The songs are masterpieces of melodic invention and artistic simplicity. The orchestra is treated throughout as a large chamber ensemble rather than as a mass of sound.

King David (F., *Le Roi David*). Oratorio by Honegger (text by René Morax), originally incidental music to a play (1921), produced as an oratorio in New York, 1925. In the latter form, the orchestra is considerably enlarged, and a narrator relates the dramatic events between musical selections. Comprising twentyseven pieces, it describes the life of David from his youth as a shepherd boy until his death. The choral writing is vigorous, and the score is marked by a highly stylized, archaic orientalism.

Kit. A small, narrow fiddle, used in the 18th and early 19th centuries by dancing masters, who carried it in the pocket of their tail coat.

Kithara (KITH-a-ra). The foremost stringed instrument of the ancient Greeks, also the legendary instrument of their god Apollo. It has a U-shaped frame, with a crossbar between the upper ends of the two arms, and five to seven (or more) strings stretched between this crossbar and the bottom part which served as a sound box. See illustration.

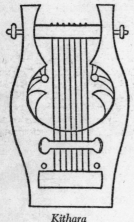

Kithara

Kl. In German orchestral scores, short for *Klarinette*, clarinet.

Klavier (klah-VEER: G.). Pianoforte (formerly also other keyboard instruments; see *Clavier*). *Klavierauszug*, piano arrangement. *Klavierstück*, piano piece. *Klavierübung* (Bach), see *Clavierübung*.

Kleine Flöte (G., small flute). Piccolo.

Kleine Nachtmusik, Eine (EYE-ne KLEYE-ne NAKHT-moo-ZEEK: A Little Night Music, or Serenade). A celebrated composition for string orchestra by Mozart (K. 525), composed in 1787. It is in four movements, similar to those of a symphony.

Kleine Trommel (G., small drum). Snare drum.

Kl. Fl. Short for *Kleine Flöte*, i.e., piccolo.

Kl. Tr. Short for *Kleine Trommel*, i.e., snare drum.

Knaben Wunderhorn, Des (G.). See *Youth's Magic Horn*.

Köchel-Verzeichnis (Catalogue). See under *K*.

Kontrabass (KON-tra-bahs: G.). Double bass.

Kontrafagott (KON-tra-fa-GOT: G.). Double bassoon.

Konzert (kon-TSAYRT: G.). (1) Concerto. — (2) Concert, recital.

Konzertstück (G.). See *Concertstück*.

Koppel (G.). Coupler (of the organ, harpsichord).

Krakowiak, Cracovienne (kra-KAW-vyak, kra-ko-VYEN). A Polish dance named after the city of Cracow. The music is in quick 2/4 time. It was in vogue in the earlier part of the 19th century, and was executed by large groups, with shouting, improvised singing, and striking of the heels. Chopin wrote a Krakowiak for piano and orchestra (op. 14).

Kreisleriana (kreyes-ler-YAH-na). The title of Schumann's cycle (op. 16, 1838) consisting of eight piano pieces in strongly contrasting moods (see under *Character piece*). The title refers to the whimsical and fantastic figure of the "Kapellmeister Kreisler," invented by the German novelist E. T. A. Hoffmann (see *Tales of Hoffmann*).

Kreutzer Sonata (KROY-tser). Nickname for Beethoven's Violin Sonata op. 47 (1803), dedicated to the French violin composer and virtuoso Rodolphe Kreutzer (1766–1831), but originally composed for the English violinist George Bridgetower (c. 1780–1860), whom Beethoven accompanied at the first performance in 1803. Its first movement is notable for its forceful expression of intense emotion. In Tolstoy's story *The Kreutzer Sonata,* the composition is made a symbol of the destruction of morals caused by violently emotional music.

Kuhreigen (KOO-reye-gen: G.). Same as *ranz des vaches.

Kujawiak (koo-YA-vyak). A Polish dance from the province of Kujawy. It is a rapid variety of the *mazurka. A number of Chopin's Mazurkas are actually in the character of a kujawiak (e.g., op. 6, no. 6; op. 30, no. 4; op. 41, no. 1).

Kunst der Fuge, Die (G.). See *Art of Fugue.*

K. V. See under *K.*

Kyrie (KEER-i-ay: Gr., O Lord). The first item of the Ordinary of the *Mass. The full text is *Kyrie eleison, Christe eleison, Kyrie eleison* (Lord, have mercy; Christ, have mercy; Lord, have mercy), each exclamation being sung three times.

L

L. or **L. H.** In piano scores, short for left hand (in German *linke Hand*). For French titles starting with *L',* see entry under the following word in the title.

La. See under *Pitch names; Solmization; Tonic Sol-fa.*

La. French for "the" (feminine singular). For titles beginning with *La,* see entry under the following word in the title.

Lac des cygnes. See Swan Lake.

Lady Macbeth of Mtsensk. Opera by Shostakovich (libretto by A. Preis and the composer, based on a novel by Leskov), produced in Moscow, 1934. The central figure is the "Russian

Lady Macbeth," Katerina (soprano), who in the course of the opera murders her father-in-law and then, with the help of her lover, kills her husband. The murderers are sent to Siberia, where the lover deserts her for another woman. Katerina drowns her rival and commits suicide. The opera became notorious because of certain unsavory scenes which represent the °verismo technique at its most degenerate. Although these scenes were omitted from later performances, the opera was officially condemned by the Soviet government as "bourgeois and formalistic" in 1936.

Ländler (LEN-dler: G.). An Austrian dance popular about 1800, in rather slow triple time and approximating the waltz (see under *Dance music*). It was also known as *Deutscher Tanz*. Mozart (K. 606), Beethoven (*Mödlinger Tänze,* 1819), and Schubert (op. 171) wrote collections of Ländler. Other examples are the third movement of Beethoven's Symphony no. 8 and the Trio of the Scherzo in Bruckner's Romantic Symphony, no. 4.

Lai, lay. A form of °trouvère poetry and music (13th century), in the character of an extended narrative of sixty, a hundred, or more lines, divided into stanzas of irregular length and of variable poetic meter and rhyme schemes. The musical form is derived from the double-versicle structure of the °sequence, but often includes sections of three or four versicles.

Lakmé (lahk-MAY). Opera by Delibes (libretto by E. Gondinet and P. Gille), produced in Paris, 1883. The plot is laid in India, where a British officer, Gerald (tenor), falls in love with Lakmé (soprano), the daughter of the Brahman priest Nilakantha (bass) who hates foreigners. In Act II the father stabs Gerald who, however, survives and is rescued by Lakmé. In Act III the lovers are together when English soldiers appear and remind Gerald of his duty in an impending campaign. He prepares to follow them and Lakmé poisons herself.

Lament. Scottish and Irish music for the bagpipes (rarely with song) used at funeral rites. Each clan had its traditional tune.

Lamentations. The Biblical Lamentations of Jeremiah, mourning the downfall of Israel. A large part of the text is used, with plainsong, in the Roman Catholic service at Matins of Thursday, Friday, and Saturday of Holy Week (before Easter). In the 16th century it was composed polyphonically by various masters, notably Palestrina, whose setting, together with that of Gregorio Allegri, is still sung by the Sistine Choir.

Landini cadence, Landini sixth (lahn-DEE-nee). A cadence named after Franceso Landini (1325–1397) in which the sixth degree is inserted between the seventh (leading tone) and the octave, for example, b-a-c'. This cadence is frequent not only in the works of Landini but also of Machaut (1300–1377) and many 15th-century composers (Dufay, Binchois).

Large. See under *Notes and rests.*

Larghetto (It.). Indication for a tempo slightly faster than *largo.* *Larghissimo,* indication for tempo slower than *largo.*

Largo (It., broad). Very slow, slower than *adagio.* See under *Tempo marks.*

Largo (by Handel). Popular name for a famous composition by Handel, originally the aria "Ombra mai fù" (Shade never was) from his opera *Serse* (Xerxes), but usually played in an arrangement for organ or other instruments. The title is taken from the original tempo indication of the piece.

Lark Quartet. Haydn's String Quartet in D major (op. 64, no. 5), so called because of the high passage of the first violin "soaring like a lark" at the opening of the first movement.

Lauda, laude (la-OO-da, la-OO-de: It., sing. and pl., praise). Songs of praise and devotion in the Italian language. They originated in the 13th century, probably in connection with the activity of St. Francis of Assisi (1182–1226). The laude of the 13th century are monophonic songs, mostly in a form somewhat similar to that of the French *virelai. In the 16th and 17th centuries there appeared a great number of laude composed in polyphonic style.

Laudon Symphony. Haydn's Symphony no. 69 in C (*c.* 1778), composed in honor of the Austrian field-marshal, Laudon.

Lauds. See under *Office.*

Lay. See *Lai.*

Le. French for "the" (masculine singular). For titles beginning with *Le,* see entry under the following word in the title.

Leading motif. See *Leitmotiv.*

Leading tone or **note.** The seventh degree of the major or minor scale, a half tone below the tonic (octave); so called because of its strong tendency to "lead up" (resolve upward) to the tonic.

Ledger lines. Short lines drawn underneath or above the staff for notes too low or too high to appear on the staff.

Legato (le-GAH-to: It., bound). Term used to indicate performance without any perceptible interruption between the notes (see Fig. 63a), as distinct from *leggiero* or *nonlegato* (b), *portato* (c), or *staccato* (d). *Lega-*

Fig. 63

tissimo (e) is either a more forceful indication of legato, or a sort of superlegato in which the preceding note is held for a moment together with the following one. *Staccatissimo* is a very short and forceful staccato, often indicated by the sign ˙ placed over the note.

Legend, Legende (G.), **légende** (F.). Romantic title for compositions based on or suggestive of a legendary narration.

Legend of St. Elizabeth. Oratorio by Liszt (words by O. Roquette), first performed in Budapest, 1865.

Leggiero (led-JAYR-o: It., obsolete form of *leggero*, light). Light (soft). See under *Legato*.

Leich (leyekh). A medieval type of German poetry and music, derived from and similar to the French °lai (13th and 14th centuries).

Leitmotiv (LEYET-mo-TEEF: G., leading motif). In Wagnerian and post-Wagnerian operas, a short theme or musical idea consistently associated with a character, a place or an object, a certain situation, or a recurrent idea of the plot. For instance, in *The* °*Ring of the Nibelung*, there are motifs characterizing (a) the Ring, (b) the Contract, (c) Valhalla, (d) the Sword (See Fig. 64). These motifs are used, not as rigidly fixed melo-

dies, but in a very flexible manner, their rhythms, intervals, etc., being frequently modified according to the dramatic requirement of the momentary situation. See also under *Transformation of themes; Parsifal*.

Lemminkäinen's Homecoming (LEM-in-KEYE-nen). A symphonic poem by Sibelius, op. 22 (1893–95), describing (after a story from the °Kalevala) the hero's journey home from Pohjola (see *Pohjola's Daughter*).

Leningrad Symphony. A title sometimes applied to Shostakovich's Symphony no. 7, op. 60, composed in 1941 when Leningrad was beleaguered by the Germans.

Lento (It.). Slow. See under *Tempo marks*.

Leonora Overtures. The three overtures which Beethoven wrote for his opera °*Fidelio* (the libretto was originally entitled *Léonore*), prior to composing the final one (1814) known as *Fidelio Overture* (or somewhat incorrectly as *Leonora Overture No. 4*). *Leonora No. 2* was written for a performance in Vienna in 1805, *No. 3* for one in Vienna in 1806, and *Leonora No. 1* for a presentation planned for Prague in 1807 but never given.

Les. French for "the" (plural). For titles beginning with *Les*, see entry under the following word in the title.

Les Adieux, l'absence, et le retour (F.). See *Farewell Sonata*.

Fig. 64

Letter notation. See *Pitch names.*

L. H. In piano scores, left hand (also German, *linke Hand*).

L'homme armé (lom ahr-MAY: The Armed Man). A 15th-century French folk song frequently used as a °*cantus firmus* for Masses (*Missa L'homme armé*), e.g., by Dufay, Ockeghem, Obrecht, Josquin, and Palestrina.

Liber usualis (L.). See under *Gregorian chant.*

Libretto (It., booklet). The text of a musico-dramatic work such as an opera, oratorio, etc. Famous writers of librettos were Rinuccini (for Peri, Caccini, Monteverdi), Metastasio (for Hasse, Handel, Mozart), Calzabigi (for Gluck), Lorenzo da Ponte (for Mozart's *Figaro, Così fan tutte,* and *Don Giovanni*), Eugène Scribe (for Auber, Meyerbeer, Halévy, Boildieu), Arrigo Boito (for Verdi's *Otello* and *Falstaff*), and William Gilbert (for Sullivan). Richard Wagner was the first composer who wrote his own librettos.

Liebeslieder (LEE-bes-LEE-der: G., love songs). Two groups of eighteen (op. 52, 1869) and fourteen (*Neue Liebeslieder*, op. 65, 1875) short pieces by Brahms. Each is in the character of a waltz, for vocal quartet and piano duet in a chamber-music relationship. The texts are taken from Daumer's *Polydora*, except for the last song in op. 65, which is by Goethe.

Lied, Lieder (leet, LEE-der: G., sing. and pl., song). Generally, a song with German words, e.g.,

the °minnesinger songs of the 13th century or a German folk song (*Volkslied*). Specifically, the "German lied" of the 19th century as represented by Schubert, Schumann, Brahms, Wolf, and R. Strauss. October 19, 1814, has been called "the birthday of the German lied," because on that day Schubert, then 17 years old, wrote his *Gretchen am Spinnrad* (Gretchen at the Spinning-wheel), which opened a new era of song writing.

Liederkreis (LEE-der-kreyes: G.). Same as °song cycle.

Lieder ohne Worte (LEE-der O-ne VOR-te: G.). °*Songs without Words.*

Lied von der Erde (leet fon dayr AYR-de: Song of the Earth). A symphonic song cycle by Mahler (who called it a Symphony), for mezzo-soprano, tenor, and orchestra, set to German translations (by Hans Bethge) of old Chinese poems: 1. *Das Trinklied vom Jammer der Erde* (The Drinking Song of Earth's Woe); 2. *Der Einsame im Herbst* (The Lonely One in Autumn); 3. *Von der Jugend* (Of Youth); 4. *Von der Schönheit* (Of Beauty); 5. *Der Trunkene im Frühling* (The Toper in Spring); 6. *Der Abschied* (The Farewell). The work was written in 1908 and first performed in Munich, 1911, after Mahler's death. Every song is patterned after the ternary form, A B A. The *Lied von der Erde* is Mahler's last work, and is considered by some his greatest.

Lieutenant Kije. See *Lt. Kije.*

Life for the Czar, A. Russian opera by Glinka (libretto by G. F. Rosen), produced in St. Petersburg, 1836. An alternative title currently in use in Russia is *Ivan Susanin*. The story takes place in the early 17th century and centers around the self-sacrifice of the peasant Ivan Susanin (bass) in order to protect the newly chosen czar from the Polish invaders. The other main characters are Susanin's adopted son Vanja (contralto), his daughter Antonida (soprano), and her fiancé Sobinjin (tenor). The opera is a landmark in the history of music because it was the first popular opera in the Russian language, inaugurating a nationalistic movement which has continued since that time.

Ligature. A group of notes connected by a slur. See also under *Neumes*.

Lincoln Portrait. A patriotic work by Aaron Copland (1942) for speaker and orchestra. Against a musical background which utilizes two traditional American tunes, the speaker reads excerpts from Lincoln's writings.

Linear counterpoint. A term originally coined for the counterpoint of Bach, but used today especially for the modern type of counterpoint (Stravinsky, Bartok, Hindemith) which emphasizes the individuality of the melodic lines, largely minimizing the harmonic aspect.

Lining, lining-out. In American and English churches, the 18th- and 19th-century practice of hav-ing each line of a psalm or hymn read by the leader before it was sung by the congregation.

Linke Hand (G.). Left hand.

Linz Symphony. Mozart's Symphony in C, no. 36 (K. 425), composed at Linz, Austria, and first performed there by the private orchestra of the Count Thun.

Lip, lipping. Same as *embouchure.

Lira (It.). A type of violin common in the 15th and 16th centuries, characterized by a heart-shaped end of the neck (instead of the scroll) with frontal pegs. For Haydn's *lira organizzata*, see under *Hurdy-gurdy*.

L'Istesso tempo. See *Istesso tempo*.

Litany. In Roman Catholic rite, solemn supplications addressed to the Lord, the Virgin, or Saints. Particularly famous are the *Litaniae Lauretaniae*, addressed to the Virgin of Loreto. They have been composed by Palestrina, Lassus, Mozart, and others. The Anglican Litany is an extended prayer consisting of recitations by the priest, interspersed with short choral or congregational answers such as "Spare us, Good Lord."

Little Organ Book. See *Orgelbüchlein*.

Little–Russian Symphony. See *Ukrainian Symphony*.

Liturgical drama or **play.** Medieval plays (12th and 13th centuries) representing Biblical stories (in Latin), with action and, occasionally, monophonic music, e.g., *Daniel, The Plaint of Rachel, The Foolish and the Wise Virgins* (Sponsus Play). In the 14th to 16th centuries they developed into the so-called *mystery plays* (corruption of *ministerium*, service) which often continued for several days and employed quite elaborate stage presentation.

Lituus (L.). A trumpet of ancient Rome, straight with a small upturned bell (resembling the letter J). The two *litui* in Bach's Cantata no. 118 are obviously tenor trumpets in B-flat.

Loco (It., place), abbr. *lo.* Indication to play at the written pitch level after *all' ottava* (see *Ottava*).

Locrian mode. See under *Church modes*.

Lohengrin (LO-en-green). Opera in three acts by Wagner, to his own libretto, composed 1846–48, produced in Weimar, 1850, by Liszt. The action takes place at the court of King Henry I (10th century) where Elsa (soprano) is accused by Count Friedrich of Telramund (baritone) of having murdered her brother Gottfried. A strange knight — Lohengrin (tenor) — arrives on a boat drawn by a swan, and offers to marry and defend Elsa on condition that she shall never ask his name (Act I). Friedrich and his wife, the heathen magician Ortrud (mezzo-soprano), are deprived of their former status and plan revenge. The latter accuses Lohengrin, when he is about to

enter the church with Elsa, of being a magician who conceals his identity for evil reasons. Elsa assures him of her confidence, however, and the marriage takes place (famous Bridal March, Act II). Later she cannot resist asking the fateful question and Lohengrin reveals his name, sorrowfully announcing that he must now return to the Holy Grail and the castle of his father Parsifal. The swan reappears and, upon Lohengrin's prayer, takes on the form of Elsa's brother who had been bewitched by Ortrud. A dove descends and leads Lohengrin away.

Lohengrin marks the transition from Wagner's early operas (*Rienzi, The Flying Dutchman, Tannhäuser*) to the late master works (*Ring, Tristan, Meistersinger, Parsifal*). Here Wagner for the first time made use of his "continuous melody" rather than the "number" style which still occurs in *Tannhäuser*. There is also a modest use of °leitmotivs. On the whole, the style is lyrical and soft, a notable exception being the ominous scene between Friedrich and Ortrud, which foreshadows the atmosphere of the *Ring*.

Lombard rhythm. See under *Dotted notes*.

London Symphony. Haydn's Symphony no. 104, in D major (1795), the seventh of the °Salomon Symphonies.

London Symphony, A. Vaughan Williams' Symphony no. 2 (1914), expressing the loneliness as well as the tumultuousness of the great city, and incorporating themes such as the Westminster chimes and London street cries. A revised, shortened version appeared in 1920.

Long, longa (L.). See under *Notes and rests.*

Lo stesso tempo (It.). Same as *istesso tempo.*

Louise. Opera in four acts by Charpentier to his own libretto, produced in Paris, 1900. The story is essentially that of the Parisian seamstress Louise (soprano) who is torn between her love for the artist Julien (tenor), who wishes to marry her, and that for her father (baritone) and mother (contralto), who will never give their consent to her marriage. She promises her father to forget Julien, but when Julien persists in wooing her, she joins him. Act III shows the lovers united at Julien's little house in Montmartre, greeted by a reveling crowd of Bohemians, when the mother appears and tells Louise that her father is very ill and that she alone can save his life. She returns to her parents (Act IV), who refuse to let her go back to Julien. This leads to a dramatic scene of struggle at the end of which Louise rushes out, the parents remaining alone with their grief.

The opera, closely related to the *verismo* movement and, particularly, to Puccini's *La Bohème,* has been called the "musical apotheosis of Paris."

Loure (loor: F.). (1) Old French name for a bagpipe. — (2) A French 17th-century dance (originally accompanied by a bagpipe?) in moderate 6/4 time (heavily accented) and with dotted rhythms.

Love of Three Kings, The. See *Amore dei tre re.*

Love for Three Oranges, The. Farcical opera (originally in Russian) by Prokofiev (to his own libretto, after a fantastic tale by Gozzi), produced (in French) in Chicago, 1921. The plot, fashioned after the manner of the 18th-century Italian *commedia,* centers around three Oranges (actually Princesses under the spell of the enchantress Fata Morgana) and a melancholic Prince who can be cured only by a hearty laugh. A comedian, Truffaldino, tries all devices in vain. Finally the prince does laugh at an unexpected fall of Fata Morgana who, enraged, curses him into unhappiness until he is loved by one of the three Oranges. In the last act the Prince and Truffaldino find the three Oranges, the last of which produces the beautiful Ninette. Numerous set pieces, particularly the March and the Scherzo, have become standard concert works.

Love-Song Waltzes. See *Liebeslieder.*

Lt. Kije. A Russian film for which Prokofiev composed the score (op. 60, 1933). A popular orchestral suite in five movements was arranged by the composer.

Lucia di Lammermoor (looCHEE-a dee lahm-mer-MOOR). Opera in three acts by Donizetti (libretto by Cammerano, after Sir Walter Scott), produced in Naples, 1835. The story takes place in Scotland about 1700. Lucia (soprano) is in love with Edgar of Ravenswood (tenor), but her brother, Lord Henry Ashton (baritone), wishes her to marry Sir Arthur Bucklaw (tenor). By intercepting the lovers' letters and making each believe that the other has been untrue, he is able to achieve his end. Immediately after the marriage, however, Lucia goes mad and kills her husband (the famous "Mad Scene"), then dies. When Edgar hears of her death, he kills himself.

Lucky Hand, The. See *Glückliche Hand*.

Ludus Tonalis (L., tonal play). A work for pianoforte by Hindemith, composed in 1942 and designed as a 20th-century *Well-tempered Clavier*. It consists of twelve fugues linked by eleven interludes and preceded by a prelude which serves, in retrograde inversion, as a postlude. The fugues are arranged according to Hindemith's principle of decreasing tonal relationship to the tonic of C: C, G, F, A, E, etc., the interludes leading from one tonality to the next. The fugues explore the various contrapuntal devices (accompanied canon, double and triple fugue, crab motion, inversion, etc.) in a modern idiom. The work is one of the most characteristic products of *neoclassicism.

Lulu. Unfinished opera by Alban Berg (to his own libretto, based on two plays by Wedekind), produced in Zurich, 1937. The story deals with the evil influence of the title character, a beautiful and unprincipled dancer who is responsible for murder, suicide, or degradation in almost all people with whom she comes in contact. Imprisoned for murdering one of her lovers, she escapes with the aid of a friend, but both finally meet a horrible death at the hands of a character recalling Jack the Ripper. The music is in *twelve-tone technique based on a single tone row throughout. Through various devices, Berg succeeds in introducing simple folk melodies as well as involved Wagnerian lines, and presents a work of infinite variety and great dramatic sensitivity.

Lunga pausa (It.). Long pause, length determined by the performer.

Lur. A prehistoric bronze trumpet, dating from the 12th to the 6th century B.C. Numerous examples are preserved in Sweden and Denmark. They are in the shape of a long contorted S, with a flat ornamented disk attached to the end of the tube.

Lute. A plucked stringed instrument with a rounded body in the shape of a halved pear from which extends a fretted finger board. There are usually six strings (the five lowest ones double strings) tuned in fourths with a third in the middle: G-c-f-a-d'-g'. Its zenith of popularity was reached in the 16th century when it was as common as the piano is today. A great number of compositions, dances, variations, fantasias, and arrangements of vocal music (motets, chansons, madrigals), are preserved in numerous lute books. The music is notated, not on a staff, but in various systems of lute *tablature, employing

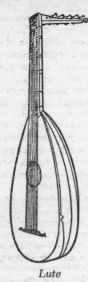

Lute

letters or figures to indicate the frets (see also *Vihuela*). See illustration.

Lydian. See under *Church modes; Greek music.*

Lyra, lyre. (1) An ancient Greek instrument, similar to the °kithara, but of lighter construction and smaller size, with a sound box often made from the shell of a turtle. — (2) A percussion instrument similar to the °glockenspiel, with the steel bars fixed on a U-shaped frame reminiscent of that of the Greek lyre. It is occasionally found in military bands. — (3) In several compositions by Haydn, the term *lyra (lyra organizzata)* is used for the medieval °hurdy-gurdy.

Lyric Suite. A suite in six movements for string quartet by Alban Berg (op. 18, 1926). Although all of the movements are in a dissonant and °expressionistic idiom, only the first and last adhere throughout to the °twelve-tone technique. A subtle unity is achieved by having the main theme of each movement introduced in the preceding movement.

M

M. Abbreviation for manual (organ) or for °metronome. Also for *mano* (It.) or *main* (F.), hand; see, for example, *M. d.,* etc.

Madame Butterfly. Opera by Puccini (libretto by Giacosa and Illica, based on a story by John L. Long), produced in Milan, 1904. The plot relates the story of Cho Cho San, a Japanese girl known as Madame Butterfly (soprano). An American lieutenant, Pinkerton (tenor), enters into an alliance with her despite the warnings of the consul Sharpless (tenor) that she considers this a binding marriage. After a three-year separation (Act II), Madame Butterfly still has unbounded faith in her "husband," a faith not shared by her maid Suzuki (mezzo-soprano).

Sharpless comes to tell Butterfly that Pinkerton has married an American wife, but she is unable to understand this and therefore refuses to listen to Prince Yamadori (baritone), who seeks her hand. Pinkerton arrives from America and comes to Butterfly's house with his wife seeking to adopt the child that Butterfly has had by him. She says that he may call for the child in half an hour and, left alone, falls upon her father's sword, dying as Pinkerton and Sharpless return.

Madrigal. A name of uncertain derivation for two types of early vocal music, one of the 14th, the other of the 16th century, both of Italian origin. The 14th-century madrigal is in a fixed form, consisting of two or three short stanzas with identical music and a final one with different music: A A B or A A A B. The composition is usually in two (sometimes three) parts, the upper in a highly florid style, the lower in larger note values. Among the composers are Jacopo da Bologna, Giovanni da Cascia (both c. 1300–1360) and Francesco Landini (c. 1325–1397).

Usually the term refers to the 16th-century type, which is based on love lyrics having no set form and is composed in four or, more often, five voices in an imitative style (similar to that of the 16th-century motet) but often interspersed with homophonic passages. The immediate ancestor of the 16th-century madrigal is the *frottola. The earliest composers were Flemish masters working in Italy,

e.g., Philippe Verdelot (c. 1500–1565) and Jacob Arcadelt (c. 1505-c. 1557), and also the Italian Costanzo Festa (c. 1490–1545). In the great period of the "classical" madrigal (c. 1540–80) we find Flemish composers (Willaert, Rore, Lasso, de Monte) as well as Italian (Andrea Gabrieli, Palestrina), while the "late" madrigal (c. 1580–1620) is represented primarily by three Italians, Marenzio, Gesualdo, and Monteverdi. Outside Italy the madrigal flourished mainly in England, from about 1580 to 1620, under Byrd, Morley, Weelkes, and Wilbye. The latter two composed madrigals of particularly great charm and native flavor.

Madrigal comedy. Composition of the late 16th century in which the madrigal style is applied, not to love lyrics, but to a text which relates a dramatic action or a short play (It., *commedia*, not necessarily comical). The best-known example is Orazio Vecchi's *Amfiparnasso*, performed in Modena, 1594. Contrary to current opinion, the presentation was not "operatic" (employing scenery, costumes, action, etc.). Vecchi states expressly in the preface that "this spectacle appeals to the imagination through the ear, not the eye."

Maestro (mah-ES-tro: It., master). Honorary title for distinguished music teachers, composers, conductors, and performers.

Magadizing. A term sometimes used for the "most primitive type of polyphony," i.e., singing in octaves. The term is derived from *magadis,* an ancient Greek harp in which each string was doubled by one giving the higher octave.

Magelone Romances (mah-ge-LO-ne). A cycle of fifteen songs by Brahms, op. 33 (1861–68), set to poems from L. Tieck's *Story of the Fair Magelone.*

Maggiore (mad-JAW-ray: It.). Major key. Also used as an inscription for variations (or for middle sections in ternary form) introducing a change from minor to major.

Magic Flute, The (G., *Die Zauberflöte*). Opera in two acts by Mozart, to a libretto (concocted of Oriental fairy tale and Freemasonry) by E. Schikaneder, produced in Vienna, 1791. Tamino (tenor), seeing a picture of Pamina (soprano), daughter of the evil Queen of the Night (soprano), falls in love with her. Accompanied by the bird-catcher Papageno (baritone), he goes out to rescue her from the temple of the high priest Sarastro (bass) where she is held captive, guarded and pestered by the moor Monostatos (tenor). Sarastro, who holds Pamina only in order to "guide her to wisdom," finds Tamino worthy, and also promises that Papageno will find a companion — Papagena (soprano). But various ordeals (injunction against speaking, passing through fire and water) are necessary before the two pairs of lovers are united.

The Magic Flute, Mozart's last opera, indicates a decided change in his approach to opera, a change which was, unfortunately, cut short by his death in 1791, two months after the

performance. The Italian *opera buffa* idea which prevails in *Figaro* and *Don Giovanni* is replaced here by a seriousness of purpose and sincerity of feeling presaging Beethoven.

Magnificat. The most important of the °canticles, beginning *Magnificat anima mea dominum* (My soul doth magnify the Lord). It contains the words of the Virgin after the Angel has announced to her that she is going to bear Christ (Luke 1: 46–55), and is sung in the Roman Catholic rites at Vespers, in the Anglican service at the Evening Prayers. Outstanding among the numerous polyphonic compositions of the text is Bach's *Magnificat,* written in 1723 in the form of an extended cantata in twelve movements (choruses, solo arias, duets, etc.).

Magnus liber organi (L., Great Book of Organum). A famous collection of organa (see *Organum*), written about 1175 by Leoninus, with additions and modifications by his successor, Perotinus (see under *Ars antiqua*).

Maid as Mistress, The. See *Serva Padrona.*

Maiden quartets. See *Scherzi.*

Maid of the Mill, The (Fair). See *Schöne Müllerin.*

Main (manh: F.). Hand. *Main droite,* right hand; *main gauche,* left hand; *à quatre mains,* for four hands.

Majeur (mah-ZHEUR: F.). Major key. Also used in the meaning explained under *Maggiore.*

Major, minor. Terms used: (1) For the distinction of intervals, for example, major third, c-e, and minor third, c-e♭ (see under *Intervals*). — (2) For two types of triads, one with a major third, c-e-g, the other with a minor third, c-e♭-g (see under *Chords*). — (3) For the two basic scales of music since about 1700, the major scale and the minor scale (melodic and harmonic), distinguished mainly by the third degree whether major, c-d-e-f- . . . , or minor, c-d-e♭-f- . . . (see under *Scales;* also *Mode*). — (4). For the two types of *keys based on these scales.

Malagueña (Sp.). See under *Fandango.*

Malinconia (mahl-in-CO-nee-a: It.). A composition in a melancholy mood.

Ma mère l'oye (F.). See *Mother Goose Suite.*

Mandolin. A descendant of the *lute, but smaller and with a nearly straight neck. It has ten metal strings forming five double courses tuned in fifths, and is played with a plectrum of tortoise shell or some other flexible material. The tones are rendered as a sustained tremolo produced by a quick vibrating movement of the plectrum.

Manfred. (1) Schumann's incidental music to Byron's famous poem, op. 115, 1848–49. Only the overture is occasionally heard today. — (2) Symphonic poem (though bearing the title "Manfred Symphony") by Tchaikovsky, op. 58 (1885), based on Byron's poem. The programmatic content of the four movements is indicated by a descriptive heading at the beginning of each.

Mani (It.). Plural of *mano.

Mannheim School. A group of German composers of the mid-18th century, located at Mannheim (near Heidelberg, Germany), who played an important role in the early development of the symphony, before Haydn and Mozart. The leading composers were Johann Stamitz (1717–1757) and Franz Xaver Richter (1709–1789). Breaking away from the Baroque tradition (Bach, Handel), they cultivated a novel style of orchestral music, purely homophonic, with extended crescendos and decrescendos, sudden changes from piano or pianissimo to forte and fortissimo, string tremolos, and rapidly ascending themes, often nothing more than scales or broken triads.

Mano (MAH-no: It.). Hand. *Mano destra,* right hand; *mano sinistra,* left hand; *a due (quattro) mani,* for two (four) hands.

Manon (ma-NONH: F.). Opera by Massenet (libretto by Meilhac and Gille, based on Prévost's novel, *Histoire de Manon Lescaut*), produced in Paris, 1884. The beautiful and fickle Manon (soprano), arriving with her cousin Lescaut (baritone) at an inn at Amiens, meets the Chevalier des Grieux (tenor), who is about to take Holy Orders. They fall in love and flee to Paris. Living in des Grieux's house, Manon starts a flirtation with the rich nobleman, de Bretigny (baritone), and forsakes des Grieux for him. Des Grieux, in despair over Manon's faithlessness, enters a monastery to take the vows, but Manon appears and persuades him to return to Paris with her. In order to satisfy Manon's wishes for luxury, des Grieux frequents a gambling house, but is accused of cheating and both are arrested. Manon is condemned to exile, and des Grieux and Lescaut wait at a road near Havre to rescue her. She arrives in a group of women to be deported, asks des Grieux's pardon for her wickedness, and, overcome with exhaustion, dies in his arms.

Manon Lescaut (ma-NONH les-KO). Opera by Puccini (libretto in Italian by Praga, Oliva, and Illica, based on Prévost's novel), produced in Turin, 1893. The plot is essentially the same as in Massenet's °*Manon*, with Geronte de Ravoir (bass) as Manon's lover instead of de Bretigny. The closing act and death scene take place on a desolate plain in Louisiana, where Manon has been deported and des Grieux has followed her.

Manual. A keyboard to be played by the hands, as opposed to the pedal keyboard of the organ. *Manualiter* (in organ music) means for the hands alone.

Manzoni Requiem. The name often given to Verdi's *Requiem*, composed in 1873 in memory of the Italian poet, Alessandro Manzoni, and performed on the first anniversary of his death.

Maracas (ma-RAH-cas). A Cuban percussion instrument (rattle) consisting of a dry gourd filled with dry seed or shot.

Marcellus Mass (mar-CHEL-us: L., *Missa Papae Marcelli*). A celebrated Mass by Palestrina, dedicated to (or to the memory of?) Pope Marcellus II who died three weeks after his accession in 1555. It is somewhat exceptional among the Masses of Palestrina because of the unusually extended use of °familiar style, resulting in a clear presentation of the text. See under *Council of Trent*.

March. Music designed to accompany marching of a large group, especially s o l d i e r s. Marches have strongly accented beats in groups of four, and regular phrases of four measures. The standard form is ternary, with a °Trio of a more melodious character as the middle section. Aside from their proper use by military bands, marches often occur in art music — operas, symphonies, sonatas, etc. These marches are usually dignified and ceremonial rather than military in character, and some of the most celebrated are slow funeral marches, such as the *Marcia funebre* of Beethoven's Symphony no. 3 (Eroica). Several attractive marches in modern idiom have been written by Prokofiev.

Marche Slave (marsh SLAHV: F., Slavic march). A concert march for orchestra by Tchaikovsky (op. 31, 1876). It utilizes traditional Russian tunes as well as the Russian national anthem.

Marcia (It.). March. *Marcia funebre*, funeral march.

Maria Theresa Symphony. Nickname of Haydn's Symphony no. 48, in C, composed in 1773 for a visit of the Austrian Empress Maria Theresa to Prince Esterházy, Haydn's employer.

Mariazell Mass (mah-ree-a-TSEL). Nickname of a Mass by Haydn, composed in 1782 for the Benedictine monastery at Mariazell in Austria.

Marienleben, Das (mar-REE-en-LAY-ben: The Life of Mary). A cycle of fifteen songs for voice and piano by Hindemith to poems by Rilke, composed in 1924 and revised in accordance with more mature musical concepts in 1950. The melodic line, one of extreme difficulty and with very little direct support from the complicated accompaniment, offers one of the most challenging vocal problems of contemporary music.

Marimba. A percussion instrument similar to the °xylophone, of larger size (five to six octaves), and with flaring and bulb-shaped wooden boxes as resonators. It is found in Africa and South America, and is particularly cultivated in Guatemala. It is now also manufactured in the United States and used by bands.

Marine trumpet. See *Tromba marina*.

Marriage of Figaro, The (It., *Le Nozze de Figaro*). Opera buffa in four acts by Mozart (libretto by da Ponte, after Beaumarchais' play *Le Mariage de Figaro*, which is the continuation of his *Le Barbier de Seville*, the source of Rossini's °*Barber of Seville*), produced in Vienna, 1786. Count Almaviva (baritone), tired of his wife, the Countess (soprano, the Rosina of Rossini's opera), tries to console himself with other women, but Figaro (baritone), now his valet, no longer assists him (as in the *Barber of Seville*) but plots against him in order to punish him for his infidelity. Around this basic idea is woven a complicated plot of love affairs and intrigue, the details of which are not always clear. Among the Count's proposed conquests are Susanna (soprano), Figaro's fiancée and the Countess' maid, and Barbarina (soprano), the gardener's daughter. Further complications result because the page Cherubino (soprano) is attached to Barbarina as well as infatuated by the Countess, and Figaro has promised to marry the elderly Marcellina (contralto) as forfeit for an unpaid debt. Figaro's difficulties are cleared up by the discovery that Marcellina is his mother. The Count's intrigues are brought to a stop by a plot involving the writing of a fictitious love letter by Susanna (dictated to her by the Countess); the use of a pin to fasten the letter (the pin to be sent back by the Count in token that he has received the letter); the loss of the pin by the messenger, Barbarina; an exchange of clothes between Susanna and the Countess, etc.

The looseness and confusion of the plot, far from being detrimental, actually enhances the value of the opera, bestowing on it a charming quality of Rococo lightness and, above all, quickly causing the listener to give up all efforts to "follow the action" and inducing him to accept the music as the central element of the opera. Needless to say, only music of such outstanding charm and artistic greatness as Mozart's could lead to this very desirable result.

Marsch (G.). March. *Marschmässig,* in the character of a march.

Marseillaise, La (mar-say-EZ: F.). See *National anthems,* 4.

Martelé (mart-LAY: F.), **martellato** (mar-tel-LAH-to: It., hammered). In violin music, see Bowing (c). In piano music, indication of a forceful technique, with the hands, frequently in alternation, acting like hammers.

Martha. Comic opera by Flotow (libretto by Friedrich W. Riese), produced in Vienna, 1847. The central figure of the plot (laid in England at the time of Queen Anne) is Lady Harriet (soprano), who persuades her cousin Lord Tristan (bass) and her maid Nancy (contralto) to join her in disguising themselves as servants and going to the Richmond Fair. There the girls, under the names of Martha and Julia, are hired for one year of service by the farmers Plunkett (bass) and Lionel (tenor). Lionel falls deeply in love with Martha, and the girls, realizing that the fun has gone too far, escape from the farmhouse during the night. Lionel, declared by the Queen as the rightful Earl of Derby, does not

recognize Martha (whom he still loves desperately) when he meets her as Lady Harriet. Finally, Plunkett and Nancy, who have become engaged, arrange for a meeting with Harriet in her servant's costume; he now recognizes her and they become betrothed.

Martyre de Saint Sébastien, Le (mar-TEER de SANH say-bas-TYANH: The Martyrdom of St. Sebastian). Incidental music by Debussy for a miracle play by d'Annunzio, composed in 1911 for solo voices, chorus, and orchestra. It is usually performed as an oratorio.

Marziale (It.). Marchlike.

Masculine, feminine cadence. A cadence is called masculine if the final note or chord occurs on the strong beat (Fig. 65a),

Fig. 65

feminine if the note is delayed to fall on a weak beat (b, c). The feminine cadence is a typical feature of the °polonaise.

Mask. See *Masque.*

Masked Ball, A (It., *Un Ballo in maschera*). Opera by Verdi (libretto by A. Somma, based on Scribe's *Gustave III, ou Le Bal masqué*), produced in Rome, 1859. The plot, laid in 18th-century Boston, centers around the love of Richard (Riccardo, tenor), governor of Boston, and Amelia (soprano), the wife of the governor's secretary and friend, Reinhart (Renato, baritone). It also involves a conspiracy against the governor's life, perpetrated by the villains Samuel (bass) and Tom (Tommaso, bass). In the second act, while Richard and Amelia meet at midnight, Reinhart arrives to warn the governor of the attempt on his life. The governor makes his escape and Reinhart recognizes his wife when a veil falls from her face. His devotion now turns to hatred and he joins the conspirators. The last act shows the masked ball from which the opera derives its name, during which Reinhart stabs the governor with his dagger.

The original play was based on historical fact; Gustave III of Sweden was shot in the back at a masked ball in Stockholm in 1792. To avoid inciting violence against royalty during a period of political unrest, Verdi was forced by authorities to change the scene of the opera from Sweden to colonial Boston. Some modern performances revert to the original Swedish setting, others set the scene in Naples.

Masque, mask. English stage production of the 16th and 17th centuries, designed for the entertainment of the nobility, lavishly produced with acting, dancing, and, to some extent, vocal and instrumental music. The most famous example is Milton's masque *Comus,* produced in 1634 with music by Henry Lawes.

Mass. The central service of the Roman Catholic rites, representing the commemoration and mystical repetition of the sacrifice of Christ on the Cross (Eucharist). The name (L. *missa*) is derived from the words "Ite, *missa* est congregatio" (Depart, the congregation is dismissed) sung at the end of the service.

The musical portions of the Mass fall into two categories, the *Proper* and the *Ordinary.* The Proper includes the items with variable texts (and music), that is, *Introit, Gradual, Alleluia, Offertory,* and *Communion.* The Ordinary includes the items with invariable texts, that is, *Kyrie, Gloria, Credo, Sanctus,* and *Agnus Dei.* For each of the latter a number of plainsong melodies (fourteen or more) are provided, according to the character of the occasion (ordinary Sundays, feasts of the Lord, of the Virgin, of Saints, etc.). The items of the Proper are much older, liturgically more important, and musically more elaborate than those of the Ordinary.

From the 12th century on, the items of the Mass were composed polyphonically. Among the earliest examples are the organa (see *Organum*) of the School of Notre Dame (Leoninus, Perotinus, *c.* 1200; see *Magnus liber organi, Ars antiqua*), based on Graduals and Alleluias. Later, however, composers mainly cultivated the Ordinary of the Mass because such compositions could be performed many times during the year, while the composition of, e.g., a given Gradual could be sung only once a year, on the day to which that Gradual was proper. Thus, in musical circles the term Mass became identified with the Ordinary of the Mass, one of the first examples being the Mass by Machaut (c. 1300–1377). In the 15th and 16th centuries, composers such as Dufay, Ockeghem, Obrecht, Josquin, and Palestrina wrote numerous Masses, some of them based on secular melodies (see under *L'homme armé*). Among later examples are Bach's °B-minor Mass and Beethoven's °Missa solemnis. In the later compositions the more extended items, notably the Gloria and the Credo, are often subdivided into several movements treated in contrasting styles. Thus, the Credo of Bach's B-minor Mass includes the following movements:

Credo in unum Deum (I believe in one God)

Patrem omnipotentem (Father almighty)

Et in unum Dominum (And in one Lord)

Et incarnatus est (And was incarnate)

Crucifixus (Crucified)

Et resurrexit (And has arisen)

Et in Spiritum sanctum (And [I believe] in the Holy Spirit)

Confiteor unum baptisma (I confess one baptism)

Master Peter's Puppet Show. See *Retable de Maese Pedro.*

Mastersingers (G., *Meistersinger*). A 15th- and 16th-century group of German craftsmen who for their pleasure cultivated poetry and music in continuation of the tradition of the aristocratic °minnesingers of the 12th to 14th centuries. The movement continued sporadically until the middle of the 19th century. They were located in various towns of southwest Germany, notably in Mainz and in Nuremberg where Hans Sachs (1494–1576), a cobbler, was one of the most important mastersingers. Their weekly gatherings, every Sunday after the church service, were governed by a rigid organization in various ranks from the "pupil" to the "master," and by rather pedantic rules (known as the *Tabulatur*) on how to write, compose, and sing. Every year, on St. John's day, a competition for prizes was held. The melodies of the mastersingers are all monophonic and in a more or less free rhythm, often clumsy and overcrowded with meaningless coloraturas. There are, however, some attractive melodies, particularly among those by Sachs.

Mastersingers of Nuremberg, The. See *Meistersinger von Nürnberg.*

Mathis der Maler (MAH-tees dayr MAH-ler: Mathias the Painter). Opera by Hindemith (to his own libretto), finished in 1934 and produced in Zurich, 1938. The story deals with the life of the German painter, Mathias Grünewald (1460–1530), who supported the peasant revolution in the early days of the Protestant Reformation. Three extracts (the overture, the scene at the painter's deathbed, and a crowd scene from the second act) were combined into a symphony in three movements for which Hindemith provided descriptive titles referring to the panels in Grünewald's famous Isenheim Altar at Colmar in Alsace: I. The Angelic Concert; II. Entombment; III. The Temptation of St. Anthony.

Matin, Le (ma-TANH: The Morning). Nickname of Haydn's Symphony no. 6, in D, which, together with *Le Midi* (Noontime), no. 7, in C, and *Le Soir* (The Evening), no. 8, in G, forms a well-known group of Haydn's earliest symphonies, all being composed about 1761.

Matins. See under *Office*.

Má Vlast (Czech, My Fatherland). A cycle of six symphonic poems by Smetana, composed 1874–79, based on various subjects pertaining to his country: 1. *Vyšehrad* (the old citadel of Prague), an evocation of Bohemia's past; 2. *Vltava* (the river Moldau); 3. *Šárka* (an Amazon of Czech legend), a drama of love and revenge; 4. *From Bohemia's Meadows and Forests*, a pastoral scene; 5. *Tábor* (an ancient city), making use of an old Hussite chorale; 6. *Blaník*, a mountain near Prague where, according to legend, the old heroes slumber, ready to rise again.

Mavra. Opera in one act by Stravinsky (libretto by B. Kokhno, based on Pushkin's story "The Little House of Kolomna"), produced in Paris, 1922. Vasili (tenor), disguised as a female cook named Mavra, succeeds in insinuating himself into the household of his beloved, Parasha (soprano), until Parasha's mother (contralto) discovers him shaving in the kitchen. The music is in a °pandiatonic style with many accompanying figures reminiscent of early *opera buffa*. It consists of solo and ensemble numbers without recitative.

Mazeppa (mah-ZEP-pa). Symphonic poem by Liszt, composed in 1854, based on a poem by Victor Hugo describing the insurrection (1708) and death of the Ukrainian Cossack chief, Mazeppa. The music incorporates elements from Liszt's *Mazeppa Etude* for pianoforte, one of the °Transcendental Etudes (1851).

Mazurka, mazur. A Polish national dance, in triple time and of moderate speed, frequently with dotted rhythms and strong accents on the second or (more often) on the third beat (see Fig. 66). It is performed by four

Fig. 66

or eight couples, with a great variety of bold steps, often improvised. Chopin's Mazurkas are artistic elaborations of this dance type, but also of some other Polish dances, such as the obertas (Mazurka, op. 56, no. 2) and the °kujawiak.

M. d. Abbreviation of *main droite* (F.) or *mano destra* (It.), i.e., right hand.

Mean-tone system. A system of tuning which was in use before °equal temperament, from about 1500 to 1700. It was purer (perfect thirds, almost-perfect fifths) than equal temperament in the simple keys (up to three sharps and flats) but hardly usable for those with many sharps or flats (which, however, were not common in that period). See under *Temperament*.

Measure. A group of °beats (equal units of time), the first of which is often accented. Set off by bar lines, such groups of two, three, four, and six (or their multiples) ordinarily recur consistently throughout a given composition. The basic scheme of beats within a measure is called *meter.

Mechanical instruments. Appliances designed to produce music mechanically, i.e., without an actual performer. Prior to about 1900 such instruments employed the barrel-and-pin mechanism, consisting of a wooden or metal cylinder bearing small pins which, acting against levers or similar gadgets, operated the hammers of a pianoforte, the clappers of a set of bells, the wind holes of an organ, etc. As early as the 14th century carillons were operated in such a manner. Mozart wrote three compositions for the *Orgelwalze* (*Walze* — rotating cylinder), that is, the *barrel organ* (street organ, also erroneously called *hurdy-gurdy*), in which the pins act upon a set of small organ pipes. While in these instruments the cylinder was turned by a handle, others were set in motion by a spring mechanism. To this type belong the *Flötenuhr* (flute clock), for which Haydn wrote a number of charming pieces, as well as the various musical toys known as *music box*, in which the pins act against the teeth (varying in length and, therefore, in pitch) of a metal comb. In the early 19th century, instruments were built for the mechanical reproduction of an entire orchestra, e.g., Mälzel's *Panharmonicon* (1804) for which Beethoven originally wrote part of his *Battle of Vittoria* (see under *Wellington's Victory*).

An important advance over the barrel-and-pin mechanism was the perforated paper roll, used in instruments such as the *Pianola, Phonola, Player-Piano,* etc. Here the hammers are made to move by air pressure, the air passing through the perforations of the paper roll which moves over a cylinder with slits, one for each key. The player rolls are sometimes reproductions of performances of famous virtuosos. Some modern composers (Hindemith, Toch), have written original compositions for such mechanical pianofortes, on which novel sound effects, such as could normally be reproduced only by three or four hands, are possible.

The most recent and most successful of all mechanical instruments is the *phonograph.

Medea. Ballet by Samuel Barber (op. 23, 1946) for Martha Graham, who retitled it *Cave of the Heart.* A suite in eight movements has been arranged by the composer for concert performance.

Medesimo tempo (me-DAY-zi-mo TEM-po: It.). The same tempo (in spite of changed meter).

Mediant. See under *Scale degrees.*

Medium, The. Opera in two acts by Gian-Carlo Menotti (to his own libretto) produced in 1946 at Columbia University. Madame Flora (contralto), a medium, is assisted in her practice by a mute gypsy boy, Toby, and by her daughter, Monica (soprano). The children play tricks on her and she becomes obsessed by an illusion of being a real medium. Her fear is brought to a climax when she imagines herself actually touched by an unseen spirit during a seance. In Act II her drunkenness and her mania mount until, frightened by the movement of a curtain, she shoots at it and kills Toby. The music is an accompanied recitative with occasional expressive arias.

Meeresstille und glückliche Fahrt (G.). See *Calm Sea and Prosperous Voyage*.

Mefistofele (mef-i-STOF-ay-lay: It.). See *Mephistopheles*.

Meistersinger (G.). See *Mastersingers*.

Meistersinger von Nürnberg, Die (dee MEYES-ter-zing-er fon NUIRN-bayrg: The Mastersingers of Nuremberg). Opera in three acts by Wagner, to his own libretto, produced in Munich, 1868. The plot, which is based on careful studies of original sources, reveals a true and lively picture of the life and customs in the °mastersinger guilds of the 16th century, with the cobbler-poet Hans Sachs (bass) as the central figure. The dramatic action is carried chiefly by the young knight Walther von Stolzing (tenor), who falls in love with Eva (soprano) and enters the guild in order to compete (victoriously, needless to say) at the yearly contest. He wins Eva's hand through his prize song "Morgenlich leuchtend im rosigen Schein," in spite of all the intrigues of his rival Beckmesser (bass buffo).

Die Meistersinger represents an artistic culmination in Wagner's work comparable to the Waldstein Sonata and the Emperor Concerto in Beethoven's. Its balance of means, its confident "C-major atmosphere," and its happy variety of scenes and expressions offer a striking contrast to the earlier *Tristan* (1865) with its all-pervading chromaticism and its overpassionate atmosphere. The overture to *Meistersinger*, frequently performed in concerts, is one of the greatest examples of 19th-century instrumental music and one which makes us wish that Wagner had not concentrated his interest exclusively on the opera.

Melisma (me-LIZ-ma). In vocal music, particularly °Gregorian chant, an extended melodic passage sung to one syllable. It is essentially like a °coloratura, but expressive rather than virtuoso in character.

Mellophone. See *Brass instruments,* IIc.

Melodic minor scale. See under *Scale.*

Melodrama (G., *Melodram*). (1). A stage presentation intermediate between play and opera, consisting of spoken text and background music. In early examples, such as Rousseau's *Pygmalion* (1762) and Benda's *Ariadne auf Naxos* (1775), text and music alternate, the latter being used for pantomimic gestures. In modern examples, such as R. Strauss's *Enoch Arden* (1898) and Stravinsky's *Persé-*

phone (1934), the music accompanies the spoken words. An interesting variety of the melodramatic principle is the *speech-song, used by Schönberg and his followers. Several operas contain melodramatic scenes, e.g., Beethoven's *Fidelio* (Grave-digging Scene) and Weber's *Freischütz* (Incantation Scene). — (2) Term sometimes applied to opera, particularly of the "folksy" type.

Melodrama (It.). Common Italian term for opera.

Melody. A succession of musical tones, as opposed to *harmony (tones sounded simultaneously). Thus, melody and harmony represent the horizontal and the vertical elements of musical *texture. More specifically, melody means a succession of tones forming a line of individual significance and expressive value, as opposed to passage work, bridge material, coloraturas, and so forth.

By its very nature, melody cannot be separated from rhythm. Each musical sound has two fundamental qualities, pitch and duration, and both of these enter into those successions of pitch-plus-duration units which constitute a melody. To consider melody and rhythm as separate, or even as mutually exclusive elements — as is often done — is misleading. If a distinction between these two elements is desired, the proper terms are *motion and rhythm. Melody may thus be said to consist of motion (up and down) and rhythm (long or short), and every melody can be separated

Fig. 67

into a motion formula and a rhythm formula, as shown in Fig. 67.

In musical composition, melody may occur either without any addition (monophonic music), in combination with other melodies (polyphonic music), or supported by harmonies (homophonic music). Since these three categories embrace the entire scope and history of music, it appears that melody is a basic element of all music (except the purely percussive type). From the creative point of view, it is different from the other musical components, such as harmony, rhythm (as such), or orchestration, in that the latter are subject to certain rational premises which make them capable of being learned systematically; many composers of mediocre rank have indeed been very adept at such studies and their practical application. Only the great artists, however, possess that power of imagination which goes into the making of a great melody.

Meno (MAY-no: It.). Less. *Meno mosso*, less quickly.

Mensural notation (MEN-soo-ral). An early system of notation which was in use from the mid-13th century (Franco of Cologne) to about 1600, when it was superseded by the simplified system of notation used today. Aside from the use of older note symbols (*longa, brevis,* etc.; see *Notes and rests*), the main differences are: (a) the absence of bar lines; (b) the absence of the tie; (c) the fact that each note could be equal to either two or three notes of the subsequent degree. In the former case they were called imperfect, in the latter, perfect. See under *Time signature.* Music written in this system is sometimes called mensural (or mensurable) music.

Menuet (F.), **Menuett** (G.), **menuetto** (It., correctly *Minuetto*). *Minuet.

Mephistopheles (It., *Mefistofele*). Opera by Boito (libretto by the composer, based on Goethe's *Faust*), produced in Milan, 1868.

Mephisto Waltzes. Four compositions by Liszt, in the character of a wild and diabolic waltz. Two are for orchestra (composed 1859 and 1881), but are also arranged for piano (both solo and duet). The two others (composed 1883 and 1885, the latter unpublished) are for piano.

Mer, La (lah MAYR: The Sea). Three symphonic poems by Debussy: 1. *De l'aube à midi sur la mer* (From Dawn to Noon on the Sea); 2. *Jeux de vagues* (Play of the Waves); 3. *Dialogue du vent et de la mer* (Dialogue of the Wind and the Sea), composed 1903–05. The work represents the culmination of *impressionistic pictorialism and of impressionistic technique, with its tendency to constant change of melodic material and orchestral color, a technique emi-

nently suited to the rendition of a "musical seascape."

Merry Wives of Windsor, The (G., *Die Lustigen Weiber von Windsor*). Comic opera by Otto Nicolai (libretto by H. von Mosenthal after Shakespeare's play), produced in Berlin, 1849. The central characters, as in the original, are Sir John Falstaff (bass), Mr. and Mrs. Ford (baritone and soprano), Mr. and Mrs. Page (bass and mezzo-soprano), and the lovers Ann Page (soprano) and Fenton (tenor). The merry escapades and misunderstandings of this lively crew are effectively mirrored in the light and ingratiating musical setting.

Messa di voce (MES-sa dee VAW-chay: placing of the voice). In vocal technique, particularly of the 18th century (see *Bel canto*), the sustaining of a long note at an unwavering pitch, often combined with a crescendo and diminuendo on that note.

Messe (mess: F.), **Messe** (MESse: G.). Mass. *Messe solennelle,* solemn Mass (see *Missa solemnis*); *messe des morts,* Mass of the Dead (see *Requiem*).

Messiah. Oratorio in three parts by Handel (libretto from the Scriptures by C. Jennens), produced in Dublin, 1742, revised afterwards and published in 1767. It is Handel's most popular work. Particularly famous are the "Pastoral Symphony" and the alto aria "He shall feed His flock" from the first part and the "Hallelujah Chorus" from the end of the second part.

Metamorphosis. See *Transformation of themes.*

Meter. In a given composition (or section), the basic grouping of °beats and accents, as found in each °measure and as indicated by the °time signature. For instance, 3/4 meter (or 3/4 time) means that the basic beats are quarter notes (lower figure) and that there are three (upper figure) of these in each measure, the first receiving an accent. See also under *Rhythm.*

The meter is either *duple* (2/2, 2/4, or rarely, 2/8), *triple* (3/2, 3/4, 3/8), or *quadruple* (4/2, 4/4, 4/8), 4/4 being also called *common meter.* All these are *simple meters,* as opposed to *compound meters,* which result from multiplying the above simple meters by three: *compound duple* (6/2, 6/4, 6/8), *compound triple* (9/4, 9/8) and *compound quadruple* (12/4, 12/8, 12/16). °*Quintuple meter* (5/4) is actually either 2/4 + 3/4 or 3/4 + 2/4, depending upon where the secondary accent in each measure lies. See also under *Time signature.*

Several new metric devices have been used during the 20th century, e.g., °multimeter (numerous changes of time signature in quick succession), irregular meter (7/4, 11/4), and such time signatures as (2 + 2 + 3)/4.

Metronome. An apparatus invented by J. N. Mälzel in 1816, and designed to indicate exactly the tempo of a composition. It consists essentially of a swinging rod (pendulum) whose speed of oscillation can be varied by moving a weight into a higher or lower position on the rod. The rod is graded from 30 to 180, each figure indicating the number of oscillations per minute. The apparatus is known as Mälzel's Metronome (M.M. or M.), and an indication such as M.♩ = 80 means that the quarter note should be played at the rate of 80, so that 80 quarter notes are played during one minute. In modern metronomes the swinging pendulum is replaced by a clock work, often electric. The metronome is useful to indicate to the performer the composer's intention as to the general pace of the composition.

Mettez (F.). Draw (an organ stop).

Mezza, mezzo (MED-za, MED-zo: It.). Half. *Mezza voce,* "half voice," i.e., with a subdued tone quality (not to be confused with °*messa di voce*). *Mezzo-forte* (abbr. *mf*), half loud: *mezzo-piano* (abbr. *mp*) half soft, i.e., a little louder than piano. *Mezzo-soprano,* see *Voices, Range of.*

Mf. *Mezzo-forte;* see under *Mezza, mezzo.*

M.g. Short for *main gauche* (F.), left hand.

Mi. See under *Pitch names; Solmization; Tonic Sol-fa.*

Microcosmos. See *Mikrokosmos.*

Microtone. A microtone (fractional tone) is an interval smaller than a half tone, e.g. °quarter tone, sixth tone (one third of a semitone), etc. Several 20th-century composers (e.g., Hába,

Stein, Carrillo, Chavez) have experimented with microtonal music, but the results have not been generally accepted partly because Western ears have not been conditioned to distinguish such small intervals.

Middle C. The C near the middle of the keyboard, that is, c' (see under *Pitch names*). It is notated on the first ledger line below the treble staff, or on the first ledger line above the bass staff.

Midi, Le (F.). See under *Matin, Le.*

Midsummer Night's Dream, A. Incidental music by Mendelssohn to Shakespeare's play. The Overture, composed in 1826, when Mendelssohn was seventeen years of age, is the most popular excerpt and is perhaps his most inspired composition, fascinating in its elfish lightness and orchestral colors. The rest of the music was written in 1842.

Mikado, The. One of the most popular of the numerous operettas of Gilbert (librettist) and Sullivan (composer), produced in London, 1885.

Mikrokosmos (MEYE-cro-COZmos: Gr., *mikros kosmos*, little world). A six-volume set of 153 short piano pieces by Bartok, arranged in order of progressive difficulty and published from 1926 to 1937. The first pieces are simple five-finger exercises, the last are intricate dances in a modified Hungarian idiom. As a "little world" of 20th-century music, the collection has outstanding value as an introduc-

tion to such aspects of 20th-century technique and style as conflicting rhythms, °bitonality, novel key signatures, °tone clusters, °wholetone scale, etc.

Military band. An instrumental ensemble, usually consisting of wood winds, brass, and percussion, used by the armed forces. The standard American military band includes 2 sousaphones, 3 trombones, 3 horns, 1 baritone (or euphonium), 5 cornets, 1 trumpet, 6 clarinets, 1 piccolo, 2 saxophones, 1 snare drum, 1 bass drum, 1 cymbal.

Military drum. Same as snare drum (see *Drums*, 2).

Military Polonaise. Nickname for Chopin's most popular polonaise, op. 53, in A-flat major, composed in 1843.

Military Symphony. Haydn's Symphony in G, no. 100 (no. 12 of the °Salomon Symphonies), composed in 1794. The second movement, *Allegretto*, employs triangles, cymbals, and bass drum in imitation of Turkish music (see *Janizary music*), and also has a trumpet fanfare.

Mimodrama. Older name for °pantomime.

Mineur (F.). Minor key. Also used in the meaning explained under °*Minore*.

Miniature score. A pocket-size, inexpensive full score of orchestral or chamber music, designed chiefly for the student and for the amateur who wants to read the music while listening to a performance. They are extremely useful for these and similar purposes.

Minim. See under *Notes and rests*.

Minnesinger (MIN-ne-zing-er: G., from *Minne,* love). A group of German poet-musicians of noble birth who flourished in the 12th to the 14th century. They were similar to and influenced by the French *troubadours and *trouvères. The start of the movement is usually traced to the marriage, in 1156, of the German Emperor Frederick Barbarossa to the French Princess Beatrix of Burgundy. Among the famous minnesingers were Walther von der Vogelweide (d. 1230), Neithart von Reuenthal (*c.* 1180-*c.* 1240), Tannhäuser (mid-13th century), and Heinrich Frauenlob (*c.* 1318). They wrote monophonic songs, love lyrics as well as devotional narratives. In the 15th century their tradition was continued by the *mastersingers.

Minor. See *Major, minor*.

Minore (mee-NAW-ray: It.). Minor key. Also used as an inscription of variations (or middle sections in ternary form) introducing a change from major to minor.

Minstrels (from L. *ministrellus,* minor servant). (1) Originally, the professional musicians of the Middle Ages, especially those employed in a feudal household (see *Jongleur*). — (2) In modern usage, the term is loosely applied to all sorts of musical entertainers, ancient and modern, especially for comedians appearing in the guise of Negroes. The Negro minstrel shows became a popular national institution in the United States in the 1830's due to the efforts of Thomas Rice, who darkened his skin and imitated the Negro's manner of speech and singing.

Minuet. A graceful French dance of the 17th century (*menuet,* probably from *menu,* small) in moderate triple time. It was much in vogue everywhere until about 1800, when the waltz appeared (see under *Dance music*). It also played an important role in art music. As early as 1700 it was adopted into the *suite, and later into the *sonata (symphony, string quartet, etc.), usually as the third movement. This "sonata minuet," as found in Haydn and Mozart, differs from the pure dance type by its somewhat faster speed and often by a character of energy and humor rather than of gracefulness. This transformation finally led to the replacement, under Beethoven, of the minuet by the *scherzo.

The sonata minuet is regularly in *ternary form, with a middle section called *Trio*: Minuet — Trio — repeat of first Minuet. Originally, the trio was a second minuet, called *menuet en trio* (F., minuet in three parts), because it was written for three instruments only, frequently two oboes and a bassoon, while the first (and last) minuet was scored for the full orchestra. Even in Haydn, Mozart, and Beethoven (e.g., Symphony no. 7), the trio often shows a lighter texture than the minuet and employs wood winds as solo instruments. Both the minuet and the trio are usually in rounded binary form, with the customary repeats omitted in the restatement of the minuet, so that the entire movement can be diagrammed as follows:

M
||:A:|| :B + A:||

T
||:C:||:D + C:||

M
||A|| B + A||

Minute Waltz. Popular name for Chopin's Waltz in D-flat, op. 64, no. 1, derived from the fact that it lasts approximately one minute when played at the proper tempo. Another name is *Dog Waltz*, because the rapidly turning figure of the beginning has been likened to a dog chasing his tail.

Mirliton (F.). See under *Kazoo*.

Miroirs (mee-RWAHR: F., Mirrors). A group of five piano pieces by Ravel, composed in 1905: 1. *Noctuelles* (Moths); 2. *Oiseaux tristes* (Mournful Birds); 3. *Une Barque sur l'océan* (A Boat on the Ocean); 4. *Alborada del gracioso* (Morning Music of a Minstrel-Clown); 5. *La Vallée des cloches* (The Valley of the Bells).

Mirror fugue. A fugue so contrived that it can also be played with each voice part inverted, resulting in a mirror reflection of the original. Famous examples are the Contrapunctus XVI

and XVIII of Bach's *Art of Fugue*. See Fig. 68.

Fig. 68

Missa (L.). Mass. *Missa pro defunctis*, Mass for the Dead; see *Requiem*. *Missa Papae Marcelli*, see *Marcellus Mass*.

Missa solemnis (MIS-sa so-LEM-nis). Solemn Mass, a title used by several composers in order to emphasize the serious and elaborate character of a Mass. The best known is Beethoven's Mass, op. 123, composed in 1818–23. Like Bach's B-minor Mass, it consists of five main sections (Kyrie, Gloria, Credo, Sanctus, Agnus Dei), most of which are subdivided into several movements.

Mixed voices. Specification for choral ensembles and compositions employing female as well as male voices.

Mixolydian. See under *Church modes; Greek music*.

Mixture stops. See under *Organ*.

M.M. Abbreviation for Mälzel's *Metronome.

Modal. In the character of a mode, either a *church mode (modal melody, harmony; see also *Modality*), or of a rhythmic mode (modal rhythm, notation). See *Mode*.

Modality. General term used with reference to melodic and harmonic formations based on the °church modes, as opposed to those based on the major and minor modes (°tonality). In particular, it is used to denote the occurrence of modal idioms in the music of the 19th and 20th centuries (see *Neomodal*). Among the earliest examples are the slow movement of Beethoven's String Quartet in A minor, op. 132 ("Song of Praise to God in the Lydian Mode"), and Chopin's Mazurka no. 15, showing the use of B-natural in the key of F major (Fig. 69a). The latter, of course, derives its modal features, not from Gregorian chant or from 16th-century sacred music, but from folk song and folk dance which, particularly in the Slavic countries and in England, often have modal characteristics. Modal formations appear, with increasing frequency, in the works of Moussorgsky, Debussy, Sibelius, Vaughan Williams, and many other 20th-century composers. Fig. 69b (Sibelius, Symphony no. 2, slow movement) is in the Aeolian mode rather than in A-minor, because it has F and G instead of F-sharp and G-sharp.

Mode. Usually a °church mode, Dorian, Lydian, etc. In a wider sense, any of the scales used in a composition, e.g., in terms such as *major mode, minor mode, pentatonic mode*. Used in this broader sense, the difference between scale and mode is that scale is usually understood as being related to a given key, as in C-major scale, while "major (or Dorian) mode" denotes the general characteristic of all the major (or Dorian) scales, transposed to any key. For another meaning of mode, see *Rhythmic modes*.

Moderato (mod-er-AH-to: It.). In moderate speed. *Allegro moderato* is less fast than allegro, *adagio moderato* less slow than adagio.

Modern music. See *Twentieth-century music*.

Modinha (mo-DEEN-ya). A type of Brazilian song, in the nature of a sentimental romance, heard mostly in the cities.

Modulation. The change of key within a composition. Such changes are found in practically every composition of some length, at least from about 1700 on. A piece in C major, for instance, will necessarily start and close in C, but will include shorter or longer passages in other keys, each new key being reached by transitional or modulatory harmonies. While in older compositions (Bach, Mozart, Beethoven) the modulations are widely spaced so that each new

Fig. 69

key becomes clearly established, Wagner developed a harmonic idiom characterized by almost continuous modulation, which resulted in a tonal ambiguity that was carried to its extremes by Franck, R. Strauss, Reger, and others, and ultimately produced the °atonal music of the 20th century. — See also under *Enharmonic*.

Moldau, The (MOL-dow). English title of the second (*Vltava*) of Smetana's symphonic poem cycle °*Má Vlast*.

Moll (mol: G.). Minor, e.g., *C moll*, C minor.

Molto (It.). Very. For example, *molto allegro*, very fast.

Moments musicals (mo-MONH mui-zee-KAHL: F., Musical Moments, correctly *Moments musicaux*). Title of Schubert's six piano pieces, op. 94 (1828?). See under *Character piece*.

Monochord (Gr., one string). An apparatus designed for the investigation and demonstration of the basic laws of acoustics, particularly the relationship between lengths of strings and intervals (see *Acoustics*, 2, 3). It consists of a single string stretched over a long wooden box, and a movable fret serving to vary the length of the string. It was widely used in the Middle Ages.

Monocordo (It.). In violin music, direction to play a certain passage on one string.

Monodrama. A dramatic work for a single singer-actor (e.g.,

Berlioz' *Lélio* or Schönberg's *Erwartung*).

Monody (Gr., one song). Literally, music for one singer, as opposed to choral music, etc. The term is sometimes used in the meaning of °monophonic music (unaccompanied song) or for accompanied solo song in general. More properly it denotes that particular type of accompanied solo song which developed about 1600 in reaction against the polyphonic style of the 16th century, and which can be characterized as a recitative with a thorough-bass accompaniment. See *Nuove musiche*.

Monophonic (Gr., one sound). Music consisting of a single melodic line, without additional parts or chordal accompaniment (see *Homophonic, polyphonic*). It is the oldest type of music, being the only one found in Greek music and Gregorian chant, and in the music of the troubadours, trouvères, minnesingers, and mastersingers. Folk music, oriental music, and primitive music are also essentially monophonic.

Monotone. (1) In Gregorian chant, the recitation of a liturgical text on an unchanging pitch, usually modified by inflections, i.e., a few ascending or descending notes at the beginning or end of phrases. It is used for the psalms (see *Psalm tones*), prayers, lessons, etc. — (2) Term sometimes used for a person who cannot sing a tune correctly.

Monothematic. Term for compositions based on one theme, as opposed to *polythematic,* for compositions based on several themes. The terms are used mainly in connection with the fugue and its ancestors, such as the *canzona and the *ricercar. The fully developed fugue, as found in Bach, is normally monothematic (except for double fugues, etc.), while the earlier compositions in fugal style were often polythematic.

Moonlight Sonata. Nickname of Beethoven's Pianoforte Sonata in C-sharp minor, op. 27, no. 2, composed in 1801. The name probably derives from a description by L. Rellstab (1799–1860) in which the first movement is likened to a boat floating in the moonlight on Lake Lucerne. Beethoven called this work, as well as its companion, op. 27, no. 1, *Sonata quasi una fantasia* (Sonata in the Manner of a Fantasy), thus indicating that the order and forms of the movements are not those usually encountered in a *sonata. See also remark under *Sordino.*

Morceau (mawr-SO: F.). Piece, e.g., *morceau de piano,* piano piece.

Mordent (MAWR-dent). A term used (very confusingly) for two or even more ornaments involving the alternation of a main note with its upper or lower neighbor. Originally, with the French clavecinists and J. S. Bach, mordent meant the ornamentation indicated as in Fig. 70 (I) and performed as in (a). The sign without the dash (II) was called *trillo* and was, in fact, nothing but a short trill starting with the upper note (c). After

Fig. 70

1750 (C. P. E. Bach and others) this sign was used for the ornament shown under (d), that is, the inversion of the mordent. Its original name was *Schneller,* but it was later called *inverted mordent.* Eventually, however, the two terms were exchanged, so that today the sign (II) is often called mordent, the sign (I) inverted mordent. The best way to avoid the confusion is to use terms such as "upper mordent" and "lower mordent." In conformity with the general trends explained under *Ornaments, the 18th-century manner of performance (a, d) changed into that shown under (b) and (e) during the 19th century.

Moresca (mo-RES-ka). A pantomimic dance popular during the 15th and 16th centuries, executed in Moorish costumes, the dancers having their faces blackened and bells attached to their legs. Although originating in Spain, it was practised particularly in England as the *Morris dance,* where it formed part of the May Games, often including solo characters such as a dancer with a hobbyhorse or the "Mayde Marian" (a boy disguised as a girl). It was accompanied by the *pipe and tabor.

Morris dance. See *Moresca.*

Mosso (MAWS-so: It.). Moved, animated.

Motet (mo-TET: from F. *mot*, word). The most important form of early polyphonic music, from *c.* 1200 to *c.* 1600. During this period it underwent considerable change, so that at least two different types of motet must be distinguished, the medieval motet (13th and 14th centuries) and the Renaissance (or Flemish) motet (15th and 16th centuries).

I. *The Medieval Motet.* This is normally in three voice parts called (from lowest to highest) *tenor, motetus,* and *triplum.* The tenor is a *cantus firmus* borrowed from a melismatic passage (sung to a single syllable or word) of a Gregorian Gradual, Alleluia, Responsory, etc. Hence it carries only a single syllable or word, e.g., *DO* (from *Benedicamus DO-mino*) or *NOSTRUM* (from *Alleluia, Pascha NOSTRUM immolatus est*). Each of the two upper voices has a full and different text, hence the name *polytextual* motet. Originally both of these texts were in Latin and expressed religious thoughts related to the text of the Gregorian chant from which the tenor was taken. About 1250, however, the *triplum* (later also the *motetus*) was provided with a French text, usually of an amorous character. The motet developed from the *clausula. Many of the earlier motets are musically identical with a clausula, the only difference being the addition of a text in the upper parts. In the 14th century the motets became more extended and elaborate, involving *isorhythmic construction (de Vitry, Machaut).

II. *The Renaissance Motet.* This type of motet, also called *Flemish* because it developed under Flemish masters, is usually meant when the word motet is used without specification. It is a sacred choral composition based on a single Latin text which is sung in all of the four or (usually) five voice parts, although the words are not normally distributed evenly, appearing at different times in the soprano, alto, etc. The texture is usually polyphonic, in the sense of "equal importance of all the parts," and from about 1500 (Josquin, Gombert, Lasso, Palestrina) imitation is consistently applied (see *Point of imitation*). This technique is so characteristic of the 16th-century motet that it is often referred to as *motet style.* However, the motets frequently include sections in *familiar style also, with notes and syllables appearing simultaneously in the various voices.

About 1600, the motet adopted various novel features, such as addition of instruments, use of solo singers, or replacement of the Latin text by the vernacular. The latter method was employed particularly in Germany, as appears from the six motets by Bach, all based on German texts.

Mother Goose Suite (F., *Ma mère l'oye*). A suite by Ravel based on fairy tales by Perrault. Translated subtitles are: 1. *Pavane of the Sleeping Beauty;* 2. *Tom Thumb;* 3. *Little Ugly One, Empress of the Pagodas;* 4. *Colloquy between the Beauty and the Beast;* 5. *The Fairy Garden.* Originally (1908) written for piano duet, it was scored for orchestra and produced as a children's ballet in 1915.

Motion. In a melody, the effect resulting from the difference of pitches (high-low), as opposed to rhythm, i.e., the variety of durations (long-short). See under *Melody*. Specific terms are *ascending* motion, *descending* motion, *conjunct* motion (progression by steps, i.e., ascending or descending seconds), and *disjunct* motion (progression by larger intervals such as thirds, fourths, etc.).

The term is also used to indicate the relative motion of two voice parts: *parallel,* if they stay at the same interval (Fig. 71a);

Fig. 71

similar, if they move in the same direction (b); *contrary,* if they move in opposite directions (c); *oblique,* if one part stays at the same pitch (d).

Motive (F., *motif*; G., *Motiv*). A brief melodic figure, too short to be called a theme, but often a fragment of a theme (of a sonata, fugue, etc.). Motives are of particular importance in the development sections of sonatas (symphonies, string quartets, etc.) where they are usually employed as building material (see under *Sonata form*). Fig. 72 shows the main theme of the first

Fig. 72

movement of Beethoven's Pastoral Symphony, together with the motives (a, b, and c) derived from it and used in the course of the movement, particularly in the development section. See also *Leitmotiv*.

Moto (It.). Motion. *Con moto,* with motion, with animation. *Moto perpetuo,* *perpetuum mobile.

Motto. A characteristic and distinctive theme stated at the beginning of a composition and quoted later on, as an allusion to some programmatic idea. Familiar examples are found in Tchaikovsky's Symphonies no. 4 and 5.

Motu proprio (L., on [the Pope's] own authority). General designation for a personal decree of the Pope. In music, a particular decree issued by Pius X in 1903, sanctioning the restoration of Gregorian chant according to the principles of the monks of *Solesmes, permitting the use of "composed music," if written in a proper style, and eliminating the use of instruments, except for a modest use of the organ.

Mount of Olives, The. Oratorio (*Christus am Ölberg*) by Beethoven, op. 85 (libretto by F. X. Huber), produced in Vienna, 1803.

Mouth harmonica, mouth organ. See *Harmonica*.

Mouthpiece. That portion of a wind instrument which is held between or applied to the player's lips. There are various types of mouthpieces, and these form a chief distinction between the various families of *wind instruments.

Mouvement (moov-MONH: F.). Tempo, pace. For example, *mouvement premier,* former tempo.

Movable Do. See under *Solmization*; also *Tonic Sol-fa*.

Movement. General term for the single pieces forming part of a composite work such as a sonata, symphony, concerto, string quartet, suite, cantata, etc.

Mp. Abbreviation for *mezzo-piano*, i.e., half soft (see under *Mezza, mezzo*).

M. S. Abbreviation for *mano sinistra* (It.), left hand.

Multimeter. A metric scheme wherein the meter of a piece changes frequently, e.g., 2 measures of 3/4, followed by one measure of 2/4, followed by 3 measures of 3/8, etc. Stravinsky has employed the device extensively.

Multitonality. A tonal scheme typical of the late 19th century in which the tonality of a composition changes frequently (see *Modulation*).

Murky bass. Name (of unknown origin and meaning) for keyboard bass patterns in broken octaves, such as occur often in the music, particularly song accompaniments, of the Rococo period (*c.* 1750–70). Beethoven, in the first movement of his Pathétique Sonata, changed the murky bass into a highly dramatic octave tremolo. A similar device is used in *boogie-woogie.

Musette (mui-ZET: F.). The French type of *bagpipe, widely used in the 17th and 18th centuries. Also, title for pieces imitating the music of the bagpipe, particularly its sustained drone in fifths.

Musica ficta (MOO-zi-ka FIK-ta: L., fictitious music). In the music of the 10th to the 16th centuries, the theory and practice of chromatic tones, other than B-flat which was regarded as a part of the regular system (see *Hexachord*). In modern writings the term usually refers to the problems arising from the scarce or incomplete indication of chromatic alterations in the sources of the period, particularly of the period from about 1450 to 1600 which, strangely enough, show considerably fewer accidentals than those of the 14th and early 15th centuries. In contrast to the methods employed by earlier musicologists, there is now a tendency to supply editorial accidentals as sparingly as possible.

Music box. See under *Mechanical instruments*.

Musical glasses. See *Glass harmonica*.

Musical Joke, A (G., *Ein musikalischer Spass*). A sextet (*divertimento) by Mozart, K. 522 (1787), for strings and two horns, in which he pokes fun at the incompetent provincial musicians of his day by using all sorts of faulty devices such as dissonances, parallel fifths, etc.

Musical Offering, The (G., *Das musikalische Opfer*). A collection of compositions by Bach, written in 1747 and occasioned by a visit with the Prussian king Frederick II, who gave him a theme to improvise upon. The pieces, two *ricercars, ten canons, and a trio sonata for flute, violin, and continuo, are all based on the "royal theme" (Fig. 73). The work thus anticipates the basic idea of the *Art of Fugue.

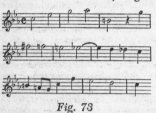

Fig. 73

Music appreciation. A type of nonprofessional musical training designed to develop the ability to listen intelligently to the music likely to be heard in concert performances, radio broadcasts, etc., thus enhancing understanding and satisfaction. It has often been criticized as leading to superficiality and presumption, without providing the thorough education indispensable for professional musicians and music scholars. Such criticism is justified only with regard to attempts on the level of the "love-life of Wagner" or the "stories behind great music," now largely a matter of the past. Basically, the idea of broadening and deepening the amateur's knowledge and understanding of music is sound, and is deserving of constructive cooperation rather than adverse criticism on the part of professional musicians.

Musica reservata (MOO-zi-ka re-ser-VAH-ta: L.). A term of obscure meaning (music "reserved" for people of high cultural standing, or for the initiated professionals?) used during the 16th century. It had the implication of Renaissance clarity, balance of means, and expressive treatment of the text, as found in the music of Josquin and his followers, in opposition to the abstract and transcendental quality of 15th-century music as represented by Ockeghem. In the late 16th century the term seems to have been used especially for picturesque and descriptive musical settings of a text such as those found in madrigals (e.g., an ascending melodic line for the words "running up the hill").

Music drama. Designation chosen by Wagner for the Wagnerian type of opera in order to distinguish his works from the conventional opera. The libretto and the action are not interrupted by set pieces, and dramatic considerations are as important as musical ones.

Musicology. The scholarly study of music, involving research based on original sources, and designed to make new contributions to knowledge of music. One of the first great achievements of musicology was the "rediscovery" of Bach, resulting in the complete edition of his works, published between 1850 and 1900.

Musikalische Opfer, Das (G.). See *Musical Offering*.

Musikalischer Spass, Ein (G.). See *Musical Joke*.

Musique concrète (F.). See under *Twentieth-century music*.

Mustel Organ. See under *Harmonium*.

Muta (It., change). Direction in orchestral parts to change the tuning of kettledrums, e.g., *muta in A,* change the tuning to A. In earlier scores, also given for horns and trumpets whose tuning could be changed by substituting different *crooks. *Mutano* is the plural.

Mutation. (1) The change from soprano or alto to tenor or bass which takes place in a boy's voice during adolescence, usually between the ages of 14 and 16. — (2) See under *Hexachord.*

Mutation stops. See under *Organ.*

Mute. A device for softening or muffling the sound of a musical instrument. The best-known example is the mute of violins, etc., a device in the shape of a small comb whose prongs are clamped on the bridge, thus reducing the vibrations and rendering the sound veiled and somewhat nasal. Brass instruments are muted by inserting a pear-shaped piece of wood into the bell, kettledrums by placing a cloth over the skin or by using sponge-headed drumsticks. In pianofortes the sound is muted by the soft pedal which, by shifting the hammers, reduces the number of strings that are struck.

The term mute should not be confused with *damper,* which properly means a device to deaden a sound. The difference between these two is particularly clear on the piano, whose left pedal is a mute, while the right pedal serves to remove the dampers from the strings. See *Pianoforte; Sordino.*

M. v. *Mezza voce.* See *Mezza, mezzo.*

My Country (Fatherland). See *Má Vlast.*

Mystery play. See under *Liturgical drama.*

Mystic chord. See under *Fourth chord.*

N

Nachschlag (NAHKH-shlahg: G.). An ornament consisting of one or several short notes attached to the preceding main note. It is usually indicated by grace notes, as shown in Fig. 74.

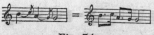

Fig. 74

Nachspiel (NAHKH-shpeel: G.). Postlude.

Nachtmusik (NAHKHT-moo-ZEEK: G.). Night music or serenade. See *Kleine Nachtmusik, Eine.*

Nachtstück ·(NAHKHT-shtuik: G., night piece). See *Nocturne.*

Nänie (L. mournful song). Title of an ode by Schiller referring to the death of the son of Aphrodite. Brahms composed a musical setting of the ode for chorus and orchestra (op. 82, 1880) on the occasion of the death of his friend, Anselm Feuerbach.

Nail violin, nail harmonica. An instrument invented about 1740, consisting of a semicircular soundboard with nails of various lengths fastened along the edge, which are made to vibrate by a violin bow.

Nakers (NAY-kers: from old Arabic, *nagarah*). Medieval name for small drums.

National anthems. Songs which represent nations, as do their flags, having been officially adopted for that purpose by their various governments. Some of the best-known anthems are listed below:

1. Austria. *Land der Berge* (Land of Mountains), text by Paula Preradovic sung to music from a cantata by Mozart, adopted in 1946. Until 1918, *Gott erhalte unsern Kaiser* (God Save our Emperor), text by L. Haschka, music by Haydn (composed in 1797; see *Emperor Quartet*), was the Austrian national anthem.

2. Canada. Although Canada has no official national anthem, both *God Save the Queen* and *O Canada* are used as such. The French text of the latter is by Routhier (English version by Weir, 1908), and the music was composed in 1880 by Calixa Lavallée.

3. England. *God Save the Queen* (author of text and music unknown; introduced about 1745). The melody is also used in the American song beginning "My Country, 'tis of Thee."

4. France. *La Marseillaise*, text and music by Rouget de Lisle, 1792. The name was acquired when it was sung in Paris by soldiers from Marseilles in 1792.

5. Germany. *Einigkeit und Recht und Freiheit* (Unity and Right and Freedom), text by Fallersleben (1841), sung to Haydn's melody for the former Austrian national anthem.

6. Netherlands. *Wilhelmus van Nassouve* (William of Nassau), text possibly by Philip van Marnix (*c*. 1570), sung to an old French soldiers' song first published in 1626. It is the oldest of all the national anthems.

7. Russia. *Hymn of the Soviet Union*, text by Mikhalkov and Registan, music by Alexandrov, adopted in 1944. From 1918 until 1944, *L'Internationale* (original French text by Pottier, music by Degeyter) was the Russian national anthem.

8. United States of America. *The *Star-spangled Banner.*

Nationalism, national schools. A musical movement which started early in the 19th century and which is characterized by a strong emphasis on the national aspect of music. This emphasis is achieved by drawing on the native folk songs and dances of the composer's country, and incorporating them into a work either literally or, more often, in free elaboration and imitation. Another common nationalistic device is the choosing of scenes from national history, legend, country life, geography, etc., as subjects for operas, songs, choral works, or symphonic poems. Well-known nationalistic composers are: Grieg (Norway); Smetana (Czechoslovakia); Moussorgsky, Rimski-Korsakov (Russia); Albéniz, Falla (Spain); Sibelius (Finland); Vaughan Williams (England); Copland, Gershwin (U.S.A.); Villa-Lobos (Brazil); Chavez (Mexico). Representative national operas are Smetana's *The Bartered Bride* (1866), Moussorgsky's *Boris Godunov* (1872), and Gershwin's *Porgy and Bess* (1935).

The term nationalism is sometimes used in a much wider sense to include all the composers who "express the spirit of their country." In one way or another, this may be said of almost every composer. The music of Bach, Beethoven, Schumann, is as thoroughly German as that of Rossini and Verdi is Italian, or that of Debussy and Ravel is French. Used in this broad sense, however, the term nationalism loses its value as a distinctive designation.

Natural. (1) A note that is neither sharp nor flat, e.g., G-natural. — (2) See under *Accidentals.*

Natural horn, trumpet. The older horn or trumpet (used until about 1800), which had no valves and therefore could only produce the *natural tones,* i.e., the harmonics of the fundamental tone corresponding to the length of the tube (see also under *Wind instruments*).

Neapolitan opera. See under *Opera,* I.

Neapolitan sixth. A sixth *chord having as its root the flattened

Fig. 75

supertonic (D-flat in C major or minor). It was frequently used in the 18th century (not limited to Neapolitan composers) in cadences such as shown in Fig. 75.

Neck. The projecting portion of violins, guitars, lutes, etc., which carries the finger board and the upper part of the strings.

Nelson Mass. A Mass by Haydn in D minor, written in 1798 while Lord Nelson was engaged in the Battle of the Nile, a battle which intrigued Haydn immensely. The Mass is sometimes called "The Imperial."

Neoclassical, neoclassicism. A movement of the 20th century which is essentially a reaction against the subjectivity and unrestrained emotionalism of late Romanticism. It is characterized by the adoption of aesthetic ideals and of forms or methods derived from the music of earlier masters, especially those of the 18th century such as Bach, Handel, Pergolesi, Mozart, etc. This influence is apparent in the emphasis on contrapuntal texture; in the revival of old forms such as the toccata, passacaglia, fugue, ostinato, concerto grosso, ricercar, motet; in the reduction of orchestral colors and sonorities; in the abandoning of program music; and in a general tendency toward an objective and detached style, antiromantic and often antiemotional. Naturally, the "return to Bach" (or other early masters) did not entail a return to the musical language of his day. On the contrary, music became even more sharply dissonant and rhythmically more complex than it had been before, because the individual lines were permitted to move according to their own melodic functions, without regard to harmonic combinations.

After isolated instances such as Busoni's *Sonata in Diem Nativitatis Christi* (1917) and Prokofiev's °*Classical Symphony*, neoclassicism became the most widespread and most important trend in music about 1920. Stravinsky's Sonata for Pianoforte (1922) and Octet for Wind Instruments (1923) are among the definitive examples of neoclassical style. Among the composers who have developed their own versions of neoclassicism are Bartok, Hindemith, Casella, Malipiero, Piston, and others.

Neomodal. Term for the use of modal idioms in 20th-century music. See *Modality*.

Neoromanticism. (1) In general usage, a term synonymous with postromanticism or late (post-Wagnerian) romanticism, embracing the period from about 1880 to about 1910, as represented by R. Strauss, Mahler, Sibelius, Rachmaninoff, etc. — (2) Recently there has been a tendency to reserve the term for the mellowing trend in contemporary composition following the ardent °neoclassicism of

the 1920's and 1930's, leaving the term postromanticism for the period defined under (1).

Netherlands Schools. Designation for the long series of 15th- and 16th-century composers who came from the Low Countries and became the leading masters in the musical centers of Italy, France, Spain, and Germany. A distinction is usually made between a first, second, and third Netherlands School, headed respectively by Dufay (*c.* 1400–1474), Ockeghem (*c.* 1430–1495), and Josquin des Prez (*c.* 1450–1521). Within the past thirty years these terms have been largely discarded. The First Netherlands School is now usually called the °*Burgundian* School, while the later masters represent various generations of the °*Flemish* School.

Neumatic style. See under *Gregorian chant*; also *Neumes*.

Neumes (newmz: from Gr. *neuma*, nod, sign). The notational signs used in the medieval manuscripts of Gregorian chant (9th century and later). They include signs for single tones as well as numerous symbols representing groups of two, three, or more tones. These symbols are designed in such a way that motion from one pitch to the next (low-to-high; high-to-low; low-to-high-to-low, etc.), is indicated much in the same way as could be done by a motion of the hand. In the earlier manuscripts (10th, 11th century) the neumes indicate only the general direction, not the exact pitches or intervals involved. Thus, the *podatus* indicates a motion from low to high, which may be an ascending second, third, fourth, etc. These neumes are called *cheironomic* (Gr., hand sign) or *staffless*. They served only as an aid to the singers who knew the melodies from memory. In later manuscripts the neumes are arranged in such a manner as to give a clear indication of the pitches, being written on a staff either imagined or indicated by one, two, and finally four lines. Such neumes are called *heightened* (also *intervallic*, *diastematic*). Hand in hand with this process went a transformation of the graphic appearance of the neumes, leading from the dots and fine lines of the earlier period to symbols with square-shaped heads. The latter became generally accepted in the 13th century, and are used to the present day in the liturgical books of the Roman Catholic Church. They were also adopted, under the name of *ligatures*, for the notation of polyphonic music, because of which they took on definite rhythmic meanings, such as *brevis-longa*, *brevis-brevis-longa*, etc. See Fig. 76.

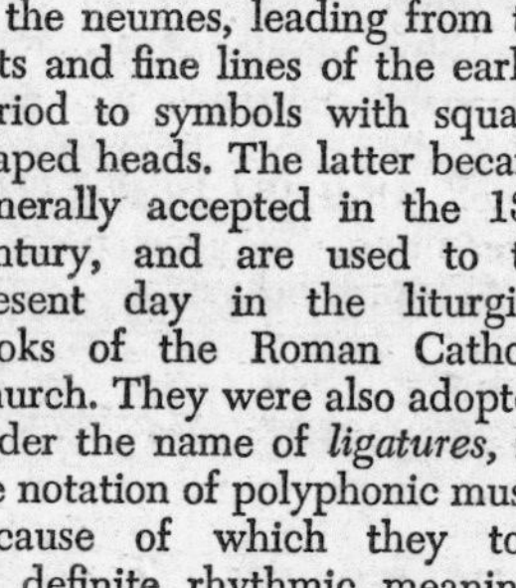

Punctum	~ ⌣	▪	♪
Virga	/ /	⌐	♪
Podatus or Pes	✔✔	▪	♫
Clivis	⌒	▶	♫
Scandicus	⠶	▪▪	♫♫
Climacus	/⠲	▶⠒	♫♫
Torculus	⌒	♪	♫♫
Porrectus	⋈	⋈	♫♫

Fig. 76

New Music. A term often used for the various radical and ex-

perimental trends in 20th-century music, beginning about 1910 and represented by such composers as Schönberg and Stravinsky, in distinction from others more inclined to continue along the traditional lines of Romanticism, Impressionism, Nationalism, etc. The term also has an interesting historical significance, as similar names were used for somewhat parallel movements 300 and 600 years ago, namely, *Nuove musiche* and *Ars nova*, meaning "new music," "new art." See *History of music*. For more details on the present-day meaning, see under *Twentieth-century music*.

New World Symphony (Dvořák). See *From the New World*.

Night on the Bald Mountain. A symphonic poem in variation form by Moussorgsky, inspired by the witches' sabbath in Gogol's story, "St. John's Eve." Composed in 1867, it was repeatedly revised (with chorus: *Night on Mount Triglav*), eventually being incorporated into his unfinished opera *Fair at Sorochinsk*. Today it is performed in an orchestral arrangement by Rimski-Korsakov.

Nights in the Gardens of Spain (Sp., *Noches en los jardines de España*). Impressionistic suite for piano and orchestra by Manuel de Falla, finished in 1915. The three movements are: (1) In the Generalife; (2) Distant Dance; and (3) In the Gardens of the Sierra de Cordoba.

Ninth chord. See under *Chords*.

Ninth Symphony. Although many composers (e.g., Bruckner, Dvořák, Haydn, Mozart) have written as many as nine symphonies, the most celebrated is Beethoven's last symphony, also known as the °Choral Symphony.

Nobilissima Visione (no-bee-LEE-see-mah vee-ZYO-nay). Ballet by Hindemith (composed 1938), based on the life of St. Francis of Assisi (1182–1226). Some of the numbers were arranged into an orchestral suite for use in concert performance.

Noces, Les (lay NOS: The Wedding). Ballet by Stravinsky (choreography by B. Nizhinska), produced in Paris, 1923. It is scored for chorus, soloists, four pianos, and seventeen percussion instruments, and consists of four scenes: 1. The Tresses; 2. In the Groom's Home; 3. The Bride's Farewell; 4. The Wedding Repast.

Noches en los jardines de España. See *Nights in the Gardens of Spain.*

Nocturne (F., night piece). Title for Romantic °character pieces, usually of a lyrical, melancholy, or reflective mood. It was first used by the Irish composer John Field (1782–1837) from whom Chopin adopted it. Most of Chopin's nocturnes are in ternary form, often with an agitated middle section.

Nocturnes. Three symphonic poems by Debussy, composed 1893–99: 1. *Nuages* (Clouds); 2. *Fêtes* (°Festivals); and, with women's voices, 3. *Sirènes* (Sirens).

Noel (F.). Christmas carol. Also (Noël) name of 17th- and 18th-century organ pieces designed to be played at Christmas time, often simple variations on popular Christmas tunes.

Nonet (no-NET). Chamber music for nine instruments, e.g., string quartet and five wood winds.

Nonharmonic tones. In harmonic analysis, tones that are foreign to the momentary harmony, being added for the sake of greater melodic interest. They may be classified into two main categories:

1. Rhythmically weak notes that occur between two notes that are part of the harmony (see Fig. 77, a–e): (a) *passing tone;*

Fig. 77

(b) *anticipation;* (c) *échappée;* (d) *cambiata;* (e) *auxiliary* or *neighboring tone* (upper or lower). With the *échappée* the motion of the nonharmonic tone is away from the note of resolution, while with the *cambiata* the two motions are in the same direction.

2. Rhythmically strong notes that occur in the place of a harmonic note: *appoggiatura* and *suspension.* An *appoggiatura* (from It., *appoggiare,* to lean) is the upper or lower neighboring note of a harmonic note, played on the beat in place of the harmonic note and resolved afterwards into the proper note. Fig. 77f shows various appoggiatura formations of the C-major triad, while Fig. 77g illustrates the *prepared appoggiatura,* with the "wrong" note anticipated in the preceding chord. The *suspension* (Fig. 77h) is the same as the prepared appoggiatura except that the nonharmonic tone is tied over from the preceding chord. Appoggiatura formations, often multiple (simultaneous appoggiaturas for two or more notes of a chord), are an important source of dissonance in the harmonic style of the 19th century, particularly in Wagner, Tchaikovsky, Franck, and R. Strauss. Fig. 77i, from the last movement of Tchaikovsky's Symphony no. 4, shows a triple appoggiatura properly resolved. In Fig. 77j is an unresolved appoggiatura (g-sharp in the final chord) from Debussy's *Pelléas et Mélisande.*

Non tanto, non troppo (non TAHN-to, non TROP-po: It.). Not so much, not too much; e.g., *non troppo allegro,* not too fast.

Nordic Symphony. Howard Hanson's Symphony no. 1, in E minor, composed in 1922.

Norma. Opera by Bellini (libretto by F. Romani), produced in Milan, 1831. The plot is laid in Gaul in pre-Christian times soon after the area had been conquered by the Romans. It centers around the love triangle of the Druid priestess Norma (soprano), the Roman proconsul Pollione (tenor), and the temple virgin Adalgisa (mezzo-soprano). Rejected by Pollione, Norma confesses her unchastity and mounts a blazing funeral pyre where Pollione, remorseful, joins her.

Notation. Generally, any set of symbols designed for the recording of music in written form. The basic elements of the present-day system are a °staff of five lines, provided with a °clef, a °time signature, and a °key signature; furthermore °notes and rests, °bar lines, °accidentals, °ties, °dots, etc. There are, however, many other systems (employed in earlier periods or for special purposes) in which music is written down by means of °neumes, syllables (see *Tonic Sol-fa*), letters or figures (see °*Tablature*), or other signs (see under *Ukulele*). The present-day system developed from an earlier one, called °mensural notation.

Notes and rests. The longest note (see under *Notation*) commonly used today is the *whole note.* Smaller values, called *half note, quarter note,* etc., are each one half as long as the preceding one. For each of these values there is a corresponding rest indicated by a special sign. Fig. 78 shows the various signs and names (the rests appear within the brackets), together with the

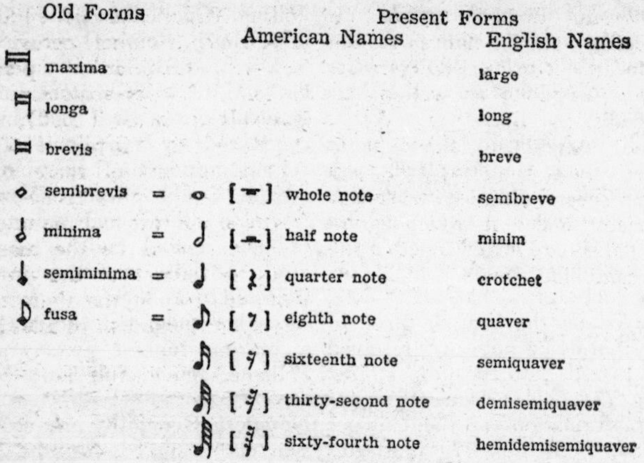

	Old Forms			Present Forms American Names		English Names
⊟	maxima					large
⊓	longa					long
⊟	brevis					breve
◇	semibrevis	=	○	[▬]	whole note	semibreve
♩	minima	=	♩	[▬]	half note	minim
♩	semiminima	=	♩	[♩]	quarter note	crotchet
♪	fusa	=	♪	[7]	eighth note	quaver
			♫	[♯]	sixteenth note	semiquaver
			♫	[♯]	thirty-second note	demisemiquaver
			♫	[♯]	sixty-fourth note	hemidemisemiquaver

Fig. 78

values employed in early music (before 1600, see *Mensural notation*). The names used in England are partly derived from the earlier system.

Although "note" properly means a written symbol, the term is also often used for the sound indicated by a note, more properly called *tone:* one sees a note and hears a tone. In English writings, however, the term note is used for both the written symbol and the audible sound, the word tone being used in the sense of whole tone (interval) or tone quality.

Notre Dame, School of. See under *Ars antiqua*.

Notturno (not-TOOR-no: It.). (1) Italian designation for °nocturne. — (2) An 18th-century name for compositions similar to a °serenade, designed to be played as an evening entertainment. They are usually in the form of a sonata, for a small chamber ensemble of strings and winds.

Nouveaux Jeunes, Les (F.). See under *Six, Les*.

Novachord. An electrophonic keyboard instrument resembling the electronic organ but differing from it in having a single manual and a simpler tone-producing mechanism.

Novellette. A designation meaning "little novel" or "short story," and used by Schumann for a group of eight piano pieces, op. 21 (1838). Each consists of contrasting sections vaguely suggestive of a narrative. See under *Character piece*.

Nozze di Figaro, Le (It.). See *Marriage of Figaro*.

Number opera. Designation for the older type of opera which consisted of separate "numbers" (arias, duets, choruses, etc.), as opposed to the continuous opera of the Wagnerian type. Typical examples of number opera are Mozart's *Abduction*, Auber's *Fra*

Diavolo, Rossini's *Barber of Seville,* and Bellini's *Norma.* Mozart's *Marriage of Figaro* and *Don Giovanni,* as well as the operas by Beethoven, Weber, and Meyerbeer, although essentially of the same type, contain several lengthy movements, mostly finales, in which various numbers are linked together into a continuous whole.

Nuove musiche (noo-O-vay MOO-zi-kay: It., new music [pl.]). Designation for the period about 1600, one of the most important landmarks in the history of music, since it marks the rise of °monody as well as of novel forms such as opera, oratorio, aria, and cantata. The movement started in Florence among a group of musicians and amateurs interested in the revival of the ancient Greek drama (see *Camerata*). Among the earliest products were the operas °*Euridice* by Peri and by Caccini (both produced in 1600); Caccini's collection of monodic songs, *Nuove musiche* (1602), after which the whole period was named; Cavalieri's operatic oratorio, °*Rappresentazione di anima e di corpo* (1600); and Monteverdi's °*Orfeo* (1607). The chief aim of these composers was a new relationship between the text and the music: "Let the word be the master, not the servant of the music" (Monteverdi, in the Preface to his *Scherzi musicali* of 1607).

Nut. (1) On violins, etc., a slightly projecting ridge at the upper end of the neck over which the strings pass in order to keep them from touching the finger board. — (2) The lower end of the violin bow, at which it is held.

Nutcracker Suite. An orchestral suite in six movements by Tchaikovsky, op. 71a (1891), arranged from his ballet, *The Nutcracker* (F., *Casse-noisette*), based on E. T. A. Hoffmann's fantastic tale, *The Nutcracker and the Mouse King.*

O

Ob. Short for oboe.

Obbligato (ob-li-GAH-to: It.). Obligatory, with reference to an instrument (*violino obbligato*) or to a part that is essential and cannot be omitted. By a strange misunderstanding, however, the term has acquired the opposite meaning, that is, of a mere accompanying part which may be omitted. The literal meaning prevails in older music (Bach, Handel), the other in 19th-century and present-day practice.

Oberon. Opera by Weber (text by J. R. Planché), produced in London, 1826. Although the whole work is rarely performed, the overture, consisting of material used throughout the opera, is a staple of orchestral concert literature.

Oberwerk (O-ber-vàyrk: G.). Swell organ.

Oblique motion. See under *Motion*.

Oboe (from F. *hautbois*, high wood, probably meaning "high-pitched instrument"). An orchestral wood-wind instrument consisting of an end-blown conical pipe about two feet long, to the upper end of which a double-reed mouthpiece is fixed. For the difference between the oboe and the similar-looking clarinet, see under *Clarinet*. The natural scale of the oboe is D, but it is not treated as a transposing instrument. Its range is from b♭ to f''' (see illustration).

and a conical bore. The *English horn* is an alto oboe, pitched a fifth below the oboe (see Fig. 79). To facilitate handling, a small curved metal tube holds the mouthpiece at the upper end of the pipe, while the lower end extends into a pear-shaped bell which largely accounts for the soft and somewhat melancholy tone color of the instrument. Its name is probably the result of a confusion of the French words *anglé* (angled) with *anglais* (English). Earlier specimens often had an angled instead of a straight pipe (see illustration below). The *bassoon* is the bass of the oboe family, corresponding in range to the cello of the violin family. It is pitched two octaves below the oboe. On account of its great length, the

RANGES
a. Oboe. b. English horn. c. Bassoon.
d. Contrabassoon.

Fig. 79

tube is bent back upon itself, first descending and then ascending (see illustration). The *double bassoon* (*contrabassoon*) sounds an octave below the bassoon. It has a tube of over sixteen feet in length, doubled on itself four times, with the bell pointing downward instead of upward, as in the bassoon.

In addition to these four main members of the oboe family there are two in-between sizes, the *oboe d'amore* and the *Heckelphone*, the former having the shape of a small English horn, the latter of a large one. The oboe d'amore (love oboe,

Oboe

Closely related to the oboe are three other instruments, the English horn, the bassoon, and the double bassoon. They have a double-reed mouthpiece

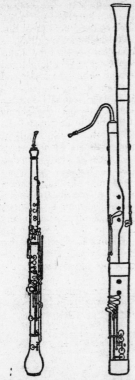

English horn *Bassoon*

or plastic material, with a protruding mouthpiece and a number of finger holes.

Octave (from L. *octavus*, eighth). The interval embracing eight *diatonic tones. Also, the eighth tone of the diatonic scale. Acoustically, this is the tone with twice the frequency of the first tone of the scale (e.g., a = 440, a′ = 880 vibrations per second). The octave is the most perfect consonance, so perfect indeed that it gives the impression of being a mere duplication of the original tone. Hence, the whole range of musical sounds is divided into almost identical segments, each called an octave. For the designation of the various octaves, see under *Pitch names*.

Octave species. See under *Greek music*.

Octet. Chamber music for eight instruments.

Ode. A poem of variable metric and verse structure, and of a festive character, frequently addressed to a deity. In musical settings, odes are usually composed in a free form, including sections for chorus, soloists, and orchestra. Famous examples are Handel's *Ode for St. Cecilia's Day* (1739, set to Dryden's poem) and Beethoven's *Ode to Joy*, which forms the last movement of his Ninth Symphony (see *Choral Symphony*). Purcell also composed four *Odes for St. Cecilia's Day*, based on various poems.

probably so called because its sound is "sweeter" than that of the oboe) was frequently used by J. S. Bach. The Heckelphone is a modern instrument (*c.* 1905) named after its inventor, W. Heckel. Also found in Bach's scores is the *oboe da caccia* (hunting oboe), which probably had a more strident sound than the oboe d'amore.

Ocarina (It.). A popular instrument in the shape of an egg, a bird (It. *oca*, goose), or a sweet potato (hence its colloquial name). It is made of terracotta

Ode to Napoleon. A composition by Schönberg, op. 41b (1944), based on Byron's poem, scored for string orchestra, piano, and a reciting voice. The text has a satirical meaning, commenting on the downfall of dictators. The work is organized as an opera without action, with an overture, arias, and recitatives, and, for dramatic and political significance current at the time of its composition, a quotation of the opening "Victory" theme from Beethoven's Fifth Symphony.

Odhecaton (od-HE-ka-ton: from Gr. *ode*, song, and *hekaton*, hundred). A famous collection of "100 songs" (actually 96) published by Petrucci in 1501. It is the earliest printed publication of polyphonic music, and contains secular compositions of the period from about 1470 to 1500. Similar collections appeared in 1502 and 1503.

Oedipus Rex (ED-i-pus: King Oedipus). Opera-oratorio by Stravinsky in two acts and separate scenes, to a Latin libretto (Cocteau and Daniélou) after Sophocles' ancient Greek drama, produced in Paris, 1927. The extensive use of the chorus for commentary, the use of a narrator, the reduction of the action to entrances and exits, the minimal stage decoration, are all reminiscent of the ancient Greek tragedy and prevent the work from being called an opera in the usual sense. Its underlying principles are similar to those of Cavalieri's °*Rappresentazione di anima e di corpo* (1600).

Oeuvre (EUR-vr: F.). Work, opus.

Offertory (1). In Protestant churches, a musical selection per-formed while offerings are being collected. — (2) In the Roman Catholic service, the fourth item of the Proper of the °Mass, sung during the placing upon the altar of the bread and wine. In the 17th and 18th centuries many composers wrote offertories for organ or instruments to accompany this liturgical action.

Office. In the Roman Catholic rites, the service of the Hours (Matins, Lauds, Prime, Terce, Sext, None, Vespers, and Compline) held approximately every three hours, as distinct from that of the °Mass. See under *Gregorian chant*.

Oiseau de Feu, L' (F.). See *Firebird*.

Old Hundred. A hymn tune which first appeared in the French Psalter of 1551 as a setting for Psalm 134. Its association with Psalm 100 began in the 16th century, hence the name.

Old Maid and the Thief, The. Comic opera by Menotti (to his own libretto), commissioned for radio performance in 1939.

Oliphant (AHL-i-funt: old English, elephant). A medieval horn for signaling, made from an elephant's tusk, often beautifully carved.

Ondes musicales (onhd mui-zee-CAHL: F., musical waves). Also called *Ondes Martenot*. An °electrophonic instrument, invented in 1928 by M. Martenot. It is based on the same principle as the °Theramin, but has a special device which makes it possible to obtain tones accurately graded according to the chromatic scale, without a transitional sliding between pitches.

One-step. American dance of the period c. 1910–20, in quick duple meter, similar to the fox trot. It was superseded by the slower two-step ("slow-fox").

Ongarese, All' (ahl on-gah-RAY-zay: It.). In the style of Hungarian music.

Op. Abbreviation for *opus.

Open fifth. A fifth or triad without the third, for instance, c-g or c-g-c'.

Open harmony. See under *Position*.

Open notes. The notes produced on violins, etc., by the unstopped strings (*open strings*). On wind instruments, the natural tones produced without keys, valves, etc.

Opera (from It. *opera in musica*, work in music). A drama or play with scenery and acting, which is in general sung throughout to the accompaniment of an orchestra. Some operas have speaking parts (e.g., Selim in Mozart's *Abduction from the Seraglio*), or *melodramatic scenes (spoken text against musical background), or spoken dialogue between musical numbers (usually in *comic opera). The opera is a highly complex form, enlisting many different arts in its service: music (both vocal and instrumental), drama, poetry, acting, dance, stage design, costuming, lighting, etc., and this fact accounts in part for both its widespread appeal and the equally widespread criticism directed against its artistic impurity. It is noteworthy that most operas have been composed by specialists in the form, such as Wagner, Verdi, Puccini, Meyerbeer, Rossini, etc. Only a few composers, such as Monteverdi, Handel, Mozart, and R. Strauss, have distinguished themselves equally in the field of opera and nonoperatic music. Following is a brief historical survey.

I. 1600–1780: *From Peri to Mozart*. Although the combination of drama with music is a very old art form, found in the tragedies and comedies of the ancient Greeks as well as in the *liturgical plays of the Middle Ages, the opera proper arose shortly before 1600, in close connection with the novel *monodic style of that day (see also *Camerata; Nuove musiche*). Operatic production started in Florence (Peri, Caccini), but soon spread to Venice (Monteverdi, Cavalli, Cesti) and Rome (Mazzochi, Rossi, Landi). From about 1670 on, opera was also cultivated in France (Cambert, Lully, Rameau), Germany (Keiser, Hasse), and England (Blow, Purcell, Handel). In the 18th century, Naples became the center of operatic activity (Neapolitan opera: Alessandro Scarlatti, Porpora, Pergolesi, Jommelli, Piccinni, Cimarosa). Growing criticism of the Neapolitan opera, with its rigid construction and lack of dramatic interest, led (about 1760) to the "reform opera" of Gluck. Of the many thousands of operas that were produced before Mozart only a handful have survived or have been revived, e.g., Monteverdi's °*Orfeo* and °*Incoronazione di Poppea*, Pergolesi's *La* °*Serva padrona* and *Il Maestro di musica*, and Gluck's °*Orfeo ed Euridice* and °*Iphigenia*. Rameau's operas contain some of the most beautiful operatic music written before Mozart, but the obsolete type of libretto presents a strong obstacle to their revival.

II. 1780–1850: *From Mozart to Wagner and Verdi*. The climax of 18th-century Italian opera is represented by Mozart's °*Marriage of Figaro* (1786) and °*Don Giovanni* (1787), while his °*Magic Flute* (1791) is a forerunner of 19th-century German Romantic opera. Mozart's operas are outstanding in sharpness and subtlety of characterization, unparalleled beauty of the music, integration of vocal and instrumental factors, and the adaptation of the classical symphonic style, particularly in their ensemble finales. The same traits are also present, although not with the same spontaneity, in Beethoven's *Fidelio* (1805–14). This, along with the *Magic Flute*, foreshadows the French "rescue opera," in which the hero or the heroine is saved after many dangers and tribulations (Cherubini, Spontini). The French "grand opera" of the early 19th century is characterized by extended historical plots, often taken from the Middle Ages or the Renaissance, as in Rossini's *William Tell* (1829), Halévy's *La Juive* (1835), Meyerbeer's *Les Huguenots* (1836), and in the early operas of Wagner and Verdi.

Somewhat aside from the main development stands the German Romantic opera (e.g., Weber's *Freischütz*) which laid the foundations for Wagner's innovations.

III. 1850–1900: *Verdi, Wagner, National Opera*. The crowning point of Italian opera, with its melodramatic plots, popular type of melodies, and concentration on "effective" vocal numbers (°number opera), is reached in Verdi's works of the 1850's: *Rigoletto* (1851), *Il Trovatore* (1853), *La Traviata* (1853), *Un Ballo in maschera* (1859). *Aida* (1871) shows unmistakable signs of the changes in style which were fully realized in Verdi's late masterworks *Otello* (1887) and *Falstaff* (1893): better librettos, continuity of presentation, a more flexible rhythm, more expressive harmony, and a closer approach to equality between vocal and instrumental elements. Simultaneously, Wagner developed an entirely new type of opera, the "music drama." While his *Tannhäuser* (1845) still retains the "number" style and has some superfluous display scenes, these remainders from the past are minimized in *Lohengrin* (1847). The music drama, characterized by a hitherto unknown unification of the constituent arts, by the use of meaningful and symbolic plots (all written by Wagner; see *Libretto*), by a highly flexible, continuous, and strongly emotional type of song ("unending melody"), by masterful handling of the orchestra and the consistent use of °leitmotivs, is fully realized in his *Ring of the Nibelung* (1853–74), *Tristan* (1857–59), *M a s t e r s i n g e r s*

(1862–67), and *Parsifal* (1877–79).

Another important development of the period is the rise of national opera (see under *Nationalism*), represented by Moussorgsky's *Boris Godunov* (1874), Smetana's *The Bartered Bride* (1866), and, in a way, Bizet's *Carmen* (1875). In France there developed a lyric, sentimental type of opera represented by Gounod's *Faust* (1859), Thomas' *Mignon* (1866), and Massenet's *Manon* (1884).

IV. 1900–present: *Modern Opera.* Wagner's musical style influenced most composers of opera in the late 19th and early 20th centuries, among whom R. Strauss is outstanding with *Salome* (1905), *Electra* (1909), and *Der Rosenkavalier* (1911). At the same time, the music drama provoked reactions in favor of so-called "realism" (*verismo), evident in the operas of Mascagni (*Cavalleria rusticana*, 1890), Leoncavallo (*Pagliacci*, 1892), Puccini (*La Bohème*, 1896), and Charpentier (*Louise*, 1900). Debussy's *Pelléas et Mélisande* (1902) represents a unique application of the impressionist technique to opera. The revolutionary tendencies and turmoil of the 1910's were not favorable to the production of opera which, more than any other art form, relies on established traditions and conventions. Within the past thirty years, however, operatic production has been pursued with renewed vigor by such composers as Stravinsky (*The Rake's Progress*), Hindemith (*Cardillac, Mathis der Maler*), Berg (*Wozzeck, Lulu*), Menotti (*The Consul, Amahl and the Night Visitors*), Britten (*Peter Grimes, The Rape of Lucretia, Turn of the Screw*), and others.

Opera buffa (O-pe-rah BOOF-fah: It.), **opéra bouffe** (o-pay-rah BOOF: F.). *Comic opera.

Opéra comique (o-pay-ra ko-MEEK: F.). See under *Comic opera*.

Opera houses. The first public opera house was the *Teatro San Cassiano* of Venice, founded in 1637, earlier operas having been performed in private rooms and for invited guests. Opera houses then were built in Paris (1669), Rome (1671), and Hamburg 1678). After 1700 opera houses were erected in nearly all the musical centers of Europe. Particularly famous are *La *Scala* in Milan and Wagner's *Festspielhaus* in Bayreuth. In the United States opera houses exist in New York (*Metropolitan Opera*, 1883), Chicago (*Civic Opera House*, 1928), and San Francisco (*War Memorial Opera House*, 1932).

Opera seria (O-pe-rah SAY-ree-ah: It.). Serious opera as opposed to *opera buffa*, *comic opera.

Operetta (It., little opera). A light and sentimental theatrical piece in simple and popular style, containing vocal and instrumental music, dancing scenes, and spoken dialogue, and designed to appeal to a wide audience. The modern operetta originated in Vienna with Franz von Suppé (1819–1895) and in Paris with Offenbach (1819–1880; *Orpheus in the Under-*

world, La Belle Hélène). J. Strauss, Jr. (1825–1899) raised the Viennese operetta to international fame with about thirty operettas written between 1871 and 1895, among them *Die °Fledermaus* (1874). At the same time A. Sullivan (1842–1900) wrote his famous English operettas (mostly on librettos by W. S. Gilbert), e.g., *Trial by Jury, H. M. S. Pinafore, The Pirates of Penzance,* and the more serious *Mikado.* In the United States operetta was established mainly by Victor Herbert (1859–1924; *Babes in Toyland,* 1903) and Reginald de Koven (1859–1920; *Robin Hood,* 1890). More recently, a typically American type of operetta has been successfully developed in such works as *Oklahoma!* by Hammerstein and Rodgers (1943), *Annie Get Your Gun* by Fields and Berlin (1946), and *South Pacific* by Hammerstein and Rodgers (1949).

Opus (L., work). Abbreviated *op.,* the term in conjunction with a figure (op. 1, op. 2, etc.) indicates the first, second, etc., work of a composer, usually in the order of publication. If several compositions are published at the same time, they are distinguished by the addition: no. 1, 2 — e.g., op. 2, no. 1, etc.

Oratorio. A musical setting, for solo voices, chorus, and orchestra, of an extended story of a religious or contemplative nature, performed in a concert hall or a church, without scenery, costumes, or physical action. The text of an oratorio is, as a rule, expressly written for the purpose of the composition, and this distinguishes the oratorio from works of a similar character which are based entirely on scriptural or liturgical texts (e.g., the Mass, the Requiem, or the Passion). The oratorio is distinguished from the sacred cantata (Bach) by its greater extension and the more narrative and continuous character of the text.

Cavalieri's *°Rappresentazione di anima e di corpo* of 1600, a work close in time and style to the first operas, is usually considered the earliest oratorio, although it was produced with scenery, costumes, and action, and may therefore more properly be termed a "sacred opera." The first oratorios fully deserving this name are those by Carissimi (1605–1674; *Jephta, Judicium Salomonis, Jonas,* etc.). While these have a Latin text, other oratorios are usually based on texts in the vernacular, e.g., H. Schütz's *Christmas Oratorio* (*Historia . . . von der Geburt Christi,* 1664), Bach's *Christmas Oratorio* (*Weihnachts Oratorium,* 1734), and Handel's *Israel in Egypt* (1737), *Messiah* (1742), and *Judas Maccabeus* (1746). A new era of the oratorio was inaugurated by Haydn's *The Creation* (1797) and *The Seasons* (1801), the latter of which, although named "Oratorio," belongs to the secular rather than to the religious field. Compared with these masterworks which stand at the summit of a long life of creative activity, Beethoven's early *Mount of Olives* (*Christus am Ölberg,* 1800) is of small significance. Outstanding among the 19th-century oratorios are Mendelssohn's *St. Paul* (1836) and *Elijah* (1846), Berlioz' *L'Enfance du Christ* (*Christ's Childhood*, 1854), Liszt's *The Legend of St. Elizabeth* (1862), and Franck's *Les Béatitudes* (1879). Important works of the 20th century are Elgar's *The Dream of Gerontius* (1900), Walton's *Belshazzar's Feast* (1931), Honegger's *King David* (*Le Roi David*, 1923), and Stravinsky's opera-oratorio *Oedipus Rex* (1927) which, because of its stage presentation, reverts to Cavalieri's *Rappresentazione*.

Orchestra (Gr., literally "dancing place," i.e., that portion of the Greek theater which was reserved for the dancing of the chorus and also for the instrumentalists). A large ensemble of instrumentalists, as distinct from the small ensembles used in *chamber music, or from ensembles consisting of special instruments (for example, the *band). The modern symphony orchestra consists of about 100 instruments which are divided into four sections: *strings* (approximately 60), *wood winds* (c. 15), *brass* (c. 15), and *percussion* (c. 10). These sections are comprised of the following instruments (with approximate numbers indicated in parentheses):

Strings. Violin I (18); Violin II (16); Viola (12); Cello (10); Double Bass (8); Harp (2).

Wood Winds. Flute (3); Piccolo (1); Oboe (3); English Horn (1); Clarinet (3); Bass Clarinet (1); Bassoon (3); Double Bassoon (1).

Brass. Horn (6); Trumpet (4); Trombone 4); Tuba (1).

Percussion. Kettledrums (4); Glockenspiel, Tenor Drum, Bass Drum, Chimes, Xylophone, Celesta, Triangle, Cymbals, etc., according to requirement.

To these may be added organ, pianoforte, and other special instruments called for in a composition, e.g., saxophones, mandolins, etc. The seating arrangement of the players is fairly uniform, with the Violins I and Violas to the left side of the conductor, the Violins II and Cellos to his right. However, many modern conductors have devised different arrangements. Fig. 80 shows the seating plan of the Boston Symphony Orchestra for Charles Munch (1958–59 season).

The earliest evidence of an orchestra is found in compositions dating from about 1600, e.g., Monteverdi's *Orfeo* (1607). During the last half of the 17th century, Lully was the conductor of the famous orchestra of the French court, called *Les Vingt-quatre violons du Roi* (The Twenty-four Violins of the King) which, in addition to twenty-four stringed instruments, included flutes, oboes, and horns. Bach's Cantata no. 119 of 1723 utilizes the following: 4 voice parts, 4 trumpets, 2 timpani, 2 flutes, 3 oboes, 2 oboes da caccia, first and second violins, violas, cellos, and organ. It was not until the late 18th century (late Haydn and Mozart, early Beethoven) that the instrumentation of the orchestra was standardized as 2 flutes, 2 oboes, 2 clarinets, 2 bassoons, 2 horns, 2 trumpets, 2 timpani, and the string section including double basses. During the 19th century Berlioz, Wagner, Rimski-Korsakov, and R. Strauss contributed greatly to the expansion

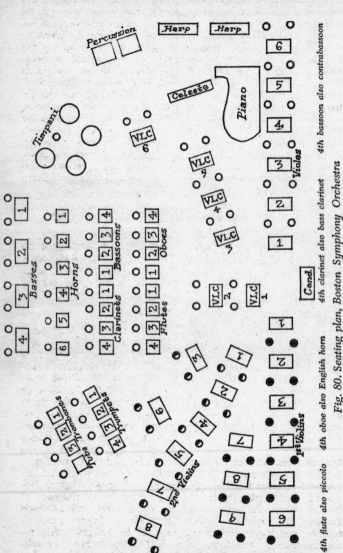

Fig, 80. Seating plan, Boston Symphony Orchestra

4th flute also piccolo   4th oboe also English horn   4th clarinet also bass clarinet   4th bassoon also contrabassoon

and skillful use of the orchestral resources, a development which culminated in the "giant orchestra" of the first decade of the 20th century (e.g., Mahler's Eighth Symphony, 1906; Schönberg's °*Gurre Lieder*, 1901–11; Stravinsky's °*Rite of Spring*, 1911–13). The reversal of this trend was a by-product of the neoclassical movement beginning about 1920. In contrast to his *Rite of Spring*, Stravinsky's *Histoire du soldat* (1918) is scored for one violin, double bass, clarinet, bassoon, cornet, trombone, and eight percussion instruments handled by one player.

Orchestral score. The conductor's copy of an orchestral work which contains all the parts (the individual players have only the part to be played by their instruments). The standard arrangement of the parts in an orchestral score is (from top to bottom): wood winds, brass, percussion, harp, strings, with vocal parts (if present) placed either above the strings or, more usually, between the violas and the cellos. The details of the arrangement can be seen from Fig. 81, which shows the beginning of Beethoven's Fifth Symphony.

Orchestration. The art of writing for the instruments of the orchestra in order to achieve the desired effects within the limitations of the various instruments. During the period lasting roughly from Haydn to Brahms, the traditional technique of orchestration (instrumentation, scoring) was to give the violins the most important melodic

parts, to use the wood winds and the French horns sparingly as color effects, to reserve the trumpets and trombones for climactic effects of massed sound and the percussion for rhythmic punctuation. More recent composers such as R. Strauss, Ravel, Stravinsky, and Bartok use the orchestral colors much more freely, often employing the strings for background effects (tremolo), the wind instruments (especially the trumpets) for leading melodic parts, and percussion instruments in a much more prominent position than formerly.

Ordinary. See under *Mass*.

Ordre (awrdr: F.). An 18th-century French term used by Couperin and others for a collection of harpsichord pieces somewhat like a °suite, but not following the normal form of the suite.

Orfeo. Opera by Monteverdi (libretto by A. Striggio), produced in Mantua, 1607. It is based on the ancient Greek legend in which Orfeo (Orpheus, tenor), the "inventor of music," grieved by the death of his beloved Euridice (soprano), sets out for the Underworld to recover her. He crosses the river Styx, guarded by the ferryman Caronte (Caron, bass), whom Orfeo enchants with his music, and appears before Plutone (Pluto, bass), the ruler of the Underworld and his wife Proserpina (mezzo-soprano). Touched by his grief, they restore Euridice to him on condition that he shall not look at her until they have left the Underworld. He cannot resist her in-

Fig. 81

sistent pleading, however, and loses her forever. As a reward for his great love, Apollo transports him to Paradise where the lovers may be reunited.

Combining the archaic style of the earliest operas (see *Nuove musiche*) with great expressiveness and dramatic impact, *Orfeo* stands out as a landmark in the history of opera (see also under *Orchestra*). It has been revived with great success.

Orfeo ed Euridice (or-FAY-o ed ay-oo-ree-DEE-chay). Opera by Gluck (libretto by Calzabigi), produced in Vienna, 1762 (produced in Paris, 1774, with French text). The story is essentially the same as in Monteverdi's *°Orfeo*, the main difference being that the tragic and heroic close of Monteverdi's work is replaced by a happy ending: Amor, the god of Love, appears and restores Euridice once more to life. *Orfeo* is the first of Gluck's reform operas.

Organ. An instrument consisting of several keyboards (manuals and pedal, the manuals to be played by the hands, the pedal by the feet), stops, a great number of pipes, an artificial wind supply (formerly by hand- or foot-operated bellows, now by an electric blower), and an action (formerly mechanical, now pneumatic or electrical) by which the movement of the keys and stops is transmitted to the valves which open and close the holes through which the wind is admitted to the pipes. Even the smallest organs have several series of pipes, each series (called a *rank*) consisting of pipes of a given tone color, different from that of another rank. These ranks (or °*registers*) are controlled by °*stops*, which make any of the ranks sound either singly or in combination with others. Modern organs often have from fifty to one hundred stops. They also have three, four, or five (occasionally up to seven) manuals and a pedal keyboard, each of which controls a separate *division* of the pipes, i.e., a section comprising a certain selection, approximately ten, of the stops. These divisions are called: *Pedal Organ* (pedal), *Great Organ* (first manual), *Swell Organ* (second manual), *Choir Organ* (third manual), *Solo Organ* (fourth), and *Echo Organ* (fifth). Each organ has its own specifications as regards selection of stops and their allotment to the various manuals. Organs also have devices which make the various divisions available on other keyboards than

their own. These are the so-called *couplers*. For instance, Coupler Swell-to-Great makes available any stop of the Swell Organ on the manual of the Great Organ. Similarly, any manual can be coupled to the Pedal and vice versa. In order to facilitate stop changes, *pistons* (*combination stops, composition stops*), usually in the shape of small round buttons, are provided. On each of these the player can arrange in advance a selection of stops, which are then brought into play by merely touching the button.

The majority of the organ stops are *foundation stops*, i.e., stops tuned in the pitch of the key (8-ft. stops; see under *Foot*), its higher octaves (4 ft., 2 ft.) or its lower octaves (16 ft., 32 ft.). In addition, there are a number of *mutation stops*, i.e., stops tuned at the pitch of one of the °harmonics of the key. For instance, a mutation stop 2⅔ ft. is tuned to the third harmonic (twelfth), hence will sound g' if the key for c is depressed. The purpose of these stops is to reinforce a certain overtone. Therefore, they must be used only together with a foundation stop of considerably greater loudness, in which case they will produce a new tone color of a very distinctive nature. Finally there are *mixture stops*, i.e., stops which combine a selection of foundation and mutation ranks, serving the same purpose as the mutation stops. Mutation and mixture stops, if properly used, are among the most valuable resources of the organ player. They figured prominently in early organs (15th-17th centuries), and have been reintroduced on modern organs of a "progressive" design, progressive meaning here a return (at least in part) to the style of the Baroque organs for which a great body of literature was composed.

The invention of the organ goes back to Greek antiquity (see *Hydraulis*). As early as the 4th century after Christ the water pressure of the hydraulis was replaced by pneumatic pressure, provided by bellows. In the 7th and 8th centuries organ building flourished at Constantinople, and several Byzantine emperors sent organs to the court of the Frankish kings (Pippin, Charlemagne) where they were greatly admired and imitated. An organ of extraordinary size, having twenty-six bellows worked by seventy men, was erected in the 10th century at Winchester in England. In the 13th to 15th centuries small organs, called *positive and *portative, were developed, in which the heavy "slides" of the earlier instruments were replaced by keys. In the 15th century the pedal as well as individual stops permitting *registration were added and, about 1500, an instrument emerged which had all the basic contrivances of a fully developed organ. See also *Organ stops*.

Organ chorale. An organ composition based on a (German Protestant) chorale, usually called *chorale prelude.

Organetto (It.). Fourteenth-century name for a small, portable organ. See *Portative*.

Organ Mass. Polyphonic compositions, for the organ, of the Ordinary of the Mass. They were written particularly in the 16th century, and consisted of organ pieces based on sections of the Kyrie, Gloria, etc., which were played in alternation with plainsong. For Bach's so-called Organ Mass, see under *Clavierübung*.

Organo (OR-gah-no: It.). Organ. *Organo pleno, pieno,* full organ.

Organ point. Same as *pedal point.

Organ stops. The term, properly denoting the levers or knobs by which the player controls ("stops" and admits) the various registers (ranks) of the organ, is also commonly employed for the registers themselves. These fall into two main categories, Flue and Reed. The flue pipes resemble an ordinary whistle or an end-blown flute, like the *recorder, while the reed pipes employ the principle of a vibrating reed, in the form of a metal tongue which beats against an opening in the metal tube, somewhat similar to the reed of a clarinet (see under *Reed*). The flue pipes are subdivided into three classes of sound: *Principal* or *Diapason, Flute* (e.g., *Claribel Flute, Concert Flute, Harmonic Flute, Gedackt, Quintation,* etc.), and *String* (*Cello, Viola, Gamba, Dulciana, Viole d'Orchestre,* etc.). Hybrids lying between two of these three classes are *Violin Diapason* (Principal-String), *Spitzflute* (Principal-Flute), and *Gemshorn* (String-Flute). The reed pipes are divided into *Chorus* reeds (*Trombone, Trumpet, Cornopean, Clarion,* etc.), *Semichorus* reeds (*Cromorne, Schalmei, Rankett,* etc.), and

Solo reeds (*Bassoon, English Horn, Clarinet, Oboe,* etc.). Only the stops of the last category are meant to imitate orchestral instruments, while the others are purely organ tones. The chorus reeds are very powerful and can be used only in "chorus" with the full organ, while the semichorus stops can also be used as solo stops or in combination with a few other stops. There is little consistency in the naming of stops and no uniformity in their sounds on different organs; therefore, a registration agreeable on one instrument will not necessarily be satisfactory on another.

Organum (OR-ga-num). (1) Latin for organ. — (2) More commonly, name for the earliest type of polyphonic music, from the 9th to the early 13th century. It is vocal music in two, three, or occasionally four parts, and shows no evident connection with the organ, although it is possible that such a connection may have existed at an early time. The following phases of its development can be distinguished:

1. *Parallel organum* (9th and 10th centuries) consists of the original plainsong (*vox principalis*) with a second voice (*vox organalis*) moving in parallel motion at the interval of the fourth or fifth below. The parallel organum of the fourth calls for oblique motion at the beginning and end of the phrase, which starts and closes with the two parts in unison.

2. *Free organum* (c. 1050 to 1150) is also in two parts, but, in addition to parallel and oblique motion, admits similar and

contrary motion. The parts frequently cross, but generally the plainsong is the lower part. Toward the end of this development contrary motion is used almost exclusively.

3. *Melismatic organum* or *organum purum* (mid-12th century), still in two parts, employs groups of notes (up to ten or more) in the upper part, now called *duplum*, against a single note of the lower part, now called *tenor*. The development of this style took place mainly in the School of °St. Martial.

4. *Measured organum* (before and after 1200) is characterized by the use of strict triple meter, according to the °rhythmic modes. This epochal innovation is the work of Leoninus, the first master of the School of °Notre Dame (see *Ars antiqua*). His successor, Perotinus, was the first to write organa in three and, occasionally, four parts (*organum triplum, quadruplum*).

Orgel (OR-gel: G.). Organ. *Orgelmesse,* see under *Organ Mass. Orgelwalze,* barrel organ; see under *Mechanical instruments.*

Orgelbüchlein (OR-gel-buikh-leyen: Little Organ Book). A celebrated collection of chorale preludes by Bach, composed in his Weimar period (1708–17) and preserved in an autograph written in Köthen (1717–22). It was planned as a cycle of pieces for the entire liturgical year, but only one third of it, from Nativity to Easter, was completed. Most of the preludes have the chorale melody in the upper part, accompanied by motives which express the basic thought of the chorale text. They are the most truly "poetic" among Bach's chorale preludes.

Orgue (awrg: F.). Organ. *Orgue positif*, choir organ. *Orgue expressif*, harmonium.

Ornaments. General designation for a number of conventional melodic formulas or methods of performance (e.g., arpeggio) which serve as a kind of decoration or embellishment of the music, enhancing its melodic, harmonic, or rhythmic interest. In earlier music (16th century) they were either written out in normal note values or improvised. In the 17th century, French harpsichord composers developed a system of ornaments indicated mostly by special signs which became the basis of the present-day system. The most important ornaments are the °appoggiatura, °arpeggio, °mordent, °trill, and °turn (see also *Grace notes; Tremolo*). Fig. 82

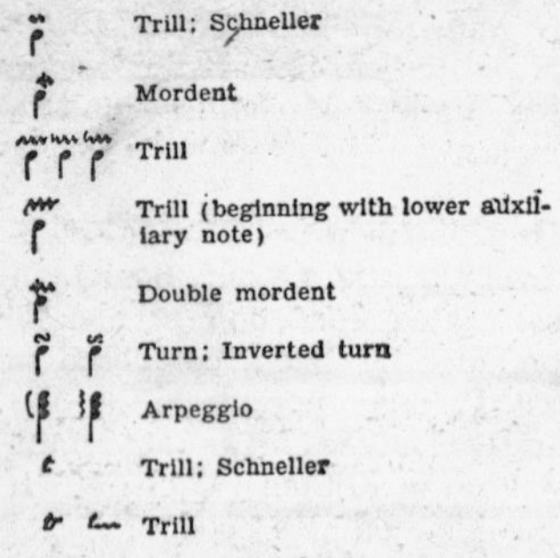

Trill; Schneller

Mordent

Trill

Trill (beginning with lower auxiliary note)

Double mordent

Turn; Inverted turn

Arpeggio

Trill; Schneller

Trill

Fig. 82

shows a variety of signs used from about 1650 on to indicate these ornaments. Regarding their execution, a distinction must be made between an older and a more recent practice, with the dividing line roughly about 1800. In the older practice nearly all the ornaments had a purely melodic significance, serving to enhance the design of the melody. They started *on* the beat and were played in moderately fast values so that they became a part of the prevailing speed pattern. After 1800 their meaning changed from melodic expressiveness to rhythmic incisiveness and virtuoso brilliance; they started *before* the main note (except for the trill) and were played as fast as possible. (For more details see the special articles.) While in the works of Bach the older method of performance is mandatory, the situation is much less clear in the music of Haydn and Mozart. In cases of doubt, preference with these two composers should be given to the older method, a remark applicable also to many examples in Beethoven and even in Chopin.

Orpheus in the Underworld (F., *Orphée aux Enfers*). Operetta by Offenbach (libretto by H. Crémieux and L. Halévy), produced in Paris, 1858. It is an amusing burlesque of the famous Greek legend (see under *Orfeo*).

Ossia (os-SEE-a: It.). Literally *o sia* (or be it, or else), the word is used in musical scores to indicate an alternative passage, usually easier to perform.

Ostinato (os-tee-NAH-to: It., obstinate). A clearly defined melodic phrase which is persistently repeated, usually in the same voice part and at the same pitch, although in extended compositions it is sometimes transferred to another voice part or to another pitch. It occurs most frequently in the bass, as *basso ostinato*. Compositions based throughout on such a *basso ostinato* are called °grounds. The *ostinato* was used mainly in the Baroque period (see *Chaconne and passacaglia*), but the 20th century has brought about a significant revival of this device. Many modern composers have been attracted by its polyphonic and rhythmic possibilities, as well as by its anti-Romantic precision and straightforwardness. Ostinato technique has also been introduced into modern jazz, especially °Boogie-woogie.

Otello. Opera in four acts by Verdi (libretto by A. Boito, after Shakespeare's *Othello*), produced in Milan, 1887. The scene is 15th-century Cyprus where the moor Otello (tenor) rules as governor. The crafty Iago (baritone), his adviser and secret enemy, devises a plot to convince Otello that his wife Desdemona (soprano) is in love with the young officer Cassio (tenor). Desdemona's handkerchief, stolen from her and secretly slipped into Cassio's room, serves as "evidence." In the last act, Otello strangles Desdemona, who in vain pleads her innocence, and then stabs himself after Emilia (mezzo-soprano), Iago's wife, has revealed the latter's treachery.

In *Otello* for the first time Verdi abandoned the fixed aria style and the number arrangement (see *Number opera*) of his earlier works, adopting something like Wagner's principle of continuous composition without, however, sacrificing his personal style.

Ôtez (F.). Take off [an organ stop].

Ottava (ot-TAH-va: It.). Octave, frequently abbreviated *8va* or 8. *All' ottava, ottava alta, ottava sopra,* or simply *8va* written above the notes indicates that they should be played an octave higher than written; *ottava bassa, ottava sotto,* or *8va* written below the notes (usually in the bass) calls for the lower octave. *Coll' ottava* means doubling in the higher (or lower) octave.

Ottavino (ot-tah-VEE-no: It.). Piccolo.

Ottoni, or **stromenti d'ottone** (ot-TO-nee, stro-MEN-tee dot-TO-nay: It.). Brass instruments.

Ours L' (loors: The Bear). Nickname for Haydn's Symphony no. 82, in C (1786), the first of the °Paris Symphonies. The name has been suggested by the opening theme of the last movement, a "growling" theme in the bass.

Ouverture (F., G.). Overture.

Overblowing. See under *Wind instruments.*

Overtones. Same as harmonics and partials (see *Acoustics,* 4). However, the first harmonic (i.e., the fundamental) is sometimes not considered an overtone, which results in a difference of numbering, the first overtone being the second harmonic, etc.

Overture. Instrumental music composed as an introduction to an opera, oratorio, stage play, etc. Such overtures are often performed separately in concerts, e.g., Wagner's *Meistersinger Overture*, or Beethoven's *Egmont Overture*. Occasionally the name has been used for independent orchestral compositions, e.g., Mendelssohn's *Hebrides Overture*, Brahms' *Academic Festival Overture*, or Tchaikovsky's *1812 Overture*.

The operatic overture developed during the 17th century in Italy, often under the name of *sinfonia*. Shortly before 1700, A. Scarlatti introduced into the *sinfonia* a definite formal scheme, consisting of three sections (or short movements), fast–slow–fast, the so-called *Italian overture*. This form is the main ancestor of the classical symphony. As early as 1650, Lully had developed anoher type, the *French overture*, which originally consisted of a slow introduction in pompous style with heavily accented rhythms, followed by an allegro in a loosely imitative style, occasionally closing with a short adagio passage similar to the introduction. In later examples this short passage is often extended into a full section, resulting in the form slow–fast–slow. The form of the Italian overture is reflected in Bach's concertos and sonatas for organ

and for accompanied violin, while the French overture occurs as the introductory movement of several of his suites, e.g., *French Overture* for harpsichord (actually a French overture followed by a suite), or in the "Ouverture" of the Partita no. 4 and of the four Orchestral Suites.

Mozart's operatic overtures to *Don Giovanni* and *The Magic Flute* were among the first designed to summarize and anticipate the high lights of the ensuing operas, an example followed in Beethoven's °Leonora Overtures (not in the final overture, the *Fidelio Overture*), in Weber's *Der Freischütz*, and in nearly all the operas of Wagner and his successors. Most of the overtures by Mozart and Beethoven (also his overtures to stage plays, *Coriolan, Egmont*) are written along the lines of °sonata form. The overtures of the French "grand opéras" (Rossini, Boieldieu, Auber, Meyerbeer) are usually a medley of most important melodies of the opera. See also under *Prelude*.

Oxford Symphony. Haydn's Symphony no. 92, in G, composed in 1788. It was performed at Oxford in 1791 when Haydn was there to receive his honorary doctor's degree from the university.

P

P. Abbreviation for *piano* (*p*), or for the *pedal* (*P*) of the pianoforte or the organ.

Pacific 231. A symphonic poem ("Mouvement symphonique") by Honegger (1923) named after an American type of heavy railway engine, and suggesting its motion from start to full speed and stop.

Paduana, Padovana (pa-doo-AH-na, pad-o-VAH-na: It.). A 16th-century name for dances of various types, some similar to the *pavane, others in quick 6/8 meter.

Paganini Etudes. Six concert etudes for pianoforte by Liszt, based on Paganini's *Capricci* for violin (except no. 3 which is taken from Paganini's *La Campanella*). Schumann also wrote twelve etudes on themes from Paganini's *Capricci*.

Paganini Variations. Variations (in two sets) for piano by Brahms, op. 35 (1866), on a theme by Paganini, the same that Liszt had used in no. 6 of his *Paganini Etudes. Brahms' variations combine utmost technical difficulty with a lucidity of design and an emotional detachment that is very unusual in the piano literature of the period.

Pagan Poem, A. Symphonic poem by Charles M. Loeffler, for orchestra and piano (1907), based on one of Virgil's eclogues, and written in impressionistic style.

Pagliacci, I (ee pah-LEEAH-chee: The Clowns). Opera in two acts with prologue by Leoncavallo (to his own libretto), produced in Milan, 1892. The story takes place in a village in southern Italy in 1865, where a group of comedians, Canio (tenor), his wife Nedda (soprano), Tonio (baritone), and Beppe (tenor), arrive to give a performance. Nedda, falling in love with the handsome villager Silvio (baritone), repulses the advances of Tonio. Swearing vengeance, Tonio helps Canio surprise the lovers, but Silvio escapes unrecognized. In the second act the players perform their comedy — a story which parallels their actual situation — and Canio, in terrible excitement, confuses play and reality and demands in vain from his wife the name of her lover. Losing all control, he stabs Nedda to death. Silvio rushes to her aid and is killed also.

Pagliacci, together with Mascagni's *Cavalleria rusticana*, is one of the outstanding examples of the Italian *verismo style. Large portions of the text are composed in a speechlike recitation which contributes to making the opera an intense and exciting representation of "true life." Particularly famous is the prologue in which Tonio explains the idea of the plot — a conscious revival of the *prologue of the earliest Italian operas.

Palestrina style. Designation for music written in the style of Palestrina, i.e., polyphonic, unaccompanied, and following more or less closely the principles of counterpoint, harmony, etc., characteristic of 16th-century music. See also *Counterpoint*.

Pandean pipes. See *Pan pipes*.

Pandiatonicism. In 20th-century music, the use of the diatonic scale as the basic tonal material, but without the harmonic restrictions inherent in the truly diatonic style of, e.g., Haydn and Mozart. Pandiatonicism therefore admits strong dissonances, for example, c-d'-e'', or an F-major triad simultaneously sounding with one built on C. Pandiatonicism was introduced about 1920 by Stravinsky (see Fig. 83, from his Piano Concerto) and others as a reaction against the chromatic idiom of

Fig. 83

impressionism and of atonal music, a reaction underlined by the almost exclusive use of the simplest keys, e.g., C major or D major. It is closely associated with the rise of °neoclassicism.

Pan pipes. A primitive wind instrument consisting of a number of graded pipes made from cane, bamboo, or clay, bound or glued together, usually in the form of a raft. This is one of the oldest instruments. It occurs in ancient Greece (where it was attributed to the god Pan, hence the name) and China as well as in the primitive cultures of Peru, Ecuador, etc.

Pantaleon, pantalon. See under *Dulcimer.*

Pantomime (Gr., everything imitated). A dramatic perform-

ance without words, the action being revealed by gestures, to the accompaniment of music. The pantomime is distinguished from the ballet by its emphasis on action and dramatic development rather than on stylized dancing. Among 20th-century examples are R. Strauss's *Josephslegende* (1914), Stravinsky's *Soldier's Tale* (1917), and Bartok's *The Miraculous Mandarin* (1926).

Papillons (pa-pee-YONH: F., butterflies). A fanciful title used by Schumann for a set of twelve short piano pieces (op. 2, 1829–31), "butterflies of different colors," as it were. The final piece suggests the close of a ball early in the morning, with the clock striking six. In various respects this work foreshadows the °*Carnival,* to which it may be said to stand in the relation of a light sketch (by no means inferior) to a finished painting. See also under *Character piece.*

Paradise and the Peri. A composition somewhat in the style of an oratorio for solo voices, chorus, and orchestra by Schumann (op. 50, 1843), based on his own German translation of a poem from T. Moore's *Lalla Rookh.*

Parallel chords. A succession of chords of identical structure, played on various degrees of the scale. In traditional harmony this device is limited to parallel sixth chords (see *Fauxbourdon*) and diminished seventh chords in chromatic succession (frequent in Chopin, Liszt). It is prohibited in connection with triads or ordinary seventh chords because of the *parallel fifths which would result in these cases. Modern composers, however, make frequent use of parallelism, for triads as well as for strongly dissonant chords, either as a "sonorous color" (Debussy; see Fig. 84a, b) or as a percussive device (Stravinsky; see Fig. 84c). Isolated examples of par-

Fig. 84

allel triads occur in the works of Rossini, Moussorgsky, Lalo, Délibes, and others. The introduction to Act II of Puccini's *La Bohème* (1896) is an early example of percussive parallelism.

Parallel fifths, octaves. Also called *consecutive fifths, octaves.* These result if the melodic motion of a voice part (for example, c-d) is duplicated in another voice part at the distance of a fifth (g-a) or an octave (c'-d'). In traditional harmony and counterpoint such progressions (Fig. 85a) are considered faulty. Occasional exceptions notwithstanding (even in Bach and Mozart), their avoidance is a basic principle of music from the 16th through the 19th centuries. Par-

Fig. 85

allel fifths and octaves are frequent, however, in early polyphony (9th-13th centuries; see under *Organum*) as well as in 20th-century music (see *Parallel chords*).

A fifth (or octave) reached not in parallel but in similar motion is called a *hidden (covered) fifth (or octave).* Such progressions are generally admissible, except for certain extreme cases, for example, when large skips occur in both voices: $\begin{smallmatrix} g\text{-}c' \\ B\text{-}f \end{smallmatrix}$. Quite frequent, and entirely proper, are *horn fifths* (Fig. 85b), so called because they are a characteristic feature of the writing for natural (valveless) horns.

Parallel key. See under *Key relationship.*

Parallel motion. See under *Motion.* Also *Parallel chords; Parallel fifths, octaves.*

Paraphrase. A free modification, arrangement, or elaboration of a composition, e.g., Liszt's paraphrases of Wagnerian operas in which the main melodies of the opera are combined into a piece for pianoforte.

Paris Symphonies. Six symphonies by Haydn, nos. 82–87, composed about 1786 for the

Concerts de la Loge Olympique in Paris. Three of them have special names, °*L'Ours* (no. 82), *La* °*Poule* (no. 83), and *La* °*Reine* (no. 85).

Paris Symphony. Mozart's Symphony in D (K. 297), written in 1778 during his stay in Paris and performed there at the *Concerts spirituels.*

Parlando, parlante (par-LAHN-do, par-LAHN-tay: It., speaking). In singing, indication that the voice should approximate the character of speech. It occurs particularly in connection with fast declamation (see *Patter song*), especially in recitatives. In instrumental music *parlando* means almost the opposite, i.e., expressive rendition suggestive of speech or song.

Parody (Gr., imitated song). In modern usage, a satirical imitation of a serious work, produced, e.g., by the substitution of a comical text or by a caricaturing version of the music. In earlier practice the term simply means reworking, without any satirical implication. See *Parody Mass.*

Parody Mass. An important type of 16th-century Mass, in which the musical material is partly derived from pre-existing compositions, such as motets, chansons, or madrigals. Usually the original work is broken up into various fragments, which occur in the (much more extended) Mass at several points, freely modified and connected by newly composed passages. About three quarters of the Masses by Palestrina and Lassus are parody Masses.

Parsifal. Music drama in three acts by Wagner (libretto by the composer, based on medieval legends), produced at Bayreuth, 1882, and intended by the composer never to be peformed anywhere else. Since the copyright expired in 1913, however, it has been performed frequently in Europe and America.

The story is somber and profound. Amfortas (baritone), guardian of the Holy Grail (the chalice from which the Savior drank at the Last Supper) and the Holy Spear (which pierced Jesus' side at the Crucifixion), has succumbed to the beguilements of Kundry (mezzo-soprano), an ageless enchantress torn between evil and good — between the service of the diabolical Klingsor (Bass) and that of the Grail. The Spear has fallen into the hands of Klingsor who has afflicted Amfortas with a wound that will not heal. The deliverer appears in the person of the "guileless fool," Parsifal (tenor), who resists the temptations of Kundry and, seizing the Spear, destroys Klingsor's power. In years of wandering he learns wisdom and, returning to the Castle of the Grail as a knight in armor, redeems Amfortas and Kundry from their sin.

Parsifal, Wagner's last work, is, in the passionate scenes, similar in musical style to °*Tristan,* but the basic expression is one of solemnity and exaltation which does not always escape the danger of monotony. Particularly conspicuous is the use of a leitmotiv representing the Holy Grail (Fig. 86).

Fig. 86

Part. (1.) In ensemble works, the music for one voice or instrument (e.g., soprano part, violin part, flute part). — (2) In contrapuntal music, a single melodic line, as in "three-part fugue." See *Voice parts*. — (3) A section of a composition, as in "three-part form" (ternary form). See *Form*.

Partials. Same as overtones and harmonics (see *Acoustics*, 4).

Partita (par-TEE-ta: It.). A term used by Bach for a set of six suites for harpsichord, published in the *Clavierübung* I (1731), and for his suites for violin solo. Usually, however, the term means variations (Frescobaldi, Pachelbel, Boehm), and Bach used it in this sense in his Chorale Partitas for the organ.

Partition (F.), **Partitur** (G.), **partitura** (It.). Score (orchestral).

Part music. Music written in separate parts, hence, in contrapuntal style. The term is used primarily in connection with 16th-century madrigals, chansons, etc.

Part song. A secular choral composition in three or more parts, such as was cultivated mainly in the 19th century (Schumann, Mendelssohn, and others). It is in a chordal, rather than contrapuntal, style.

Paso doble (PAH-so DO-blay: Sp.). A kind of dance (one-step, although the name means "double step") in 6/8 meter which became popular about 1926.

Passacaglia. See *Chaconne and passacaglia*.

Passage. A term loosely used for a short section of a composition, often one of secondary importance (transitional, final passage) or involving display of virtuosity (scale passage, etc.).

Passamezzo (pah-sa-MED-zo: It.). An Italian dance of the mid-16th century, in moderate 4/4 time, involving steady quarter-note or eighth-note rhythms. It is usually followed by the *saltarello.

Passepied (pahs-PEEAY: F., "pass-foot"). A French 17th-century dance in rather quick 3/8 or 6/8 meter and of a gay and spirited character. It occurs in the optional group of Baroque suites, e.g., in Bach's English Suite no. 5.

Passing tone. See under *Nonharmonic tones* (1).

Passion music. A musical setting of the story of the Crucifixion, as told by one of the four Evangelists (St. Matthew, St. Mark, St. Luke, St. John). The earliest examples (12th century) are in plainsong and were performed as a sort of dramatic play, with different singers for the parts of Christ, the Narrator, and the

Crowd (°*turba*). Beginning in the 15th century, the text was composed polyphonically. Particularly famous are the Passions by Schütz and by Bach. Schütz's *Die sieben Worte Jesu Christi am Kreuz* (The Seven Words of Jesus Christ on the Cross), composed about 1645, uses a thorough-bass accompaniment (organ) for the recitative of the Evangelist (Narrator), and three-part instrumental accompaniment for the words of Christ, a treatment adopted by Bach in his *St. Matthew Passion* (1729) and *St. John Passion* (1723). In both of these the scriptural text is amplified by the insertion of free poetic texts (by Brockes for the *St. John Passion*, by Picander for the *St. Matthew Passion*) which serve as the basis for arias and for large choruses. Also inserted are a great number of °chorales.

Pasticcio (pahs-TEET-cho: It., pastry, pie). A type of 18th-century opera for which the music was largely put together from melodies of famous operas of the day, for the purpose of entertaining the audience with their favorite songs. Most of the °ballad operas are of this kind.

Pastorale (pahs-to-RAH-lay: It., shepherdlike). Instrumental or vocal music suggestive of a pastoral scene. Typical features are 6/8 or 12/8 meter in moderate tempo, a tender and flowing melody in the rhythm of a lullaby, and long-held drones in imitation of the shepherd's bagpipes. This type of music originated in Sicily, hence the alternative name *siciliano*. Typical examples are the Sinfonia which

opens Part II of Bach's *Christmas Oratorio*, the Pastorales in Corelli's °*Christmas Concerto* and Handel's °*Messiah*, and the last movement of Beethoven's °Pastoral Symphony.

Pastoral Sonata. Nickname of Beethoven's Piano Sonata op. 28, in D (1801), a name which, although not authentic, properly indicates the lyrical character of the work, particularly of the first and last movements.

Pastoral Symphony. Beethoven's Symphony no. 6, in F major, op. 68, published in 1809 under the title "Sinfonia Pastorale, No. 6." The five movements portray, according to Beethoven's inscriptions: (1) Awakening of Cheerful Feelings on Arrival in the Country; (2) A Scene at the Brook; (3) Merry Meeting of Country Folk; (4) Thunderstorm and Tempest; (5) Song of the Shepherds, Glad and Thankful Feelings after the Storm. It is interesting to note that Beethoven expressly distinguished this work from the more obvious type of program music of his day (battle pieces, etc.) by the remark: "Expression of feelings rather than tone-painting."

Pastoral Symphony, A. Vaughan Williams' Symphony no. 3 (1922) for orchestra and soprano voice (without text).

Pathétique Sonata (pah-tay-TEEK). Beethoven's Piano Sonata op. 13, in C minor, published in 1799 under the title "Sonate pathétique." It should be noted that the French word *pathétique* does not mean "pathetic" (sad, pitiful) but "emotional," "full of pathos." The sonata is in three movements, with an Introduction which reappears twice during the first movement.

Pathétique Symphony (pah-tay-TEEK). Tchaikovsky's Symphony no. 6, in B minor, op. 74, composed in 1893 shortly before his death. (For the meaning of *pathétique,* see under *Pathétique Sonata*). The fact that Tchaikovsky rejected the name *Tragic,* first suggested to him by his brother Modeste, would seem to indicate that he considered the work as an expression of passionate grandeur rather than of tragic melancholy, although both traits are present in it. The symphony consists of an Introduction and four movements in an unusual order, the slow movement, remarkable for its genuine expression of "tragic failure," being placed at the end. The second, dancelike movement is in *quintuple meter.

Patter song. A humorous type of song involving extremely rapid declamation of syllables. Many familiar examples, representing the English counterpart of the Italian *parlando, occur in the operettas of Sullivan.

Pauke (POW-ke: G.). Kettledrum. For Haydn's *Paukenmesse,* see *Drum Mass.*

Pause. The sign ⌒, also called "hold" or "fermata," which indicates that the note (or rest) over which it appears should be prolonged. As a rule, a duration of approximately (but not exactly) double the normal value is appropriate. It should be noted that the foreign terms *pausa* (It.), *pause* (F.), and *Pause* (G.) always mean rest.

Pavane (pah-VAHN: F.). A court dance of the 16th century, probably of Spanish origin, in rather slow duple meter, and performed in a dignified, ceremonial style. Possibly the name is derived from L. *pavo,* peacock, referring to the proud deportment of the exotic bird. The pavane (sometimes also called *paduana) is usually combined with a following dance in faster triple meter, the *galliard (see also under *Dance music*). Of particular artistic importance are the pavanes and galliards composed in England, c. 1575–1620, by Byrd, Bull, and Gibbons. A modern example is Ravel's *Pavane pour une infante défunte* (i.e., "for a dead Princess") for piano (1899) or orchestra (1912).

Pavillon en air (pa-vee-YONH ahh ayr: F.). "Bell upwards" (for horns or trumpets).

Peasant Cantata. A secular cantata by Bach, written to a text by Picander in Saxonian dialect ("Mer hahn en neue Oberkeet," We Have a New Magistrate) and performed in 1742 to celebrate the installment of a new magistrate in a rural district of Saxony. The music includes several popular tunes of that day.

Pedal. (1) In musical instruments, an action operated by the feet. The pedal of the organ is a full keyboard on which feet produce sounds; the pianoforte pedals serve to prolong or to mute the sound; the harp pedals enable the player to alter the pitch of the strings; and those of the harpsichord are *stops (registers) operated by the feet. See under the various instruments. — (2) In composition, see *Pedal point*.

Pedalflügel (G.). Same as *pedal piano.

Pedal harp. The modern *harp, so called because it has pedals, in contrast to the chromatic harp or early types of harps.

Pedal note. Same as *pedal tone.

Pedal piano. A pianoforte equipped with a full pedal keyboard, similar to that of the organ, so that bass notes can be played with the feet. The instrument, which had a passing success during the 19th century, is known chiefly through Schumann's *Studien* and *Skizzen für den Pedalflügel*.

Pedal point. A long-held note, normally in the bass, sounding against changing harmonies, etc., in the upper parts. Such notes create tension by sounding with chords that normally could not be combined with it, for example, a low C with a D-flat or B-flat triad (see Fig. 87). In orchestral music, pedal points (often performed as a long roll on the kettledrum) are an effective device for climactic mo-

ments and have been used as such particularly by Bruckner and Tchaikovsky. Terms such as tonic pedal or dominant pedal refer to the scale degree of the sustained note. Inverted pedal and internal pedal denote sustained tones in the upper or in a middle part.

Pedal tone. On wind instruments, the lowest tone, being the pitch produced by the entire length of the pipe. On many brass instruments this tone is difficult or impossible to obtain, so that the practical range starts with the first overtone, an octave above the pedal tone.

Peer Gynt Suite (payr gint). Two orchestral suites by Grieg, op. 46 and 55, arranged from his incidental music to Ibsen's play *Peer Gynt*. The first suite consists of Morning Mood; The Death of Aase; Anitra's Dance; In the Hall of the Mountain King; the second, The Abduction of the Bride and Ingrid's Lament; Arabian Dance; Peer Gynt's Homecoming; Solvejg's Lament.

Peg. In violins, etc., the wooden pins set in the neck, which serve to tighten or loosen the strings.

Pelléas et Mélisande (pe-lay-AHS ay may-lee-ZAHND). Opera in five acts by Debussy, based on Maeterlinck's play of the same name, produced in Paris, 1902. The story, in a medieval setting, begins when Golaud (baritone) finds the beautiful Mélisande (soprano) in a forest, marries her, and brings her to the gloomy castle of his grandfather Arkel (bass).

Fig. 87

There she and Golaud's younger half brother, Pelléas (tenor), fall in love with each other. Golaud ignores what he believes to be a childlike sympathy but, upon discovering the truth, is enraged with jealousy and kills Pelléas. After bearing Golaud's child, the innocent Mélisande dies.

Pelléas et Mélisande, being the most significant opera that impressionism produced, stands in a class by itself. The story is told not as a continuous plot with a closely knit action, but in a succession of scenes filled with mystic and symbolic significance. In opposition to the Wagnerian opera, Debussy wrote a score which deliberately avoids emotional stress, providing only a "tonal envelope" of pale colors. In this respect it comes closer than any other modern opera to realizing the ideal of the earliest Florentine operas, i.e., of music as an unobtrusive support and setting for the poetry.

There also exists incidental music to *Pelléas and Mélisande* by Fauré (1898) and Sibelius (1905).

Pelleas und Melisande (G.). A symphonic poem by Schönberg (completed in 1905), based on Maeterlinck's play. It is written in numerous sections in which the tragic love story is detailed. The music combines the Wagnerian principle of the leitmotiv with the orchestral technique and harmonic language of French impressionism, as represented in Debussy's opera on the same story.

Penitential Psalms. Psalms 6, 32, 38, 51, 102, 130, and 143, so called because of the character of their texts. Particularly famous is Lasso's musical setting of the whole group (1565).

Pentatonic scale. A scale consisting of five different tones (Gr., *penta,* five) as distinguished from the familiar diatonic (seven tones) and chromatic (twelve tones) scales. The most common one has an intervallic structure represented by the notes c d f g a (c'). The same scale (in transposition) is formed by the black keys of the piano: c♯ d♯ f♯ g♯ a♯ (c♯'). Pentatonic scales occur in many early music cultures, in China, Africa, and Polynesia, as well as among the American Indians, the Celts, and the Scots.

Percussion instruments. In the modern orchestra, all instruments whose sounding agent is a stretched membrane or some solid material, such as steel and wood (see under *Instruments*). They are usually defined as instruments played by being struck or shaken, but this definition is misleading, and has indeed led to the erroneous notion that the pianoforte is a percussion instrument because its strings are struck by hammers. On this basis it could also be argued that the violin, if played *°col legno* or *°pizzicato,* is a percussion instrument.

Percussion instruments can be divided into two groups, according to whether or not the sound produced has a definite pitch. The instruments of *definite pitch* are the kettledrum, glockenspiel, xylophone, celesta, and chimes; those of *indefinite pitch* are the snare drum, tenor drum, bass drum, tambourine, triangle, cymbals, castanets, and gong (also the various types of °rattles used occasionally in modern scores).

Perfect, imperfect. See under *Cadence; Intervals.*

Period. See under *Phrase.*

Perpetuum mobile (per-PET-yoo-um MO-bi-lee: L., continuous motion). Title for pieces proceeding from the beginning to the end in the same rapid rhythmic motion, with few rests or slower notes.

Persephone (per-SEF-o-nee). A melodrama in a series of tableaux by Stravinsky, commissioned by Mme. Ida Rubenstein for her ballet, based on a poem by André Gide, and composed in 1933 (in Paris) for orchestra, chorus, children's chorus, solo tenor, dancers, and narrator.

Peter and the Wolf. An orchestral fairy tale for children, by Prokofiev (op. 67, completed in 1936), for a small orchestra and a narrator. The narrator tells the story of a boy's capturing a large and ferocious wolf with the aid of friendly animals. Each figure (cat, duck, Peter, etc.) is characterized by a specific instrument and melodic phrase, making the work an excellent introduction to the orchestra for young children.

Peter Grimes. Opera by Britten (libretto by M. Slater, based on part of Crabbe's poem *The Borough*), produced in London, 1945. The hero of the opera is Peter Grimes, a morose and eccentric fisherman, who is disliked and distrusted by all but a few of his fellow villagers. The hos-

tility reaches a climax when an orphan boy who assists Grimes dies, presumably from maltreatment. The opera ends with Grimes setting out to sea alone in an open boat.

Peter Ibbetson. Opera in three acts by Deems Taylor (libretto by the composer and C. Collier, after a novel of the same name by George du Maurier), produced in New York, 1931.

Petite flute (F.). Piccolo.

Petrouchka. See *Petrushka.*

Petrushka. Ballet by Stravinsky (choreography by M. Fokine), produced in Paris, 1911, by Diaghilev's Russian Ballet. The action takes place at a Russian fair (Popular Festivities at Mardi Gras; Dance of the Drunken Crowd; The Organ-Grinder and a Ballerina), with a Magician showing three dolls — Petrushka, the Moor, and the Ballerina — who, brought to life by the showman, begin to dance. Petrushka, a lovable but clumsy peasant boy, falls in love with the Ballerina (Scene II), but the resplendent and fascinating Moor wins her (Scene III). Scene IV shows the evening of the fair, with a Nurses' Dance, a Bear Dance, a Merchant's Dance, a Coachmen's Dance, and a General Dance. This stops with the sudden appearance of Petrushka, pursued by the Moor, who kills him with a blow of his sword, whereupon they all become lifeless dolls again.

The work, often heard in the form of an orchestral suite at concerts, is one of the landmarks in the evolution of 20th-century music. Among the many notable features are the percussive parallel chords in the opening scene, the clever caricature of a sentimental valse, and the bold use of bitonality, particularly in the "Petrushka chord" (see under *Bitonality*).

Pezzo (PED-zo: It.). Piece.

Pf. Short for pianoforte.

Phantasie (G.). Fantasy. *Phantasiestück,* fantasy piece; *Phantasiebilder,* fantasy pictures.

Philharmonic pitch. See under *Pitch.*

Philosopher, The. Nickname (unexplained) for Haydn's Symphony no. 22, in E-flat, composed in 1764.

Phoebus and Pan. See *Streit zwischen Phöbus und Pan.*

Phonographs and records. The phonograph (Gr., *sound* and *writer*) traces its origin to Thomas A. Edison who, in 1877, produced a recording made of tin foil from which his own voice could be heard reciting "Mary had a little lamb." Numerous improvements have led to the phonograph of the present day, by far the most nearly perfect of all the °mechanical instruments. The most recent major innovation, comparable in its revolutionary character to the replacement of the old cylinder by discs, is the changing of the normal speed of the turntable from 78 revolutions per minute (RPM), to 33⅓ or 45 RPM. The slower speed combined with more grooves on the surface of the disc make possible a period of about 20 minutes of uninterrupted performance as compared to a previous maximum of about 5 minutes. This advantage of the long-playing (LP) records, in addition to the greater convenience of storage and transportation, has made the older 78 RPM discs almost obsolete. Fortunately, many records made at 78 RPM have been transferred onto LP discs. Recent advances in recording technique (particularly with stereophonic sound and magnetic tape) and phonograph production have made possible a °high fidelity of sound which often equals and in some cases surpasses that of most "live" performances.

The continually increasing availability of recorded music is one of the most significant aspects of musical life in the 20th century. The more familiar selections of the standard repertory are obtainable in a variety of performances, but especially notable as a unique advantage of recorded music is the accessibility of new works by contemporary composers and of works which for practical reasons are seldom performed (e.g., operas and compositions for large orchestras and choruses). Furthermore, records have brought to life many less-familiar works of the great composers, as well as a considerable amount of early music formerly thought to be of "historic" interest only. Notable examples of the latter category are the series entitled *Masterpieces of Music before 1750* (Haydn Society), *Archive Production* (*Deutsche Grammophon Gesellschaft*), and the *Anthologie Sonore.*

The most useful reference books in the field are: Clough and Cuming, *The World's Encyclopedia of Recorded Music* (London, 1952); Hall, *The Record Book* (New York, 1950), and *The Gramophone Shop Encyclopaedia of Recorded Music* (New York, 1948, with Supplements). Current releases of LP records are listed in the monthly *Schwann Long Playing Record Catalog*. In addition to periodicals devoted primarily to recorded music (*American Record Guide, The New Records, High Fidelity*) and professional musical journals (e.g., *Notes*, published by the Music Library Association, Washington, D.C.), several general periodical publications (e.g., *Saturday Review*) give evidence of the widespread popularity of recorded music by devoting space regularly to critical evaluation of new releases.

Phonola. See under *Mechanical instruments.*

Phrase. A division or section of a musical line, somewhat comparable to a clause or a sentence in language. Other terms used for such divisions are period, half phrase, double phrase, etc. There is no consistency in applying these terms, nor can there be, in view of the infinite variety of situations and conditions found in compositions. Only with melodies of a very simple type, especially those of some dances, can the terms be used with a certain degree of consistency, e.g., half phrase for a unit of two measures, phrase for one of four, double phrase or period for a unit of eight measures, double period for one of sixteen.

Phrasing. In musical performance, the proper separation of the various divisions of the musical line, not only of its *phrases, etc., but often of its smaller units such as motives or other groups of notes that "belong together." Phrasing is achieved by slightly shortening and softening the last note of the group, and is usually indicated by a slur extending over the group. In a larger sense, phrasing is also understood to include other details of the performance, such as observance of staccato or nonlegato, the various types of bowing on stringed instruments, and the control of breath in singing and in the playing of wind instruments.

Phrygian. See under *Church modes; Greek music.*

Phrygian cadence (FRIJ-i-an). Name for cadences proper to the Phrygian mode (mode on E), characterized by the progression f-e (rather than f#-e, as in E minor). They give the impression of half cadences, and in this meaning they occur frequently in Baroque sonatas (Corelli, Handel), as a transition from one movement to the next. See Fig. 88.

Fig. 88

Pianino. A small upright piano.

Piano (It.). Soft; *pianissimo*, very soft. Also, word commonly used for *pianoforte.

Piano concerto. A concerto featuring a pianoforte as the solo instrument (see under *Concerto*).

Piano duet. A composition for two pianoforte players, playing either on one or two instruments. The repertory for duets on one instrument, which includes outstanding masterworks by Mozart and Schubert, has been overshadowed by the recent interest in playing on two pianos.

Pianoforte (It., soft-loud). The pianoforte (most often called simply "piano") may be briefly described as a stringed instrument with a separate string (or sets of two or three strings tuned in unison) for each tone, the strings being struck by hammers which are put in motion from keys (keyboard) by means of a complicated lever mechanism called *action*. Its name refers to the fact that it is possible to play louder or softer by striking the keys more or less vigorously, an effect impossible to the harpsichord which it superseded during the latter part of the 18th century. The earliest pianofortes were built about 1709 by Bartolommeo Cristofori (1655–1731) of Florence, but it was not until about 1770 that they came into general use. J. S. Bach probably saw his first such instrument late in life (1747) when he visited the Prussian king, Frederick the Great. Mozart, on the other hand, composed all of his mature clavier works for the pianoforte.

In addition to the above-described parts, the pianoforte has *dampers*, i.e., small rectangular pieces of wood whose underside is covered with felt. The dampers lie above the strings and, by means of stiff wires, move together with the key, making the string free for vibration when the hammer strikes, and checking (damping) the vibration the moment the key is released. Without the dampers the strings would continue to sound for a considerable time, thus leading to a blurred noise. For special purposes, however, this continued sounding is desirable and can be effected by the so-called *damper pedal* (right pedal) which raises all the dampers, allowing the strings to vibrate at will. It is therefore, properly speaking, a "nondamper pedal." The *soft pedal* (left pedal) causes the entire keyboard and action to shift a little to the right, so that the hammers strike only two (or one) of the three (or two) strings tuned in unison for a given tone (see *Mute; Una corda*). Large modern instruments usually have a third pedal, the *sostenuto* (or *sustaining*) *pedal* (middle pedal), which is a modification of the damper pedal. It raises the dampers only for the key or keys which are depressed when the pedal is put into action. It can be used to sustain a low bass note (*pedal point), leaving both hands free for playing in the higher registers.

Pianofortes are built in two basic shapes, the wing-shaped *grand piano and the box-shaped upright piano. Grand pianos exist in various sizes from the *Concert Grand* (about nine feet long) to the *Baby Grand* (about five feet). See also *Spinet*.

Pianola. See under *Mechanical instruments*.

Piatti (It., plates). °Cymbals.

Picardy third. A major third, if used in the final chord of a composition that has been in a minor key; for example, an E-major triad at the end of a composition written completely in E minor. Many examples of this device, suggestive of "light after darkness," occur in the compositions of Bach, e.g., in nearly all the minor-key fugues in the *Well-tempered Clavier*. The origin of the name is unknown.

Piccolo. See under *Flute*.

Pictures at an Exhibition. A collection of descriptive piano pieces by Moussorgsky composed in 1874, each piece illustrating a picture by the Russian painter Victor A. Hartmann (d. 1873) shown at a memorial exhibition of his paintings in 1874. The highly "picturesque" pieces are preceded and connected by a recurring "promenade" theme suggesting the walk from one picture to the next. The work is often heard in an orchestral version by Ravel.

Pieno (PEEAY-no: It.). Full. *Organo pieno*, full organ; *a voce piena*, with full voice.

Pierrot lunaire (peeay-RO lui-NAYR: Pierrot in the Moonlight). A cycle of twenty-one short pieces, for a "singing narrator" (°speech song) and chamber orchestra (flute, violin, clarinet, cello, piano, etc.) by Schönberg, op. 21 (1912), based on poems by A. Giraud in the German translation of O. E. Hartleben. The poems, highly decadent and macabre (one of them describes Pierrot contentedly smoking his tobacco out of a human skull), are composed in a novel melodramatic style, accompanied sometimes by the full group of instruments, sometimes by only one or two.

Pinafore (full title: *H. M. S. Pinafore*). Operetta by Sullivan (libretto by W. S. Gilbert), produced in London, 1878. It was the first in the series of highly successful works by Gilbert and Sullivan.

Pines of Rome (It., *Pini di Roma*). Symphonic poem by Respighi (1924), showing four musical "landscapes" near Rome, the *Villa Borghese*, a *Catacomb*, the *Janiculum* (a hill named after the god Janus), and the *Appian Way* (famous road built by the ancient Romans). In the third picture a phonograph recording of the song of an actual nightingale is introduced.

Pipe and tabor. A combination of two instruments played by one man, used as a dance accompaniment as early as the 13th century and to the present day in Spain (see *Sardana; Farandole; Moresca*). The pipe, a small recorder, is held in the right hand, while the left hand beats the tabor, a small drum suspended from the player's shoulder or waist.

Pirates of Penzance, The. Operetta by Sullivan (libretto by W. S. Gilbert), produced in London and New York, 1879.

Piston. (1) On brass instruments, same as °valve. *Cor à* *pistons* and *cornet à pistons* (F.) are the modern French horn and cornet, both of which have valves. The French term *piston* is sometimes used as a colloquial name for the cornet. — (2) On organs, a small button or toe stud by which the °registration may be changed by a slight motion of a finger or toe.

Pitch. A term referring to the high–low quality of a musical sound (see under *Tone*). The pitch is determined by the frequency of the tone, i.e., the number of vibrations per second (see under *Acoustics*, 1). In a special sense, pitch means standard pitch or the pitch nationally accepted as standard in order to assume identical tuning for instruments everywhere. Great Britain and most European nations have recently adopted the United States standard which assigns 440 vibrations per second to a' (the A above middle C). Formerly, the standard pitch varied greatly at different times and localities. Generally speaking, it has constantly been rising since the time of Bach, so that some compositions originally sounded at least a half tone lower than they do today. For instance, Beethoven's Fifth Symphony, in C minor, originally was heard at the present-day B-minor pitch level. See also *Absolute pitch*.

Pitch names. The designations used to indicate the various tones (pitches). The tones within an octave are called c, d, e, f, g, a, b, with c-sharp, d-flat, etc., for the chromatic alterations. The various octaves, each beginning on a *c*, are usually (always in the present book) indicated as shown in Fig. 89. The French (Italians) use the Guidonian syllables: *ut (do), ré (re), mi, fa, sol, la, si*, with *dièse (diesis)* for sharp, and *bémol (bemolle)* for flat. Hence, c-sharp is *ut dièse* in French, *do diesis* in Italian. The German names for the white keys are the same as the English, except for the tone b, which is called *h* (pronounced *hah*). The sharp tones are called: *cis, dis, eis, fis, gis, ais, his* (b-sharp); the flat ones: *ces, des, es* (e-flat), *fes, ges, as* (a-flat), *b* (b-flat).

Più (peeoo: It.). More, e.g., *più allegro*, faster.

Piuttosto (peeoo-TOS-to: It.). Rather, somewhat.

Pizzicato (pit-see-KAH-to: It.). An indication (often abbr. *pizz.*) that the strings of a violin, etc., are to be plucked with the fingers instead of being bowed. Usually the plucking is done with the right hand, but occasionally, in virtuoso performance, the left hand is used, in quick alternation with bowed notes.

Pk. In German orchestral scores, short for *Pauke* (kettledrum).

Fig. 89

Plagal (from Gr. *plagios*, slanting, i.e., collateral, subsidiary). See under *Cadence; Church modes*.

Plainsong (also *plainchant*). Common designation for °Gregorian chant. Derived from L. *cantus planus*, the term carries the connotation of liturgical music without accompaniment (monophonic) and without strict meter. It can also be applied, in a descriptive sense, to similar repertories such as Ambrosian chant, Hindu chant, all of which are "in plainsong."

Planets, The. A programmatic suite for orchestra, organ, and female chorus, by Holst (1916), describing in successive movements the astrological characters of the seven planets.

Player-Piano. See under *Mechanical instruments*.

Plectrum. A small piece of hard, elastic material (horn, quill, metal, plastic, etc.) used to pluck the strings of certain instruments, e.g., the mandolin and the zither. Today it is often attached to a ring placed on the thumb. See also under *Harpsichord*.

Plein jeu (planh zheu: F.). Full organ.

Pleno (It.). Same as °pieno.

Pochette (po-SHET: from F. *poche*, pocket). A pocket violin (see *Kit*).

Poco (It.). Little, e.g., *un poco adagio*, somewhat slow. *Poco a poco*, little by little, or gradually. Diminutive forms are *pochetto, pochettino, pochissimo* (very little).

Poème (po-EM: F., poem). Title used by several composers for compositions of a lyric, poetic nature. The best known is a piece for violin and orchestra, op. 25, by Chausson, composed in 1896.

Poem of Ecstasy. Symphonic poem, op. 54, by Scriabin, composed in 1907–08. The underlying programmatic idea is the ecstasy of freedom and action.

Pohjola's Daughter (PAW-hewlah). Symphonic poem by Sibelius, op. 49 (1906), based on a story from the °Kalevala, in which the old magician Vainamoinen, traveling homeward, encounters the daughter of Pohjola (i.e., the North Country) seated on a rainbow. He tries to win her by performing magic feats, but he does not succeed and resumes his journey.

Poi (PAW-ee: It.). Then, afterwards; e.g., *Scherzo D. C. e poi la coda*: repeat the scherzo and then [play the] coda.

Point of imitation. In imitative counterpoint, a section including at least one statement of the theme in each voice part. The term is useful mainly in connection with 16th-century °motets, which usually include and sometimes consist entirely of points of imitation each based on a different subject.

Polacca (po-LAHK-ka: It.). °Polonaise. *Alla polacca*, in the style and rhythm of a polonaise.

Polka. A Bohemian (not Polish) dance in quick duple meter, with rhythmic patterns such as

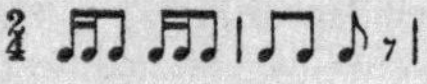

Fig. 90

shown in Fig. 90. It originated about 1830, and was extremely popular until the end of the century.

Polo. A 19th-century Spanish (Andalusian) dance in moderate 3/8 meter, often in syncopated rhythms, and with rapid *coloraturas sung to exclamations such as "Ay" or "Olé." The music as well as the dance movements, being movements of the body rather than of the feet, show Oriental influence.

Polonaise (pol-o-NAYZ). A Polish dance of a stately character in moderate 3/4 meter, with rhythmic patterns such as shown in Fig. 91, and with

Fig. 91

*feminine cadences, the last note of a phrase being delayed to fall on the second or the third beat of the measure. It is not a folk dance, but originated in the 17th century at the Polish court as an accompaniment for festive processions. The earliest known examples occur in works by Bach (Brandenburg Concerto no. 1, French Suite no. 6) and Handel (Concerto Grosso no. 3). Later, polonaises were written by W. F. Bach, Mozart (Piano Sonata in D, K. 284), Beethoven (op. 89), Schubert (for four hands), and Weber, but it remained for Chopin to imbue this dance with the full life and spirit of its native country and to make it a symbol of national heroism

and chivalry. Particularly famous is his *Military Polonaise.

Polovtzian Dances. See under *Prince Igor*.

Polychoral (from Gr. *polys*, many). Descriptive term for compositions employing several (usually two or three) distinct groups of singers and/or instrumentalists producing effects of alternation, answering, or echoing. This technique, also termed antiphonal, was developed in the *Venetian School of the late 16th century under Andrea Gabrieli and, especially, his nephew Giovanni Gabrieli (1557–1612). In the performance of these magnificent works at St. Mark's Cathedral in Venice, the effect was heightened by placing the various groups in different parts of the church, a practice which is sometimes preserved in modern performances.

Polymeter. The simultaneous sounding of two or more different meters, e.g., 2/4 in one part, 3/4 in another. See *Polyrhythm*.

Polyphonic, polyphony (pol-i-FON-ik, po-LIF-o-nee: Gr., many-voiced). One of the three basic musical textures (see *Monophonic; Homophonic*). Music is said to be polyphonic if it is composed of two or more voice parts, each having individual melodic significance. Hence, polyphony is practically synonymous with *counterpoint. In current usage, counterpoint carries the connotation of musical instruction (counterpoint versus harmony), especially in its application to the styles of Palestrina, Bach, etc., while polyphony is used in a more general sense in reference to musical texture and its historical evolution. The earliest extant polyphonic music dates from the 9th century; polyphony was the prevailing texture from that time until the end of the 16th century. See *History of music*.

Polyrhythm. The simultaneous use of conflicting rhythms and accents, often as a result of combining different meters (see *Polymeter*). Simpler types, such as the use of 6/8 against 3/4, are usually called *cross rhythm, while the term polyrhythm is used for the bold rhythmic

Fig. 92

clashes often encountered in 20th-century music (see Fig. 92, from Hindemith's *Klaviermusik*, op. 37). Strongly syncopated passages, such as occur in jazz, also produce a polyrhythmic effect.

Polythematic. See under *Monothematic*.

Polytonality. The simultaneous sounding of several tonalities or *keys. The term is frequently applied (incorrectly) to *bitonal music. While bitonality occurs frequently in 20th-century music, real polytonality is rare.

Pomp and Circumstance. Five concert marches for orchestra by Elgar, op. 39 (nos. 1 to 4 composed in 1901–07, no. 5 in 1930). The title is taken from Shakespeare's *Othello*, III.iii. 354: "Pride, pomp and circumstance of glorious war."

Ponticello (pon-ti-CHEL-lo: It., little bridge). The bridge of the violin, viola, etc. See *Sul ponticello*.

Porgy and Bess. A three-act folk opera by George Gershwin (libretto by his brother, Ira, adapted from DuBose Heyward's play, *Porgy*), produced in New York, 1935. The music features the styles of the blues, jazz, and Negro spirituals.

Portamento (por-ta-MEN-to: It., carrying). A special manner of singing, with the voice gliding gradually from one tone to the next. The same effect is possible on the violin and trombone, where it is somewhat incorrectly called *glissando. The term is also used for an *appoggiatura performed in the same manner, i.e., gliding toward a note from its upper or lower neighbor note. See also under *Portato*.

Portative (POR-ta-tiv). A small portable organ of the Middle Ages, held in the left arm of the player, and played with the right hand only, while the left hand supplied the wind by means of a small bellows. This was a melody instrument, used to play one of the parts of a polyphonic composition. It was particularly popular during the 14th century in Italy where it was called *organetto*.

Portato (por-TAH-to: It., carried). A manner of performance halfway between legato and staccato (see under *Legato*). The use of the term **portamento* for this is misleading and should be avoided.

Port de voix, portez la voix (por de VWAH, por-tay la VWAH: F.). **Portamento.*

Portuguese Hymn. See *Adeste fidelis.*

Pos. Abbreviation for (1) Position (in violin playing); (2) *positif* (in French organ music); and (3) *Posaune* (in German orchestral scores).

Posaune (po-ZOW-ne: G.). Trombone.

Position. (1) In connection with chords, the term refers to the various possibilities of placing the notes of a chord in different octaves, thus changing the spaces between them. When the three upper notes of a chord are as close together as possible, the position is said to be *close* (close harmony, close spacing; see Fig. 93a, b). Sometimes this term is reserved for positions not exceeding a twelfth between

Fig. 93

the bass and the soprano (93c, d). The other arrangements frequent in vocal music, are called *open position* (93e, f). For another meaning in reference to chords, see *Inversion.* — (2) On the violin, etc., the various places to which the left hand is shifted in order to obtain higher or lower tones. The first position is the normal one, giving, on the G-string, the tones a, b, c', d' (in addition to the open string, g). The second position gives b, c', d', e', etc. The term is also used for the sliding mechanism of the trombone, the home position being called the first.

Positive (F., *positif;* G. *Positiv*). In the Middle Ages, name for a small organ which several men could move from one place to another, in contrast to the large organs which were built into churches. A famous illustration, showing an angel playing on a positive, is found on van Eyck's Altar of Ghent (*c.* 1420). Later the term was used for the **Choir Organ division of large organs.

Post horn. A valveless brass instrument similar to the military bugle or a small horn, formerly used by postilions to announce the arrival and departure of their coaches. Like the bugle, it could produce only the natural tones.

Postlude. An organ piece played at the conclusion of a church service while the congregation is leaving. Sometimes the term is used in the meaning of *coda.*

Potpourri (po-poo-REE: F., literally, rotten pot). A medley of popular tunes, operatic airs, patriotic songs, etc., loosely strung together with brief connecting phrases and presented as a popular entertainment.

Poule, La (la pool: The Hen). Nickname of Haydn's Symphony no. 83, in G minor (1786), no. 2 of the *Paris Symphonies. The name seems to refer to the second theme of the first movement, which vaguely suggests the cackling of a hen.

Pp. *Pianissimo*, very soft. Sometimes *ppp* or *pppp* is used to indicate extreme softness.

P. R. In French organ music, abbreviation for *Positif-Récit*, i.e., Choir Organ and Swell Organ coupled.

Praeludium (pray-LOO-dee-oom). See *Prelude*.

Prague Symphony. Mozart's Symphony in D (K. 504), composed in 1786 in Vienna and first performed (1787) in Prague where it was enthusiastically received. It has no minuet. See under *Symphony*.

Préambule (pray-anh-BUIL: F.). See *Prelude*.

Prelude. A piece of music designed to be played as an introduction, e.g., before the singing of a church hymn (*chorale prelude) or before another composition, particularly a *fugue (prelude and fugue; see *Well-tempered Clavier*) or a *suite. This connotation was lost in the 19th century when Chopin used the word as a fanciful title for a collection of twenty-four short Romantic *character pieces.

Chopin's example was followed by Scriabin (op. 11), Debussy, and Shostakovitch. In Debussy's collection (two sets of twelve each, composed 1910–13) each piece has a programmatic title given at the end.

The term prelude is also used for operatic overtures, especially those that do not follow a strict form, which derive their material from the opera to follow and which lead directly into the first scene, as in Verdi's *Traviata* and *Aida* or in Wagner's *Lohengrin* and *Tristan*.

Prélude à l'après-midi d'un faune. See *Afternoon of a Faun*.

Préludes, Les (lay pray-LUID). Symphonic poem by Liszt (composed in 1848–50), based on a poem of the same title by Lamartine.

Preparation. A term used in harmonic analysis to indicate that a dissonant note is properly introduced ("prepared") according to certain rules. A dissonance is fully prepared if the dissonant note, or its lower or upper neighbor note, appeared in the preceding chord as a consonance.

Prepared piano. A pianoforte the sound of which is artificially altered by various devices, e.g., metal clips or metal bolts attached to the strings; strips of paper, rubber, felt, etc., inserted across the strings; altered tuning of the two or three unison strings that are struck by a hammer, etc.

Presto (It.). Very fast; *prestissimo*, as fast as possible. See under *Tempo marks*.

Prick song (Old English, to prick, to write in by means of notes). Old term (16th century) for written or printed music, i.e., composed music as distinct from music handed down orally (folk song) or improvised.

Prima donna (PREE-ma DON-na: It., first lady). The singer of the principal female role in 18th-century opera. In the 19th century the term also gained the meaning of a conceited and capricious operatic star.

Prima vista (PREE-ma VEES-ta: It.). First sight, performance in *sight reading, without preparation.

Prima volta, seconda volta (PREE-ma VOL-ta, se-CON-da VOL-ta: It., first time, second time). The two different endings frequently found at the close of a repeated section (e.g., the exposition in *sonata form), indicated 1. and 2. . The first ending leads back to the beginning, the second leads on to another section or to the conclusion.

Primo, secondo (PREE-mo, se-CON-do: It., first, second). Terms used to indicate the upper and lower parts of a piano duet, or the first and second violin, flute, etc., in orchestral scores (*Violino primo*, etc.)

Prince Igor. Opera by Borodin (to his own libretto), composed between 1871 and the year of his death, 1887, completed by Rimski-Korsakov and Glazunov, produced in St. Petersburg, 1890. The setting is in the Russian town of Poutivl during the 12th century when the ruler Prince Igor (baritone) finds it necessary to go to war against the barbaric Polovtzy tribes. While away, he leaves his wife Yaroslavna (soprano) under the protection of her brother, the crafty Prince Galitsky (bass), who plots to usurp Igor's authority. After a period of captivity during which his son Vladimir (tenor) falls in love with the Polovtzian princess Kontchakovna (mezzo-soprano), Igor escapes and returns to Poutivl amid general rejoicing.

Best known are the Polovtzian Dances, which are often heard in concerts, and the selections adapted for the Broadway musical, *Kismet.*

Prix de Rome (PREE de rom: F., Prize of Rome). A famous prize awarded annually by the *Académie des Beaux-Arts* of Paris to composers (as well as to other artists) on the basis of a competition. It entitles the winner to a four-year stay at the Villa Medici in Rome. Among the successful competitors were Halévy (1819), Berlioz (1830), Bizet (1857), Debussy (1884), Charpentier (1887), and Florent Schmitt (1900).

Prodaná Nevěstá. See *Bartered Bride.*

Prodigal Son, The. See *Enfant prodigue.*

Program chanson. See under *Chanson* (2).

Program music. Music inspired by and suggestive of an extra-musical idea which is usually indicated in the title and sometimes further explained in a preface or additional remarks. The program idea may be taken from literature (Liszt, *Faust Symphony*), from history (Tchaikovsky, *1812 Overture*), from geography (Smetana, *The Moldau*, Sibelius, *Finlandia*), from the composer's own imagination (Berlioz, *Fantastic Symphony*), from visual impressions (Debussy, *Reflections in the Water*), etc. Although compositions of a descriptive character can be found as early as the 14th century, it was not until the 19th century that program music appeared as a serious rival of absolute music, particularly in its orchestral form, the °symphonic poem (tone poem). Early in the 20th century, however, composers generally turned away from program music and from the symphonic poem in particular. This was one of the manifestations of the °neoclassical aesthetic.

There is a certain weakness inherent in the underlying principle of program music. Music is basically an art in its own right, and too great a reliance on extraneous associations is likely to weaken rather than to enhance the artistic value of a composition. The great vogue which program music enjoyed during the 19th century led to a deplorable misunderstanding of the fundamental nature and purpose of music, resulting in the tendency to interpret all the great compositions in terms of a "story." Hundreds of such stories and "interpretations" have been contrived in the mistaken belief that they would help to facilitate an understanding of such works.

In the final analysis, there are two kinds of program music: that which is good music regardless of the program, and that which is poor music although it may have an interesting program. Unfortunately, the majority of program pieces belong to the latter category.

Program notes. Short historical and/or descriptive notes found in concert programs or record folders, written to enhance the listener's understanding and enjoyment of the music to be performed.

Program symphony. A composition written in the general form of a symphony (in several movements), and based on a programmatic idea (see *Program music*). Examples are Beethoven's °*Pastoral Symphony*, Berlioz' °*Fantastic Symphony*, Liszt's °*Faust Symphony*, and Strauss's °*Alpine Symphony*. Each movement of these has a separate title, representing one aspect of the general program. See under *Symphonic poem*.

Prologue. In early operas, an introductory scene containing a brief statement about the work, or an address to a noble patron present at the first performance. This practice, largely abandoned after 1700, was revived in Leoncavallo's °*Pagliacci* (1892).

Prometheus. A legendary Greek hero who created man and brought fire from the sun to the earth in defiance of the gods. The legend is the basis of: (1) A ballet by Beethoven; see *Creatures of Prometheus.* — (2) A symphonic poem by Scriabin, *Prometheus, Poem of Fire* (op.

60, 1910), written for large orchestra, piano, organ, choruses, and color organ (see *Color music*). The first (and only?) performance with the color organ took place in New York, in 1915. The music is based on the so-called mystic (or *Promethean*) chord (see under *Fourth chord*).

Proper. See under *Mass*.

Prosa (L.), **prose** (F.). Medieval name, preferred in France, for the liturgical sequence (see *Sequence*, 2).

Prussian Quartets. (1) A set of three string quartets (also called "King of Prussia Quartets") by Mozart, in D, B-flat, and F (K. 575, 589, 590), composed in 1789–90 and dedicated to Frederick William III, king of Prussia, who in 1789 had invited him to Berlin. The cello parts are unusually elaborate, obviously intended to please the king, who played this instrument. — (2) The name is also applied, for uncertain reasons, to Haydn's string quartets op. 50, nos. 1–6 (1786–87).

Ps. Abbreviation for Psalm, or for G. *Posaune*.

Psalms. The Book of Psalms (150 in number) has been the most productive single source of texts for musical compositions. More than three fourths of the chants of the Roman Catholic Church (*Gregorian chant) are Psalms or contain single verses of Psalms (see *Verse*). The Psalms are equally important in the services of most of the various Protestant churches (the music of the Lutheran Church is based on the *chorale or hymn). There also exist numerous elaborate compositions of Psalms, by Binchois, Josquin, Gombert, Palestrina, Lassus (see *Penitential psalms*), Marcello, Schubert, Mendelssohn, Liszt, Stravinsky, and many others.

Psalm tones. In the Roman Catholic Church, recitation melodies used for the singing of complete Psalms at the various Office Hours, especially Vespers. There are eight such tones, one for each of the eight church modes. Each psalm tone consists of Intonation–Tenor–Mediation–Tenor–Termination, the tenor being the reciting note, while the other members are connecting formulas of three or more notes.

Psalter. The Book of Psalms translated into the vernacular (English, French, Dutch Psalter), frequently in rhymed versions (metrical psalter), and provided with music for congregational singing. Particularly important are the *French Psalter* by Marot and Bèze of 1562 (music, in four parts, by Bourgeois, Goudimel, Jannequin, and Sweelinck), and the *English Psalter* of Sternhold and Hopkins (1562). The early American settlers used the *Ainsworth Psalter* (1612), which was replaced by the *Bay Psalm Book*, published in 1640 in Cambridge, Mass.

Psaltery. A medieval stringed instrument similar to the *dulcimer, but with the strings plucked instead of struck by hammers.

Pulcinella (pul-chee-NEL-lah). Ballet by Stravinsky, produced in Paris, 1920. The music is a modern setting of numerous passages from anonymous works formerly thought to be by the 18th-century composer, Pergolesi. Many of the melodies are maintained intact, while the accompaniment is cleverly altered into a sophisticated 20th-century idiom that is often *pandiatonic. See *Neoclassical*.

Punta d'arco (POON-tah DAR-co: It.). Point of the bow (of the violin, etc.).

Purfling. The inlaid border of violins, etc., consisting of three small slips of wood. Aside from its ornamental value it serves to prevent chipping of the edges.

Pythagorean scale. A scale, possibly devised by Pythagoras (c. 550 B.C.), in which all the tones are derived from the interval of the fifth, 3/2 (see *Acoustics*, 2). Thus, the third (e, if being derived from c) is obtained as the fourth successive fifth (c-g-d'-a'-e''), $3/2 \times 3/2 \times 3/2 \times 3/2 = 81/16$ (reduced two octaves downward, from e'' to e, 81/64). This third is slightly higher (8 *cents) than that of equal temperament, and considerably higher (22 cents, almost a quarter tone) than that of just intonation.

Q

Quadrille. A French dance of the early 19th century, performed by two or four couples moving in a square. It consisted of five figures for which the music, alternately in 6/8 and 2/4 meter, was chosen from popular tunes or operatic airs.

Quadruple counterpoint. See under *Invertible counterpoint*.

Quadruple fugue. See under *Double fugue*.

Quadruplets. A group of four notes to be played in the time of three, e.g., 4 eighth notes replacing 3 eighth notes in 6/8 meter.

Quartal harmony. Designation for a harmonic idiom based upon the interval of the fourth, as opposed to the traditional system based on the third (see *Tertian harmony*). Thus in quartal harmony, the *fourth chord (for example, c-f-bb) takes the place of the triad (for example, c-e-g) as the basic sonority.

Quarter note. See under *Notes and rests*.

Quarter tone. An interval equal to one half of a half tone (one quarter of a whole tone; see *Microtone*). Such intervals were used in ancient Greek music (enharmonic tetrachord, see under *Greek music*), and are also found in Arabian and Hindu music, but only at certain points of the scale, e.g., between b and c'. During the 20th century, several composers (e.g., Hába, Barth, Carrillo) have written quarter-tone music based on a complete scale of 24 notes to the octave. Fig. 94 shows the usual

Fig. 94

notation and the beginning of Hába's String Quartet, op. 9. Only a few instruments, mainly strings and the trombone (also the singing voice), can be used for quarter-tone music. Special quarter-tone pianos have been built, usually with two keyboards, the second keyboard tuned a quarter tone higher than the first.

Quartet. A composition for four instruments or voices; also the four performers assembled to play or sing such compositions (Budapest Quartet; barbershop quartet). By far the most important type is the °string quartet. See also under *Chamber music.*

Quasi (It.). As if, almost; e.g., *allegro quasi presto*, allegro, almost presto. *Quasi niente*, as if nothing, i.e., *ppp*.

Quattro (It.). Four. *Quattro mani*, four hands; *quattro voci*, four voices.

Quatuor (KAH-tui-or: F.). Quartet.

Quaver. See under *Notes and rests*.

Queen, The. See *Reine*.

Quick step. In military parlance, a march in quick steps, about 108 per minute. Also the music for such a march.

Quinten Quartet (G., *Quinten*, fifths). Nickname of Haydn's String Quartet op. 76, no. 2, in D minor, so called because of the prominent use of the descending fifth throughout the first movement.

Quintet. A composition for five instruments or voices. See under *Chamber music.*

Quintole. Same as °Quintuplet.

Quintuple meter. Music with five beats to the measure, usually 5/4. Well-known examples occur in Chopin's Piano Sonata op. 4 (slow movement), Tchaikovsky's °Pathétique Symphony (second movement, see Fig. 95), Wag-

Fig. 95

ner's *Tristan* (Act III, scene ii), and in numerous 20th-century compositions.

Quintuplet. A group of five notes played in the place of four or (occasionally) three notes.

Quodlibet (L., as it pleases). A composition in which well-known tunes or folk melodies are presented in a polyphonic setting so that different melodies sound simultaneously or in close succession. Quodlibets containing a great number of fragments of folk tunes were quite frequent about 1500 and later. The best known example is the final number of Bach's *Goldberg Variations, in which two folk songs, "Ich bin so lang nicht bei dir g'west" (Long have I been away from thee) and "Kraut und Rüben haben mich vertrieben" (Cabbage and turnips have driven me away), are artfully combined (see Fig. 96). More recent examples are found

Fig. 96

in Brahms' *Academic Festival Overture* and in Hindemith's *Der *Schwanendreher.*

R

R. In French organ music, *récit.*

Radical bass. See *Root bass.*

Radio broadcasting (of serious music). Although radio broadcasting as a regular public service in the United States was inaugurated in November 1920, it was not until the establishment of large networks (e.g., National Broadcasting Company, 1926; Columbia Broadcasting System, 1927) that broadcasts of serious music became available to the general public. Since that time, radio broadcasting of serious music has flourished in three general categories: (1) performances by existing musical organizations, which are incidentally relayed to radio listeners, (2) performances arranged especially for broadcasting, and (3) broadcasts of recorded music. Of the programs broadcast incidental to regular performances, the two annual series that have endured longest and are the most popular are the Sunday afternoon subscription concerts (changed in the 1958–59 season to Saturday evening) of the Philharmonic Society of New York (since 1930) and the Saturday afternoon performances of the Metropolitan Opera (since 1931). About eighty different operas have been heard during the past thirty years.

In the category of music performed especially for radio listeners, all of the networks have made significant contributions. This was particularly true in the 1930's and 1940's. For example, CBS offered a wide variety of unusual musical experiences in such series as "Exploring Music," "Essays in Music," and "The Story of Song." NBC broadcast a series of 110 programs of "Music of the Americas." The most ambitious effort along this line was NBC's assembling in 1938 a virtuoso orchestra under the direction of Arturo Toscanini. The orchestra, generally conceded to be peerless, was disbanded upon the retirement of the maestro in 1954. Occasionally such leading composers as Piston, Copland, Harris, etc., have been commissioned to write works especially for broadcasting, and several operas have been conceived primarily for radio performance. Of these, Menotti's *The Old Maid and the Thief* (NBC, 1939) has proved the most durable.

The third category — broadcasts of recorded music — is a comparatively new development that has resulted mainly from the growing number of independent radio stations, especially FM stations. Station WQXR in New York pioneered in this development, devoting about 80 per cent of its broadcasting time to recordings of serious music. Many newer independent stations, particularly those sponsored by colleges and universities, have followed this pattern. The combination of this sort of small station with the tremendous repertory now available on long-playing records provides the listening public with a magnitude of musical experience equaled at no other time in history.

Ragtime. A style of American popular music which originated at the end of the 19th century, one of the earliest known examples being the "Harlem Rag" of 1895. It probably derived from the early minstrel show tunes of the 1840's and from marches, especially those improvised for street parades in New Orleans. Its main feature

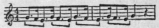

Fig. 97

was a slight rhythmic complexity which produced simple effects of syncopation (Fig. 97). Ragtime was made popular by the pianist Ben Harvey, who published his *Ragtime Instructor* in 1897. It reached its peak about 1910–15, afterwards merging into jazz.

Raindrop Prelude. Popular name for Chopin's Prelude in D-flat, op. 28, no. 15, so called because the continuously repeated note A♭ (G♯ in the middle section) suggests the dripping of raindrops.

Rake's Progress, The. Opera in three acts by Stravinsky (libretto by W. H. Auden, inspired by the set of prints by Hogarth), produced in Venice, 1951. The libretto, generally admired for its excellence, combines elements of *Don Giovanni* and of *Faust*. Tom Rakewell (tenor) is betrothed to a gentle country girl, Anne (soprano), but Nick Shadow (baritone), a personification of the devil, convinces him to leave her. They go to London where Tom enters into a fantastic marriage with a bearded lady, Baba (mezzo-soprano). Nick brings him to moral and financial ruin, and finally, when the agreed-upon time (a year and a day) has passed, demands his soul. Tom, however, wins a wager and a reprieve which puts him in Bedlam thinking he is Adonis awaiting the arrival of Venus. It is Anne who appears and lulls him into his final slumber. The work is a modern revitalization of late 18th- and early 19th-century opera (Mozart — Bellini), with recitative and frequent reminiscences from scores of that period.

Rákóczi March (RAH-kot-see). A Hungarian national air, composed by Janos Bihari in 1809, in homage to Prince Ferencz Rákóczi (1676–1735) who led the Hungarians in a revolt against Austria. The melody was used by Berlioz in his *Damnation of Faust* and *Marche Hongroise*, as well as by Liszt in his Hungarian Rhapsody, no. 15.

Rallentando (rahl-en-TAHN-do: It., slowing down). Abbr. *rall.*; same as *ritardando*.

Range. See *Voices, Range of*.

Rank. In organs, a complete set of pipes of the same type, e.g., Diapason, Gamba, etc. See under *Organ; Register*.

Ranz des vaches (RAHNH day VAHSH: F., cow's procession). A type of Swiss mountain melody sung or played on the *alphorn by herdsmen to call the scattered cows. There exist about fifty such melodies in the various districts of the Alps. One of

them is used in the overture of Rossini's *William Tell*, another in Liszt's piano piece, *Vallée d'Obermann* (from the *Années de Pélerinage*, I).

Rape of Lucretia, The. Opera in two acts by Britten (libretto, after Livy, by R. Duncan), produced in Glyndebourne, 1946. It presents the tragic tale of Lucretia (contralto), the faithful wife of the Roman general Collatinus (bass), who had been ravished by the Etruscan general Tarquinius (baritone), and who commits suicide before her husband when he returns. The work is organized in the manner of a Greek tragedy, with two characters representing the male and female choruses who comment on the action from the viewpoint of each sex. The score is of chamber music dimensions, calling for only twelve instruments.

Rapsodie Espagnole. See *Spanish Rhapsody*.

Rappresentazione di anima e di corpo, La (rahp-re-zen-taht-see-O-nay dee AHN-ee-ma ay dee COR-po: The Representation of Soul and Body). Stage work by Emilio de'Cavalieri, produced in Rome, 1600. It is usually regarded as the first *oratorio. The music consists almost exclusively of recitative and short choruses.

Rasgado (rahs-GAH-ttho: Sp., scraped). In guitar playing, sweeping of the strings with the thumb to produce a rapid arpeggio.

Rasumovsky Quartets (rahz-oo-MOV-skee). See *Russian Quartets*.

Ratsche (G.). See *Rattle*.

Ratswahlkantate (RAHTS-vahl-kahn-TAH-te: Council Election Cantata). A cantata (no. 71) by J. S. Bach, *Gott ist mein König*, written in 1708 for the election of the town council of Mühlhausen (Thuringia), where he was organist in 1707–08.

Rattle. A percussion instrument which consists of a cogwheel revolving against a flexible spring of wood or metal (similar to a familiar children's toy). It is used, under the German name *Ratsche*, in Strauss's *Till Eulenspiegel*. Rattle is also a generic term for various noise-producing instruments found in primitive cultures, e.g., gourds filled with pebbles, etc.

Razor Quartet. Popular name for Haydn's String Quartet no. 61 (op. 55, no. 2), in F minor, composed in 1787. Haydn gave it to his publisher Bland in a humorous exchange for a new razor which he needed.

Re. See under *Pitch names; Solmization; Tonic Sol-fa*.

Reading Rota. See *Sumer is icumen in*.

Real answer (fugue, sequence). See under *Tonal and real*.

Rebab (re-BAHB). Name for various primitive bowed stringed instruments, often of unusual shapes, found in Moslem countries (Arabia, Persia, Egypt, North Africa).

Recapitulation. See under *Sonata form*.

Rechte Hand (G.). Right hand.

Récit (ray-SEE: F.). In French organ music, the entire °Swell Organ or a solo stop used for the playing of melodies.

Recital. A public performance given by a soloist. A performance given by an orchestra or an ensemble is called a concert.

Recitative (re-see-tah-TEEV). A vocal style designed for the speechlike declamation of narrative episodes in operas, oratorios, or cantatas. Its main characteristic is a strictly syllabic treatment of the text with careful attention to word accent. The early recitative (about 1600–1700) combined this with a musical line of a fairly expressive and lyrical character (see Fig. 98a); but there developed in the 18th century a "parlando" style of recitative, in rapid tempo with

Fig. 98

frequent reiteration of the same pitch, in irregular rhythmic patterns dictated by the length of the words and phrases, and of a deliberately inexpressive character, hence called *secco* (It., dry) recitative (Fig. 98b). During the 17th and 18th centuries, recitative was usually sung to a °thorough-bass accompaniment consisting mainly of sustained chords. For narratives of special importance, however, a more elaborate orchestral accompaniment was used, together with a vocal line of a more expressive and more strictly measured type. This is known as *accompanied* recitative (*recitativo accompagnato* or *stromentato*). Bach, in his *St. Matthew Passion*, uses *secco* recitative for the Evangelist and accompanied recitative for Christ and for the recitatives preceding arias.

Recorder. An old instrument (15th through 18th centuries) of the flute family, differing from the modern flute in being held vertically and blown through a mouthpiece containing an obstructive block (°fipple) which leaves only a narrow slit for the passage of the breath. Recorders (also called blockflutes, G. *Blockflöte*) were usually made in four sizes: bass, tenor, treble (alto), and descant (soprano). The soprano size was still in common use at the time of Bach under the name of *flauto*, while the modern flute was called *flauto traverso* (transverse flute). Beginning about 1920, through the efforts of the Dolmetsch family in England, playing of recorders has been revived and they have been manufactured for the performance of old as well as of

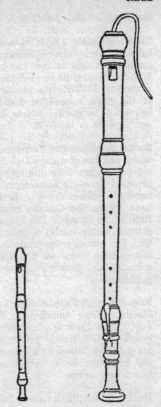

Recorder   *Bass recorder*

new music. They have a delightfully mild sound and are relatively easy to play. See illustrations.

Records. See *Phonograph and records.*

Reed. A vibrating tongue, made from a small piece of reed (cane) or metal, and used in the tone production of certain instruments, e.g., oboes and clarinets, hence the collective term "reeds" for all such instruments. The members of the °oboe family have a *double reed*, i.e., two reeds vibrating against each other, while those of the °clarinet type have a *single reed* vibrating against a slot at the upper end of the pipe. See also under *Wind instruments; Organ stops*.

Reel. A dance performed by two or more couples, who stand face to face and execute a variety of figures, each of which lasts for eight measures. The music consists of simple tunes in fairly fast tempo, which are repeated over and over again. The dance is common in Scotland, Ireland, and America, the American variety being known as the Virginia Reel.

Reformation Symphony. Mendelssohn's Symphony no. 5, op. 107, in D minor, composed in 1830 for the tercentenary of the Augsburg Conference (at which Luther openly declared the establishment of the German Reformed — the Protestant — Church).

Refrain. A recurring section of music (and text). The basic structure of a refrain song is therefore: a r b r c r . . . ; where a, b, c . . . stand for the sections with varying texts, although these are often (in strophic songs) also sung to identical music. Among the earliest examples of refrain structure in literature is Psalm 136, in which each verse ends with the refrain "For his mercy endureth forever." In early Christian chant the Psalms were regularly sung with a refrain (the *antiphon* or *response*) stated at the beginning and re- peated after each verse. In the later Middle Ages (13th and 14th centuries) there developed three types of French refrain song, the °ballade, the °virelai, and the °rondeau.

The term refrain is also used for a short instrumental piece repeated after each stanza of a song (see *Ritornello*), or for recurrent sections in purely instrumental compositions, particularly in the °rondo.

Regal (REE-gul). A small portable organ of the 15th and 16th centuries which had reed pipes only, hence producing a very peculiar sound, nasal and metallic. In his *Orfeo* (1607), Monteverdi prescribed its use for the accompaniment of the song of Charon, the mythical ferryman of the Underworld.

Register. (1) On the organ, a full set of pipes controlled by one stop. It may include one or (in mixture stops) several °ranks. — (2) In singing, term for the lower or higher parts of the range of the human voice, differing as to method of sound production and as to tone quality, e.g., "head register" (head voice, with resonance chiefly in the head) or "chest register" (chest voice, with resonance concentrated in the chest).

Registration. In organ playing, the use of the °registers to obtain variety in loudness and in color, according either to the composer's indication or, in the case of older music (Bach), to the player's own interpretation. Such interpretation, of course, should be governed by a knowledge of the relatively limited resources of old organs. A certain

REINE 244 REPEAT

amount of registration is also possible and required on the harpsichord.

Reine, La (ren: The Queen). Nickname of Haydn's Symphony no. 85, in B-flat (no. 4 of the °Paris Symphonies), composed about 1786. The name refers to Queen Marie Antoinette, who is said to have been particularly fond of this work.

Réjouissance (ray-zhui-SAHNHS: F., enjoyment). A light and playful movement sometimes found in Baroque suites (e.g., Bach's Orchestral Suite no. 4).

Related key, relative key. See under *Key relationship*.

Relative pitch. (1) The pitch of one tone (for example, E) in relation to another tone (for example, C), usually indicated as an interval (e.g., major third). — (2) The ability to recognize a relative interval in sense (1) above, e.g., to recognize and identify the tone E (when played after the tone C) as a major third, or, if the major third above C is demanded, to sing the tone E. This faculty is one of the most important requirements of a musician, functionally more valuable than °absolute (perfect) pitch.

Renaissance. Designation for a period of music history roughly coinciding with the Renaissance in the other Fine Arts, that is, from about 1400 or 1450 to 1600, between the Middle Ages and the Baroque period (see *History of music*). Among the outstanding masters are Dufay

(c. 1400–1474), Ockeghem (c. 1430–1495), Obrecht (c. 1453–1505), Josquin (c. 1450–1521), Willaert (c. 1485–1562), Palestrina (1525–1594), Lassus (1532–1594), Byrd (1542–1623), and Giovanni Gabrieli (1557–1612). Throughout the Renaissance the numerous members of the °Flemish School played a leading role in the development of a musical style which can be characterized as a vocal polyphony (see *A cappella*) in from four to six parts, related to each other by extended use of imitation (see *Motet, II*) and by increasingly refined methods of counterpoint (see *Palestrina style*).

The chief musical forms of universal cultivation were the Mass and the motet. To these were added the various national types of secular music, e.g., the Italian and English °madrigal (see also *Frottola*), the French polyphonic °chanson, and the German polyphonic °lied. Instrumental music acquired considerable importance in numerous compositions (°prelude, °toccata, °variations, °ricercar, °canzona), for the organ, clavier, and lute, and also for small instrumental ensembles. Dance music was extensively cultivated in the °basse danse, °pavane, °galliard, °passamezzo, and many other types of lesser importance.

Repeat. The signs ||: and :|| calling for the repetition of the section enclosed by them. If the latter sign appears alone, the repetition starts from the beginning of the movement (e.g., the exposition of sonata form). Unfortunately, repeat signs are frequently disregarded in performance, a liberty that often leads to a distortion of the musical structure. See under *Sonata form*.

Repetition. As a device of composition, repetition is one of the fundamental principles of musical structure, providing *unity* (as opposed to the *variety* of contrasting material). It occurs, not only as recurrence of entire sections in musical forms such as A B A, A A B A, etc. (see under *Form*), but also in more subtle manifestations, such as imitation, sequence, ostinato, motival technique, and as "varied repetition" in the numerous types of variation and in the *twelve-tone technique.

Replica (It.). Repeat. *Da capo senza replica*, often found at the end of minuets or scherzos, indicates that the minuet should be repeated after the trio, but without the internal repeats for its first and second sections. This practice is generally observed in performance, even when there is no such indication. See under *Minuet*.

Reprise (re-PREEZ). Same as recapitulation in *sonata form.

Requiem, Requiem Mass (from L., *requies*, rest). The Mass of the Dead in the Roman Catholic rites, so called because it begins with the Introit "Requiem aeternam dona eis, Domine" (Give them eternal rest, O Lord). The complete Mass in plainsong (Gregorian chant) consists of the above-mentioned Introit, followed by the *Kyrie*, a Gradual, a Tract, the Sequence *Dies Irae*, an Offertory, the *Sanctus*,

Agnus Dei, and a Communion. Elaborate musical settings (e.g., by Ockeghem, Palestrina, Victoria, Mozart, Verdi) usually omit some of the Gregorian items. For instance, Mozart's *Requiem* opens with a movement including both the Introit and the *Kyrie*, then proceeds to an extended treatment of the *Dies Irae* (nos. 2–7), after which follows the Offertory (*Domine Jesu Christe*, nos. 8, 9), the *Sanctus* (nos. 10, 11), and the *Agnus Dei* (no. 12). Verdi's *Requiem*, often called *Manzoni Requiem*, uses the same items, with the addition of the Communion *Lux aeterna* and of the Responsory *Libera me*, which properly belongs to the Burial Service. See also *German Requiem* (Brahms).

Rescue opera. A term sometimes used to refer to a type of early 19th-century opera, of French origin, based on a fairly realistic plot involving trials, dangers, and eventual rescue of the hero and/or heroine. Among the best-known examples are Cherubini's *Deux Journées* (1800) and Beethoven's *Fidelio* (1805).

Resolution. In harmony or counterpoint, the process of passing from a dissonant chord or tone into a consonance. For instance, a seventh chord is "resolved" into a triad, or an appoggiatura into its lower or upper neighbor note.

Resonance. The reinforcement of a musical tone by a vibrating body (*resonator*) attached to or in close proximity to the source of the sound. In the xylophone, for example, each key has its own resonator, in the form of a metal cylinder suspended below the key. The sounding board of the piano and the belly of the violin are *general resonators*, reinforcing all the sounds produced on the instrument. Another type of resonator is the set of °sympathetic strings of the viola d'amore.

Respond. Either the Roman Catholic responsory or, less frequently, the Anglican (Episcopal) °response.

Response. In Anglican (Episcopal) churches, the choral or congregational replies (e.g., "Amen" or "And grant us Thy salvation") to the versicles, petitions, etc., of the priest.

Responsorial. A method of performance consisting of the alternation between a soloist and a group, as opposed to antiphonal performance (see *Antiphon*), i.e., alternation of two groups. The prototypes of these effects occur in Gregorian chant where, according to the original method of performance, chants are classified as either responsorial (e.g., Graduals, Alleluias, Responsories) or antiphonal (e.g., Introits, Communions). The responsorial chants are more elaborate (melismatic) than the others.

Rest. A sign indicating that, for a specified time, the music ceases, at least in one of the parts. See under *Notes and rests*.

Restatement. Same as recapitulation in °sonata form.

Resultant tone. In musical acoustics, term for a third tone which is heard when two relatively

loud tones are sounded simultaneously. They are also called *combination tones* or *differential tones*. The most important of these is the so-called *Tartini's tone*, a low tone whose pitch is given by the difference of the frequencies of the two original tones. Fig. 99 shows this tone

Fig. 99

(black note) for various intervals (c' arbitrarily = 300 cycles). Tartini's tone can easily be heard on the harmonium, organ, and violin. Tartini and Leopold Mozart recommended it as a means of controlling the intonation of double stops, since a slight inaccuracy results in a more clearly noticeable change of the low-pitched tone.

Resurrection Symphony. Mahler's Symphony no. 2, in C minor, completed in 1894. The fourth movement is a setting for alto solo and orchestra of *"Urlicht"* (Primordial Light, a song from *Des Knaben Wunderhorn*); the fifth and last movement is a setting of Klopstock's poem, *"Auferstehung"* (Resurrection), for soprano solo, chorus, and orchestra.

Retablo de Maese Pedro, El (ray-TAH-blo day mah-ES-ay PAY-tthro: Master Peter's Puppet Show). A one-act opera for marionettes by Manuel de Falla to his own libretto, produced in Seville, 1923. It is based on a chapter from Cervantes' *Don*

Quixote, in which Don Quixote attends a puppet show depicting a fight between the Christians and the Saracens, and, believing the puppets to be real, draws his sword to assist the Christians.

Retardation. A rarely used term for suspension (see under *Nonharmonic tones*) or, particularly, a suspension which resolves upward.

Retrograde. A term indicating reverse or backward motion, e.g., beginning with the last note of a melody and ending with the first. Synonymous terms are crab motion, *cancrizans* (from L. *cancer,* crab), and *al rovescio* (It.). See Fig. 100a and b. Although,

Fig. 100

from the listener's point of view, this procedure completely obscures the original melody, it has been quite frequently used by composers as a constructive device. Some examples are the canons in Bach's *Musical Offering,* the *Menuetto al rovescio* of Haydn's Sonata no. 4 for piano and violin, and the final fugue of Beethoven's *Hammerclavier Sonata,* op. 106, in which the fugal theme occurs in retrograde motion. Retrograde motion is one basic element of the *twelve-tone technique. Retrograde inversion ("inverted crab") is the combination of retrograde motion and inversion, as shown in Fig. 100c. In Hindemith's *Ludus Tonalis* the Postlude is the retrograde inversion of the Prelude which can be played by turning the pages upside down, the Prelude becoming the Postlude and vice versa when allowance is made for accidentals.

Revolutionary Etude. Nickname of Chopin's Etude in C minor, op. 10, no. 12, written in 1831 after he heard that Warsaw had been taken by the Russians.

Rf., rfz. Short for *rinforzando.

Rhapsody. A term of Greek origin, properly meaning something like "fragmentary song," used in music chiefly as a designation for free fantasies of a somewhat epic, heroic, or national character (e.g., Liszt's *Hungarian Rhapsodies;* also works by Raff, Lalo, Dvořák, Bartok), or for compositions which, although in strict form, have a certain epic or archaic flavor (Brahms' Rhapsodies for piano). Gershwin's *Rhapsody in Blue* (1924) is a free fantasy in jazz idiom, modeled somewhat after Liszt's Rhapsodies. In Brahms' *Rhapsodie* in C, op. 53, for contralto solo, male chorus, and orchestra (often called *Alto Rhapsody*), the title seems to refer to the fact that it is based on a *fragment* from Goethe's *Harzreise im Winter.*

Rheingold, Das. See under *Ring of the Nibelung.*

Rhenish Symphony. Schumann's Symphony no. 3, in E-flat, op. 97, composed in 1850–51 after a trip along the Rhine. The fourth movement was inspired by the Cathedral of Cologne.

Rhumba. See *Rumba*.

Rhythm. Rhythm may be broadly defined as everything pertaining to the duration quality (long–short) of musical sounds. Thus it forms the counterpart of °motion, i.e., everything pertaining to the pitch quality (high–low) of the musical sound (see also under *Melody*). Rhythm may be entirely free, i.e., employing temporal values not derived from a basic unit. Such rhythms occur in some primitive and Oriental music, and are also present when passages are played in °ritardando, °accelerando, °rubato, etc. Normally, however, rhythm is metrical, i.e., its values are multiples or divisions of a temporal unit, the beat, which is normally represented by the quarter note or the eighth note, occasionally by the half note (see *Alla breve*). The beats are arranged in groups of two, three, four, six, etc., according to the meter (4/4, 6/8, etc.), each group constituting a measure. Rhythm, in the more specific sense of the word, denotes the innumerable patterns formed, within the basic metric framework, by the various arrangements of smaller or larger note values, as illustrated in Fig. 101. For related topics, see *Beat; Measure; Meter; Polyrhythm; Rubato; Tempo; Syncopation.*

Rhythmic modes. A 13th-century system of rhythm, based on a few simple rhythmic patterns, all in triple meter. Usually six modes are distinguished, as shown in Fig. 102. In a given composition

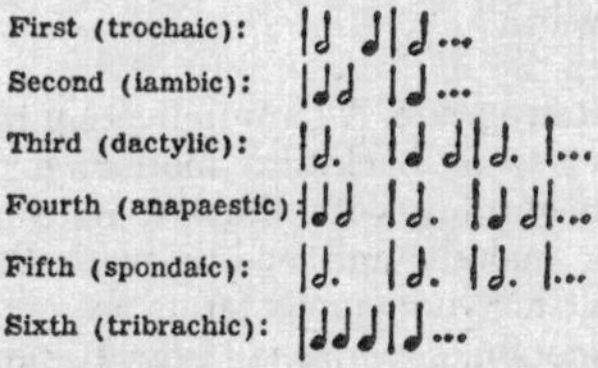

First (trochaic):

Second (iambic):

Third (dactylic):

Fourth (anapaestic):

Fifth (spondaic):

Sixth (tribrachic):

Fig. 102

such as a 13th-century motet, each part adheres throughout to one mode, e.g., the 6th mode in the upper voice, the 1st mode in the middle voice, and the 5th mode in the lowest (tenor) part. There may be certain modifications of the basic pattern (occasional rests, groups of two or three eighth notes instead of a quarter note, etc.).

Ricercar (ree-chayr-KAHR: It., *ricercare*, to search out). A 16th- and 17th-century type of instrumental music, particularly for the organ, written in imitative counterpoint and of a solemn, restrained character. Ricercars are usually polythematic, that is, they employ several themes each of which is treated in a separate section, often with the aid of special devices of "learned counterpoint," such as augmentation, diminution, inversion, invertible counterpoint, stretto, combination of themes,

Fig. 101

etc. The ricercar is derived from the 16th-century motet, but differs from it in various aspects, particularly the much more extended treatment of each subject (fugal section versus *point of imitation). The most important composers were Willaert, Girolamo Cavazzoni, Andrea Gabrieli, Frescobaldi, and Froberger. Bach closed and climaxed the development of the ricercar in his *Musical Offering, inscribed: Regis Iussu Cantio Et Reliqua Canonica Arte Resoluta (Upon the King's Demand, the Theme and Additions Resolved in Canonic Style), a sentence whose initial letters spell RICERCAR. The ricercar style is also evident in several fugues from the Well-tempered Clavier, particularly the C♯ minor of vol. I and the E major of vol. II. As with so many forms of old music, the ricercar has been revived by 20th-century composers, e.g., Martinu, Casella, and Malipiero.

The term was also occasionally applied to nonimitative compositions, especially for the lute. The general meaning of the term was probably something like "study."

Ricochet (F.). See Bowing (e).

Riddle canon. See Enigmatic canon.

Ridotto (ri-DAWT-to: It.). Reduced, i.e., arranged (for pianoforte, etc.).

Riduzione (ree-doo-tsee-O-nay: It.). Arrangement (for pianoforte, etc.).

Rienzi (ree-EN-zee). Opera by Wagner (libretto by the composer, based on Bulwer-Lytton's novel), produced in Dresden, 1842. It is an early work reflecting the styles of Italian and French opera.

Rigaudon (ree-go-donh: F.). A Provençal dance of the 17th century, used in French operatic ballets and also in the optional group in the *suite. It is in lively 4/4 meter, without upbeat. In England it was called rigadoon.

Rigoletto (rig-o-LET-to). Opera in three acts by Verdi (libretto by F. M. Piave, after Victor Hugo's drama, Le Roi s'amuse), produced in Venice, 1851. The scene is in 16th-century Italy where the handsome and profligate Duke of Mantua (tenor), aided by his deformed jester Rigoletto (baritone), pursues the wives and daughters of his courtiers. One of the latter, Count Monterone (baritone), arrives during a party to berate the Duke for having betrayed his daughter. When Rigoletto ridicules him, Monterone pronounces a father's curse upon the jester (Act I). In revenge for his barbed mockery, some of the courtiers conspire to kidnap Rigoletto's daughter Gilda (soprano), believing her to be his mistress. She is taken to the palace, and seduced by the Duke (Act II). In reprisal, Rigoletto hires the bandit Sparafucile (bass) to murder the Duke, who (Act III) comes to Sparafucile's inn to amuse himself with the latter's sister Maddalena (mezzosoprano). Implored by his sister, Sparafucile agrees to murder, instead of the Duke, the first person to enter the inn, and Gilda, overhearing this, sacrifices herself. Rigoletto receives from Sparafucile a sack which he believes to contain the corpse of the Duke; opening it, he discovers that of his own daughter — Monterone's curse has been fulfilled.

Its gruesome plot places *Rigoletto* in the category of the "horror opera" which had a great vogue about 1850. The action is full of moments of genuinely dramatic tension effectively underlined by the music, which also includes arias of touching tenderness. Together with *Il Trovatore* (1853) and *La Traviata* (1853), *Rigoletto* represents the crowning point of the Italian opera with melodramatic plots, popular type of melodies, and concentration on effective vocal "numbers." See *Number opera.*

Rinforzando (reen-for-TSAHN-do: It., reinforcing). Abbreviated *rf., rfz., rinf.* A sudden stress on a single note or chord (*°sforzando*), or a sudden and short crescendo.

Ring of the Nibelung, The (NEE-be-loong: G., *Der Ring des Nibelungen*). A cycle of four operas by Wagner: *The Rhinegold* (*Das Rheingold*), 1853–54; *The Valkyrie* (*Die Walküre*), 1854–56; *Siegfried,* 1856–71; and *The Twilight of the Gods* (*Götterdämmerung*), 1869–74. The libretto is by the composer, based on the Scandinavian *Edda* and the German *Nibelung Saga* (12th to 13th century). First full performance in Bayreuth, 1876, for the dedication of the Wagner Festival Theatre. Wagner designated *Rhinegold* as a

Prologue, the other three operas as a Trilogy.

The basic idea of the cycle is the ancient Germanic conception of the world consisting of three realms struggling against each other: I, the realm of the gods (Valhalla, with Wotan; his wife, Fricka; the goddess of youth, Freia; and the god of fire, Loge). II, the realm of men (Earth, represented by Wotan's son, Siegmund; his sister, Sieglinde; their son, Siegfried; Sieglinde's husband, Hunding; and, in the *Twilight of the Gods,* Hagen, Gunther, and Gutrune). III, the dark realm of the Nibelungs, a race of dwarfs living beneath the earth (Alberich, Mime). In addition, there are the Valkyries, Wotan's daughters (Brünnhilde and her sisters), the Giants (Fasolt and Fafner), and the Norns, representing the eternal destiny to which even the gods are subject. Two basic plots are merged in the action. The first is a legendary plot centering around the magic ring which, forged by Alberich out of the gold hidden in the Rhine, makes its possessor master of the world and which falls successively into the hands of Wotan, of Fafner (who obtains it in return for the goddess Freia and guards it in the form of a dragon), and of Siegfried, who kills the dragon and gives the ring to Brünnhilde as a sign of his love (in *Siegfried*) but who, in the *Twilight of the Gods,* takes it away from her. The second is a human plot centering, in the *Valkyrie,* around the incestuous love of Siegmund and Sieglinde and in *Siegfried* around the love of their son Siegfried and Brünnhilde. In the *Twilight of the Gods,* Siegfried, blinded by a love potion, falls in love with Gutrune, but, immediately before his death, once more remembers Brünnhilde and calls her name with his last breath.

In order to forge together this gigantic plot, Wagner relies here more than in any other of his operas upon the °leitmotiv as a means of unification. Not only has each of the acting persons his own characteristic motive, but also basic ideas, such as "the curse," "the ring," "the sword," are thus represented. Moreover, in contrast to the earlier operas such as *Tannhäuser* and *Lohengrin,* Wagner completely discards here the aria, the song, or the chorus of the °number opera, adopting instead the "unending melody," a highly expressive declamation which, purposely avoiding cadences and sectional construction, continues almost from the beginning to the end of each act in an uninterrupted flow.

Ripieno, pl. **ripieni** (ree-pee-AY-no, ree-pee-AY-nee: It., replenished, supplementary). In the Baroque concerto grosso (Bach, Handel), an indication for sections to be played by the full orchestra, as distinguished from those to be played by the soloists (marked *concertino*). The term properly denotes the "reinforcing section" or "rear section" of the orchestra. Therefore, *senza ripieni* does not mean "without orchestra" but calls for a small number of "front players" to accompany the soloists.

Ripresa (ree-PRAY-za: It.). Repeat, repetition.

Ritardando (ree-tar-DAHN-do: It.). Abbreviated *rit., ritard.* Gradually slackening in speed.

Ritenuto (ree-te-NOO-to: It.). Same as °ritardando, but often suggesting a marked reduction of speed.

Rite of Spring, The (F., *Le Sacre du printemps*). Ballet by Stravinsky (choreography by Nijinsky), produced in Paris, 1913. It represents an ancient pagan rite which is climaxed with the sacrifice of a virgin to the gods of fertility. The two parts (I, *The Adoration of the Earth;* II, *The Sacrifice*), now often performed as a concert piece, are divided into several scenes. The work is one of the major landmarks in the evolution of 20th-century music, establishing Stravinsky's revolutionary °dynamism. Its harsh sounds and barbaric rhythms, willingly accepted and admired today, caused a riot of indignation among the audience at the first performance.

Ritmo (REET-mo: It.). Rhythm. For Beethoven's *ritmo di tre* (*quattro*) *battute,* see under *Battuta.*

Ritornello (ree-tor-NEL-lo: It.). In the early 17th century, term for short instrumental sections designed as introductions, interludes, or postludes for a vocal composition. In spite of the implication of the term ("little return"), they are not necessarily a refrain (i.e., the same music). They did adopt this character, particularly in 17th-century German songs (Adam Krieger) in which they were played at the end of every stanza. Modern writers have adopted the term for the recurring *tutti* sections of the concerto grosso. Hence, the name *ritornello form* applies to movements (usually the first, often also the last) written in this manner.

Rococo (ro-CO-co: from F. *rocaille,* shell). A period of music history, extending roughly from 1710 to 1775, which forms the transition from the Baroque to the Classical period (see under *History of music*). The name is borrowed from a nearly contemporary movement in the Fine Arts characterized by an abundance of merely decorative scroll and shell work (e.g., on furniture) and by a general tendency toward superficial elegance, luxury, and frivolity. Similar traits are noticeable in the music of the period, which emphasizes pleasantness and prettiness, in contrast to the seriousness and dignity of Baroque music. The general character of Rococo music is well described by the term *gallant style.* Among the earliest examples are the harpsichord pieces of F. Couperin, composed between 1710 and 1725. Later representatives are Daquin, Telemann, Grazioli, Rutini, and many others. Rococo elements are still present in the works of C. P. E. Bach, Haydn, and Mozart.

Rodeo. Ballet by Copland (choreography by Agnes de Mille), produced in New York, 1942. The scene is set in the American Southwest, and several traditional cowboy tunes are incorporated into the score. A suite of four numbers has become a popular selection for orchestral concerts.

Roi David, Le. See *King David.*

Roll. A drum effect produced by the rapid alternation of strokes by the sticks, essentially a °tremolo. See *Drum Roll Symphony.*

Rollschweller (ROLL-shvel-ler: G.). The crescendo pedal of the organ.

Roman Carnival, The (F., *Le Carnaval romain*). Concert overture by Berlioz, op. 9, composed in 1843. The themes were taken from his unsuccessful opera, *Benvenuto Cellini* after its failure in the Paris production, 1838.

Romance. Properly a lyrical and sentimental song. Also instrumental pieces of a similar character.

Roman chant. Same as °Gregorian chant.

Roman Festivals (It., *Feste Romane*). Symphonic poem by Respighi, composed in 1928, in four movements: "Circus Maximus," "Jubilee," "October Festival," and "Epiphany."

Roman School. A group of Roman composers who continued the style of sacred *a cappella* music established by Palestrina (1525–1594). Among the leading figures were Giovanni Maria Nanino (*c.* 1543–1607), Gregorio Allegri (1582–1652), Orazio Benevoli (1605–1672), Antonio Lotti (1667–1740), and Antonio Caldara (1670–1736). These composers generally rejected the current forms of Baroque music (opera, oratorio, cantata, sonata, etc.) and devoted themselves to liturgical music (Masses, motets, Psalms, etc.) composed in the traditional style of Palestrina (see *Palestrina style*), with the inclusion of certain later idioms such as *polychoral treatment and Baroque harmony.

Romantic, Romanticism. Designation for the major musical movement of the 19th century, succeeding the *Classical school of the late 18th century. It may be divided into three periods: early Romanticism, c. 1820–50, represented by Weber, Berlioz, Mendelssohn, Schumann, and Chopin; middle Romanticism, c. 1850–90, by Liszt, Wagner, Franck, Bruckner, Smetana, Brahms, Tchaikovsky, and Dvořák; late Romanticism, c. 1890–1920, by Elgar, Mahler, MacDowell, R. Strauss, Sibelius, Reger, Holst, and many other composers born between 1860 and 1880. Beethoven and Schubert are transitional composers, their early works adhering to the Classical tradition and their later ones exhibiting more Romantic tendencies.

The Romantic movement (as well as the term "Romantic") originated in an English-German literary school of the late 18th century formed by writers such as Walter Scott, Wackenroder, Tieck, and Novalis, who, in search of new themes, turned for subject matter to the *Romanesque* period of the Middle Ages (11th and 12th centuries), the period of valiant knights, gracious ladies, and pious monks. From this movement,

musicians took over the same general "longing for something nonexistent," a propensity for dream and vision, for the fantastic and the picturesque, for strong emotion and vivid imagery. Musical Romanticism, therefore, may be characterized as an art which emphasizes subjective and emotional elements, translating into music the feelings of the human soul — joy and sorrow, passion and tenderness, exuberance and despair. In the music of the Classical masters, such feelings, if presented at all, may be said to form an unconscious stratum underlying the musical realities. In Romantic music, on the other hand, they themselves become the realities, of which the music is but the reflection. Modifying a famous sentence written by Monteverdi in 1607 (see under *Nuove musiche*), the gate leading to Romanticism may be said to carry the inscription: "Let Emotion be the master, not the servant, of music."

From the technical point of view, the most important achievements of Romanticism are the full exploitation of chromatic harmony (carried to its ultimate degree and leading to the disintegration of tonality), development of a rich and varied palette of tonal colors, particularly in orchestral music, and the cultivation of expressive devices such as tempo *rubato, dynamic fluctuation, etc. Of musical forms, the *character piece (for piano) and the *symphonic poem are particularly distinctive and typical.

Romantic Symphony. (1) Nickname for Bruckner's Symphony

no. 4, in E-flat major, composed in 1874 (rev. 1878, 1880). — (2) Name for Hanson's Symphony no. 2, composed in 1930.

Romanze (ro-MAHN-tze: G.). Romance.

Romeo and Juliet. Among the many compositions based on Shakespeare's play are: (1) Symphony by Berlioz, op. 17 (1839), for solo voices, chorus, and orchestra. — (2) Opera by Gounod (1864). — (3) Symphonic poem (Fantasy Overture) by Tchaikovsky (1869-70). — (4) Ballet, op. 64, by Prokofiev (1935).

Rondeau (ronh-DO: F.). (1) An instrumental form of the 17th century, consisting of a recurring section, the °refrain, played in alternation with three or more varying sections called *couplets:* A B A C A D . . . A. This is a favored form of French harpsichord music (Chambonnières, Louis Couperin, d'Anglebert, F. Couperin, Rameau), and is also frequent in contemporary orchestral and operatic music (Lully). In the late 18th century the rondeau developed into the °rondo form of the sonata. — (2) The medieval rondeau (13th–15th centuries) is a vocal composition (monophonic or polyphonic) with the form A B a A a b A B (capital letters indicate a literary as well as a musical refrain, e.g., repetition of text as well as music). — (3) In sonatas (Beethoven), see *Rondo*.

Rondo, rondo form (RON-do). A form often used for the final movement of classical sonatas, string quartets, symphonies, and concertos, as well as for independent pieces. It was developed from the °rondeau of the French clavecinists by limiting the number of couplets to three, and by using the same material for the first and third couplet (usually called *episode*), thus leading to the standard structure A B A C A B' A. The sectional structure of the rondeau is changed into a more continuous one by the addition of bridge passages, and the first and third episodes are respectively in the dominant and tonic keys. In this latter stage it appears that the structure of the rondo merges with elements of sonata form, inasmuch as B and B' correspond to exposition and recapitulation, C occupying the position of the development section. (See *Rondo–sonata form*.) A clear example is the last movement of Beethoven's Pathétique Sonata, op. 13.

The term rondo form is also used for shorter and more elementary forms involving alternation, for example, A B A ("first rondo form") and A B A B A or A B A C A ("second rondo form"). These forms usually lack the continuous character as well as other features of the true rondo, and are more appropriately termed °ternary form and extended ternary form (or five-part form). See under *Form*.

Rondo–sonata form. A hybrid structure combining elements of °rondo form and °sonata form. It differs from rondo form in that the second episode is replaced by a development section, resulting in the form A B A

Development A B A. Except for the second and fourth recurrences of the refrain (A), it is similar to the sonata form.

Root. The fundamental note upon which a chord is constructed by superimposing intervals of a third, for example, C in the case of a C-major or C-minor triad. If this fundamental is the lowest note, the chord is said to be in root position (see Fig. 103, chords a and b); if one of the other chord members is below the root, the chord is said to be inverted, or in inversion (chords c-f). See also under *Chords; Inversion.*

Fig. 103

Root bass. A bass formed by harmonies all of which are in root position, e.g., I III IV II V I, as opposed to, e.g., I III IV₆ II⁶₄ V₆ I. See *Root.*

Rosalia (ro-ZAHL-ya). A disparaging term for a type of sequence found in the works of mediocre composers of the early 19th century, involving exact repetition of the intervals (real sequence; see under *Sequence*)

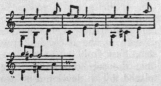

Fig. 104

and, therefore, modulation (see Fig. 104). The term is derived from a popular Italian song, "Rosalia, mia cara," in which this device occurs.

Rosamunde (RO-zah-MOON-da). Incidental music by Schubert for a play by Helmina von Chézy, produced in Vienna, 1823. It contains, in addition to some choral numbers, an overture (originally written for a melodrama, *Die Zauberharfe*), three entr'actes, and two ballets which are often played in concerts.

Rose. Ornamental escutcheon of carved wood inserted in the circular soundhole of lutes, guitars, harpsichords, etc., frequently as the maker's trademark.

Rosenkavalier, Der (RO-zen-kah-vah-leer: The Knight of the Rose). Opera by R. Strauss (libretto by H. von Hofmannsthal), produced in Dresden, 1911. The plot, taking place in an 18th-century Viennese setting, presents characters and love intrigues not dissimilar to those of Mozart's *Figaro:* the aging but still beautiful Princess of Werdenberg (soprano); the young cavalier Octavian (mezzo-soprano) who, disguised as the princess' maid, attracts the unwelcome attentions of the coarse and profligate Baron Ochs of Lerchenau (bass); and the fair Sophie (soprano), who is betrothed to the Baron but is secretly in love with Octavian. The title refers to a silver rose, the Baron's betrothal token, which, in Act II, is delivered to Sophie by Octavian. In Act III, the Baron is lured into a hotel-room tryst with the "maid" (Octavian) where he is tormented and punished by the appearance of a "deserted wife" with four children who call him "Papa," ghostly faces at the window, etc. The music, full of lush and delightful tunes, is well known through numerous orchestral excerpts, particularly the waltzes.

Rosin, resin (RAH-zin, RE-zin). A preparation made from gum of turpentine, and applied to the hair of the violin bow in order to give it the necessary grip on the strings.

Rota (RO-ta). Medieval term for a round, particularly for the canon, *Sumer is icumen in.*

Roulade (roo-LAHD: from F. *rouler*, to roll). A term applied to highly ornamental *coloratura passages present in some operatic arias of the 18th and 19th centuries.

Round. Common name for a canon so devised that it can be repeated indefinitely (circle canon, perpetual canon, infinite canon), as shown below:

```
 I   a  b  c  ‖   a  b  c  ‖
II      a  b  ‖ : c  a  b : ‖  c
III        a  ‖   b  c  a  ‖  b  c
```

Most examples of this type (e.g., *Three Blind Mice*) are designed for popular entertainment and therefore employ a simple melody falling into distinct phrases (a, b, c, of the above scheme) and imitated at the unison. Fig. 105 shows an example by M. Praetorius (1571–1621). Rounds enjoyed an extreme popularity in 17th-century England, where they were usually called *catches.

Vi-va vi-va la Mu-si-ca

Fig. 105

Roundelay (rown-de-LAY). A 14th-century term, found in literary sources (Chaucer), for round dances and dancing songs, possibly in the form of the medieval French *rondeau.

Rovescio, al (ahl ro-VESH-o: It., in reverse). Designation for either *retrograde motion (e.g., in the "Menuetto al rovescio" of Haydn's Sonata no. 4 for violin and pianoforte), or *inversion (melodic), as in Mozart's Serenade K. 388.

Row. Same as tone row. See *Twelve-tone technique.*

Roxelane, La. Nickname for Haydn's Symphony no. 63, in C, composed in 1777. The second movement is a set of variations on the French tune, "La Roxelane."

Rubato (roo-BAH-to: It., robbed). Term denoting a certain elasticity and freedom of tempo, i.e., slight accelerandos and ritardandos alternating according to the musical expression, thus "robbing" the duration of some beats and adding to others. The practice of rubato originated in the late 18th century, and was first applied to the melody only, in such a way that the accompaniment was played in strict tempo while the notes of the melody were allowed to sound slightly before or after the notes of the accompaniment. Modern jazz also makes use of this device, in which the plus-and-minus deviations compensate each other so that, after two or three measures, both melody and accompaniment coincide again. Romantic music of the 19th century (Schumann, Liszt, etc.) often calls for a "full rubato," a freedom of tempo which affects the accompaniment as well as the melody.

About 1800, the term rubato was also used to indicate free modification not of tempo, but of dynamic values such as accents on weak beats. This usage possibly explains the rather mystifying indication of rubato found in several mazurkas by Chopin (also in the final movement, written in mazurka style, of his F-minor Concerto). The dancelike rhythm of these pieces seems to exclude the possibility of tempo modification, but readily admits accents on the normally unaccented second or third beats.

Rückpositiv (RUIK-po-zi-teef: G., *Rücken, back*). In older German organs, a small group of the pipes located at the back of the organist, screening him from the nave. Also (in several of Bach's organ pieces), the upper manual from which that section of pipes was played.

Rugby. A "symphonic movement" by Honegger (1928), suggested by the English game of the same name.

Rührtrommel (RUIR-trom-mel: G.). Tenor drum.

Ruins of Athens, The (G., *Die Ruinen von Athen*). Incidental music by Beethoven, op. 113, for a play by Kotzebue, produced in Budapest, 1812. It contains, among other movements, an overture and a Turkish march (the latter adapted from a Theme with Variations for piano, op. 76, composed 1809).

Rumba. A Cuban dance which, about 1930, became a popular ballroom dance in the U. S. and Europe. It is of African Negro origin and character, with strong emphasis on rhythm, complicated syncopations, and indefinite repetitions of an eight-measure theme, while melody and text are of subordinate importance. The dancing emphasizes movements of the body rather than of the feet.

Russian Easter Overture. A programmatic orchestral work by Rimski-Korsakov, op. 36, 1888. Using themes from the *obikhod*, a collection of Russian church music, it depicts the Easter celebration in vivid orchestral colors.

Russian horns. Brass instruments, in a straight or a slightly bent shape, which were used in Russia from about 1750 to 1825 in large groups, each player sounding only one tone at the required moments. Such bands were trained at the courts of wealthy noblemen, and gave most remarkable performances of harmonized music. The principle of performance is the same as that used today, for a melody only, by a group of handbell ringers (or bottle whistlers).

Russian Quartets. (1) Beethoven's String Quartets, op. 59, nos. 1–3, composed in 1807, also known as the Rasumovsky Quartets because they were commissioned by the Russian Count Rasumovsky, then ambassador to the Austrian court. A "Thème Russe" is used in the fourth movement of no. 1 and another one in the third movement of no. 2. — (2) For Haydn's Russian Quartets, see *Scherzi.*

Russlan and Ludmilla (ROOS-lahn and lood-MEE-la). Opera by Glinka (libretto by Shirkov and Bakhturin, based on a poem by Pushkin), produced in St. Petersburg, 1842.

Rustic Chivalry. See *Cavalleria rusticana.*

Ruy Blas (RUI-ee BLAHS). Overture and chorus for Victor Hugo's drama *Ruy Blas,* composed by Mendelssohn for a production at Leipzig, 1839.

S

S. Abbreviation for *°segno, sinistra* (see *M.s.*), or *°subito.*

Sacbut, sackbut (SAK-but: from old F. *saquebute,* pull-push). Old English name for the medieval trombone.

Sacre du printemps, Le (F.). See *Rite of Spring.*

Saga, En (en SAH-ga: A Saga). A symphonic poem by Sibelius, op. 9 (1892, rev. 1901), of a narrative, balladlike character, although without a definite descriptive program.

Sainete (sah-een-AY-tay: Sp.). A Spanish type of comic opera of the late 18th century, portraying scenes from everyday life and approaching the character of low comedy.

St. Anne's Fugue. Nickname of Bach's great organ fugue in E-flat, from the *°Clavierübung III* (1739), so called because its theme is similar to the beginning of an English hymn tune called *St. Anne* (usually sung to the poem beginning "O God, our help in ages past") with which Bach was not familiar, of course.

St. Anthony Variations. Same as *°Haydn Variations* (Brahms).

St. Elizabeth. See *Legend of St. Elizabeth.*

St. John Passion (Bach, Schütz). See under *Passion music.*

St. Martial, School of (sanh mar-SHAHL). A group of composers who were active at the abbey of St. Martial at Limoges (southern France), an important music center in the 9th to 12th centuries. They played a leading role in the development of *sequences and *tropes (9th-11th centuries) as well as in polyphonic music (12th century), preceding the School of Notre Dame (see *Ars antiqua; History of music;* also *Organum*).

St. Matthew Passion. Bach's last and greatest Passion, based on the story as related by St. Matthew, with free poetic insertions by Picander, first performed at St. Thomas' Church in Leipzig on Good Friday, 1729. The first performance after Bach's death, produced in Berlin by Mendelssohn in 1829, was the decisive step toward the "rediscovery" of Bach. See *Passion music.*

St. Paul. Oratorio by Mendelssohn, op. 36, produced in Dusseldorf, 1836.

St. Paul's Suite. A suite in four movements for string orchestra by Gustav Holst. It was composed in 1913 for the orchestra of St. Paul's Girls' School, where he taught. The folk songs "Dargason" and "Greensleeves" appear in the last movement.

Saite (ZEYE-te: G.). String. *Leere Saite,* open string. *Saiteninstrumente,* stringed instruments.

Salmo (It., pl. *salmi*). Psalm, psalm composition.

Salome (SAHL-o-may). Opera by R. Strauss (libretto by H. Lachmann, translated from Os-

car Wilde's play), produced in Dresden, 1905. The story outlines the unholy love of Salome (soprano), stepdaughter of Herod (tenor), for Herod's prisoner Jochanaan (John the Baptist, baritone), who repulses her. Herod, desiring Salome, gives her an unconditional promise of reward if she will dance for him. She performs the famous "Dance of the Seven Veils" and then demands the head of the prophet. Herod grants her wish, but is so repelled by her passionate fondling of the severed head that he orders her killed. Except for the passages associated with Jochanaan, the music is some of the most intensely emotional ever written.

Salomon Symphonies. Haydn's last twelve symphonies, nos. 93 to 104, written 1791–95 in London for the concerts managed by Johann Peter Salomon. They are also known as *London Symphonies,* but the name *London Symphony specifically applies to no. 104 (which, however, is also sometimes called the Salomon Symphony). Others in this group are the *Surprise (no. 94), the *Military (no. 100), the *Clock (no. 101), and the *Drum Roll (no. 103). It should be noticed that the numbering of the complete series of Haydn's symphonies is not in agreement with the numbering within this group. Thus, the nos. 94 and 104 of the complete series are nos. 3 and 7 (rather than 2 and 12) of the Salomon Symphonies.

Salón México, El (sah-LON MAY-hee-co). A descriptive piece for orchestra by Copland, composed in 1933–36, inspired by the composer's visit to Mexico in 1932. It uses several popular Mexican melodies that might be heard in the dance hall called *El Salón México*.

Saltarello (sahl-ta-REL-lo: from It., *saltare*, to jump). An Italian 16th-century dance in fast triple meter, often paired with (and following) the °passamezzo. In the 19th century the name was applied to dance music in very rapid tempo and of a violent character, somewhat similar to the °tarantella. An example occurs in the last movement of Mendelssohn's °Italian Symphony.

Saltato, saltando (It.). See *Bowing* (d).

Salve regina (sahl-vay ree-JEYE-na: L., Hail, O Queen). A celebrated chant in praise of the Virgin Mary (see under *Antiphon*). The text has often been used for elaborate compositions, first by Dunstable and Ockeghem (15th century), more recently by Pergolesi (five compositions), Schubert, and Fauré.

Salzburg Festivals. Summer musical festivals founded at Salzburg, Austria (Mozart's birthplace), in 1920 by Max Reinhardt, R. Strauss, and others. Dramatic music, church music, chamber music, etc., of old and new composers is performed, with prominence given to the works of Mozart.

Samba. A Brazilian dance in duple meter, derived from the maxixe (the predecessor of the °tango). It became popular in the United States in 1939.

Samson and Delilah (F., *Samson et Dalila*). Opera by Saint-Saëns (libretto by F. Lemaire), produced in Weimar, 1877. It is based on the story from the Scriptures, to which the music provides a background of lush oriental colors.

Sanctus (SAHNK-toos). The fourth item of the Ordinary of the °Mass.

Saraband (SAR-a-band: F., G., *Sarabande*). A 17th- and 18th-century dance in slow triple meter and of a dignified character, usually without upbeat and frequently with an accent on the second beat of the measure. It occurs as the third movement of the Baroque °suite. The saraband appeared in Spain during the 16th century, probably coming from the Orient. At that time it was described and attacked by several writers (e.g., Cervantes) as being wild and lascivious. However, no trace of this character is suggested by the surviving examples, dating from 1600 on.

Sardana (sar-DAH-na: Sp.). The national dance of Catalonia (northeastern Spain), usually in quick 6/8 meter and danced in a circle to the music of the °pipe and tabor.

Sarrusophone (sa-ROOZ-o-fon). A type of instrument with a double-reed mouthpiece and a metal pipe, instead of the wooden pipe of the oboe family, invented in 1856 by the French bandmaster Sarrus. Various sizes, closely corresponding to those of the saxophone group, have been used in military bands, but only one of these (the contrabass size in C) has occasionally been used in French orchestral scores, to replace the contrabassoon.

Sassofono (sah-SO-fo-no: It.). Saxophone.

S. A. T. B. On title pages of vocal scores, abbreviations for soprano, alto (i.e., contralto), tenor, bass.

Satz (zahts: G., sentence). Movement of a sonata, symphony, etc.

Saudade (sow-DAH-da: Portuguese, longing, nostalgia). A type of Brazilian dancing song of a nostalgic, melancholy character. It has been introduced into art music by Villa-Lobos and Milhaud (*Saudades do Brazil*).

Saul. Oratorio by Handel, produced in London, 1739.

Sautillé (F., springing). See *Bowing* (d).

Saxhorn. See under *Brass instruments*, II.

Saxophone. A type of instrument, invented about 1840 by Adolphe Sax of Paris, which combines features of various other instruments: made of metal (as in brass instruments), having a single reed (as in clarinets), having a conical bore (as in oboes). The complete family of saxophones numbers six sizes, alternately pitched in E-flat and B-flat, of which the *alto* (E-flat, range starting from e♭) and the *tenor* (B-flat, range

starting from B♭) are the most common. They are regularly used in dance bands and often in military or marching bands. The alto saxophone has occasionally been used in symphonic orchestras, particularly by French composers (Bizet, Delibes, Saint-Saëns, d'Indy, Ravel). R. Strauss scored for a quartet of saxophones in his *Domestic Symphony. See illustration.

Saxophone

The sound of the saxophone is extremely fluid. Being intermediate between the timbres of wood and brass, it may pass from the softness of the flute to the broad, mellow tone of the cello to the metallic strength of the cornet. It blends well with either the wood winds or the brass instruments.

Sax tuba. See under *Brass instruments*, II.

Scala, La (SKAH-lah: It.). Short for *Teatro alla Scala*, the great opera house of Milan

(Italy), so called because it was erected, in 1778, at the site of the church Santa Maria alla Scala (St. Mary's by the Stairs).

Scala enigmatica (It.). See *Enigmatic scale*.

Scale (from L. *scala*, ladder). A succession of notes, normally either a whole tone or a half tone apart, arranged in ascending or descending order. The basic scales of most music heard today are the *major* and the *minor* scales, both consisting of seven different notes forming five whole tones (w) and two half tones (h), the former in the arrangement w w h w w w h, the latter, w h w w h w w. Starting from c, the tones of the major scale (C major) are: c d e f g a b c', those of the minor (C minor), c d eb f g ab bb c' (brackets indicate half tones).

as descending, combines the flat sixth (ab) with the natural seventh (b). This is called *harmonic minor* because it includes the tones contained in the main harmonies of the minor key (c-eb-g; g-b-d'; f-ab-c').

A scale is identified by the name of the first note on which it starts, for example, D major scale: d e f# g a b c# d'; B-flat minor scale: Bb c db eb f gb ab bb. All of the tones required by these scales are found in the *chromatic* scale, consisting of twelve different tones, all at the distance of a half tone. A chromatic scale, therefore, represents a "ladder" with the steps all having equal distance, and this scale can be conveniently used for the schematic representation of all the other scales, major and minor, in all the keys, *pentatonic scale, *whole-tone scale, *church modes, etc., as shown below:

	1	2	3	4	5	6	7	8	9	10	11	12	13	(= 1)
Chromatic:	c	c#	d	d#	e	f	f#	g	g#	a	a#	b	c'	
Major:	c		d		e	f		g		a		b	c'	
Minor														
natural:	c		d	eb		f		g	ab		bb		c'	
melodic														
(ascending):	c		d	eb		f		g		a		b	c'	
(descending):	c		d	eb		f		g	ab		bb		c'	
harmonic:	c		d	eb		f		g	ab			b	c'	
Pentatonic:	c		d		e			g		a			c'	
Whole-tone:	c		d		e		f#		g#		a#		c'	
Lydian:	c		d		e		f#	g		a		b	c'	

The minor scale given above is the *natural minor*. In actual melodic usage the sixth and seventh tones of the minor scale are raised in an ascending motion (. . . g a b c'), but retained in the descending scale (c' bb ab g . . .). Since this minor scale results from melodic considerations (upward and downward movement), it is called *melodic minor*. There exists a third type of scale which, ascending as well

Using the figures 1 to 13 for the chromatic scale, each scale can be identified by a definite succession of numbers, and these are useful particularly for the determination of scale formation at all pitches. For example, the major scale is characterized by 1 3 5 6 8 10 12 13 (= 1), and the same figures used with another starting point (e.g., f# = 1) give the correct tones of the desired scale (F-sharp major).

Scale, scaling. In organ building, a term used to indicate the ratio of length to width of a pipe. All pipes of the same *rank have the same scale, which, however, differs from one rank to another. Wide scaling (length about 10 to 15 times the width) gives a soft sound with few overtones (Principal flue stops), while narrow scaling (length about 20 to 24 times the width) makes the sound thin, sharp, and rich in overtones (Gamba, Violin, etc.).

Scale degrees. Functional and numerical (Roman numerals) designations for the notes of a scale, used particularly in *harmonic analysis to denote the various tones of the scale as used as the basis of chords. These designations are: tonic (I), supertonic (II), mediant (III), subdominant (IV), dominant (V), submediant or superdominant (VI), leading tone or subtonic (VII). The most important ones are the *tonic, *dominant, and *subdominant (see, e.g., under *Cadence*).

Scaramouche (skar-a-MOOSH). A suite of three pieces for two pianofortes derived (1939) by Milhaud from his incidental music to *Le Médecin volant*, produced at the Théâtre Scaramouche in Paris, 1937.

Scat singing. A style of singing introduced into jazz about 1930 (Cab Calloway), characterized by the interpolation of nonsense syllables and other peculiar vocal effects, expressing an attitude of uninhibited exuberance.

Scenario (se-NAYR-ree-o). An outline of an opera, indicating plot, main characters, scenes, entrances and exits of singers, etc.

Schauspieldirektor, Der (G.). See *Impresario*.

Scheherezade (she-hayr-e-ZAHD). A symphonic suite by Rimski-Korsakov, op. 35 (1888), based on some tales from the *Arabian Nights* and named after the woman who tells the stories. In 1910 it was presented in Paris as a ballet, produced by the Russian Ballet (Fokine). The lush and sensuous atmosphere of Oriental tales is successfully captured in the music, which is notable particularly for its rich orchestration. See also *Shéhérazade* (Ravel).

Schellen (SHEL-len: G.). Little bells played with a hammer.

Schellentrommel (SHEL-len-TROM-mel: G.). Tambourine.

Schenker System. A method of musical analysis introduced by Heinrich Schenker (1868–1935) in order to show the "principles which govern the creation and foundation of all music." Schenker's point of departure is "nature," which supplies the raw materials of music, i.e., the *overtone series (C-c-g-c'-e'-g'). From this is derived the major triad as well as all intervals, scales, and basic structures found in music. By successive processes of reduction Schenker's analysis leads from the actual composition, the "foreground," over a "middle ground" to the "background," which he calls *Ursatz* (primordial or fundamental structure). The middle ground, according to Schenker and his disciples, enables one to distinguish the work of a great master from that of a lesser talent. Opinions as to the merits of the Schenker System are divided.

Scherzi, Gli (lyee SKAYR-tzee: It.). Nickname of Haydn's six string quartets, op. 33, so called because the minuets bear the inscription "Scherzo" or "Scherzando" and, accordingly, are faster than the usual minuets of the period (see under *Scherzo*). They are also called, for unknown reasons, Russian Quartets or Maiden Quartets (G., *Jungfern-Quartette*).

Scherzo (SKAYR-tzo: It., joke, humor). (1) A movement, usually the third one, of sonatas, symphonies, string quartets, or other compositions written in the form of the *sonata (except the *concerto, in which the scherzo is usually missing). It was tentatively introduced by Haydn, particularly in his string quartets *Gli *Scherzi*, and definitely adopted by Beethoven to replace the *minuet, from which it differs mainly in its faster tempo, varying from allegretto to a full presto, always in triple meter. Other characteristic traits are a vigorous rhythmic element, strongly marked accents, often a certain abruptness of thought involving elements of surprise, and a capricious character ranging from the playful to the sinister. The great masters of the true scherzo are Beethoven, Schubert, and Bruckner. The form of the scherzo is the same as that of the minuet, i.e., Scherzo-Trio-

Scherzo, with each section in rounded *binary form. Chopin's four Scherzos (also one by Brahms) for piano are independent compositions of considerable extension generally modeled after Beethoven's scherzos, in rapid triple meter and with an alternation of highly dramatic and somewhat somber episodes (in the scherzo) with others of a more lyrical nature (trio).

Schicksalslied (SHIK-zahls-leet: Song of Destiny). A setting by Brahms for chorus and orchestra, op. 54 (1871), of a poem from Hölderlin's *Hyperion.*

Schlaginstrumente, Schlagzeug (SHLAHG - in - stroo - men - te, SHLAHG-tzoyg: G.). Percussion instruments.

Schlummerlied (SHLUM-erleet: G.). Slumber song.

Schmetternd (SHMET-ternd: G.). Same as *cuivré* (see under *Horn*).

Schnarre (SHNAHR-re: G.). Rattle. *Schnarrtrommel*, snare drum.

Schneller (SHNEL-ler: G.). Same as inverted mordent (see under *Mordent*).

Schöne Müllerin, Die (SHEUne MUIL-le-rin: The Fair Maid of the Mill). A cycle of twenty songs by Schubert, op. 25, composed in 1823 after poems by Wilhelm Müller.

Schübler Chorales (SHUI-bler kor-ALZ). A collection of six chorale preludes by Bach, published about 1747 by Schübler.

They are all arias from cantatas arranged for the organ.

Schwanda the Bagpiper (SHVAHN-da). Folk opera in two acts by Jaromir Weinberger, produced in Prague, 1927. The story deals with a marvelous bagpipe player whose tunes can make the most unfortunate situations come out well. His greatest triumph takes place in Hell where his gay playing induces the Devil to allow Schwanda to return to the world. The opera, although translated into more than ten languages, is little known in America except for two excerpts, the Polka and the Fugue, which are played frequently in orchestral concerts.

Schwanendreher, Der (der SHVAH-nen-dray-er). A concerto by Hindemith for viola and small orchestra (the only strings used are cellos and basses), composed in 1935. The music is a skillful elaboration of four old German songs, in three movements: I. A setting of "Zwischen Berg und tiefem Tal" ('Twixt Hill and Deep Dale; c. 1500); II. An introduction on "Nun laube, Lindlein, laube" (Burst forth in leaves, little linden; 16th century) and a fugato on "Der Gutzgauch auf dem Zaune sass" (The cuckoo sat upon the fence; by Lemlin, c. 1520); III. A set of variations on "Seid ihr nicht der Schwanendreher?" (Are you not the *Schwanendreher?* This word, literally "swan turner," may refer to an organ grinder who had a swan turning on the top of his instrument.).

Schwanengesang (SHVAH-nen-ge-ZAHNG; G., swan song).

Schubert's last songs (composed in 1828), on seven poems by Rellstab, six by Heine, and one by Seidl, published posthumously by Haslinger (Vienna), who chose that title in reference to Schubert's death. They are often performed as a song cycle, although they do not properly fall under that category.

Schwellwerk (SHVEL-vayrk: G.). Swell (of the organ).

Scordatura (skor-dah-TOO-ra: It., off-tuning). Abnormal tuning of a violin, lute, etc., for the purpose of obtaining unusual chords or additional notes, facilitating difficult passages, or changing the tone color. It was widely used in the 17th century (particularly by Heinrich Biber) and occasionally by Bach and later composers. In more recent violin music, the G-string is sometimes lowered to F♯ or F in order to increase the compass, or raised to A in order to obtain a more brilliant sound.

Score. The notation (in printed or manuscript form) showing all the parts of an ensemble (orchestra, band, etc.), with a separate staff for each part (sometimes for two parts, e.g., Flute I and II), and with simultaneously sounded notes aligned vertically. The score is used by the conductor, while the performers use copies of the individual parts. A *full score* (for symphonies, etc.) is one containing all the parts separately indicated; a *vocal score* (for operas, oratorios, etc.) shows the vocal parts separately indicated but combines the instrumental parts into an arrangement for piano; a *piano score* is the arrangement of an orchestral or chamber music composition for piano alone. The normal arrangement of the parts in an orchestral score is explained under °orchestral score.

Score reading is the facility of grasping the essential details (harmony, leading melodies, etc.) of a score and reproducing them on the piano. This task, not easy in itself, is rendered still more difficult by the practice of using, for some instruments, special clefs (alto clef, tenor clef) and transposed notation (see *Transposing instruments*).

Scoring. The art and process of making an orchestral score on the basis of a sketch (°short score). The term is also used in a critical sense ("good scoring for flutes," etc.).

Scotch snap. See under *Dotted note.*

Scotch (Scottish) Symphony. Mendelssohn's Symphony no. 3, in A minor, op. 56, inspired by a visit to Scotland in 1829. It was begun in Italy in 1830 and finished in Berlin in 1842.

S. C. T. B. Short for soprano, contralto, tenor, bass (in a vocal score).

Seasons, The. Oratorio by Haydn, composed 1798–1801, on a German libretto (original title: *Die Jahreszeiten*) by G. van Swieten, based on an English poem by Thomson. Its four parts portray spring, summer, fall, and winter. Although its subject is not strictly religious, as is normally the case in oratorios, it is treated with such a profound feeling of devotional gratitude that it fully deserves the designation Oratorio which Haydn gave to this work.

Sea Symphony. Vaughan Williams' Symphony no. 1 (1910), for solo voices, chorus, and orchestra.

Secco (SEK-ko: It., dry). See under *Recitative.*

Second. See under *Intervals.*

Secondary dominant. In harmonic analysis, the dominant of a scale degree other than the tonic, usually indicated by a symbol such as V of V, V of II, V of III, etc., or V/V, V/II, V/III, etc.

Seconda volta. See under *Prima volta.*

Segno (SAY-nyo: It., sign). A sign in the form of :S: which is used to indicate the beginning or the end of a section to be repeated. In the former case, the remark *Dal segno, Dal S.,* or *D. S.* (from the sign) appears at the end of the section; in the latter case, *Al segno* (to the sign), *Sin' al segno* (until the sign) or *Fin' al segno* (end at the sign) is stated. See also under *Da capo.*

Segue (SAY-gway: It., follows). Direction to continue with the subsequent movement or section without a pause (*Segue l'aria, Segue la coda*). It is also used as a direction to continue in the same manner, e.g., with a certain pattern of broken chords written out fully only at the beginning (see under *Abbreviations*, Fig. 1).

Seguidilla (say-gee-DEEL-ya: Sp.). A national dance from Andalusia (southern Spain) in fast triple meter, similar to the *bolero, but quicker. It is danced to the accompaniment of guitars and castanets. Although Bizet uses the term for a song in the first act of *Carmen*, it is not a representative example of the type.

Semi- (L., half). For *semibreve, semiquaver*, see under *Notes and rests. Semichorus*, a part of the chorus, usually less than one half, used for special purposes of contrast or variety of color.

Semitone. Same as half tone (see under *Intervals*).

Sempre (SEM-pray: It.). Always, e.g., *sempre legato*, always legato.

Sennet (SEN-et). In the plays of Elizabethan dramatists, a direction calling for a fanfare to be played. The term has been explained as a variant of "sonata" (sounding piece) or of "signet" (sign). See *Tucket*.

Senza (SEN-tza: It.). Without. *Senza tempo, senza misura*, without strict tempo or meter. For *senza sordini*, see under *Sordini*.

Septet. Chamber music for seven players, usually strings and winds mixed. Also a composition for seven singers, e.g., in an opera.

Septimole, septuplet. A group of seven notes to be played in the time of four or six.

Septuor (SEP-tui-or: F.). Septet.

Sequence. (1) In musical composition, the repetition of a short figure in one and the same voice part(s) at different pitches, usually at the second above or below. A sequence is called *melodic* if the repetition takes place in the melody alone, *harmonic* if it affects all the parts. If the sequence progresses within a given scale or key (without accidentals or modulation), it is called *tonal*. In this case the repeats involve modifications of intervals, e.g., from a major to a minor third, or from a perfect to a diminished fifth (see Fig. 106a). If, on the other hand, the intervals are strictly imitated, resulting in changes of key, the sequence is called *real* (Fig. 106b; see also *Tonal and real*). Most sequences

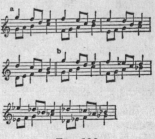

Fig. 106

found in compositions belong to a mixed type, called *modulatory* or *chromatic*. See also *Rosalia*. — (2) In Gregorian chant, the sequence is a type of chant which developed in the 9th century, as an addition to the Alleluia (Alleluia trope; see *Trope*). It consists of an extended, freely poetic text, usually cast in the form of long paired lines (except for the first and last line, which are single) with identical music for the two lines of each pair: a b b c c d d . . . g g h. Paired lines have the same number of syllables (the musical style is strictly syllabic), but there is great variation in length from one pair to another, so that, for example, b may have 10 syllables while c has 23, etc. In the 12th century this free sequence was replaced by the rhymed sequence (Adam of St. Victor) whose text is in regular versification with rhymes, and whose music consists entirely of repeated sections: a a b b c c. . . . From the 9th to the 16th century, there accrued a vast number of sequences, nearly all of which were abolished by the *Council of Trent (1545–63). Only five are used today: the Easter Sequence, *Victimae paschali laudes* by Wipo (11th century, the only one of the early type); the "Golden Sequence," *Veni sancte spiritus* for Whitsunday; *Lauda Sion* for Corpus Christi; *Stabat mater* for the Feast of Seven Dolours; *Dies Irae* for the *Requiem Mass.

Serenade. Evening music, properly for outdoor performance, e.g., a lover's wooing song, or instrumental music presented as an homage. The latter type was cultivated by Mozart, Haydn, Beethoven, and others, the most famous examples being Mozart's *Haffner Serenade and *Eine *Kleine Nachtmusik*. In form

and style the serenade is similar to the *divertimento.

Series. See under *Twelve-tone technique*.

Serious Songs (Brahms). See *Vier ernste Gesänge*.

Serpent. An obsolete wind instrument consisting of a long leather-covered wooden tube shaped like a serpent, with a cupped mouthpiece similar to that of modern brass instruments. It was the bass of a family known as *cornetts* (16th century; not to be confused with the modern cornet), and the only one to survive as late as 1850. It was often used in early French church music — hence the strange name *church serpent* — and is prescribed in scores by Rossini, Mendelssohn, Wagner (*Rienzi*, 1842), and Verdi (*Sicilian Vespers*, 1855).

Serva padrona, La (SAYR-va pah-DRO-na: The Maid as Mistress). A short comic opera in two acts by Pergolesi, produced in Naples, 1733, as an *intermezzo between the three acts of his serious opera, *Il Prigioniero superbo* (The Haughty Prisoner). It is a delightful miniature, employing only three characters: the elderly and wealthy bachelor Uberto (bass), his maid Serpina (soprano), who wants to become the mistress of the house, and his servant Vespone (mute role), who is cleverly employed by Serpina to force Uberto into marriage. *La Serva padrona* is an important landmark not only in the field of opera (see *Comic opera; War of the Buffoons*), but also in the general development of musical style, anticipating some practices of the later 18th century.

Service. In the Anglican (Episcopal) church, the musical setting of the canticles and certain other items (Kyrie, Sanctus, Creed, etc.), as distinct from the harmonized plainsong (see *Anglican chant*) and from *anthems. A *Full Service* consists of three divisions; Morning Service, Evening Service, and Communion. A wealth of Service music was written in the 16th century (after the Reformation) by Tallis, Byrd, Weelkes, and others. After a long period of stagnation or mediocrity, a turn for the better occurred in the 19th century, under Thomas A. Walmisley (1814–1856) and Samuel Sebastian Wesley (1810–1876). Several 20th-century composers (e.g., Vaughan Williams) have composed services in a more contemporary idiom.

Seven Words of the Savior on the Cross, The. A composition (originally for orchestra) by Haydn, commissioned in 1785 by the Bishop of Cadiz (Spain) and consisting of seven slow movements (called "Sonatas") which were played in the cathedral of Cadiz during Lent, one after the recitation of each of the "Seven Last Words" of Christ. In 1787 Haydn arranged the work for string quartet (Quartets, op. 51, nos. 1–7) and later for pianoforte. There also exists a choral version, with the text of the "Words" underlaid, probably by Haydn's brother, Michael. For a composition of the Scriptural text by Schütz, see under *Passion music.*

Seventh. See under *Intervals.*

Seventh chord. See under *Chords.*

Sextet. Chamber music for six performers, in various combinations, e.g., two violins, two violas, and two cellos (Brahms, op. 36), or string quartet and two winds, etc. Also a vocal composition for six singers (e.g., in operas).

Sextolet, sextuplet. A group of six notes played in the time of four. Various methods of writing are used, as shown in Fig. 107.

Fig. 107

Sf. Abbreviation for *sforzando, sforzato.*

Sforzando, sforzato (sfor-TZAHN-do, sfor-TSAH-to: It.). Abbreviated *sf* or *sfz*. Forcing, forced, i.e., with a strong accent on a single note or chord. *Sfp* means *sforzato* followed immediately by *piano.*

Sfp, sfz. See under *Sforzando.*

Shake. Older name for the trill.

Shanty (properly *chanty, chantey*, from *chant*). Working songs of English and American sailors, sung when engaged in pulling the ropes or in other work calling for concerted effort. Well-known examples are "The Drunken Sailor," "The Banks of Sacramento," and "The Rio Grande."

Shape note. See under *Fasola.*

Sharp. See under *Accidentals.*

Shawm. An earlier type of oboe, used before 1700.

Shéhérazade (shay-hayr-a-ZAHD). A song cycle by Ravel (poems by T. Klingsor, inspired by the *Arabian Nights*), composed in 1903 and containing three songs: "Asie" (Asia), "La Flûte enchantée" (The Enchanted Flute), and "L'Indifférente" (The Indifferent One). See also *Scheherezade* (Rimski-Korsakov).

Shift. The change of *position in the playing of violins, etc., or of the trombone.

Shimmy. A type of dance music which was popular in America after World War I. It was in the character of a fast fox trot, danced with shaking movements of the shoulders or of the entire body. Hindemith was one of several German composers who transferred the shimmy into the realm of art music, in his *Suite 1922.*

Shofar (SHO-far). An ancient Jewish instrument, dating back to Biblical times, made of a ram's horn. The instrument has been used for more than three thousand years at the celebration of the New Year. It produces two crude and awe-inspiring sounds, roughly corresponding to the second and third harmonics (see *Acoustics*, 4), i.e., about a fifth apart.

Short score. A preliminary score, with musical ideas sketched on a few staffs, to be elaborated later into a full score.

Si. See under *Pitch names; Solmization.*

Siciliano (It.). See under *Pastorale.*

Side drum. See *Drums* (2).

Side-holes. On wood winds, same as *finger holes.

Siegfried (G.). See under *Ring of the Nibelung.*

Siegfried Idyll (ZEEG-freed). A composition for small orchestra by Wagner, composed in 1870 and first performed in his house at Triebschen (hence also called *Triebschen Idyll*) on the birthday of his wife, Cosima. The title refers to their son, Siegfried, then just over one year old. It is based on themes from Wagner's opera *Siegfried,* but also includes the cradle song "Schlaf, Kindchen, schlaf" (Sleep, baby, sleep).

Sight reading (singing). The ability to read or perform music at first sight, i.e., without preparatory study of the composition. Such a rendition puts entirely different demands on the performer than a carefully prepared performance given in a recital. A finished result is not expected, the aim being to obtain or to convey a satisfactory general impression of the music. An ability of playing from sight is an invaluable asset to music students and amateurs, because it opens to them a wide field of music literature beyond the necessarily limited "repertory" of pieces they have carefully studied. Unfortunately, music teachers generally do not realize the importance of sight reading. The problems of sight reading are somewhat different in the various fields of performance. In singing and in playing of melody instruments (violin, clarinet, etc.) the main requirement is a thorough acquaintance with the elements of melody (intervals) and rhythm, and with their notation. In recent years this basic study has been emphasized in a number of music schools (where it is sometimes called °solfeggio). In piano playing, the difficulties are considerably greater, owing to the greater complexity of the music. The greatest obstacle to sight reading on the piano is the customary emphasis on memorization of a few selections. This causes the pianist to rely on his memory and to control his fingers by the eye, while in sight reading his eyes must remain fixed on the music page. Proficiency in sight reading at the keyboard depends, therefore, on the player's ability to guide his fingers by the sense of touch. This feeling of tactile security can be developed by simple exercises such as playing various intervals and simple chords by touch, without looking at the keyboard, in much the same way that typists develop skill.

Signature. Signs placed at the beginning of the composition, indicating the key (°key signature) and the meter (°time signature).

Similar motion. See under *Motion.*

Simile (SEE-mee-lay: It.). Indication to continue "in a similar manner," e.g., with the same kind of bowing, phrasing, etc.

Sin' al fine, sin' al segno (seen ahl FEE-nay, seen ahl SAY-nyo: It.). Until the end, until the sign. Direction indicating repeat of a previous section to a place marked *Fine* or by the sign :S: (see under *Segno*).

Sincopas. See *Cinquepace.*

Sinfonia (seen-fo-NEE-a: It.). (1) Symphony. — (2) A name chosen by Bach, for an unknown reason, as the title of his Three-Part °Inventions. — (3) In Baroque music (1600–1750), name for orchestral pieces of various kinds, particularly the introductions (overtures) of operas. See under *Overture* (Italian). In his Partita no. 2, Bach transferred the orchestral Sinfonia to the harpsichord.

Sinfonia concertante (seen-fo-NEE-a con-chayr-TAHN-tay: It.). A term used by Mozart and others for a symphony with one or more solo instruments. The most famous example is Mozart's Sinfonia Concertante in E-flat for violin, viola, and orchestra (K. 364), composed in 1779.

Sinfonietta (sin-fo-nee-ET-ta: It.). A short symphony, usually for a small orchestra.

Sinfonische Dichtung (sin-FO-ni-she DEEKH-toong: G.). Symphonic poem.

Singspiel (ZING-shpeel: G.). A popular type of 18th-century German comic opera, with spoken dialogue and simple folk-like tunes, similar to the English °ballad opera from which it developed. The earliest examples, set to music by Johann Standfuss (c. 1750), were based on German translations of Coffey's ballad operas (e.g., *The Devil to Pay*; G., *Der Teufel ist los*). The most important composers were Johann Adam Hiller (1728–1804) in Leipzig, Georg Benda (1722–1795) in Berlin, and Carl Dittersdorf (1739–1799) in Vienna. Mozart's *Abduction* may be said to represent the artistic culmination of this type, of which his *Bastien and Bastienne* is an earlier and simpler example of great charm.

Sinistra (It.). Left [hand].

Sinkapace, sink-a-pace. See *Cinquepace*.

Sistine Choir (Chapel). The papal choir of thirty-two singers who provide music for the services in which the Pope officiates in person. It developed from the ancient *Schola cantorum*, organized by St. Gregory about 600, and received its present name from the *Cappella Sistina*, the chapel built by Pope Sixtus IV, 1471–84.

Sistrum. An ancient Egyptian rattle used especially in the worship of the goddess Isis. It consisted of a pear-shaped metal frame attached to a handle and hung with loose metal plates.

Six, Les (lay SEES: The Six). A name applied in 1920 to a group of six French composers: Louis Durey, Arthur Honegger, Darius Milhaud, Germaine Tailleferre, Georges Auric, and François Poulenc, who about 1916 formed a loose association on the basis of their common attachment to the aesthetic ideals championed by Eric Satie. Although their individual styles differed considerably, they shared an opposition to the vagueness of *impressionism and an allegiance to simplicity, clarity, and other aspects of the then-dawning *neoclassicism. See *Twentieth-century music*. They were originally called *Les Nouveaux Jeunes* (The New Youth).

Six-four chord. See under *Chords*.

Sixteen-foot. See under *Foot*.

Sixth. See under *Intervals*.

Sixth chord. See under *Chords; Fauxbourdon*.

Skolie (SKO-lye: G., from Swedish *skol*, a drinking salutation). Name used by Schubert for a drinking song.

Skyscrapers. Ballet by John Alden Carpenter (choreography by H. Kröller), produced in Monte Carlo, 1925 (Russian Ballet); New York, 1926.

Sleeping Beauty, The. Ballet by Tchaikovsky (choreography by M. Petipa), produced in St. Petersburg (now Leningrad), 1890. It is based on the familiar fairy tale.

Slentando (zlen-TAHN-do: It.). Slowing up, *rallentando*.

Slide. (1) In violin playing, a technique of passing quickly from one note to another by moving the same finger along the string. — (2) The movable portion of the *trombone. — (3) An ornament like the *appoggiatura, but including two grace notes, for example, c and d leading up to e.

Slide trumpet. See *Tromba da tirarsi.*

Slur. An arching line drawn over a group of notes to indicate that they should be played legato. In connection with dots placed over the single notes it indicates *portato. A slur connecting two successive notes of equal pitch is properly called a *tie.

Snare drum. See *Drums* (2).

Soft pedal. See under *Pianoforte.*

Soggetto (so-JET-to: It.). Subject, fugal theme.

Soir, Le (swahr: The Evening). See under *Matin.*

Sol. See under *Pitch names; Solmization.*

Soldier's Tale, The. See *Histoire du soldat.*

Solesmes method (so-LEM). A method of singing Gregorian chant, named after the Benedictine monks of Solesmes (a village near Le Mans in France), who were primarily responsible for the restoration of the old tradition of the chant. On the basis of early manuscripts (9th to 12th centuries) they prepared a carefully collated edition of Gregorian chant which was officially adopted in 1904 under the name of *Vatican Edition* (see also *Motu proprio*), supplanting the corrupt versions that had been used since the

16th century. They also worked out definite rules (Solesmes method) for the singing of the chants.

Sol-fa. See *Tonic Sol-fa.*

Solfeggio (sol-FEJ-o: It.), **solfège** (sol-FEZH: F.). (1) Vocal exercises sung to syllables of *solmization, e.g., sol-fa (hence the name *solfaggio, solfeggio*), each tone receiving its proper pitch name. A similar exercise sung throughout to one vowel (a—, o—, etc.) is more properly called *vocalise.* The true solfeggio method combines technical training with musical instruction, since the student is required to recognize the pitches and intervals quickly. — (2) The term has sometimes been adopted to denote general instruction in all the fundamentals of music, i.e., the study of pitches, intervals, rhythm, notation, harmony, etc. See *Ear training.*

Soli (It.). See under *Solo.*

Solmization (sol-mi-ZAY-shun: from *sol-mi*). A system of designating the degrees of the scale by syllables rather than by letters. The syllables mostly used today are: do (doh), re (ray), mi (me), fa (fah), sol (soh), la (lah), si (te) — the syllables in parentheses are those used in *Tonic Sol-fa. There are two methods of applying them to the scale degrees, known as *fixed do* and *movable do.* In the fixed-do system, the syllables are invariably applied to the notes of the C-major scale: do = c, re = d, mi = e, etc. In the movable-do system, the syllables can be moved to any scale position, e.g., in D major: do = d; re = e, mi = f♯, etc. The fixed-do method is used in Italy and France (see under *Pitch names*), the other in the English Tonic Sol-fa system.

The inventor of solmization was Guido of Arezzo (c. 995–1050), who used the six syllables *ut re mi fa sol la* as partly movable names, to be located on three degrees of the diatonic (C major) scale, i.e., on G (G A B c d e), on c (c d e f g a), on f (f g a b♭ c′ d′). The reason for this procedure is that in each of these six-note segments (hexachords) there is a half tone between the third and fourth degrees which, therefore, is always represented by *mi-fa*. Guido derived his syllables from an 8th-century hymn to St. John the Baptist, the melody of which has six lines starting successively on c, d, e, f, g, and a:

c ...
Ut quant laxis
d ...
Re-sonare fibris
e ...
Mi-ra gestorum

f ...
Fa-muli tuorum
g ...
Sol-ve polluti
a ...
La-bii reatum, Sancte Johanne

The syllable *si*, adopted later, was derived from the initials of *Sancte Johanne*. See also *Hexachord*.

Solo (It., alone). (1) Designation for pieces executed by one performer (soloist), e.g., *piano solo*; also by two or more performers if one is featured, e.g., *violin solo* with piano accompaniment. — (2) In orchestral scores the term denotes passages to be performed by one player, particularly the soloist of a con-

certo, or a group of soloists (*soli*).

Solo Organ. See under *Organ*.

Solovox. An *electrophonic instrument, consisting of a small keyboard of three octaves, which is mounted just below the right-hand end of a piano keyboard, and which produces sounds electronically by means of a vacuum tube oscillator, with controls affording a considerable variety of tone color. The performer plays the melody on the Solovox with the right hand, the accompaniment on the piano keyboard with the left hand.

Soltanto (sol-TAHN-to: It.). But only, for example, *allegro soltanto moderato*, fast, but only with moderation.

Sombrero de tres picos, El (Sp.). See *Three-Cornered Hat*.

Sonata (so-NAH-ta: It., from *sonare*, to sound). The most important form of instrumental music from the Baroque period to the present. It usually consists of four independent pieces called *movements*, each of which follows certain conventions of character and structure. Two different types of sonata must be distinguished: the *Classical sonata*, which became fully established about 1760 (Haydn, Mozart, and their predecessors), and the *Baroque sonata*, from about 1660 to 1760 (Vivaldi, Bach, Handel).

I. *The Classical Sonata.* The normal scheme of movements is as follows:

Movement	Character	Form
1. Allegro (sometimes with a slow introduction)	fast, usually dramatic, exciting	sonata form
2. Adagio (andante, largo, lento)	slow, lyrical or intensely emotional	sonata form ternary form binary form variations
3. Minuet, scherzo	dancelike, usually in triple meter; minuet in moderate speed, scherzo very fast. Also other dance types (waltz).	ternary form (see under *Minuet*)
4. Allegro (presto)	fast or very fast, energetic conclusion	sonata form rondo

Sonatas are written for piano (*piano sonata*) or for a solo instrument with piano accompaniment (*violin sonata, cello sonata,* etc.). It must be noted, however, that practically all the features of the sonata are also found in other types of contemporary instrumental music, namely the *symphony*, the various species of chamber music (*string quartet, trio, quintet,* etc.), and, with certain modifications, the *concerto*. The difference is mainly one of the medium of performance, so that the symphony may be called a "sonata for orchestra," the string quartet a "sonata for four strings," the concerto a "sonata for a soloist plus orchestra," etc. Naturally, this difference entails considerable variation in treatment and style, but does not, as a rule, affect the basic scheme. The piano sonatas by Haydn and Mozart have only three movements, one of the two inner movements (or, in Haydn, occasionally the final one) being omitted. Their string quartets and symphonies, however, show the full form which was adopted by Beethoven and his successors for all the various types of sonata (except for the concerto, which usually has no scherzo or minuet). Occasionally the position of the two inner movements is reversed, e.g., in Beethoven's *Hammerklavier Sonata or in his Symphony no. 9 (*Choral Symphony). Tchaikovsky, in his *Pathétique Symphony, placed the slow movement at the end. Other notable modifications are found in Beethoven's *Moonlight Sonata, which begins with the slow movement, and his last piano sonata, op. 111, which consists of Introduction, Allegro, and Adagio. Later in the 19th century Liszt used the term for a long rhapsodic, one-movement piano piece. On the whole, however, the form has remained fairly stable to the present day (Stravinsky, Hindemith, Bartok).

Regarding the internal structures of the individual movements, the above indications apply chiefly to the period from Haydn and Mozart to Brahms, Bruckner, and Tchaikovsky; later composers (Mahler, Sibelius, and others), often treat the movements more freely. See the individual entries, especially *sonata form. Concerning keys, the first and the last movements are in the key of the composition itself, as indicated in titles such as Symphony in D major, while the slow movement is in another key. The minuet or scherzo, if present, usually is in the same key as the first and last movements. For possible thematic relationship between the various movements, see under Cyclic.

II. The Baroque Sonata. The Baroque sonata was written mostly for small ensembles, the most important type of which was the *trio sonata. During the last half of the 17th century there developed, under Torelli (1658–1709) and Corelli (1653–1713), two standard forms of the Baroque sonata, the sonata da chiesa (church sonata) and the sonata da camera (chamber sonata). The former usually has four movements, Slow-Fast-Slow-Fast, while the latter has mostly dancelike movements taken over from the suite, e.g., Prelude-Allemande-Courante-Saraband-Gigue (or Gavotte).

Bach used the sonata da chiesa form in his six Sonatas for Violin and Harpsichord and in the three Sonatas for Violin Solo, while the sonata da camera (practically identical with a suite) is represented by his three Partitas for Violin Solo and six Suites for Violoncello Solo. Numerous examples of both types exist also in the works of Handel. Johann Kuhnau was among the first to write such sonatas for the harpsichord alone (about 1690).

Sonata allegro. Same as *Sonata form.

Sonata form. A form frequently used for single movements of the sonata (symphony, etc.), consisting essentially of three sections called exposition, development, and recapitulation (also statement, fantasia, and restatement), usually followed by a closing section called the *coda. Each of these sections has a special function and design. In the exposition the main musical ideas are "exposed" — usually two themes or theme groups (consisting of two or more themes each) connected by transitional or bridge passages. The development serves to "develop" the thematic material introduced in the exposition. This is done in a great variety of ways, all designed to bring about that special feeling of dynamic growth, tension, and dramatic conflict which is characteristic of the development section. The basic procedure is the motival technique, i.e., the working with short *motives derived by segmentation from some of the themes of the exposition. Another important trait of the development section is the extended use of modulation, leading into various keys, often far removed from the main key. The *recapitulation* is essentially a restatement of the exposition (though it can be shortened or extended) with a modification of the key scheme (see below). The *coda* varies greatly in length and importance; in earlier compositions (Haydn, Mozart) it is often hardly more than a short phrase designed to lead to a definitive close of the movement. With Beethoven and his successors the coda often assumes considerable proportions and great importance, amounting to a second development section which may incorporate the most impressive climax of the whole movement, e.g., in the first movement of Beethoven's Eroica Symphony (which also introduces a new theme in the development section).

There is also a standard tonal scheme in sonata form. The exposition begins in the tonic key, but modulates (in a transitional passage) to the dominant for

different tonal color. In the recapitulation, the modulation to the dominant, which is typical of the exposition, is not made, both themes (or groups of themes) being in the tonic key — a change necessary to bring the entire movement to its proper close in the tonic key.

Sonata form is similar to *ternary form in that it consists of three sections, the last essentially identical with the first. However, the mature sonata form as found in the symphonies of Mozart, Beethoven, and Schubert (see 2 below) nearly always calls for a repetition of the exposition (E), and the somewhat shorter examples found in Haydn's and Mozart's piano sonatas, string quartets, and early symphonies (see 1 below) actually have also a repeat of the development plus recapitulation (D, R). Sonata form, therefore, has gone through three stages of development in its evolution from *binary form. The first is rounded binary form, the last a simple tripartite form:

1. $\|: E :\|: \ D \ R :\|$ $(= E \ E \ D \ R \ D \ R)$
2. $\|: E :\| \quad D \ R$ $(= E \ E \ D \ R)$
3.   E   D R

the second theme or theme group (or, if the movement is in a minor key, the modulation is to the relative major key). The development section moves freely through various keys, often with quick and striking modulations. In fact, an unexpected modulation into a remote key is often found at the very beginning of the development section, so as to impress the hearer immediately by its

It is to be deplored that in examples of the second type the repeat of the expositions, clearly prescribed by Beethoven, Schubert, and others, is often disregarded by modern performers and conductors.

Sonata form is almost invariably employed for the first movement of a sonata (symphony, string quartet, etc.), often also for the second and for the last (see under *Sonata*).

The name sonata form is misleading, since it does not denote the "form of the sonata" (as consisting of four movements), but the form used frequently for single movements of the sonata. The term *sonata allegro*, used interchangeably with sonata form, is also misleading in that the form appears in slow (andante, adagio, etc.) movements as well as in fast (allegro) ones. The term *first-movement form* has been suggested, but this is also inaccurate as the same form occurs frequently in the second and fourth movements. A proper name would be "development form," since the development section and technique is of basic importance in this form, while in other forms (e.g., in ternary form proper) it is either absent or incidental.

Sonatina (so-nah-TEE-na: It.). A short sonata, also usually easy to play and often designed for instruction (Clementi, Kuhlau). Beethoven's Sonatas op. 49, nos. 1 and 2, also belong to this type. Modern composers, such as Busoni and Ravel, have written sonatinas of considerable technical difficulty.

Song. A short composition for solo voice, usually accompanied by the piano, based on a poetic text and composed in such a way as to enhance rather than to overshadow the significance of the text. In a song the words and the music are of equal importance, while in the *aria the emphasis is on the musical elaboration. Practically every age of music has contributed to the song literature, not to mention the universal tradition of *folk song. Important repertories of an early date (12th to 16th centuries) are the songs of the *troubadours, *trouvères, *minnesingers, and *mastersingers, as well as the devotional *laude and *cantigas. All these are monophonic songs. A great flowering of songs accompanied by one or two instruments took place in the 14th century in France (Machaut) and in Italy (Landini). See under *Ars nova*. In the 16th century, songs with lute accompaniment were cultivated in Spain (Luis de Milan) and in England. In the Baroque period (c. 1600–1750) the preoccupation with the aria led to a neglect of the song proper, except in Germany (Krieger, Erlebach) and in France, where a popular type of song was cultivated (see under *Chanson*). In this period, the harpsichord became the chief instrument for accompaniment.

Modern song is characterized by an expression of personal feelings that encompass the whole range of human emotion, which was new to musical expression; by an intimate fusion of poetry and music, reflected in the most careful attention given to the text; and by an elaborate piano accompaniment rising to full partnership with the vocal melody. This development started with Mozart (*Das Veilchen*, 1785) and Beethoven (*An die ferne Geliebte*, 1816), and reached an early culmination, never surpassed, in the songs and song cycles of Schubert. Schubert and his successors (Schumann, Brahms, Wolf, R. Strauss) firmly established Germany's leadership in the field of 19th-century song (see *Lied*). In France, the development of modern song started about 1870, with Duparc and Fauré. In 1897 Debussy composed his *Chansons de Bilitis*, which marked a decisive turn away from German models toward a typically French (impressionistic) style and expression. Russian composers like Glinka, Tchaikovsky, Rachmaninoff and Glière, wrote mostly songs of a lyrical and somewhat sentimental character, while Moussorgsky created a vigorous and novel type of song, often employing a realistic recitative. The songs of Rimski-Korsakov, Balakirev, and Borodin are in a strongly nationalistic idiom. In the United States, Stephen Foster created a national type of song, approaching folk song; the romantic type is represented by MacDowell, Hadley, Carpenter, and Cadman; the impressionistic, by Loeffler and Griffes.

Compared to the 19th-century activity, song composition has waned considerably during the 20th century. Most of the major contemporary composers have produced some song literature, however, reflecting all the numerous and diversified trends of this period. Among these, to mention a few, are Ives, Copland, and Barber in the United States; Schönberg and Hindemith in Germany; Ravel, Roussel, Reynaldo Hahn, Honegger, Milhaud, and Poulenc in France; Stravinsky and Prokofiev in Russia; Vaughan Williams, Cyril Scott, Bax, Bliss, and Britten in England; Casella and Respighi in Italy; Villa-Lobos in Brazil.

Song cycle. A group of songs based on poems (usually by the same poet) which are connected by a general idea, the songs being designed to form a musical unit and to be performed as such. Famous examples are Beethoven's *An die ferne Geliebte* (1816), Schubert's *Die Schöne Müllerin* (1823) and *Winterreise* (1827), Schumann's *Frauenliebe und Leben* (1840) and *Dichterliebe* (1840), Brahms' *Magelone* (1861–68), Fauré's La *Bonne chanson* (1892), Mahler's *Lied von der Erde* (1908), and Hindemith's *Marienleben* (1925).

Song form. An ambiguous designation frequently used for small sectional forms such as A B A (*ternary), A B (*binary), A A B A, etc. The term is inappropriate because such forms are rarely used in songs, though frequently used for piano pieces (e.g., Chopin's Nocturnes) or in dances (minuet, scherzo). Some writers make a distinction between "ternary song form" and "binary song form," but here the word "song" may just as well be omitted.

Song of Destiny. See *Schicksalslied.*

Song of the Earth. See *Lied von der Erde.*

Songs of a Wayfarer (G., *Lieder eines fahrenden Gesellen*). Four songs for contralto and orchestra by Mahler (1883) set to his own poems. They were inspired by his youthful love affair with Johanna Richter in Cassel.

Songs without Words (G., *Lieder ohne Worte*). Forty-eight piano pieces by Mendelssohn, published in eight groups of six each (op. 19, 30, 38, 53, 62, 67, 85, 102; 1830–45), and written in the form and style of a song, i.e., with a singable melody and a simple uniform accompaniment. The songlike character is also evident in the absence of contrasting middle sections such as are usually found in the *character pieces of the 19th century (see under *Ternary form*). The individual titles given in modern editions ("Spring Song," "Hunting Song," "Spinning Song") are not authentic, except for the three "Venetian Boat Songs" (*Venezianisches Gondellied*), nos. 6, 12, and 19, the "Dialogue" (*Duetto*), no. 18, and the "Folk Song" (*Volkslied*), no. 23.

Sonnenquartette (G.). See *Sun Quartets.*

Sopra (It.). Above. *Come sopra,* as above, as previously. *M.d. sopra* means right hand above the left (in piano playing); *m.s. sopra* means left hand above the right.

Sopranino (so-prah-NEE-no: It.). Term for instruments of very high range; especially the highest saxophone, in E-flat.

Soprano. The highest female voice (see under *Voices, Range of*). Soprano soloists are classified as dramatic, lyric, or coloratura according to tone quality and range. Voices of similar type are the unchanged boy's voice, *boy soprano,* and the *male soprano,* either a *falsetto or a *castrato. The term is also used to denote instruments of a simi-

lar high range, e.g., soprano saxophone or soprano recorder.

Soprano clef. See under *Clefs.*

Sorcerer's Apprentice, The (F., *L'Apprenti sorcier*). A symphonic poem by Paul Dukas, composed in 1897, based on Goethe's ballad *Der Zauberlehrling*, in which an apprentice sorcerer, by a magic word, brings a broom to life and directs it to fetch water. He does not know the word that would return the broom to inactivity, so the broom continues its job with ever-increasing speed and fury until the master sorcerer comes home and, with the proper magic word, stops the deluge and restores order and quiet. The music is a vivid portrayal of these lively happenings.

Sordino (sor-DEE-no: It.). The *mute of the violin, etc., hence *con sordini,* with the mutes, canceled by *senza sordini* or *sordini alzati* (removed), *levati* (lifted). Similarly on the piano, *con sordini* means "with the mutes," i.e., with the left (soft) pedal. In the early 19th century, however, before the invention of the soft pedal, the *sordini* of the piano were the dampers. This change of meaning has led to a widespread misunderstanding of the indication *senza sordini* given by Beethoven in the first movement of his Moonlight Sonata. It means "without the dampers," i.e., "with the damper (right) pedal," equivalent to the modern indication *P.* Later editors have thought this to be an error, and have changed it into *con sordini* (in the meaning of "with the soft pedal") or even into *una corda*. The movement should be played with the normal pedal, not with the soft pedal.

Sorotchintsy Fair. See *Fair at Sorochinsk.*

Sostenuto, also **sostenendo, sostenente** (sos-te-NOO-to, sos-te-NEN-do, sos-te-NEN-tay: It.). Sustained, either in the sense of holding notes and chords to their full value (more properly called *tenuto), or of holding back the tempo, e.g., in *Andante sostenuto*.

Sostenuto pedal. See under *Pianoforte.*

Sotto (It.). Under. *Sotto voce,* in an undertone, with subdued sound. In piano music, *m.d.* (*m.s.*) *sotto* means right (left) hand underneath the other.

Soubrette (soo-BRET: F., from old French *soubret,* cunning). An operatic soprano of a light type, usually cast as an intriguing or lighthearted servant, e.g., Zerlina in Mozart's *Don Giovanni.*

Soundboard. In pianofortes, zithers, etc., a thin flat wooden board serving as a resonator over which the strings are stretched. Most defects in sound, such as develop in pianos after a number of years, are due to the cracking or bending of the soundboard.

Sound holes. In violins, etc., openings in the form of an *f* (F-holes) which are cut in the table in order to give its central portion greater freedom of vibration. In earlier instruments (*viols) these holes were in the shape of the letter *c* (C-holes). Sound holes of a circular form are customary for lutes, guitars (see *Rose*), and for the soundboard of the pianoforte.

Sound post. In violins, etc., a small pillar of pine wood fixed between the table and the back, slightly behind the right foot of the bridge. It serves to support the pressure of the strings and, especially, to communicate and coordinate the vibrations of the table and of the back.

Sourdine (soor-DEEN: F.). Used in the same meaning as *sordino. Also name for an obsolete type of oboe and bassoon.

Sousaphone. See *Brass instruments,* IIe.

Sp. Abbreviation for G. *Spitze,* tip, either of the bow (in violin music, i.e., *punta d'arco*) or of the foot (in organ music).

Spacing. See *Position.*

Spanish Rhapsody. A descriptive suite for orchestra by Ravel, composed in 1907. Its four movements, distinguished by impressionistic technique in the first one and by brilliant orchestral color throughout are: (1) *Prelude to the Night,* (2) *Malagueña,* (3) *Habanera,* and (4) *Fair.*

Spanish Song Book (G., *Spanisches Liederbuch*). A collection of forty-four songs by Hugo Wolf, composed 1890, to German translations of Spanish poems.

Speaker key. In wood-wind instruments, special keys facilitating the production of tones by overblowing. If depressed, the key opens a small hole in the pipe which causes the air column to vibrate in one half or one third of its entire length. The oboe has two speaker keys; the clarinet, one.

Speaking stops. On organs, all the stops that produce sounds, as distinct from those merely operating couplers, etc.

Speech song. Translation of G. *Sprechgesang* or *Sprechstimme*, a type of half singing and half speaking introduced by Schönberg in his *°Pierrot lunaire* and *°Glückliche Hand* (also used by Berg in *Wozzeck* and *Lulu*). It consists of a recitation with higher and lower inflections of individual words or syllables indicated by special signs, but avoids exact intonation of pitch.

Spiccato. See *Bowing* (d).

Spiegelfuge (SHPEE-gel-FOO-ge: G.). Mirror fugue.

Spieldose (SHPEEL-do-se: G.). Music box.

Spieloper (SHPEEL-O-per: G. play opera). Name for German 19th-century operas of a playful, light character.

Spinet (SPIN-et). Originally a name for small harpsichords with only one manual. Today the name is also used for the small, oblong pianofortes of the mid-19th century, or for small pianos of modern make.

Spirituals. Religious songs of the American Negro, often based on Biblical stories of promise and redemption, such as the crossing of the river Jordan, Daniel's deliverance from the lions' den, or Moses' leading the children of Israel to the Promised Land. They are sung in four-part harmony derived from the standard hymns, but with certain native characteristics, such as a preference for pentatonic melodies and a frequent use of syncopation. Negro institutes such as Fisk University, Hampton, and Tuskegee have been instrumental in furthering the tradition of singing spirituals, and the concert tours of their choral groups have made available this type of music sung in an authentic style.

Sprechgesang,   Sprechstimme (SHPREKH-ge-zahng, SHPREKH-shtim-e: G.). *°Speech song.

Spring Sonata. Nickname of Beethoven's Sonata for Violin and Piano in F, op. 24 (1801), referring to its gentle and lyrical character, especially in the first movement.

Spring Song. Nickname of one of Mendelssohn's *°Songs without Words* in which the ornamented melody suggests the chirping of birds.

Spring Symphony. (1) Nickname of Schumann's Symphony no. 1, in B-flat, op. 38 (1841), referring to its gentle and idyllic character. — (2) A work for solo voices, chorus, and orchestra by Benjamin Britten, composed in 1949.

St. See under *Saint*.

Stabat mater (STAH-baht MAH-ter: The Mother Was Standing). A celebrated religious poem of the 13th century, probably written by the Franciscan monk Jacopone da Todi (c. 1228–1306), and still sung today in the Roman Catholic rites at the Feast of the Seven Dolours. The liturgical melody belongs to the type known as *sequence. The famous text has also often been used for elaborate compositions, e.g., by Josquin, Palestrina, Pergolesi, Haydn, Schubert, Rossini, and Verdi.

Staccato (sta-KAH-to: It., detached). The shortened performance of a note (or group of notes) so that it sounds only for a moment, the major part of its written value being replaced by a rest. It is indicated either by the word *staccato* or, more frequently, by dots placed over the notes (see under *Legato*). In piano and violin playing as well as in singing there exist various types of staccato produced by different touch, bowing, attack, etc. Earlier composers such as C. P. E. Bach, Haydn, Beethoven, indicated the normal staccato by a wedge-shaped sign (ɤ), reserving the dot for a less pronounced staccato, more like a *portato. Today the dot is used as the normal sign, and the wedge for a very pronounced and forceful staccato. See also *Bowing* (f).

Ständchen (SHTENT-chen: G.). Serenade, open-air music.

Staff (stave). Five parallel horizontal lines, upon and between which musical notes are written, thus indicating their relative pitch and, in connection with a clef, their absolute pitch (see under *Notation*). The invention of the staff is ascribed to Guido of Arezzo (c. 995–1050), who recommended the use of three or four lines, denoting f a c' or d f a c'. Even before him, rudimentary staffs of two lines, a red one for f and a yellow one for c', were used. The four-line staff was generally accepted, and is retained to the present day for the notation of Gregorian chant. Five-line staffs, for polyphonic music, were used as early as 1200. In the 16th century staffs with up to seven or eight lines were employed for keyboard music, particularly for the lower staff (left hand) which otherwise would require numerous ledger lines.

Staff notation. The ordinary music notation employing a staff, in distinction from staffless notations such as *Tonic Sol-fa and earlier systems employing letters, figures, or other symbols (see *Tablature*).

Star-Spangled Banner, The. The national anthem of the United States, officially adopted by a bill passed on March 3, 1931. The words were written by Francis Scott Key (1779–1843) in September of 1814, while he watched the British bombardment of Fort McHenry, near Baltimore. It is sung to a tune by John Stafford Smith (1750–1836), an Englishman who originally composed the music for a poem beginning "To Anacreon in Heaven." It is not known whether Key had this tune in mind when he wrote the poem, or whether text and music were united later (possibly by Joseph Hopper Nicholson).

Stave. See *Staff.*

Steel guitar. An electrophonic instrument (also called electric guitar), widely used in popular dance orchestras in the place of the normal guitar, its advantages being widely variable amplification, greater sustaining power, and control of tone quality. In appearance it bears little resemblance to the traditional guitar, its body consisting of a small boxlike structure which merely serves to support the strings. The sound is produced by an electric pickup system, with an amplifier contained in a separate cabinet connected by cable to the pickup.

Steg (shtayg: G.). Bridge (of the violin, etc.). *Am Steg*, same as *°sul ponticello.*

Steppes of Central Asia, In the. Title commonly used in English-speaking countries for a symphonic poem by Borodin. Its correct Russian title is translated simply as *In Central Asia*. It was composed in 1880, and its ingratiating tunes and oriental pictorialism have made it one of the most popular of Borodin's compositions.

Stesso tempo. Same as *°istesso tempo.*

Stimme (SHTIM-e: G.). Voice or voice part. Also applied to individual parts in orchestral or chamber music.

Stimmen (SHTIM-en: G.). (1) Plural of *°Stimme. —* (2) To

tune. *Nach G stimmen,* indication to change the tuning (e.g., of a kettle drum) to G.

Stimmungsbild (SHTIM-ungs-bilt: G.). "Mood picture," title for Romantic pieces expressing a definite mood.

Stop. On the organ, a hand-operated device by which the player can control one of the various registers. Formerly they were in the form of knobs to be pulled out or pushed in. On the modern organ, which has electric action, they consist of small ivory tablets that are lowered or raised by a touch of the finger. The term is also used for the set of pipes connected with a given stop, as in "foundation stops," "mixture stops," etc. Stops also occur in a limited number on the °harpsichord. See *Organ stops.*

Stopping. On violins, guitars, lutes, etc., the pressing of a string against the finger board by the fingers of the left hand in order to shorten the vibrating length of the string and, thereby, raise the pitch. See *Double stop. —* (2) See under *Horn.*

Streicher (SHTREYEK-er: G., bowers). String players.

Streichinstrumente (SHTREYEK-in-stroo-MEN-te: G.). Stringed instruments. *Streichquartett* (*Streichquintett,* etc.), string quartet (string quintet, etc.).

Streit zwischen Phöbus und Pan, Der (shtreyet TSVISH-en FEU-bus unt pahn: The Strife between Phoebus and Pan). Secular cantata by J. S. Bach (1732), text by Picander after Ovid's contest between Phoebus Apollo legend relating to the musical (god of the Muses, representing the high art of music) and Pan (god of the Earth, representing the peasant or folk music), at the conclusion of which Apollo transforms the ears of Midas, advocate of Pan, into those of an ass. The work is probably a satire against Bach's critic, Scheibe (represented by Midas).

Stretta (It.). Same as *stretto* (2).

Stretto (STRET-to: It., close). (1) In a fugue, the imitation of the subject at a close distance, so that two (or more) statements overlap (see Fig. 108).

Fig. 108

This device brings about an increase of density and intensity, and is therefore often employed for a climactic conclusion of a fugue. — (2) In nonfugal compositions, *stretto* (*stretta*) means a concluding section in increased speed as, e.g., at the end of the last movement of Beethoven's Fifth Symphony, also frequently in operatic arias (Verdi); see *Cabaletta*.

Strich (shtrikh: G.). Bow stroke, for example, *mit breitem Strich*, with a broad stroke.

String bass. Colloquial name for the *double bass.

Stringed instruments. Instruments in which the sound-producing agent is a stretched string. The most important members of this group are the violin (and its family), the harp, and the pianoforte. In the violin the strings are made to vibrate by bowing, in the harp (also guitar, lute, harpsichord) by plucking, in the piano by the strokes of hammers. Ordinarily, the name (particularly in the abbreviated form "strings") denotes the four members of the *violin family which constitute the "string section" of the orchestra, i.e., violin (first and second), viola, cello, and double bass.

String quartet. A chamber-music group consisting of two violins, viola, and cello. Also the music written for such a group, e.g., String Quartet op. 18, no. 1, by Beethoven. The string quartet is not only the most universal type of *chamber music, but is also frequently considered, by serious musicians as well as by many amateurs, the ideal type of music. As a musical form, the string quartet is, for all practical purposes, identical with the *sonata.

The present-day repertory of string quartets begins with the later quartets of Haydn, written between 1770 and 1790 (*Sun Quartets, Gli *Scherzi, Tost Quartets, *Prussian Quartets, *Emperor Quartet, etc.), and those by Mozart composed in the same decades (*Haydn

Quartets, *Prussian Quartets, etc.). This heritage was passed on to Beethoven, whose earlier works (op. 18, nos. 1–6, 1801; op. 59, *Russian Quartets, 1808) are what may be called "Haydn quartets in Beethoven's language," while his late quartets (op. 127, 130–133, 135) lead far away from "distinguished entertainment" into a realm of sublime thought and transcendental subjectivism. A contemporary of Beethoven was Schubert, whose late string quartets (A minor, 1824; D minor, subtitled *Death and the Maiden, 1826) have only recently gained the recognition they deserve.

During the Romantic period, chamber music waned considerably as a result of the new interest in coloristic and programmatic effects, but a new peak was reached in the works of Brahms (op. 51, 67; 1859–75), who filled the traditional form with a new expression of restrained Romanticism. The Romantic period of the string quartet came to its conclusion with the works of Dvořák (eight quartets, 1874–95), Franck (D minor, 1889), d'Indy (op. 35, 45, 96; 1897–1930), and Reger (op. 54, 74, 109, 121, 133; c. 1900–15).

With the advent of *neoclassicism in the 20th century, quartet writing has taken on new vitality (e.g., Bartok's six quartets, Hindemith's seven quartets), and all of the new techniques and materials developed since 1900 have been utilized in this medium.

String quintet. Chamber music for five strings, usually for two violins, two violas, and cello (18 by Boccherini, 12 by Dittersdorf, 6 by Mozart, 3 by Beethoven, 3 by Mendelssohn, 3 by Brahms, 1 by Bruckner, 1 by Vaughan Williams, 1 by Reger, etc.). The less usual combinations of two violins, viola, and two cellos was preferred by Boccherini (113), but is represented later only in Schubert's famous Quintet in C, op. 163.

Strings. (1) The chords, either of gut or wire, which are used in stringed instruments. — (2) Colloquial abbreviation for *stringed instruments.

String trio. Chamber music for three stringed instruments. See under *Trio* (1).

Stromento (stro-MEN-to: It.). Instrument. *Stromenti a corde,* stringed instruments; *s. d'arco,* bowed; *s. di legno,* wood wind; *s. d'ottone* or *di metallo,* brass; *s. a percossa,* percussion; *s. a fiato* or *di vento,* wind; *s. da tasto,* keyboard.

Strophic. A song is termed strophic if all the stanzas of the poem are sung to the same music. Hymns and folk songs are usually strophic, as are most of the art songs written before 1800. The opposite treatment, with new music to each stanza, is called *through-composed* (the translation of G. *durchkomponiert*).

Strumento (It.). Older spelling for *stromento. For Mozart's *strumento d'acciaio,* see under *Glockenspiel.*

Stück (shtuik: G.). Piece, composition; for example, *Klavierstück,* piano composition.

Stürze (SHTUIR-tse: G.). Bell, particularly of the horn or trumpet. *Stürze hoch,* direction to turn the bell upward.

Style. "Distinctive or characteristic mode of presentation, construction, or execution in any art" (Webster). Musical style, therefore, means "characteristic language" or "characteristic manner of composition," particularly with reference to the treatment of melody, harmony, rhythm, etc. The term is also used to denote the characteristic language of composers (e.g., Beethoven's style), of types of composition (operatic style, church style), of mediums of performance (instrumental style, vocal style), of periods (Baroque style, Romantic style), etc.

Style galant (steel gal-ANH: F.). Gallant style. See *Rococo.*

Subdominant. The fourth degree of the scale (F in C major or minor), so called because it is a fifth below (*sub*) the tonic, just as the dominant is a fifth above it (see *Scale degrees*). Subdominant triad is the triad built on the fourth degree (for example, f-a-c′ in C major).

Subito (SOO-bee-to: It.). Sudden, e.g., *subito piano,* suddenly soft.

Subject. A melody which, by virtue of its characteristic design, prominent position, or special treatment becomes a basic element in the structure of a composition. The subject (or, if there are several, the main subject) is stated at or near the beginning of a composition, and

recurs several times during its course. In *sonata form there are normally two subjects or, in more extended examples, two groups of subjects. A *fugue usually has only one subject, except in special cases such as double or triple fugues. The term is almost synonymous with *theme.

Submediant. See under *Scale degrees.*

Subtonic. See under *Scale degrees.*

Subtonium. See under *Church modes.*

Suite. An important instrumental form of Baroque music, consisting of a number of standardized movements, each in the character of a dance and all in the same key. Also a form of modern music (*c.* 1870 and later), but without adherence to standard dance types, uniformity of key, and other details.

1. *The Baroque Suite.* As represented in the works of Bach, the suite consists of Prelude (not always present), Allemande, Courante, Saraband, Optional dance(s), Gigue. The optional dances are one or several of various types, chiefly minuet, bourrée, gavotte, passepied, polonaise, and rigaudon. This form is observed in all the harpsichord suites of Bach (see *English Suites; French Suites; Partita*), as well as in his three suites for violin plus harpsichord and in the six suites for cello solo. The three suites for violin solo and the orchestral suites show a freer form, characterized by a higher incidence of the

optional dances. The single dance movements are almost invariably in °binary form. Occasionally some of the optional dances appear in pairs, e.g., Gavotte I, Gavotte II, implying repeat of the first dance after the second (I II I), so that the whole group is in ternary form. This arrangement, applied to minuets, survived in the °minuet (later °scherzo) of the Classical sonata, symphony, etc. An important difference in style exists between the four standard dances (A, C, S, G) on the one hand and the optional dances on the other, the standard dances being idealized dances written in an elaborate contrapuntal style, while the optional ones are simpler and more clearly suggestive of real dance music. The reason for this difference is that the standard dances are of older origin (before 1600) than the optional ones (c. 1650).

The central figure in the pre-Bach development of the suite was Johann Jacob Froberger (c. 1617–1667), whose suites (for harpsichord) show the form A–C–S or A–C–G–S, always with the saraband at the end. About 1690 the arrangement A–C–S–G became customary, and optional dances were introduced either at the end (A–C–S–G–O) or in the middle (A–C–O–S–G). Bach seems to have been the first to place the O group just before the gigue. The suites of Handel often include free (i.e., not dancelike) movements. In Italy the suite was cultivated mainly for chamber music, under the name of *sonata da camera* (see under *Sonata,* II).

II. *The Modern Suite.* In the later part of the 19th century the designation "suite" was revived for orchestral compositions which are only remotely, if at all, related to the Baroque suite. Some of these are extensions of the °symphonic poem — programmatic or characteristic compositions divided into movements, e.g., Rimski-Korsakov's °*Scheherezade* or Debussy's *La* °*Mer.* Many are excerpts from stage music or ballets, arranged for concert performance, e.g., Bizet's °*Arlésienne Suite* (1872), Grieg's °*Peer Gynt Suite* (1875), Tchaikovsky's °*Nutcracker Suite* (1892), or Stravinsky's °*Petrushka Suite* (1911). Hindemith incorporated modern ballroom dances in his *Suite 1922.* More recently composers have returned to the dance types of the Baroque, e.g., Schönberg in his Suite for String Orchestra in G major (1934), which consists of Overture, Adagio, Minuet, Gavotte, and Gigue; but the designation is still freely applied to any unified collection of movements of smaller dimensions than a symphony (e.g., Milhaud, *Suite Provençale* and *Suite Française*).

Suite Bergamasque (sweet bayrga-MAHSK). A piano composition by Debussy, consisting of Prélude, Menuet, °Clair de lune, and Passepied. Its title is probably derived from a line in Verlaine's poem *Clair de lune,* ". . . masques et bergamasques."

Suivez (swee-VAY: F.). Follow; an indication used in the sense of either °*attacca* or °*colla parte.*

Sul (sool: It.). On, at. *Sul G,* on the G-string of the violin; *sul* *ponticello,* bowing near the bridge; *sul tasto, sulla tastiera,* bowing near the finger board.

Sumer is icumen in. A famous composition, probably dating from *c.* 1300, in the form of a four-voice canon, with two additional bass parts (called *pes,* i.e., foot, in the original) forming a short ground bass (essentially f-g-f) which is reiterated throughout the piece. Its former ascription (now generally considered erroneous) to John of Fornsete, a monk of Reading Abbey, accounts for the title "Reading Rota" sometimes applied to it. Although of rather limited artistic significance, its folklike melody and full-sounding harmony have made this piece the only example of medieval music (one not at all representative) generally known today. Brahms imitated its strucure in no. 13 of his *Kanons,* op. 113.

Sun Quartets. Nickname for Haydn's six string quartets op. 20, nos. 1–6, composed in 1772. An early edition had an engraving of a rising sun as part of its frontispiece.

Suor Angelica. See under *Trittico.*

Supertonic. See under *Scale degrees.*

Surprise Symphony. Haydn's Symphony no. 94, in G major (no. 3 of the *Salomon Symphonies), composed in 1791, so called because of the loud chord in the midst of the quiet and peaceful second movement (Haydn stated that that would make the ladies jump).

Suspension. See under *Nonharmonic tones.*

Sustaining pedal. See under *Pianoforte.*

Sw. Abbreviation for Swell Organ.

Swan Lake, The. Ballet by Tchaikovsky (choreography by M. Petipa and L. Ivanov), composed in 1876. The story deals with the conflict of Prince Siegfried against the Evil Power in his attempt to woo the Swan Queen, Odette. The ballet is one of the first to utilize the *leitmotiv technique, with a specific melody representing the Queen. The suite from the ballet consists of five sections: Scene, Waltz, Dance of the Swans, Scene, and Czárdás.

Swan of Tuonela (TWON-e-lah). Symphonic poem by Sibelius, op. 22 (1895), based on a legend from the *Kalevala. Tuonela, the Finnish Hades, is surrounded by a river of black water on which a swan swims majestically and sings. In the music, sustained strings represent the dark waters and the gliding movements of the swan, while a solo English horn presents its song.

Swan Song. See *Schwanengesang.*

Swell. In organs, a contrivance to control volume. It consists of a wooden enclosure (*swell box*) built around a division of the pipes and provided with frontal shutters similar to vertical Venetian blinds, hence the name *Venetian swell.* The enclosed division is called *Swell Organ,* a name also applied to the manual from which its pipes are played. The shutters are opened and closed by the *Swell Pedal*, operated by the feet. On modern organs, the other divisions (Great, Choir, Solo, etc.) are also enclosed and provided with shutters.

Swing. A term applied to the style of jazz that originated about 1935, particularly in the music of the Benny Goodman orchestra. Difficult to define precisely, it seems to refer to (1) the increase in number and variety of instruments; (2) a subtle rubato; (3) crispness of attack, especially in the rhythm section; (4) precision of ensemble. A simultaneous development in jazz was the introduction of performances divorced from dancing (swing concerts).

Sympathetic strings. Strings which are not played upon but which serve to reinforce the sound of bowed or plucked strings, to which they run parallel at a close distance, being tuned at the same pitch or at the octave. Various old instruments had such strings, e.g., the °baryton, the °viola d'amore, and the °tromba marina.

Symphonia Domestica. See *Domestic Symphony*.

Symphonic poem. A type of music in which an extramusical idea (literary, descriptive, etc.) serves as the basis of an orchestral composition. Thus the symphonic poem belongs to the general category of °program music, of which it represents the most recent and the most ambitious realization. The term is usually restricted to compositions in one movement, while a programmatic work divided into several movements is called a symphonic °suite or, if it follows the scheme of a four-movement symphony, a °program symphony. The symphonic poem grew out of the program symphony (e.g., Berlioz' *Fantastic Symphony*) when Romantic composers sought to be freed from the formal restrictions of the symphony. It was inaugurated by Liszt in such works as *Tasso* (1849, after a poem by Byron), *Mazeppa* (1851, after a poem by Victor Hugo), *The Slaughter of the Huns* (1857, after a painting by Kaulbach), etc. His idea was seized upon by a great number of composers to whom literary, pictorial, and other subjects provided a new source of inspiration. Particularly favored were works descriptive of national life and scenery, and it was a happy circumstance that the symphonic poem came into being at the time when musical °nationalism was flourishing. The first contributions in this latter field were Smetana's six symphonic poems *°Má Vlast* (1874–79). His example was followed by a host of successors, and there is scarcely a country that has not been described in music. Compositions such as Borodin's *In the °Steppes of Central Asia*, Saint-Saëns' *Africa*, Sibelius' *°Finlandia*, Vaughan Williams' *°London Symphony*, Respighi's *°Fountains of Rome*, and Bloch's *America* illustrate the scope of the "musical atlas." The poetic type initiated by Liszt was continued in Tchaikovsky's

Romeo and Juliet and Franck's *Eolides,* among others.

A new period of the symphonic poem began shortly before 1900 with Richard Strauss, who preferred the designation *tone poem* for his realistic works such as *Death and Transfiguration,* *Till Eulenspiegel's Merry Pranks,* *Thus Spake Zarathustra,* and A *Hero's Life.* Others of the same generation are Sibelius (*Swan of Tuonela; Lemminkainen's Homecoming; Pohjola's Daughter; Tapiola*) and Debussy (*Afternoon of a Faun; La Mer*). Although some modern composers occasionally try to instill new life into the form, the symphonic poem, born of Romantic conceptions, has waned since the advent of *neoclassicism in the 1920's.

Symphonic Studies (F., *Études symphoniques*). A set of twelve piano pieces by Schumann, op. 13 (1834), in the form of a theme (by Fricken) with variations and a concluding finale. The term "symphonic" probably refers to the highly virtuoso treatment of the piano, occasionally with distinctly "orchestral" effects. The variation technique is extremely advanced for the time when the work was written (see under *Variations*), and some of the pieces have, at best, a very tenuous connection with the theme. This probably is the reason why Schumann discarded the original title, *Études en forme de variations.*

Symphonic Variations. Generally, a set of variations for orchestra. Specifically, the title (F., *Variations symphoniques*) of a work for piano and orchestra by Franck (composed 1885) in which the expected theme-and-variations structure is expanded by a developmental treatment more characteristic of a symphony of two themes.

Symphony (Gr., sounding together). The most important form of orchestral music, essentially a sonata for orchestra. For all the details of form, see the explanations under *Sonata, Sonata form,* etc.

The symphony originated about the middle of the 18th century, having its roots in several earlier forms. Among these, the most direct ancestry can be traced to the Italian operatic *overture, often called *Sinfonia avanti l'opera.* To the three movements of the *sinfonia,* fast–slow–fast, a minuet was occasionally added between the last two by various pre-Classical composers such as Georg Monn (1717–1750), G. B. Sammartini (c. 1698–1775), and the group known as the *Mannheim School (1740 and later); however, it was not until the middle symphonies of Haydn (beginning with no. 31) that the four-movement form became standard.

The present-day repertory begins with the later symphonies of Mozart and Haydn. Mozart, although nearly twenty-five years younger than Haydn, was the first to write truly great symphonies, namely the *Prague Symphony (K. 504, 1786) and his last three symphonies, in E-flat (K. 543), G minor (K. 550), and C (*Jupiter Symphony, K. 551), written in 1788. The total number of his symphonies is forty-seven. Among Haydn's symphonies, which number over one hundred, only the last twelve, written in 1791–95 for the Salomon Concerts in London (see *Salomon Symphonies*), show the same maturity of style as those by Mozart. The advance of these works over the earlier ones is chiefly one of thematic invention, development technique, and *obbligato* accompaniment (emancipation of the lower instruments from their former role as a mere chordal support).

Beethoven, who wrote only nine symphonies, established the character of the symphony as an "individual creation," rather than as an "example of a type." His first two symphonies (op. 21, in C, 1800; op. 36, in D, 1802) already show, if compared with those of Haydn and Mozart, a greater seriousness of purpose, a more dynamic vitality, and a more advanced orchestration. The later ones, except perhaps the no. 4, stand out as masterworks of symphonic literature (see *Eroica*, no. 3; *Pastoral Symphony*, no. 6; *Choral Symphony*, no. 9). Beethoven's heir to the symphonic tradition was Schubert (eight symphonies), notable mainly for his lyrico-dramatic *Unfinished Symphony in B minor (1822) and his magnificent last Symphony in C major (1828). Berlioz initiated a new trend (see *Program music*) in his *Fantastic Symphony (op. 14, 1830), while the four symphonies of Mendelssohn (C minor, 1824; *Scotch Symphony, 1830–42; *Italian Symphony, 1833; *Reformation Symphony, 1830–32) and the four symphonies by Schumann (*Spring Symphony, 1841; C major, 1846; *Rhenish Symphony, 1850; D

minor, 1841, revised 1851) adhere to the conservative tradition, although they are somewhat weaker in substance and craftsmanship.

It was not until about 1875 that symphonic art arrived at a new culmination with the four symphonies of Brahms (C minor, op. 68, 1875; D major, op. 73, 1877; F major, op. 90, 1883; E minor, op. 98, 1885) and the nine symphonies of Bruckner (particularly no. 4, *Romantic Symphony, 1874; no. 6, 1879; no. 7, 1883; no. 8, 1885; no. 9, 1894). Brahms took over the basic idea as well as the form of the Beethoven symphony, modifying its style from a straightforward dynamism to a pliable lyricism. He is perhaps the only master whose development technique matches that of Beethoven. Bruckner created a symphonic form and style — derived from Schubert rather than Beethoven — whose a r t i s t i c greatness many feel is even today far from being sufficiently recognized. His symphonies are architectural structures of vast dimensions, and his music is filled with a profound religious conviction, expressed in a fervent musical language. Much better known are the six symphonies by Tchaikovsky, although only the last, the *Pathétique Symphony, can be included in the list of truly great symphonies. It was written in 1893, the same year in which Dvořák composed the last of his symphonies, the popular *From the New World.

New trends are noticeable in Franck's D-minor Symphony (1888) with its *cyclic treatment and chromaticism, and in the nine symphonies (1888–

1909) of Mahler, who discarded the traditional forms of the symphony and its individual movements and took a definite step in the direction of the dissonant harmonies and the polyphonic texture of the 20th century. Similar tendencies are present in the seven symphonies of Sibelius, particularly nos. 4 to 7 (1911–24), remarkable for their novel orchestral effects, interesting treatment of thematic material (see *Transformation of themes*), and somber intensity. Other 20th-century composers of symphonies are Vaughan Williams (nine: no. 1, *Sea Symphony; no. 2, *London Symphony; no. 3, *Pastoral Symphony), Rachmaninoff (three), Prokofiev (seven, including the *Classical Symphony), Howard Hanson (five), Roy Harris (seven), William Schuman (seven), and Walter Piston (six). A special recognition must be given to two Russians, Miaskovsky (about 25 symphonies) and Shostakovich who has written eleven symphonies, among which nos. 1, 5, and 7 (*Leningrad Symphony) have been particularly successful owing to a skillful blending of modernistic and popularizing elements. Of the leading composers of the 20th century Stravinsky and Hindemith have made some contributions to the symphonic repertory, Stravinsky mainly with his Symphony in Three Movements, Hindemith with his Symphony *Mathis der Maler* and Symphony *Harmonie der Welt*, both derived from operas of the same titles.

Symphony of Psalms. A work for chorus and orchestra (with- out violins or violas) by Stravinsky, completed in 1930. Its three movements are based on Psalms (in Latin): I. Psalm 38, v. 13–14, treated in an archaic chordal style; II. Psalm 39, v. 12–13, a double fugue with one subject for the orchestra, the other for the chorus; III. Psalm 150, in a free, sectionalized form.

Syncopation   (sing-ko-PAY-shun). An abnormal metric pattern produced by an emphasis on the normally weak beats, e.g., the second or fourth in 4/4 time, or the second or third in 3/4 time. This can be done (a) by tying over the strong beat, (b) by placing a rest on the strong beat, or (c) by placing an accent on the weak beat (see Fig. 109,

Fig. 109

a-c). Syncopation is best known today through its extensive use in jazz. Its earliest occurrence, in a strikingly bold manner, is in French compositions of the late

14th century. It is featured also in the late works of Beethoven, as a means of obscuring the basic beat (Fig. 109d), and occurs frequently in the works of Schumann and Brahms, usually with similar effects of blurring. Modern composers such as Stravinsky and Bartok employ the device frequently as an adjunct of changing and asymmetric patterns of meter.

Syrinx (SIR-ingks). Ancient Greek name for *Pan pipes.

System. The group of staffs (see *Staff*) used for the notation of music, e.g., two for piano music, four for a string quartet.

T

T. Abbreviation for tonic, *tutti*, trill, or toe (in pedal parts of organ music).

Tabarro, II. See under *Trittico*.

Tabatière à musique (ta-ba-TYAYR a mui-ZEEK: F.). Music box (see under *Mechanical instruments*). Also title of piano pieces imitating the sound of a music box (e.g., the popular one by Anatol Liadov).

Tablature (TAB-la-tyoor: G., *Tabulatur*). (1) General name for various early (15th–17th centuries) systems of notation in which the tones are indicated, not by notes placed on a staff, but by letters, figures, or other symbols. At present tablature notation is used only for the guitar and the *ukulele. — (2) The set of rules which regulated the composition and performance of the *mastersingers.

Tabor (TAY-ber: from F. *tambour*). A medieval type of drum, in the shape of a long cylinder, about twice as high as it was wide. See *Pipe and tabor*.

Tabulatur (G.). *Tablature.

Tacet (L., it is silent). In an orchestral part, indication that the instrument is not needed for a long section or for a whole movement.

Tales of Hoffmann, The (F., *Les Contes d'Hoffmann*). Opera ("opéra fantastique") in three acts with prologue and epilogue, by Offenbach (libretto by J. Barbier and M. Carré, based on stories by the German novelist, E. T. A. Hoffmann, 1776–1822), produced in Paris, 1881. In the prologue Hoffmann (tenor) is shown drinking with his friends in a tavern, relating the tales of three of his love affairs, each ending tragically owing to the magic influence of some evil spirit. These episodes are shown in three acts (Act I: Olympia; Act II: Giulietta; Act III: Antonia), while in the epilogue the scene is the same as at the end of the prologue, the friends in the process of leaving Hoffmann.

The opera, left unfinished by the composer and completed by Guiraud, was produced shortly after Offenbach's death. Its musical style stands midway between that of the operetta, which Offenbach had cultivated before, and that of a more serious type of opera.

Talon (tah-LONH: F.). The frog of the violin bow. *Au talon,* indication to use the lower part of the bow.

Tambour (tamh-BOOR: F.). Drum, particularly the snare drum (*tambour militaire*). *Tambour de basque,* tambourine.

Tambourin (tahm-boo-RANH: F.). (1) The modern orchestra tambourine. — (2) In older usage, the °tabor. Also, with reference to the latter, an old Provençal dance accompanied by a steady drum beat.

Tambourine. See *Drums* (5).

Tamburin (G.), **tamburino** (It.). Tambourine.

Tamburo (tahm-BOO-ro: It.). Drum. *T. militare,* snare drum; *t. rullante,* tenor drum; *t. grande,* old name for the bass drum, now called *cassa grande,* or *gran cassa.*

Tampon (TAHM-pon). A two-headed drumstick used to produce a roll on the bass drum. The stick is held in the middle and moved by rapidly turning the wrist.

Tam-tam. See *Gong.* Not to be confused with °tom-tom.

Tangent. See under *Clavichord.*

Tango. A modern dance which originated about 1900 in the suburbs of Buenos Aires from elements of the °habanera and the milonga, having the same rhythmic pattern as the habanera, but at a slightly faster speed and with syncopation. About 1910 the tango was imported into the ballrooms of the Western world, creating a sensation because of the sensuous character of the dance steps, and about 1920 it made its way into art music, especially in the suites of composers such as Hindemith, Beck, and Křenek. Stravinsky included a tango in his *L'Histoire du soldat* (1918).

Tannhäuser (TAHN-hoy-zer: subtitle, *Der Sängerkrieg auf der Wartburg,* The Singers' Contest at the Wartburg). Opera in three acts by Wagner (to his own libretto, based on a medieval legend), produced in Dresden, 1845. The plot centers around the minnesinger Tannhäuser (tenor), who longs for freedom after a year of sinful life spent in the Venusberg, the abode of Venus (soprano), and who breaks Venus's unholy spell by imploring the Virgin Mary for help (Scene 1). In Scene 2 he is found by the Landgrave (bass) and his knights — among them Wolfram von Eschenbach (baritone) — who take their long-lost friend to the Wartburg, where the Landgrave's niece, Elizabeth (soprano), has been waiting faithfully for his return. Act II shows the Singers' Contest in which Elizabeth's hand is to be the prize. While Wolfram and the other minnesingers praise virtuous love, Tannhäuser in shameless defiance extols the pleasures of sensuous love, and all the ladies leave the hall except Elizabeth. Deeply touched by her faithfulness, Tannhäuser expresses his penitence and joins a procession of pilgrims. In Act III the pilgrims return from Rome without Tannhäuser, and Elizabeth goes away broken-hearted. Finally Tannhäuser appears, seeking again the grotto of Venus, since the Pope has not forgiven him. At this moment a funeral procession arrives carrying the body of Elizabeth, and Tannhäuser, overwhelmed with emotion, joins her in death. Pilgrims enter carrying Tannhäuser's staff, which has put forth fresh leaves in evidence that he has found forgiveness in heaven.

The score of *Tannhäuser* shows Wagner working with the tools of the "grand opera" of Meyerbeer and Bellini. The formal structure is essentially that of the traditional *number opera, although the actual numbering of different items is abandoned. The harmonic style is fairly traditional. It is by reason of its expressive qualities, evident in the story as well as in the music, that *Tannhäuser* opens a new period in the history of opera.

Tanto (TAHN-to: It.). So much. *Non tanto*, not too much.

Tanz (tahnts: G.). Dance. *Tanzstück*, dance piece.

Tapiola (tah-pee-O-la). Symphonic poem by Sibelius, op. 112 (1926). The name is derived from *Tapio*, the forest god of Finnish legend. (*Kalevala).

Tarantella (tahr-an-TEL-la). A Neapolitan dance in rapid 6/8 meter, probably named after the town of Taranto in south Italy and later associated with the spider *tarantula* whose poisonous bite it was believed to cure. In the mid-19th century it was frequently composed in the style of a brilliant *perpetuum mobile* in accelerating speed (Chopin, Auber, Weber, Heller, Thalberg).

Tardo, tardamente (TAHR-do, tahr-dah-MEN-tay: It.). Slow. *Tardando*, slowing, retarding.

Tartini's tone. See under *Resultant tone.*

Tasso (TAHS-so). Symphonic poem by Liszt, based on a poem by Byron, composed 1849–51 and first performed as an overture to Goethe's drama *Torquato Tasso*. See under *Symphonic poem.*

Tastiera (tahs-tee-AY-ra: It.). The finger board of the violin, also called *tasto*. *Sulla tastiera* (*sul tasto*), same as *flautando.*

Tasto (TAHS-to: It.). (1) See *Tastiera.* — (2) Key [of a keyboard]. *Tasto solo*, in compositions with a thorough bass, indicates that the bass note should be played alone, without the addition of harmonies.

Tattoo. The military signals, sounded on bugles and drums, by which the soldiers are called to their quarters at night.

T. c. Abbreviation for *tre corde* (see under *Una corda*).

Tedesca (te-DES-ka: It., German [dance]). About 1800, name for *Ländler and similar waltzlike dances in rather quick triple time.

Te Deum (L., Thee, O Lord [we praise]). A celebrated hymn of praise and rejoicing, sung in the Roman Catholic liturgy at Matins of greater feasts of a joyful character and in the Anglican liturgy during Morning Prayer. It has been erroneously attributed to St. Ambrose (hence the designation *Ambrosian hymn). The text has often been used for compositions designed for occasions of thanksgiving, e.g., after great victories. Well-known examples are by Handel, for the peace of Utrecht (1712) and the victory of Dettingen (1743); by Berlioz for the Paris Exhibition of 1855; by Bruckner, 1884; Dvořák, 1896; Sullivan, for Queen Victoria's Diamond Jubilee, 1897; and Verdi, 1898.

Telephone, The. One-act comic opera by Menotti, completed in 1947 as a companion piece to *The *Medium.* There are three characters: Lucy (soprano); her suitor, Ben (baritone); and the telephone itself which, throughout most of the opera, prevents Ben from completing his proposal to Lucy.

Telharmonium. See under *Electrophonic instruments.*

Tema (TAY-ma: It.). Theme, subject.

Temperament. General designation for various systems of tuning in which the intervals are "tempered," i.e., they deviate from the acoustically correct intervals of the *Pythagorean scale and of *just intonation. Such adjustments are necessary since systems based on the pure intervals are very limited, restricting choice of keys as well as harmonic progressions. During the 16th and 17th centuries various systems of tempered tuning were in use which provided for partial adjustments, so that a number of keys (up to three sharps or flats) could be used (see *Mean-tone system*). These are called *unequal temperament,* in contrast to the system of *equal temperament which was universally adopted during the 18th century.

Temple blocks. Same as *Chinese blocks.*

Tempo. The rate of speed of a composition or section, as indicated by *tempo marks or by *metronome indications. Only the latter provide a means of determining the exact tempo desired by the composer, while inscriptions such as *Adagio, Allegro molto,* etc., are general indications, leaving the interpreter considerable latitude in his choice of tempo. On the whole, composers seem to have favored this less specific practice, since original metronome marks are fairly rare, even in the works of modern composers. There often arises, therefore, the question of the "right" tempo for a composition — one of the most controversial topics in the field of musical interpretation. The discrepancy in tempo encountered in two performances of, e.g., the second movement of Beethoven's Seventh Symphony is amazing. Despite the "authority" with which each conductor and his disciples defend their position, the choice of tempo is largely a matter of personal preference. Generally it can be said that, as far as the classical repertory is concerned (Mozart, Beethoven, and especially Bach), modern conductors and performers play the fast movements too fast, the slow ones too slow.

Tempo giusto (TEM-po JOOS-to: It.). Normal, proper speed; strict tempo.

Tempo marks. Indications (usually in Italian) of the speed of a composition or a section. These are, proceeding from the slowest to the fastest: *larghissimo* (very broad), *largo* (broad), *lento* (slow), *adagio* (slow), *andante* (walking), *moderato* (moderate), *allegretto* (rather fast), *allegro* (fast), *vivace* (lively), *presto* (very fast), *prestissimo* (very, very fast). Gradual changes of speed are indicated by *ritardando* (slackening), *ritenuto* (holding back), and *accelerando* (quickening). See under the individual entries, particularly *Andante*.

Ten. Short for °tenuto.

Tenebrae (TEN-e-bray: L., dark [hours]). The early morning services on Wednesday, Thursday, and Good Friday of Holy Week, preceding Easter, so called because of the gradual extinction of the candles. Among the chants sung during this service are the °Lamentations and the °Improperia.

Tenor (from L. *tenere,* to hold). (1) The highest male voice; see under *Voices, Range of.* — (2) In part music, the part above the lowest; see under *Voice parts.* — (3) Originally (12th-13th century) tenor was the name for that part (then the lowest, but corresponding in range to the modern tenor) which had the °cantus firmus, a Gregorian melody presented in long note values, so that tenor originally meant "part in sustained notes."

Tenor clef. See under *Clefs.*

Tenor drum. See *Drums* (3).

Tenuto (tay-NOO-to: It., held). Fully sustained, occasionally even a bit longer than the note value requires.

Ternary form. A common musical form consisting of three distinct and self-contained sections, the third being a repeat (often modified) of the first, while the second forms a noticeable contrast to the first (and third): A B A. Numerous examples exist in the Romantic °character pieces, e.g., Chopin's Nocturnes and Brahms' piano pieces. The minuets and scherzos of sonatas (symphonies, string quartets, etc.) are regularly in ternary form, the middle section being called °trio. The same form is also used for marches (Schubert's *Marches militaires*), waltzes (Chopin's *"Minute" Waltz*), and occasionally in the suites of Bach for a pair of dances (e.g., Gavotte I, Gavotte II; see *Alternativo*), which invariably call for repeat of I after II: I II I (= A B A). Finally, the slow movements of °sonatas are frequently written in ternary form. In these, as well as in the Romantic character pieces, the middle section serves to introduce a change of mood, e.g., from the lyrical to the dramatic, or from the cheerful to the somber.

Occasionally one meets with examples of "continuous" ternary form, in which the middle section continues with the material of the first, but is set apart by some device such as a change of key, e.g., the first movement of Beethoven's *Moonlight Sonata* and a number of Mendelssohn's *Songs without Words*. See also under *Sonata form*.

Tertian harmony. A harmonic system based on the interval of a third, i.e., on the triad; hence our common system of harmony as opposed, e.g., to *quartal harmony.

Terzett (ter-TSET: G.), **terzetto** (ter-TSET-to: It.). A vocal piece, usually operatic, for three solo singers.

Tessitura (tes-see-TOO-ra: It., texture). The prevailing compass of a vocal or instrumental part in relation to the total range of that voice or instrument. Thus, if a certain soprano part ranges mostly from c" to g" (see *Voices, Range of*), that part is said to be in a "high" tessitura, otherwise "medium" or "low."

Testo (TES-to: It., text). In oratorios, passions, etc., designation for the part of the narrator who relates the Biblical story.

Tetrachord. In ancient *Greek music, a succession of four descending notes consisting nor-

mally of a whole tone, whole tone, and half tone, for example, e'-d'-c'-b or a-g-f-e. Nowadays the term is loosely applied to any four-note segment of a scale, descending or ascending, and without regard to intervallic structure.

Tetralogy (Gr., four ideas). A term sometimes used for the four operas constituting Wagner's *Ring of the Nibelung*. Wagner designated the first as a prologue, the other three as a trilogy.

Texture. The horizontal (melodic lines) and vertical (chords) relationships of musical materials, comparable to the interweaving of the warp and woof of woven fabric. There are three basic musical textures: *monophonic, *homophonic, and *polyphonic. The first is represented by a single melodic line. The second exists in what is commonly called "accompanied melody," and consists of a single melodic line (horizontal) supported at various points by chords (vertical). Polyphonic texture, on the other hand, consists of two or more horizontal lines of individual design, connected with each other by the vertical relationship of consonance or harmony. In the dissonant polyphony of some 20th-century music, however, this vertical relationship is governed by other considerations.

In addition to these three basic types, there are combinations which might be called hybrid textures, e.g., three melodic lines (polyphony) supported by some subsidiary chordal accompaniment (homophony).

Theme. In sonatas, fugues, etc., same as *subject. Sometimes theme has the connotation of a complete and self-contained melody, as in "theme with variations" (see *Variation*).

Theorbo(e) (the-AWR-bo). A large lute of the 17th century having, in addition to the ordinary strings of the lute, a number of bass strings stretched over a second neck.

Theory of music. Originally the philosophical, speculative, and scientific explanation of musical phenomena such as acoustics, scales, intervals, etc. In current usage, however, the term is applied in academic circles to courses which more properly could be called "elementary musicianship" or "techniques and materials of music" — studies of notation, part writing, harmonic analysis, sight singing (see *Solfeggio*), ear training, counterpoint, form analysis, orchestration, etc. See the separate entries.

Theremin (THAYR-a-min). An *electrophonic instrument invented about 1924 by the Russian scientist Leon Theremin. It consists essentially of two oscillators and a loudspeaker contained in an upright box to which are attached a vertical rod antenna at the right side and a horizontal loop antenna on the left. The player holds both hands in space, and by moving his hands back and forth, changes the pitch with the right hand, the loudness with the left. Its main drawback is the impossibility of obtaining distinct pitches without an intervening glissando. This disad-

vantage has been eliminated in the *Ondes musicales*.

Theresienmesse (te-RAY-zee-en-MES-se: Theresa's Mass), Nickname (unexplained) for Haydn's Mass in B-flat, composed in 1799.

Third. See under *Intervals*; also *Triad; Tertian harmony*.

Thirty-second note. See under *Notes and rests*.

Thorough bass (old spelling of through bass, translation of It. *basso continuo*, i.e., bass continuing throughout the composition). A method of representing a keyboard accompaniment by the bass notes only, while the chords to be played with the right hand are improvised, usually with the aid of figures written above or underneath the bass notes (*figured bass*). This stenographic system was universally used in the Baroque period (1600–1750), for which it is so characteristic that the name "Thorough-bass Period" is sometimes applied to that period. Each figure indicates the interval above the bass note — for instance, with g as the bass note, 7 indicates f, and $\frac{6}{5}$ with a indicates e and f (or, depending on the key signature, e and $f\sharp$, or $e\flat$ and f). The intervals of the third, fifth, and octave are frequently not indicated by figures (3, 5, 8), the understanding being that these are to be added wherever suitable. Chromatic alterations are indicated by a sharp, flat, or natural placed after the figure. If these signs occur without a figure, they refer to the third degree, making this a major or a minor third. Sharpened degrees are also frequently indicated by a diagonal stroke through the figure or by an apostrophe. The accompanying examples (Fig. 110) illustrate these principles;

Fig. 110

needless to say, this constitutes only the rudiments of the art of thorough-bass accompaniments, numerous details and additions being left to the player's skill and ingenuity. *Basso continuo* or simply *continuo* is the name for bass parts to be played in this manner. However, these terms were also used for "continuous" bass parts to be played without additional chords.

Three-Cornered Hat, The (Sp., *El Sombrero de tres picos*). A comedy ballet by Falla, produced in London, 1919. Based on a novel by Alarcón, the story relates the marital mix-ups of a village official, a miller, and their wives. The music, largely taken from Andalusian sources, has a strong Spanish flavor, and some of the dances (particularly the Miller's Dance) have become popular concert pieces.

Threepenny Opera, The (G., *Die Dreigroschenoper*). Operetta by Kurt Weill (libretto by Brecht), produced in Berlin, 1928. It is a modern *ballad opera, based on the plot of Gay's *The Beggar's Opera* (1728), with attractive music in a sophisticaed jazz style.

Through-composed. See under *Strophic*.

Thunder machine. A device introduced by R. Strauss in his *Alpine Symphony to imitate thunder. It consists of a big rotating drum with hard balls inside which strike against the drumhead.

Thus Spake Zarathustra (G., *Also sprach Zarathustra*). Tone poem by R. Strauss, op. 30, completed in 1896. It is based on the well-known literary work of the German philosopher Nietzsche, in which the concept of the superman is propounded in speeches of Zarathustra (Zoroaster, founder of the ancient Persian religion, *c.* 1000 B.C.). The work is divided into several sections: Of the People of the Hinterlands, Of the Great Longing, Of Happiness and Misfortune, Song of the Grave, Concerning Science (an extremely dissonant and pedantic fugue), The Convalescent, Dance Song, Song of the Night, and Song of the Night Wanderer.

Tie. An arching line connecting two successive notes of the same pitch, indicating that the second note should not be played, but should be added to the value of the first.

Tierce de Picardie (F.). See *Picardy third*.

Till Eulenspiegel's Merry Pranks (til OY-len-shpee-gel: G., *Till Eulenspiegels lustige Streiche*). Tone poem by R. Strauss, op. 28 (1895), based on the 16th-century German folk tale of Till

Eulenspiegel (Tyl Owlglass), perpetrator of numerous pranks. The music develops, in a free rondo form, around two themes, one representing Till as a popular hero, the other as a vagabond and prankster. There are no specific programmatic connotations except for the close, which clearly suggests the sentencing and hanging of Till. The introductory material, which also serves as a coda, establishes the fairy-tale touch, "once upon a time."

Timbale (tanh-BAHL: F.). Kettledrum.

Timbre (tamhbr: F.; also English). Same as °tone color.

Timbrel. Older English term for the tambourine.

Time. Same as °meter, e.g., 4/4 time equals 4/4 meter.

Time signature. A sign given at the beginning of a composition to indicate its °meter (time). It consists of two figures written like a fraction, the lower figure indicating the chosen unit of measurement, whether half note, quarter note, etc. (half note = 2; quarter note = 4; eighth note = 8, etc.), the upper figure indicating the number of such units in a measure. Thus, 3/2 means that there are three half notes to the measure; 4/4, four quarter notes; 6/8, six eighth notes, etc. In addition there are two special signs, $\mathbb{C}$ for 4/4, and $\mathbb{¢}$ for 2/2. Both survive from the old system of °mensural notation, in which the full circle was used to indicate "perfect time" (*tempus perfectum*), i.e., triple division; the half cir-

cle for "imperfect time" (*tempus imperfectum*), i.e., duple division. While in both of these mensurations the *semibrevis* was the unit, the sign $\mathbb{¢}$ indicated that the *brevis* was to be considered as the unit. Hence, the circle and the half circle were called *alla semibreve*, and the $\mathbb{¢}$ was called *alla breve*, a term which still survives today. About 1700 the symbol $\mathbb{CO}$ was used to indicate measures of double length, i.e., 8/4 instead of 4/4 (Bach, Partita no. 6, Gigue), a method of designation also encountered in the original sign $\mathbb{¢¢}$, i.e., 4/2 instead of 2/2, of Schubert's Impromptu op. 90, no. 3.

Timpan. Old English for *tympanon*, a medieval instrument similar to the °dulcimer. See also under *Tympani.*

Timpani (TIM-pah-nee: It.). Kettledrums. *Timpani coperti* or *sordi*, muffled kettledrums.

Tin-Pan Alley. Designation for the industry, centered in New York City, which publishes popular music. The name is often used with derogatory connotations.

Tipping. See under *Tonguing.*

Tirarsi (It., to be drawn). See under *Tromba.*

Tira tutti (TEE-rah TOO-tee: It., draw all). In organ music, direction to use the full organ, i.e., "pull out all the stops."

Tirasse (tee-RAHS: F.). Organ coupler.

Tirer, tirez (tee-ray: F., draw). (1) Retard. — (2) In organ music, indication to draw a specified stop.

Toccata (to-KAH-ta: It., from *toccare,* to touch [the keys]). An important type of early keyboard music, originating in the 16th century but cultivated mainly during the Baroque period. Its chief characteristic is the combination of various styles, improvisatory, virtuoso, fugal, etc., the whole being designed to exhibit the resources of the instrument (particularly the organ) as well as the ingenuity of the composer and the virtuosity of the performer. The earliest toccatas, by Andrea Gabrieli (1510–1586), consist of full chords and intervening scale passages only. Claudio Merulo (1533–1604) introduced one or two fugal (F) sections (in *ricercar style) alternating with sections in free toccata (T) style (T F T or T F T F T). While Frescobaldi created a highly personal type of toccata characterized mainly by frequent change of musical ideas, the Merulo type was developed during the 17th century under the North German composers (Weckmann, 1621–1675; Buxtehude, 1637–1707; Bruhns, *c.* 1665–1697), reaching its culmination in the works of J. S. Bach. These compositions combine sections in toccata style with fugues, in various arrangements (such as T F T, T F T F T, T F, etc.). Bach used the toccata style also for some of his preludes, e.g., in the great A-minor Prelude and Fugue for organ. Italian composers of the late 17th century (Pasquini,

1637–1710; A. Scarlatti, 1660–1725) developed the toccata (without fugue) in the direction of superficial keyboard virtuosity, gradually leading to the etudes of Clementi and Czerny.

Both the free, rhapsodic type of the North Germans and the etude type of the Italians have been revived by later composers. Examples of the etude type (*perpetuum mobile*) are the toccatas by Schumann, Debussy (in *Pour le piano*), Honegger, Prokofiev, and Casella, while the *Toccata* by Busoni is a fascinating re-creation of the Bach toccata.

Tod und Verklärung. See *Death and Transfiguration.*

Tombeau (tonh-BO: F., tombstone). A composition written in memory of a deceased person. French composers of the Baroque period wrote such pieces in commemoration of friends or famous composers, e.g., d'Anglebert for his teacher Chambonnières, F. Couperin for Lully and for Corelli. Ravel revived this custom in his *Le Tombeau de Couperin,* a suite in six movements (Prélude, Fugue, Forlane, Rigaudon, Menuet, Toccata) written originally for piano (1917), and orchestrated (without the fugue and toccata) in 1919.

Tom-tom. American Indian or Oriental drum of indefinite pitch, imitations of which are occasionally used in dance bands.

Tonada (to-NAH-ttha: Sp.). General Spanish term for song;

also used in the Latin American countries.

Tonadilla (to-nah-TTHEE-ya: Sp.). A short Spanish comic opera of popular type, somewhat in the character of the Italian *opera buffa* (see under *Comic opera*). It flourished from about the middle of the 18th to the early 19th century. Chief composers were Luis Misón (d. 1766), Pablo Esteve, and Blas de Laserna (1751–1816).

Tonal and real. In a fugue, an answer is called real if it is an exact transposition of the subject; tonal, if certain intervals are changed. Such changes frequently take place if the subject contains the interval of a fifth (for example, d-a), this being answered, not by the transposed fifth (a-e'), but by the fourth (a-d') as in Fig. 111 (from

Fig. 111

Bach's *Art of Fugue*). Fugues having a tonal answer, at least in the beginning, are sometimes called *tonal fugues;* those having a real answer being called *real fugues.* For a somewhat different application of the terms tonal and real, see under *Sequence* (1).

Tonality. A term essentially synonymous with °key (C major tonality equals key of C major), but also often used in more general and vague connotations, e.g., in the distinction between tonality and modality,

in which tonality denotes the entire system of all the major and minor keys, modality denoting the system of the church modes. Yet another meaning, of a more recent date, is indicated in the use of the term "tonality" as the opposite of "atonality." Here tonality means "loyalty to a tonic" (i.e., to a tonal center which, of course, may change frequently during a composition) and therefore includes not only the music of the 17th to 19th centuries but also the works of some modern composers such as Stravinsky and Hindemith, in contradistinction from those of Schönberg, who rejected the traditional concept of tonality.

Tondichtung (TON-dikh-toong: G.). Tone poem, °symphonic poem.

Tone. A sound of well-defined pitch and quality, as distinct from a noise or a diffused sound such as that of a bass drum or a gong. Tone, therefore, is the basic building material of music. It has four distinct properties: pitch (for example, c'), duration (e.g., a half note), intensity (e.g., forte), and timbre or °tone color (e.g., flute sound, trumpet sound). The term is also used (especially in England) in the meaning of whole tone (i.e., major second) as opposed to half tone or semi-tone. In American usage, a distinction is usually made to the effect that one "hears a tone" and "sees a note," a note being the written symbol for a tone.

Tone cluster. In modern music, a strongly dissonant group of tones lying close together (d-d#-e-f-f# or e-f-g-a-b, etc.). The term was invented by Henry Cowell who, along with Charles Ives, has used the device extensively, sometimes prescribing that an entire section of the keyboard be depressed by the forearm or by a board of specified length. For an example see under *Chords*, Fig. 22r.

Tone color. The peculiar quality of a tone as sounded by a given instrument or voice. The term, therefore, indicates the difference between two tones of the same pitch, duration, and intensity (see under *Tone*) if performed on, e.g., a violin and a flute. The tone color (also called quality or timbre) is determined by the harmonics (see *Acoustics*, 4).

Tone poem. Same as *Symphonic poem.

Tone row. See under *Twelve-tone technique*.

Tonguing. In playing wind instruments, the use of the tongue for greater precision of attack, the tongue moved as in pronouncing the letters t or k: t-t-... (single tonguing), t-k, t-k... (double tonguing or tipping). *Flutter tonguing* is produced by rolling an r with the tip of the tongue (as in Italian pronunciation).

Tonic. The first and main note of a key, c in C major (minor), d in D major (minor), etc. See *Scale degrees; Key; Tonality; Chords.*

Tonic accent. An accent resulting from higher pitch. It plays an especially important role in Gregorian chant, where accented syllables often have a note of higher pitch, for example, a-g-g on *Dómino*.

Tonic Sol-fa. A method of notating music by means of syllables (see *Solmization*), developed about 1840 by John Curwen and now widely used in England, particularly for instruction and choral singing. The syllables (borrowed from the old system of solmization) are: *doh, ray, me, fah, soh, lah, te,* and are indicated in the notation by the letters d, r, m, f, s, l, t. They are used as "movable" syllables ("movable do"), that is, they indicate not fixed notes but the seven degrees of the key in which the composition is written (e f# g# a ..., if the key is E major). Higher and lower octaves are indicated by horizontal dashes above or below the letters, and time values are indicated by the placement of the letters within each bar.

Tonic Sol-fa is useful for the specific purposes for which it was devised, i.e., sight singing and ear training, but is practically useless for more complex types of music such as for piano, orchestra, etc.

Tonsatz, Tonstück (TON-zahts, TON-shtuik: G.). Piece of music, composition.

Tosca (TAWS-ka). Opera by Puccini (libretto by G. Giacosca and L. Illica, based on Sardou's drama of the same title), produced in Rome, 1900. The plot takes place in Rome in 1800, and the main characters are Angelotti (bass), a political offender who has escaped from prison; his friend Cavaradossi (tenor), a painter; Tosca (soprano), a singer in love with Cavaradossi; and Baron Scarpia (baritone), the chief of police who is in amorous pursuit of Tosca. In Act II, Scarpia questions Cavaradossi about Angelotti's hiding place, sending him to the torture chamber when he refuses to answer. Tosca agrees to come to supper with Scarpia, where she hears Cavaradossi's cries of pain under torture and, in despair, divulges Angelotti's hiding place. Scarpia sends Cavaradossi to prison to be shot, but assures Tosca that blank shells will be used. When Scarpia advances to embrace her, she stabs him to death. In Act III Tosca sees Cavaradossi in his cell, and tells him about the mock execution. The bullets are real, however, and she discovers that her lover's "marvelous acting" is bitter reality. When the police come to arrest her for Scarpia's murder, she throws herself over the battlements of the prison.

Touch. In pianoforte playing, the way of approaching and depressing the keys in order to obtain a satisfactory sound, as well as a variety of tone qualities, ranging from the soft and lyrical to the harsh and percussive. The basic idea of touch is that piano playing permits not only dynamic gradations (*pp, p, mf*, etc.), obtained by differing the force applied to the keys, but also of additional variations of tone color, so that a *mf* may be

either "lyrical," "vigorous," "percussive," etc. Scientifically, this idea is unsupportable since the sound of the pianoforte is produced by hammers whose movement can be varied only as regards the speed with which they hit the strings. However, piano playing is not a scientific and mechanical process, but is largely conditioned by mental attitudes, and, to project them, the idea of "touch" with its numerous subtleties is useful and often indispensable.

Touche (toosh: F.). Key (of the pianoforte) or finger board (of the violin). *Sur la touche,* same as *°flautando.*

Tourte bow (toort). Designation for the type of violin bow made by F. Tourte (1747–1835). See under *Bow.*

Toye. Title of short and playful pieces of the Elizabethan period.

Toy Symphony. A playful composition usually ascribed to Haydn and scored, aside from the 1st and 2nd violins and double bass, for toy instruments such as cuckoo, quail, nightingale, trumpet, drum, rattle, and triangle. It is a delightful little symphony to be played and enjoyed by children and adults alike. Recent investigations indicate that it is not by Haydn but by Mozart's father, Leopold (1719–1787).

Tp. Abbreviation of timpani.

Tr. Abbreviation of trumpet or trill (*tr*).

Tract. In Gregorian chant, an item of the Proper of the Mass, used occasionally instead of the Alleluia. Historically, the tract is the older of the two chants. From about 600 on, the Alleluia took the place of the tract, which was retained only for feasts of a somber character.

Traduction (trah-duiks-YONH: F.), **traduzione** (trah-doot-see-O-nay: It.). *Arrangement.

Tragic Overture (G., *Tragische Ouvertüre*). An orchestral composition by Brahms, composed in 1880 as a companion piece to the *Academic Festival Overture.

Tragic Symphony. Subtitle, provided by Schubert, of his Symphony no. 4, in C minor, composed in 1816. The work is clearly more serious and somber than his first three symphonies.

Transcendental Etudes. Twelve concert etudes by Liszt, published in 1851 under the title of *Études d'exécution transcendantes,* referring to their great technical difficulty.

Transcription. Essentially the same as *arrangement, but admitting considerable freedom in the handling of the original material, as, e.g., in the numerous transcriptions by Liszt in which themes from Wagnerian operas or other sources are freely presented in the glittering light of a highly virtuoso pianism.

Transfigured Night (G., *Verklärte Nacht*). Sextet in one movement, for two violins, two violas, and two cellos, by Schönberg (op. 4, 1899). It was inspired by a poem of R. Dehmel describing how the happiness of two lovers, despite their personal tragedy, can transfigure a bleak winter's night into a thing of great beauty. The style of this early work derives from the "love music" of Wagner and R. Strauss, with occasional impressionistic effects. It was later arranged for full string orchestra, and finally became the music for the ballet, *Pillar of Fire.*

Transformation of themes. The modification of a theme made in such a way as to "change its personality." This is a 19th-century device (also called *metamorphosis*) which differs from earlier, more technical, methods of modification, such as augmentation and diminution, inversion, or ornamentation. A characteristic example exists in the various appearances of the *idée fixe* of Berlioz' *Fantastic Symphony. The method was more fully exploited in Liszt's symphonic poems, in Wagner's operas, where it is applied to the *leitmotivs (see Fig. 112, from *Siegfried*), and in Sibelius' symphonies.

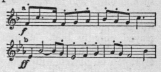

Fig. 112

Transition. A passage designed to connect two sections of a composition, e.g., two movements of a sonata (frequently in Handel), or two sections of ternary form, or two successive themes in sonata form (here also called *bridge passage).

Transposing instruments. Instruments for which the music is written not in its actual pitch, but in a different key. An example is the clarinet in A, that is, a clarinet whose fundamental tone (with all keys depressed) is A. Since for a player of such an instrument A major is the simplest key, it has become customary to present this key to him in the simplest notation, C major. Music for the clarinet in A, therefore, is always notated a minor third higher than it sounds and, as a result, sounds a minor third lower than written (see Fig. 113). The use of trans-

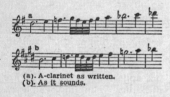

(a). A-clarinet as written.
(b). As it sounds.

Fig. 113

posing instruments (more accurately, of transposing notation) dates back to the period (18th century) when wind instruments such as horns and trumpets were valveless (see *Natural horn, trumpet*) and therefore could be played only in their "natural" key. Modern instruments, however, can be played with almost equal facility in all the keys, so that there is no reason why their music should not be notated according to actual pitch. It is very unfortunate that a mere archaism has been preserved which greatly, and quite unnecessarily, adds to the difficulty of reading orchestral scores. The most important among the transposing instruments are the clarinet (in Bb or A), the English horn (in F), the French horn (in F), the trumpet (in Bb and A), and the cornet (in Bb and A). The term "transposing" is also applied to instruments such as the piccolo which, quite sensibly, is notated an octave lower than it sounds in order to avoid the extensive use of ledger lines.

Transposition. The playing or rewriting of a composition in a key different from the original, for example, E-flat instead of D. The music remains the same, except for a change of pitch. Accompanists particularly are often required to transpose in order to accommodate the vocal range of a singer. The easiest transposition is that of a chromatic semitone, for example, from F to F-sharp or from E to E-flat, since here most of the written notes remain unaltered, and it is only necessary to imagine a different key signature. Other transpositions (a second, third, etc., down or up) are considerably more difficult, particularly in the case of modern music involving modulations, chromatic alterations, etc.

Transverse flute. An older name for the flute, used in the 18th century to distinguish this instrument, held horizontally, from the *recorder, held vertically.

Traps. In jazz parlance, the various noise-producing devices attached to the drum (trap drum) and played by the trap drummer.

Trauermarsch (TROW-er-marsh: G.). Funeral march.

Trauer-Ode (TROW-er-O-de: Funeral Ode). A choral work by Bach, written in 1727 on the death of the Electress Christiane of Saxony. It is based on an ode by Gottsched, and is in the form of a cantata, with choruses, arias, and recitatives.

Trauer-Symphonie (TROW-er-zim-fo-NEE: Mourning Symphony). Nickname (because of its somber character) for Haydn's Symphony no. 44 (*c.* 1771), in E minor.

Traversière (trah-vayr-see-AYR: F.), **traverso** (trah-VAYR-so: It.), **Traversflöte** (TRAH-vers-FLEU-te: G.). °Transverse flute.

Traviata, La (trah-VEEAH-ta: The Erring Woman). Opera in three acts by Verdi (libretto by F. Piave, after Dumas' *La Dame aux camélias*), produced in Venice, 1853. The scene is Paris of the 1850's, with the courtesan Violetta (soprano) as the central figure. Falling in love with Alfred Germont (tenor), she gives up her life of pleasure and lives with him (Act II) but, implored by Alfred's father (baritone), leaves his home and resumes her former life. Alfred, not knowing that her change of mind is only a pretext, insults her, but in Act III he and the dying Violetta are again united in love.

Traviata is one of the earliest instances of the use of a contemporary plot in opera, a practice which became established, about 1890, by the °verismo movement. Musically it follows the tradition of the Italian opera with its mixture of lyrical and pathetic elements, its melodies of a popular type, and its concentration on effective vocal numbers.

Tre (tray: It.). Three. *Sonata a tre*, trio sonata. *Tre corde*, see *Una corda.*

Treble. An older term for the highest part of a choral composition, i.e., soprano. It is derived from L. *triplum*, a 13th-century designation for the "third," i.e., the highest part of a three-voice composition. For treble recorder, treble viol, see under *Recorder; Viol.*

Treble clef. Same as G clef (violin clef).

Tremolo (TREM-o-lo: It., treble). On stringed instruments the quick reiteration of the same note, produced by a rapid up-and-down movement of the bow. It is indicated as shown in Fig. 114a. The string tremolo is an important orchestral effect frequently used for moments of dramatic impact or as a vibrating background for melodies played by other instruments.

Fig. 114

The term tremolo is also used for the rapid alternation of two notes (Fig. 114b), this being called *fingered tremolo,* because it is produced by a rapid motion, not of the bow, but of a finger.

In pianoforte music, the term tremolo is used, not for a rapid repetition of the same note, but for its rapid alternation with the higher octave. This effect is used mainly in piano arrangements of orchestral works to imitate the string tremolo or sustained chords. In singing, tremolo denotes a fluctuation of pitch resulting from a lack of control on the singer's part. See under *Vibrato*.

Tremulant (TREM-ew-lant). An organ stop producing alternating increases and decreases of wind pressure, thus causing mechanical pulsations which have an expressive effect similar to a violinist's vibrato.

Trenodia (tre-no-DEE-a: It.). Threnody, dirge.

Trepak (tray-PAHK). A Russian dance in quick duple time.

Triad (TREYE-ad). A chord consisting of three tones: a fundamental note, its upper third, and its upper fifth. It may also be described as consisting of two superimposed intervals of a third. Depending on whether the intervals are major or minor (see under *Intervals*), there are four species of triad (Fig. 115): (a) *major,* consisting of a major third plus a minor third (c-e-g); (b) *minor,* consisting of a minor third plus a major third (c-eb-g); (c) *diminished,* consisting of two minor thirds (c#-e-g); (d) *augmented,* consisting of two major thirds (c-e-g#). The major and minor triads are consonant (see *Consonance and dissonance*), and form the basis of the entire system of *chords.

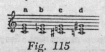

Fig. 115

Triangle. A percussion instrument consisting of a steel bar bent in the shape of a triangle and suspended from a hook or chord. It is struck with a steel rod and produces a high, tinkling sound of indefinite pitch.

Trill. A musical ornament consisting of the rapid alternation of a given tone with its upper neighbor. It is indicated by the sign *tr* or *t,* to which, in the case of extended trills, a long wavy line is added. Regarding details of performance, a distinction must be made between the "modern trill," which came into use early in the 19th century, and the "old trill," which is the only proper one for the works of Bach and Handel (very likely also for Haydn, Mozart, and early Beethoven). The modern trill starts on the written note, is played as rapidly as possible, and usually closes with a five-note turn introducing the lower neighbor note. This closing turn is required when the next principal note is higher than the main note of the trill, especially

Fig. 116

when it is a second above; the turn may often be omitted when the trill leads to a lower note (see Fig. 116a,b). The old trill differs from the modern one in two main details: it invariably starts on the upper neighbor note (regardless of the pitch of the preceding note), and it is performed in small rhythmic values, but not "as fast as possible." It is often indicated by a zigzag line (wrongly called inverted mordent). See Fig. 116c. See also under *Ornaments.*

Trillo del diavolo (It.). See *Devil's Trill Sonata.*

Trilogy (Gr., three ideas). Wagner's subtitle for the *°Ring of the Nibelung.* See also *Tetralogy.*

Trinklied (TRINGK-leet: G.). Drinking song.

Trio (It., group of three). (1) Designation for a group of three performers; also for the music that they perform. The most important type is the piano trio for piano, violin, and cello. Particularly famous are Beethoven's Trios, op. 70 (°Ghost Trio) and 97, and Schubert's, op. 99 and 100. The string trio for violin, viola, and cello was rarely used in the 19th century, but has received some attention by modern composers (Hindemith, Schönberg). An unusual combination is Brahms' °Horn Trio. — (2) In older music, trio means a composition in three contrapuntal parts, irrespective of the number of instruments, which may vary from one (harpsichord, organ, e.g., in Bach's six organ sonatas) to four (see under *Trio sonata*). Modern examples of a "Trio for pianoforte" (not to be confused with a "Pianoforte trio") have been written by Hindemith. — (3) Name for the middle section of the scherzo or minuet movement of sonatas, symphonies, etc.; see under *Minuet.* Also for the middle section of other compositions in °ternary form, e.g., military marches and some of the Impromptus by Schubert.

Trio sonata. The most important type of Baroque chamber music, so called because it is composed in three parts, two upper parts of similar range and design, and a supporting thorough-bass part. The trio sonata is usually performed on four instruments: two violins (or violin and flute) for the upper parts, a cello (or viola da gamba) for the bass part, and a harpsichord (or organ) for the bass part and the improvised harmonies (see *Thorough bass*). For the form, see under *Sonata,* II. Trio sonatas were written by Corelli, Purcell, Handel, d'Abaco, and many other composers from about 1680 to 1750. Bach preferred the trio sonata without thorough-bass accompaniment, e.g., in his sonatas for violin and harpsichord (calling for two instruments) or in his organ sonatas (for only one). There are practically no examples of trio sonatas performed on three instruments.

Triple concerto. A concerto for three solo instruments (and orchestra), e.g., Beethoven's Concerto, op. 56, for piano, violin, cello, and orchestra.

Triple counterpoint. See under *Invertible counterpoint.*

Triple fugue. See under *Double fugue*.

Triplet. A group of three notes to be performed in the place of two of the same value, indicated by a 3 and usually by a slur (see Fig. 117). Occasionally the pat-

Fig. 117

tern shown at the end of the measure is notated as a dotted rhythm; see *Dotted notes*, Fig. 34d.

Triple meter (time). See under *Meter*.

Tristan and Isolde (TRIS-tahn and ee-SOL-de: G., *Tristan und Isolde*). Opera in three acts by Wagner to his own libretto (based on a medieval legend of Celtic origin), produced in Munich, 1865. The main characters are Isolde (soprano), an Irish princess, and Tristan (tenor), a knight who is escorting her from Ireland to Cornwall, to be married to the English king Marke (bass). Isolde, learning from Tristan that he has killed her former betrothed in combat, is torn between hatred and love, and orders her companion Brangäne (mezzosoprano) to prepare a poisoned drink for Tristan and herself. Brangäne, however, mixes a love potion, and the potion takes effect just as the ship arrives at the Cornish coast (Act I). The lovers, meeting while the king goes hunting (Act II), are spied upon by Melot (baritone), who wounds Tristan in a duel. Tristan, brought to his own castle by his servant Kurvenal (baritone), dies (Act III) in the arms of Isolde, who has come to nurse him. Heartbroken, she joins him in death.

Tristan is without doubt the fullest musical incarnation of love and passion ever presented on the stage. Acts II and III are practically an "unending love duet" in which feeling and sensation, ranging from the tenderest to the most passionate, are portrayed. Owing to the relative simplicity and unimportance of the story, the *leitmotiv plays a secondary role in this opera, if compared with the *Ring*. The most conspicuous features of the music are the "unending melody" and a harmonic vocabulary full of daring chromatics and appoggiaturas.

Tritone (TREYE-tone). The interval of the augmented fourth (c-f#) or diminished fifth (c-gb), so called because it spans three whole tones. It has always been considered a "dangerous" interval (see *Diabolus in musica*) which was to be avoided or treated with special precaution. As a melodic progression, it was rarely used before 1900, except in combinations such as c-f#-g, in which f# becomes the leading tone before g. In modern music, however, it has been established as a legitimate interval, e.g., in the *whole-tone scale in which it replaces the perfect fourth; in bitonal formations (Petrushka chord; see under *Bitonality*); and in various experimental devices based on the fact that the tritone is exactly one half of the octave, the interval c-f# being the inversion of f#-c'.

Trittico (TREET-ti-co: It., Triptych, i.e., a painting on three panels as often found over altars). Name for a cycle of three independent one-act operas by Puccini, composed in 1918: (1) *Suor Angelica* (Sister Angelica) has a sentimental plot centering around a Florentine girl with an unfortunate past who has retired to a convent. When she hears that her child, born in sin, is dead, she kills herself, but her soul is borne to heaven by the Virgin. (2) *Gianni Schicchi* has a comical plot (laid in the 13th century) involving a rich merchant, Donati, who has died and left his entire estate to charity. His friend Gianni, by a clever ruse (he climbs into the deathbed and impersonates the dying Donati), succeeds in making a new will in his own favor. (3) *Il Tabarro* (The Cloak) is a tragic story in which Michele, a boatsman, kills Luigi, a longshoreman, who is the lover of Michele's wife Giorgetta. He covers the corpse with his cloak and, when the woman returns, flings back the cloak and reveals the dead body of her lover.

Trojans, The. See *Troyens*.

Tromba (TROM-ba: It.). Trumpet, also called *tromba cromatica, tromba a macchina, tromba ventile*, i.e., valve trumpet. *Tromba da tirarsi* is the slide trumpet, an 18th-century type having a short slide underneath the mouthpiece and therefore capable of producing more notes than the natural trumpet. The same instrument (possibly also the trombone) is occasionally prescribed by Bach under the name of *tromba spezzata* ("pieced," with reference to its consisting of several pieces).

Tromba marina (TROM-ba mah-REE-na: It.). A stringed instrument of the later Middle Ages, consisting of a long tapering body (5 to 6 feet in length), narrower at the top, over which a single string was stretched. The string was not stopped, but slightly touched to produce harmonics. No satisfactory explanation of the strange name has been given.

Tromba spezzata. See under *Tromba*.

Trombone. A brass instrument with a cup-shaped mouthpiece and a cylindrical tube bent into an oblong shape with two long parallel sides, and expanding into a bell. A sliding mechanism

Trombone

takes the place of the valves used on the other brass instruments and, like these, serves to fill in the gaps between the natural tones (see *Wind instruments*). See illustration.

The trombone can be regarded as the tenor member of the trumpet family, although its tone is more mellow, less brilliant, than that of the trumpet. This difference in tone color is due mainly to the larger mouthpiece of the trombone. In addition to the normal trombone pitched in B-flat (*tenor trombone*), with a range from E to bb′, the *bass trombone*, with a range a fourth below the tenor, is used. Historically, the trombone is interesting because it was the first of all the orchestral instruments (except for drums) to appear in its present shape. The earliest extant representations, in paintings of the late 15th century, show all the essential features of the modern trombone.

Trommel (TROM-el: G.). Drum. *Grosse Trommel*, bass drum; *Kleine Trommel*, snare drum.

Trompete (trom-PAY-te: G.), **trompette** (tronh-PET: F.). Trumpet.

Trope. (1) In the Roman Catholic liturgy of the 9th century and later, an addition, textual and/or musical, to the chants that had become standardized under Pope Gregory (*c.* 600) or later. Among the simplest and shortest examples are the Kyrie tropes, in which a few words, such as *fons bonitatis* (fountain of goodness), are in-serted between the two original words (*Kyrie, fons bonitatis, eleison*) and set syllabically to the melisma of the original melody. Frequently, however, long sentences and even entire poems were placed between two words of the authentic text. A special type of particular importance are the *sequences. All the tropes, numbering many thousands, were abolished by the *Council of Trent, except for a few sequences. — (2) In 20th-century music, the term trope has been used by Josef Hauer (b. 1883) in connection with his special system of twelve-tone music, differing from that developed by Schönberg. Hauer distinguishes 44 tropes (each including about 100,000 different tone rows), and considers each trope as a sort of "key." Any change from one trope into another is modulation. His system has not been widely accepted.

Troppo (TROP-po: It.). Too much, usually in combinations such as *Allegro ma non troppo* (fast, but not too fast).

Troubadour, The (Verdi). See *Trovatore.

Troubadours. A medieval class of poet-musicians active in southern France (Provence) from about 1100 to 1300. Most of them were members of the nobility, devoting themselves not only to fighting and hunting, but also to cultivating poetry and music in romantic service to chivalrous love. About 2500 poems are preserved and about 250 of their melodies. They are all monophonic songs, a considerable number showing the form of the *ballade* (see *Ballade*, 1), while the majority are through-composed. Possibly there was, at least on occasion, some instrumental participation, e.g., by a fiddler (*jongleur) playing in unison with the singer, or extemporizing a short prelude. Outstanding members of the group were Guillaume de Poitiers (*c.* 1070–1127), Marcabru (a commoner, died *c.* 1150), Bernart de Ventadorn (died 1195), Raimon de Miraval (died *c.* 1220), and Guiraut Riquier (died 1294), known as the "last of the troubadours."

Trout Quintet. Schubert's Quintet in A, op. 114 (1819), for violin, viola, cello, double bass, and piano, in five movements, the fourth being a set of variations on his song *The Trout* (G., *Die Forelle*).

Trouvères (troo-VAYR). A medieval class of poet-musicians active in central and northern France from about 1150 to 1300. The movement developed from the *troubadours, and showed the same general traits. About 4000 poems are preserved, 1400 of them with melodies. Most of these show the form of the *ballade* (see *Ballade*, 1), a relatively small number being through-composed. Other forms associated with the trouvère movement are the *lai, the *rondeau, and the *virelai. Outstanding members of the group were Blondel de Nesles (*c.* 1150–*c.* 1200), Thibaut IV (1201–1253; king of Navarre), Perrin d'Angecourt (fl. *c.* 1250), and Adam de la Halle (a commoner, *c.* 1230–1288).

Trovatore, Il (eel tro-va-TAW-ray: The Troubadour or The Minstrel). Opera by Verdi (libretto by S. Cammarone, based on a Spanish play), produced in Rome, 1853. The plot (Spain, 15th century) centers around the beautiful Countess Leonora (soprano), the young troubadour Manrico (tenor), with whom she is in love, and the Count di Luna (baritone), who loves her. In the opening scene we are told by Ferrando (bass), Luna's Captain of the Guard, that the Count's younger brother, when a baby, had been stolen by a gypsy woman, Azucena (contralto). Unknown to the Count, this child is Manrico, who has grown up as Azucena's son. In Act III, Azucena has been captured by Luna and cast into prison. Manrico, about to be united with Leonora, hears that his "mother" is to be burned and rushes out to her rescue. He is also captured (Act IV), and Leonora now implores the Count for mercy, offering herself to him in marriage. In the last scene, Azucena and Manrico are both in the dungeon. Leonora comes to tell him that he is free, but dies of poison she has taken in order to escape the dreaded marriage with the Count. The Count orders Manrico's execution, and is finally told by the dying Azucena that he has killed his own brother.

Troyens, Les (lay trwah-YENH: The Trojans). Opera by Berlioz, to his own libretto (after Virgil), in two parts: *Le Prise de Troie* (The Taking of Troy) and *Les Troyens à Carthage* (The Trojans at Carthage), composed

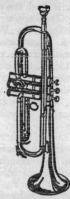

Trumpet

1856–59. Only the first part was produced during Berlioz' lifetime (Paris, 1863), the whole work being first performed in 1898.

Trumpet. A brass instrument with a cup-shaped mouthpiece and a narrow tube which is cylindrical for about three quarters of its length, then widening out into a moderate-sized bell. The tube is bent into an oblong shape, with two short parallel sides. The trumpet has three valves (rotary or piston), hence the name valve trumpet in distinction to the earlier natural trumpet. The trumpet is pitched in B-flat (the pitch can be lowered to A by means of a short slide or a special valve) and has a chromatic compass of two octaves and a half, from f♯ to c'''. It has a brilliant and penetrating tone color, and is capable of great agility. The development of a virtuoso trumpet technique has enabled composers to use the trumpet as a melody instrument equal in agility to the wood winds. The scores of Sibelius, Stravinsky, Shostakovich, and others contain many interesting trumpet passages, frequently of a caricaturing character. Within the past thirty years the trumpet has also found a prominent place in jazz bands, replacing the cornet. See illustration.

Trumpet marine. See *Tromba marina.*

T. s. Abbreviation for *tasto solo.*

Tsigane (F.). See *Tzigane.*

Tuba. A term somewhat loosely applied to any sort of brass instrument with the range of a bass, except the trombone. Orchestral tubas combine the conical bore of the horn with the oblong shape and the cupped mouthpiece of the trumpet. They have four or five valves and exist in three sizes: *tenor tuba* in B-flat, a fifth below the horn; *bass tuba* in E-flat (*EE-flat bass tuba*), an octave below the horn (also in F, one tone higher); and the *double-bass*

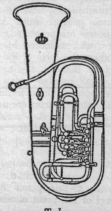

Tuba

tuba (*BB-flat bass tuba*), an octave below the tenor tuba. *Wagner tuba* is the name given to instruments designed for Wagner's *Ring*. They have a somewhat narrower bore and a funnel-shaped mouthpiece like that of the horns. They combine the agility of the cornet with the mellow timbre of the true tubas. See illustration.

Generically, the term tuba also includes the various bass instruments used in brass bands. The most important of these, such as the euphonium, helicon, sousaphone, and baritone, are described under *Brass instruments*, II.

Tubular bells. See *Chimes*.

Tucket. In plays of the Elizabethan period, a stage direction indicating a fanfare to be played on trumpets and drums. See also *Sennet*, which meant much the same thing.

Tune. (1) Popular term for a simple and easily remembered melody, e.g., a folk song or an attractive theme from a symphony. — (2) "In tune" means singing or playing in proper pitch, "out of tune," the opposite. See *Tuning*.

Tuning. In stringed instruments (violins, etc., pianoforte, harp), the adjustment of the tension of the strings in such a way that they sound at their proper pitches. Also similar adjustments for the pipes of an organ and for the other instruments. The term is used particularly with reference to the piano which, because of the great number of strings, presents a special prob-

lem of tuning. The modern method of piano tuning is based on the pure ocatve and the tempered fifth (see under *Equal temperament*). The octaves are tuned so as to give no *beats, while the fifths are obtained empirically by lowering the pure fifth (no beats) to the point where it gives one beat per second.

Tuning fork. A two-pronged fork made from steel and used to indicate the correct absolute pitch, usually for the tone *a'* (440 vibrations per second; see under *Pitch*).

Turba (L., crowd). In oratorios, passions, etc., name for the choral movements representing a shouting crowd, e.g., the high priests or the heathens. They are usually fast movements in fugal style using short motives in close imitation. Numerous examples exist, e.g., in Bach's *St. Matthew Passion*.

Turca, Alla (AHL-lah TOOR-ca: It., in the Turkish style). Title used for pieces written in imitation of the Turkish military music (see *Janizary music*), which was popular in Europe in the late 18th century.

Turkish crescent. See *Crescent, Turkish*.

Turn. An ornament consisting essentially of four notes, that is, upper neighbor, principal, lower neighbor, and principal note, e.g., if d is the written note, e-d-c-d. It is indicated by a curved line, placed above the note or, in compositions of the Classical period (Haydn, Mozart), by writing the first three notes as grace notes (Fig. 118a). If, as is often the case, the sign appears between two notes, this means that the four-note ornament, instead of replacing the first note, should be played after it, as shown under (b). Very often the turn appears after a dotted note, as under (c). As regards the rhythmic execution, a great deal of freedom is left to the discretion and taste of the player, who should always take the tempo into consideration. The *inverted turn*, starting with the lower neighbor note, is indicated by the ordinary sign upside down (∾) or in a vertical position (?) or, more frequently, by grace notes (Fig. 118d).

Fig. 118

Tutte le corde. See under *Una corda.*

Tutti (TOO-tee: It., all). In orchestral works, particularly concertos, the passages or sections for the whole orchestra, as distinct from those of the soloist.

Twelve-tone technique. A 20th-century method of musical composition devised by Schönberg (*c.* 1920) as a means of motivic construction and unification within the general framework of °atonal music, replacing traditional principles of melody, harmony, and tonality. The main principles of the twelve-tone technique are as follows:

1. Every composition is based on a so-called *series* or *tone row*, containing all the twelve chromatic tones in a succession chosen by the composer. The chosen order of tones remains unchanged throughout the composition, except for the modifications explained below. The entire composition, therefore, consists of nothing but restatements of the series in any of its numerous formations (horizontal and vertical).

2. The octave position of any tone can be changed at will.

3. In addition to its original form (S), the series can be used in its inversion (S^i), in its retrograde form (S^r), and in its retrograde inversion (S^{ri}).

4. The above four forms of the series can be used in transposition to any step of the chromatic scale. Thus the series becomes available in 48 (12 x 4) modifications.

5. From this basic material innumerable formations can be derived, differing as to rhythm, chordal grouping, polyphonic juxtaposition, etc., and it is with these that the actual process of

composition begins. The technical premises explained above are no more restricting (actually, less so) than those of any other method (e.g., the triads and harmonic progressions as employed by Classical composers), especially since so many liberties are taken with the fundamental "rules." See Fig. 119.

Schönberg's method has been adopted by Alban Berg, Anton von Webern, Ernst Křenek, and numerous other composers. Although twelve-tone music is usually atonal, and although any reference to traditional harmonic practices was originally avoided, there is nothing in this technique that precludes the inclusion of tonal elements such as triads. Some of the more recent twelve-tone compositions show tendencies in this direction. See also *Trope* (2).

Twentieth-century music. The music of the 20th century has developed along two general lines: (1) the expansion and final working out of trends established in the 19th century (*Romanticism, *Impressionism), and (2) the more or less novel practices distinctive of the 20th century, which are essentially anti-Romantic. Some of the more radical of these practices are often distinguished from the others by the designation of *New Music. By and large, the musical development during the first half of the century can be divided into three periods: Impressionism and post-Romanticism (*c.* 1900–15); experimentation along the lines of *Expressionism, *Dynamism, etc. (*c.* 1910–25); and *Neoclassicism (*c.* 1920–present).

The second decade of the century, dominated by World War I, encompassed the most widespread and daring experimentation. Of basic importance was the activity of Schönberg who, casting away the harmonic system and the formal methods of the past, arrived, about 1910, at a radically novel style, the most distinctive feature of which was *atonality. (To this he

Schönberg, Suite op. 25

Fig. 119

added, in 1923, his equally revolutionary method of composition, the *twelve-tone technique.) Simultaneously, new possibilities in the field of rhythm were exploited, e.g., by Bartok in his *Allegro barbaro* (1910), inspired by the fanatical drumbeating of primitive African tribes, and by Stravinsky in the folkloristic ballet *Petrushka* (1911) and the primordial *Rite of Spring* (1913). The French writer, Cocteau, aptly expressed the spirit of this period in the words, "After the music with the silk brush, the music with the axe." Provocative slogans such as bruitisme (noise music), *futurism, motorism, and machine music appeared without leaving a lasting imprint on the future evolution. Experimentation in the field of tonal material led to *quarter-tone music. Aside from the above-mentioned leaders, composers such as Kodaly, Malipiero, Casella, Honegger, Milhaud, and Berg contributed to the developments of this experimental period.

The neoclassical movement, which started in the early 1920's, brought with it a certain degree of unification and consolidation by a return to the formal and aesthetic ideals of the 18th century (and earlier), now revitalized in a modern musical language. Once more, Stravinsky took the lead with such compositions as the Octet for Wind Instruments (1923). Bartok and Hindemith, who were destined to become the major composers of the half century (along with Schönberg and Stravinsky), began to receive international recognition. Hindemith was active in the development of *Gebrauchmusik and also devised a useful theoretical explanation of the new harmonic and tonal concepts. Bartok represents another main development of the period since 1920: the assimilation and synthesis into a colorful and expressive musical language of most of the experimental techniques of the second decade. One other noteworthy feature of the period around 1920 is the impact of American jazz on serious music, resulting in such works as Stravinsky's *Ragtime* (1918), Hindemith's *Suite 1922*, and Křenek's jazz opera *Jonny Spielt Auf* (1926).

The materialistic trend of our century is reflected particularly in the numerous attempts to expand the materials of music, often at the expense of (or without concern for) its spiritual and expressive values. Many new instruments (chiefly *electrophonic instruments) have been invented, and even typewriters and motorcycle engines have been given musical status. Unusual coloristic effects on string and wind instruments have become common practice in modern scores, and the piano has been "prepared" to produce new tonal effects (see *Prepared piano*). Recently, a school of French composers led by Pierre Boulez has been experimenting in what they call *musique concrète* (concrete music), i.e., music which uses recordings of assorted sounds and noises rather than musical tones as its basic material. Other composers, notably Karlheinz Stockhausen, have used electric resonators to produce compositions recorded on tape. Such experimentation does not belong to the main stream of musical development at present, however. Since about 1935 there has been a general tendency to lessen the gulf between modern music and the listening public, and most composers are showing a renewed concern for euphony and expressiveness, discarding some of the more esoteric techniques and materials.

Twilight of the Gods, The. Wagner's *Götterdämmerung.* See under *Ring of the Nibelung.*

Two-step. See under *One-step.*

Tympani (TIM-pa-nee). Less correct spelling for It. *timpani,* i.e., kettledrums. *Tympanon* is the ancient Greek term (*tympanum* in Latin) for a big drum. Medieval writers, confusing it with *cymbalon,* used it as a term for the dulcimer, a meaning which still persists here and there.

Tyrolienne (tee-ro-LYEN: F.). A popular dance of the early 19th century, imitating Tyrolian folk music. It combines the rhythm of the Ländler (slow waltz) with the melodic figurations suggestive of the °yodel.

Tzigane (tsee-GAHN: F.). Gypsy; gypsy music (*à la tzigane*).

U

U. c. Short for °*una corda.*

Ukelele. See *Ukulele.*

Ukrainian Symphony. Tchaikovsky's Symphony no. 2, in C minor, op. 17 (1872), also called *Little-Russian Symphony,* "Little Russia" being the common name for the Ukraine in the 19th century.

Ukulele (yoo-ku-LAY-lee). A small Hawaiian guitar, with four strings, tuned g'-c'-e'-a'. It developed from a Portuguese guitar, and became popular in America about 1920. The music is notated in a manner similar to (though not derived from) the

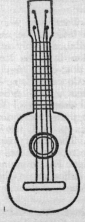

Ukulele

lute *tablatures of the 16th century. Each chord is indicated by a symbol of four vertical lines representing the four strings, and of small dots indicating the position of the fingers on the frets. See illustration.

Umfang (UM-fahng: G.). Compass, or the vocal or instrumental range.

Umstimmen (UM-shtim-en: G.). To change the tuning, e.g., of kettledrums.

Un Ballo in maschera (It.). See *Masked Ball*.

Una corda (OO-na KAWR-da: It., one string). In piano music, a direction (abbr. *u. c.*) to use the left pedal (soft pedal) which, if depressed, moves the entire action (keyboard and hammers) a little to the right, thus causing the hammers to strike a single string (in modern instruments usually two strings) instead of all three. The indication is canceled by *tre corde or tutte le corde* (*t. c.*). Beethoven, who was the first to indicate the use of the soft pedal, not only calls for a gradation in three steps: *una corda, due, e poi tre corde* (G-major Concerto, op. 58, slow movement), but even for a gradual execution of the shift: *poco a poco due corde* (Piano Sonata, op. 101, slow movement). The latter request obviously represents an unattainable ideal. For an erroneous *una corda* indication in the Moonlight Sonata, see under *Sordino*.

Una Cosa rara (OO-na CO-sa RAH-ra: A Rare Thing). Opera by Vicente Martín y Soler, a Spanish composer (1754–1806). It was produced in Vienna, 1786, and is remembered today only because Mozart included an extended section from it in the finale of Act II of *Don Giovanni*, as part of the music played during Don Giovanni's supper.

Undertow. Ballet by William Schuman (choreography by A. Tudor), produced in New York, 1945. Symphonic excerpts of the intensely dramatic music have been arranged by the composer for concert performance.

Unequal temperament. See under *Temperament*.

Unequal voices. Designation for vocal compositions using male as well as female voices.

Unfinished Symphony. Schubert's Symphony no. 8, in B minor, so called because only the first two movements exist. These were written in 1822, six years before the composer's death. That Schubert intended to complete the work appears from the fact that he had sketched out the beginning of the scherzo. Preoccupation with other compositions is the probable reason why the symphony remained unfinished. Schubert sent the two movements to his friend Hüttenbrenner, and it was not until the latter's death in 1868 that the work was published, having had its first performance in 1865.

Ungherese, All' (ahl-oon-gay-RAY-se: It.). In the Hungarian (gypsy) style; also, incorrectly, *all' ungarese*.

Unison. (1) Different instruments or voices are said to be "in unison" if they jointly perform the same melody, either at identical pitches or in octave duplication, the latter method being properly called octave unison (see *All' unisono*). — (2) Name for the "zero" interval, for example, c-c (see under *Intervals*).

Unit organ. A modern type of organ in which one rank of pipes is made to serve for several stops. Thus, a rank of 8' Principal pipes can be employed to provide 16' Principal, 8' Principal, and 4' Octave, which normally would require 183 pipes. This method, called *unification* (also *extension*), is widely used for theater organs and in small church organs.

Un poco (oon PAW-co: It.). A little, e.g., *un poco più lento*, a little more slowly.

Unterwerk (UN-ter-vayrk: G.). Choir Organ.

Upbeat. A note or a group of notes occurring on the weak beat at the beginning of a musical phrase, immediately before the bar line.

Up-bow. See under *Bowing*.

Upright piano. See under *Pianoforte; Grand piano*.

Urlinie, Ursatz (G.). See under *Schenker System*.

Ut. See *Pitch names* (French); *Solmization*.

Utility music. See *Gebrauchsmusik*.

Utrecht Te Deum (Handel). See under *Te Deum*.

V

V. Abbreviation: (1) For violin. — (2) In older Italian music, for *voci* (voices). — (3) In liturgical books, with a slash line through it, for verse (℣).

Va. Abbreviation for viola.

Valkyrie, The (VAL-kui-ree). Wagner's *Die Walküre*. See under *Ring of the Nibelung*.

Valse (F.). *Waltz. Valse à deux temps* (in two beats) is

a special type in which the melody proceeds in notes having a value of two beats, hence in syncopation and in cross-rhythm to the triple meter of the accompaniment. A familiar example occurs in Gounod's *Faust*.

Valse, La. "Poème chorégraphique" (dance poem) for orchestra by Ravel (composed in 1920), imitating and cleverly parodying the Viennese waltz of Johann Strauss. It is often used for ballet performance.

Valse Triste (vahls treest). A popular waltz for orchestra by Sibelius, originally composed (1903) as part of the incidental music to the play *Kuolema*.

Valses nobles et sentimentales (vahls nobl ay sanh-ti-manh-TAHL). A set of waltzes for piano by Ravel, composed in 1911 and orchestrated by the composer to serve as the music for the ballet *Adélaïde, ou le Langage des Fleurs*. The adjectives "noble" and "sentimental" (already used by Schubert) are used to distinguish between the "elegant" and the "lyrical" types of waltz.

Valve. A mechanism, invented by Blühmel in 1813, by which all the tones of the chromatic scale become available on the brass instruments (trumpets, horns, tubas, etc.), the only exception being the trombone, on which they are produced by the slide. The essential part of the mechanism is not the valve as such, but the short pieces of tubing inserted between two points of the main tube which form a detour, thereby increasing the actual length of the pipe. Thus an instrument normally sounding B-flat (and its harmonics) can quickly be changed into a longer one sounding A (and its harmonics). Horns and trumpets usually have three valves (three detour tubings of varying lengths) which lower the pitch a half tone, a whole tone, and a minor third, respectively. By combining two or all three valves, the pitch can

be lowered further, down to six half tones. See also under *Wind instruments*.

Valve horn, trumpet, etc. The modern horn, trumpet, etc., built with °valves, as distinguished from the earlier types which had none, e.g., the natural horn or the slide trumpet. Valve trombones (which have not been popular) are trombones having valves instead of the sliding mechanism.

Vamp. An extemporized accompaniment or introduction for popular songs, consisting of simple chords in familiar rhythmic patterns. Hence, vamping tutor, a book of instruction in this type of playing.

Variation canzona. See under *Canzona* (2).

Variations. More fully, theme with variations. An important musical form, the principle of which is to present a given melody, called the *theme*, in a number of modifications, each of which is a *variation*. Variations occur as independent compositions (Bach's °Goldberg Variations, Beethoven's °Diabelli Variations) or as a movement, usually the slow one, of sonatas, symphonies, etc. (e.g., in Beethoven's °Appassionata Sonata and Ninth Symphony). The theme is usually a simple tune in binary (often rounded binary) form, either invented by the composer (Goldberg Variations) or borrowed (Diabelli Variations; also Brahms' °Handel Variations). Variations often close with an extended and elaborate final section, in the character of an improvisation, or with a fugue whose subject is derived from the theme.

For an understanding of variation technique it is important to realize that a variation always has something in common with the theme (otherwise it would not be a variation of the *theme*), and that it also deviates from it in some way (otherwise it would not be a *variation* of the theme). These two aspects can be conveniently distinguished as the "fixed" and the "variable" elements. Regarding the fixed aspect, the whole field can be roughly divided into four types of variation, depend-

ing on which features of the theme are retained:

Type A: Melody, harmonies, and structure retained.

Type B: Harmonies and structure retained.

Type C: Structure retained.

Type D: Motives retained. (Structure means here the general outline of the theme, indicated by the number of measures, number and length of phrases, basic scheme of harmonies, cadential points, etc.)

Type A prevails in the variations of Haydn and Mozart; type B in Beethoven and Schubert, also in Bach's Goldberg Variations; type C in Brahms; type

Fig. 120

D, often called "free variations," in modern works (d'Indy's *Istar Variations; R. Strauss's *Don Quixote; Reger's Variations and Fugue on a Theme by Mozart; also in Schumann's *Symphonic Studies).

Regarding the variable element, some of the standard procedures are illustrated in Fig. 120, a-g: (a) *ornamenting variation;* (b) *contrapuntal;* (c) *melodic* (new melody); (d) *figural* (use of a characteristic figure); (e) *canonic* (two or more voices in canon); (f) *harmonic* (modified harmonies); (g) is an example of the *character variation,* in which a well-defined musical type, e.g., a waltz or a funeral march, is used as a model. It also illustrates three other methods of variation technique, i.e., change of meter, change of tempo (usually from fast or moderate to slow), and change of mode, from major to minor or vice versa.

A special kind of variation, frequently used in the Baroque period and revived in modern music, is the *chaconne or passacaglia.

Variations on a Theme by Diabelli (Handel, etc.). See under *Diabelli Variations.*

Varsovienne (vahr-so-VYEN: F.). A Polish dance, named after the city of Warsaw (F., *Varsovie*), in slow mazurka rhythm, usually with an accented dotted note on the first beat of each second measure. It was popular in ballrooms from about 1850 to 1870.

Vatican Edition. See under *Solesmes method.*

Vaudeville (vode-VEEL: F.). Originally (17th, 18th centuries) a short satirical poem sung to a simple, tuneful (often pre-existing) melody. The name is probably derived from *vaux de Vire* (valley of Vire), birthplace of a 15th-century poet who is said to have invented this type. The vaudeville was the principal type of song in French comic operas of the 18th century. In the 19th century the name was applied to short comedies interspersed with popular songs, and today it is used for various kinds of light entertainment presented on the stage.

Vc., Vcl. Abbreviations for violoncello.

Venetian School. A 16th-century school of Flemish and Italian composers active in Venice. It was inaugurated by Adrian Willaert (*c.* 1485–1562) and included, among others, Andrea Gabrieli (*c.* 1510–1586), Cypriano de Rore (1516–1565), Claudio Merulo (1533–1604), and Giovanni Gabrieli (1557–1612). Its most outstanding achievement is the "Venetian style" of G. Gabrieli with its broad masses of sound, *polychoral treatment, echo effects, and extensive use of instruments, alone and in combination with voices. The group also included two of the most progressive theorists of the century, Niccola Vicentino (1511–1572) and Gioseffo Zarlino (1517–1590).

Venetian swell. See *Swell.*

Vent (vanh: F.). Wind. *Instruments à vent,* wind instruments.

VENTIL 327 VIBRAPHONE

Ventil (ven-TEEL: G.). Valve. *Ventilhorn*, valve horn.

Ventile (ven-TEE-lay: It.). Valve. *Corno a ventile*, valve horn.

Verbunko (VAYR-boon-ko: Hungarian, from G. *Werbung*, draft). An 18th-century Hungarian dance performed by soldiers in full uniform with sword and spurs. The *csárdás is said to be a 19th-century revival of the *verbunko*.

Verismo (vay-REEZ-mo: It., realism). An Italian operatic movement of the late 19th century which represents the musical counterpart of the literary "realism" of Zola, Flaubert, and Ibsen. Instead of the heroic, mythological, or historical libretti of Rossini, Verdi and Wagner, realistic subjects from everyday life were chosen. Coloratura arias and the tuneful melodies of the earlier Italian opera were abandoned in favor of a melodramatic and naturalistic recitative. Outstanding examples are Mascagni's *Cavalleria rusticana* (1890), Leoncavallo's *Pagliacci* (1892), and Puccini's *La *Bohème* (1896), the latter showing a somewhat modified verismo of a more lyrical character.

Verkaufte Braut, Die (G.). See *Bartered Bride*.

Verklärte Nacht (G.). See *Transfigured Night*.

Verse. In Gregorian chant, a verse (abbreviated ℣) of a Psalm or a canticle, occasionally also a sentence from other Scriptural texts. Such verses occur in the Graduals, Alleluias, Introits (where they are indicated by Ps., i.e., Psalm), Responsories, etc., in combination with antiphons or responses. They are always sung by the soloists (except for a short choral ending), and this connotation was taken over into the *Verse Anthem* and *Verse Service* of the Anglican Church. These latter terms denote settings including sections for solo voices, as distinguished from the purely choral *Full Anthem* and *Full Service*. — For organ verse, see *Verset*.

Verset (VER-set: from It. *versetto*, little verse). Organ verse, i.e., a short organ piece, usually in fugal style, so called because it was used in the Roman Catholic service of the 16th to 18th centuries to replace the even-numbered verses of the Psalms or canticles. The odd-numbered verses were performed in plainsong.

Versicle. Same as *verse, particularly in the Anglican service.

Vespers. The evening service of the Roman Catholic and of the Anglican Church (see under *Office*). The Roman Catholic vespers consist mainly of singing the five vesper Psalms, nos. 109–113 (110–114 of the King James Bible) and the *Magnificat. Mozart wrote two *Vespers* (K. 321, 339) for voices, orchestra, and organ, each consisting of the above-named items.

Via (VEE-a: It.). Away, e.g., *via sordini*, remove the mutes.

Vibraphone. An instrument of the marimba type, in which the resonators are kept vibrating by means of electric impulses. This imparts a pulsating quality to the sound produced on the metal bars, a sort of artificial tremolo (see under *Vibrato*).

Vibrato (vee-BRAH-to: It.). On violins, cellos, etc., a minute fluctuation of pitch produced by a shaking motion of the left hand. Modern players use it as a basic technique in order to increase the emotional quality of the tone, although some great violinists have insisted that it be reserved for moments of heightened expression, as it was in the earlier days of violin playing. In singing, the term usually denotes a slight wavering of pitch, an effect which corresponds to the violin vibrato since it increases the emotional quality of the tones without resulting in a noticeable fluctuation of pitch. Cultivated by many singers, it is avoided by others as likely to degenerate into a real wobble, which is then called *tremolo. In singing, therefore, vibrato and tremolo are essentially the same effect, varying only in degree, while in violin playing they denote two entirely different effects, vibrato denoting a fluctuation of pitch, whereas tremolo denotes a rapid reiteration (or pulsation) of an unchanged pitch or rapid alternation between two pitches. The *Bebung* of the °clavichord is a vibrato. The Tremulant stop on organs produces a tremolo, the Voix Céleste stop a vibrato.

Victory Symphony. A nickname for Beethoven's Symphony no. 5, coined during World War II when the opening theme of the first movement became associated with the Morse code signal for V (· · · —). The nickname was only briefly popular, and is rarely if ever used today. See *Fate Symphony*.

Vida breve, La (lah VEE-ttha BRAY-vay: The Short Life). Opera by Falla (libretto by C. F. Shaw), composed in 1905 and produced (in French translation) in Nice, 1913. The story relates the love of Salud, a gypsy girl, for a young man above her caste who loves her, although he is engaged to marry a girl of his own class. At the wedding party for her lover and his fiancée, Salud sings of her love and betrayal, but her lover denies everything, and she falls dead. The music includes many °Flamenco melodies and other authentic Spanish dances and chorus songs.

Vide (veed: F.). Empty. *Corde à vide*, open string.

Vide (L.). See. The term is used, with its two syllables (*vi-de*) placed at separate points of the score, to indicate an optional shortening, the player being permitted to skip from the point marked *vi-* to the point marked *-de*.

Vielle (vyel: F.). The medieval type of violin (12th to 15th centuries), later superseded by the °viol (16th century). It had four fingered strings and a drone string. The instrument has been revived for the performance of medieval music. After it had become obsolete, the name was applied to the wheel viol (see *Hurdy-gurdy*, 1), properly called *vielle à roue*.

Viennese Classics. See under *Classicism.*

Vier ernste Gesänge (feer ERN-ste ge-ZENG-e: Four Serious Songs). Four songs by Brahms, op. 121 (1896), for baritone and piano, to words from the Bible: 1. It befalleth the Man as the Beast (Eccl. iii: 19–22); 2. I returned and considered (Eccl. iv: 1–3); 3. O death, how bitter (Ecclus. xli: 1, 2); 4. Though I speak with the tongues of men and angels (I Cor. xiii: 1–3, 12–13).

Vihuela (vee-WAY-lah: Sp., from *vielle*). The Spanish guitar of the 16th century. The number and tuning of the strings, as well as the notation and manner of playing, were the same as on the °lute. An impressive repertory of music for the vihuela has come down to us in the books of Luis Milan (1536), Luis de Narvaez (1538), Miguel de Fuenllana (1554), and others.

Villancico (veel-yan-THEE-ko: Sp.). A type of 15th- and 16th-century Spanish poetry, idyllic or devotional as to subject matter, and consisting of several stanzas linked by a reiterated refrain. The poems were set to music for three or four voices either in a simple note-against-note style, or as solo songs with lute accompaniment. After 1600 the villancico adopted an entirely different meaning, i.e., of a composition resembling a cantata or an anthem, based on a religious text and written in several movements for chorus, soloists, and orchestra.

Villanella, villanesca (veel-ah-NEL-a, veel-ah-NESS-ka: It., rural song). A 16th-century type of vocal music which originated in Naples and which forms a sharp contrast to — probably a parodistic reaction against — the refinements of the contemporary madrigal. Although probably suggested by folk music, the villanella had as little in common with the Italian peasants as had the gallant style (see under *Rococo*) of the 18th century with the shepherds of France. The sophisticated and parodistic character of the villanella appears particularly in the frequent use of parallel triads, strictly prohibited in 16th-century style. Thomas Morley, in his *Plaine and Easie Introduction to Practicall Musick* (1597), aptly describes it as "clownish music to a clownish matter."

More recent composers, such as Berlioz, Chabrier, Dukas, Granados, and Loeffler, have used the term *villanelle* (F.) or *villanesca* for instrumental pieces in the style of a rustic dance, usually in quick 6/8 meter.

Viol (VEYE-ul). Name for a family of stringed instruments used mainly during the 15th to 17th centuries, following the various types of medieval fiddles (rebec, °vielle) and being superseded in turn by the violin family. The viols differ from the violins mainly in that: (a) the shoulders slope down from the neck instead of being at right angles; (b) the normal number of strings is six instead of four, tuned in fourths with a third in the middle, for example, D G c e a d′ for the bass viol (*viola* *da gamba*); (c) the sound holes have the shape of a *c* instead of an *f* (see *Sound holes*); (d) the viols were not pressed against the shoulder but were held downward, resting on or between the legs of the player. See illustration.

Viol

The viols have a delicate and soft tone color, lacking the brilliance and intensity of the violins. During the 17th century they existed in three sizes, *treble viol* (tuned d g c' e' a' d''), *tenor viol* (A d g b e' a'), and *bass viol* (D G c e a d'). According to T. Mace's *Musick's Monument* (1676), a good "chest of viols" consisted of "two basses, two tenors, and two trebles." Viol music was cul-

tivated mainly in England for chamber music (see *Fancy*) until about 1660, when the violin made its appearance there. Only the bass viol or *viola da gamba* was largely used as a solo instrument in England as well as in Italy, France, and Germany. Bach used it in three sonatas and in the aria "Komm süsses Kreuz" of the St. Matthew Passion. There also existed a double-bass viol, which is the ancestor of the modern °double bass. See also *Baryton; Viola d'amore; Violone.*

Viola (vee-O-la). The second member of the °violin family, tuned a fifth lower than the violin, c g d' a'. Its size, however, is only one seventh larger than that of the violin, a disproportion which results in a more veiled and slightly nasal tone color, different from that of the violin and the cello.

Viola da braccio (vee-O-la dah BRAHT-cho: It., *braccio,* arm). Originally (17th century) the Italian name for all the stringed instruments held "in the arm," i.e., against the shoulder. Later identified with the °viola (hence the German name *Bratsche*).

Viola da gamba (vee-O-la dah GAHM-ba: It., *gamba,* leg). Originally (17th century) the Italian name for all stringed instruments held "on the leg," i.e., all the viols. Later it was identified with the bass viol (see under *Viol*).

Viola d'amore (vee-O-la dah-MAW-ray: It.). An instrument similar in size and shape to the treble °viol, from which it was distinguished by the addition of *sympathetic strings made of thin wire and stretched behind the bowed strings, thus producing a silvery resonance. The name probably refers to the scroll which was usually fashioned as a blindfolded face of the god Amor. The instrument was used chiefly in the 18th century (Bach, St. John Passion and Cantata no. 132; Haydn, Divertimento in E-flat), but survived in the 19th- and 20th-century works of such composers as Meyerbeer (*Les Huguenots*), Charpentier (*Louise*), Puccini (*Madame Butterfly*) R. Strauss (*Sinfonia Domestica*), Loeffler (*The Death of Tintagles*), and Hindemith (Sonata, op. 25, no. 2; Concerto, op. 46, no. 1). See *Baryton*.

Viola pomposa (vee-O-la pom-PO-sa: It.). An 18th-century instrument of the violin (not viol) family, probably a larger viola with five strings. Its invention has been erroneously ascribed to J. S. Bach.

Violin (veye-o-LIN). The most important of the stringed instruments, in the orchestra as well as in chamber and solo music. Its main parts are: (a) the body, consisting of the table (soundboard), the back, and the ribs (side walls); (b) the finger board, ending in the pegbox and the scroll; (c) the string holder (tail piece); (d) the bridge. Other details are shown in the illustration below. Inside the body there is the *bass-bar, the *sound post, and reinforcing blocks glued to the corners and to the back. The violin has four

strings tuned in fifths: g d′ a′ e″.

The prominent position held by the violin results from its appealing tone color, an expressiveness ranging from the softest

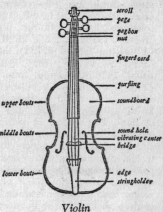

Violin

lyricism to the highest dramatic excitement, a dynamic flexibility and subtlety unsurpassed by any other instrument, its ability to blend well in an ensemble, and a great variety of special coloristic effects, including many types of *bowing as well as the *pizzicato and the use of *harmonics.

The violin emerged about 1600, gradually superseding the *viols during the 17th century. A singular glory surrounds the "old violins." While all other modern instruments have reached their highest degree of perfection within the past fifty years, the great period of violin making extends from about 1600 to 1750. During this time the center of the craft was in Cremona in northern Italy where the three greatest masters of all, Nicolo Amati (1596–1684), Antonio Stradivari (1643–1737), and Giuseppe Guarnieri (1686–1744; also known as Giuseppe del Gesu) were producing their unsurpassed instruments. The most renowned of all is Amati's pupil, Stradivari, who created (c. 1700) the model for his most celebrated instruments, e.g., the "Betts" (1704), the "Viotti" (1709), the "Rode" (1722), the "Sarasate" (1724), the "Wilhelmj" (1725), and the "Swan" (1735). Stradivari is believed to have made 1116 instruments in all between 1666 and 1737; of these, 540 violins, 12 violas, and 50 cellos are known to exist, all priceless instruments for which fabulous sums have been paid. Although the craftsmanship and beauty of these old violins have never been equaled, modern makers have produced instruments whose sound can hardly be distinguished from that of a genuine Stradivari. The widespread belief that the varnish has a decisive influence on the sound of a violin has been shown to be untrue. The incomparable luster of the old instruments adds greatly to their beauty, but nothing tangible to their tonal quality.

In the *orchestra, the violin is regularly used in two groups, distinguished as Violin I and Violin II (see Fig. 80 for a seating plan of a symphony orchestra). Both employ the same kind of instrument, but for different parts. The same remark applies to the Violins I and II in chamber music, e.g., the *string quartet. See also Violin family.

Violin family. The chief members of this family are the *violin, the *viola, and the *cello. They form the nucleus of most chamber music ensembles, and, along with the *double bass, comprise the string section of the orchestra. Numerous other sizes, ranging from the violino piccolo (Bach, Cantata no. 140 and Brandenburg Concerto no. 1) to the giant Octobass (13 feet in height), have been made, but none of these has achieved a permanent place in instrumental music.

Violoncello (It.). See Cello.

Violone (vee-o-LO-ne: It., big viol). A low-pitched member of the *viol family, approximately the size and range of a double bass and used in that function in the scores of Bach and his contemporaries. The modern double bass is directly descended from the violone or, possibly, from a larger variety known as violone grosso.

Virelai (VEER-e-lay: F.). A form of medieval French poetry and music, consisting of three stanzas with a refrain before and after each stanza. The form is as follows (considering only the first stanza): A b b a A (A is the refrain, b b a the stanza). The virelai was cultivated mainly during the 14th and 15th centuries by Machaut and his successors. There also exist a few monophonic virelais of the 13th century. The virelai structure occurs also in many of the 13th-century *cantigas and *laude, as well as in the Italian *ballata of the 14th century.

Virginal (VUR-ji-nal). A 16th-century type of harpsichord used mainly in England, but described first in a German book of 1511. It is uncertain whether it is so called because it was played by young ladies or with reference to the Latin word *virga* (rod or twig, i.e., jack — part of the playing mechanism). The instruments were of various shapes: rectangular, wing-shaped, or in the form of a trapezoid. A common designation, of obscure origin and meaning, was "pair of virginals."

Among the English composers of the late 16th and early 17th centuries who wrote music for the instrument, the three outstanding masters were William Byrd (1543–1623), John Bull (*c.* 1563–1628), and Orlando Gibbons (1583–1625). The most important source is the *Fitzwilliam Virginal Book*, a manuscript of *c.* 1620 containing 297 compositions, among which the numerous pavanes and variations on secular tunes are of particular interest. The virginalists were the first to develop an idiomatic harpsichord style, including many elements of the later piano style, e.g., rapid scales, broken-chord figurations, broken octaves, quick passages in parallel thirds and sixths for one hand, full chords, etc.

Virtuoso. A performer who excels in technical ability. The term is sometimes used as a derogatory reference to one who excels in technique only, lacking comparable understanding and musical taste.

Vivace (vee-VAH-chay: It.). Lively, quick. *Vivacissimo,* very lively.

VI. Abbreviation for violin; *vla.,* viola; *vlc,* violoncello, *vll.,* violins.

Vocalise (F.), **vocalizzo** (It.). *Vocalization, *solfeggio.

Vocalization. An extended melody or an entire composition for voice(s) sung on a vowel (usually *a*), hence, without text. This method, which played an important role in the early history of music, is used today mainly for instructive purposes, as a vocal exercise (see *Solfeggio*). Occasionally, however, modern composers have used vocalization as an artistic medium, treating the human voice as a pure "instrument," unencumbered by words. Examples are the "Chorus of Heavenly Spirits" in Spontini's opera *Nurmahal* (1821), Debussy's *Sirènes* (1899), Ravel's *Vocalise en forme d'Habanera* (1907), Medtner's *Sonata-Vocalise*(1921), and Villa-Lobos' *Bachianas Brasileiras* no. 5 (1945).

Vocal music. Music written for voices, either solo or chorus, with or without instrumental accompaniment.

Voce (VAW-chay: It., pl. *voci*). Voice. *A due voci,* for two voices or instrumental voice parts; *a tre voci,* for three such parts. *Colla voce,* see under *Col. Voci pari* or *eguali,* equal voices. *Voce di gola,* throat voice, guttural voice; *di petto,* chest voice; *di testa,* head voice, *falsetto.

Voice. The human voice is essentially a wind instrument, with the lungs supplying the wind, the vocal cords setting up the vibrations, and the cavities of the upper throat, mouth, and nose forming the resonator. Different pitches are obtained by varying (subconsciously) the tension of and the opening between the vocal cords. A unique feature of the human voice is that the resonator may be varied in shape, thereby producing different tone colors — the vowel sounds. The same pitch can be sung to different vowels and, on the other hand, complete melodies can be sung to one and the same vowel sound (see *Vocalization*). Usually, however, the human voice is employed with the vowel sounds varying according to the words of the text, which also introduce consonants between the vowels. Vocal timbre and style of singing are strongly influenced by tradition and taste. Until about 1500 much use was made of the °falsetto, which later fell into disrepute. The celebrated °castrati of the 17th and 18th centuries possessed a type of voice which today few people would consider ideal. Even in the 19th century a decisive change in vocal color and style of singing took place, leading from the clarity and brilliance of the 18th-century °bel canto (Mozart) to the powerful and highly dramatic voice demanded by the Wagnerian operas. In modern popular music we are witnessing the cultivation of special manners of singing (see *Crooning*) which, although not recognized as artistic, help to illustrate the variability of the human voice. See also *Voices, Range of; Register* (2).

Voice parts, voices. The individual parts of a choral composition called, from top to bottom, soprano, alto, tenor, and bass.

Voices, range of. The human voices are usually classified in six types: three female voices: soprano, mezzo-soprano, contralto; and three male voices: tenor, baritone, bass. The normal ranges of these voices are approximately an octave (more safely, a seventh) below and above the notes b′, g′, e′ and a, f, d, as shown in Fig. 121. Trained soloists frequently exceed these ranges, however. Particularly the singers of the 18th century possessed ranges which seem miraculous. The soprano Lucrezia Agujari (1743–83) could reach c″″, and a bass part in Handel's *Acis and Galatea* (1708), written for Giuseppe Boschi, shifts, within one measure, from a′ to C♯, more than 2½ octaves. Russian basses are found who can sing down to F_1, a fifth below C.

Fig. 121

Voicing. In organ building, the mechanical adjustments necessary in order to obtain and maintain the proper tone color throughout a rank of pipes. In pianos, voicing is the rehabilitation of the hammer felts, necessary in order to obtain an even quality of sound.

Vokalise (vo-ka-LEE-ze: G.). °Vocalization, °solfeggio.

Volkslied (FOLKS-leet: G.). Folk song, also popular songs of a similar character which may be of fairly recent origin and of known authorship, such as the *Loreley* (by Silcher, 1789–1860).

Volles Werk (FOL-les vayrk: G.). Full organ.

Volta (It.). See *Prima volta*.

Volteggiando (vol-tej-JAHN-do: It.). Crossing the hands (in piano playing).

Volti (VOL-tee: It.). Turn over [the page]; *volti subito* (abbr. *v. s.*), turn quickly.

Voluntary. English organ pieces to be played in connection with the church service, as preludes, postludes, etc. They are often improvised.

Vorspiel (FOR-shpeel: G.). Prelude, operatic overture (Wagner).

V. s. *Volti subito.*

Vuota (VWO-ta: It.). Open string, on violins, etc.

Vv. Abbreviation for violins.

W

Wachet Auf (VAHKH-et owf: G.). Bach's Cantata no. 140 ("Sleepers, Awake"), for the twenty-seventh Sunday after Trinity. The three choral movements (the first, fourth, and seventh) are based on a chorale of the same title by Philip Nicolai (1599).

Wagner tuba. See under *Tuba.*

Waldhorn (VAHLD-horn: G., forest horn). The French horn, either natural or with valves.

Waldstein Sonata (VAHLD-shteyen). Beethoven's Piano Sonata in C, op. 53 (1804), dedicated to Count Ferdinand Waldstein. It consists of three movements, the second being a rela-

tively short Adagio in a somewhat improvisatory style, serving as an introduction to the Finale, an extended movement in rondo form.

Walküre, Die (vahl-KUI-re: G.). Wagner's *The Valkyrie*. See under *Ring of the Nibelung.*

Waltz. A dance in moderate triple time characterized chiefly by an accompaniment pattern consisting of a low bass note on the first beat and two chords in the middle register on the second and third beats. It developed, about 1800, from an Austrian peasant dance, the *Ländler*. The waltzes by Beethoven still resemble the Ländler, as also to some extent do those by Schubert. Weber's *Invitation to the Dance* (1819) is the first example showing the irresistible sway and characteristic accompaniment of the true waltz. For its later history the important names are those of Chopin, Johann Strauss, father and son, Brahms (*Liebeslieder Walzer*), R. Strauss (in *Rosenkavalier*), and Ravel (*Valses nobles et sentimentales; La *Valse*).

Walze (VAHL-tse: G.). The crescendo pedal of the organ.

Walzer (VAHL-tser: G.). Waltz.

Wanderer Fantasy. Nickname of Schubert's Fantasy (actually a sonata) in C for piano, op. 15 (1822), so called because the second movement is a series of variations on a theme derived from his song *Der Wanderer* (1816). The initial pattern of this theme is used also at the beginning of the other three movements, making this work the earliest example of a completely *cyclic sonata.

War of the Buffoons (F., *Guerre des bouffons*). A famous quarrel which developed in 1752 between two parties of Parisian musicians and opera enthusiasts, those favoring the French serious opera (exemplified by works of Lully and Rameau) and those extolling the Italian comic opera (such as composed by Pergolesi). The immediate cause of the quarrel, which found its expression in dozens of pamphlets, books, and speeches, was a performance of Pergolesi's *La Serva padrona* by a troupe of Italian comedians (*buffi*). Essentially,

the War of the Buffoons was a conflict of the rising *Rococo against the dying *Baroque— of simple, natural expression against the pompous heroics of French Baroque opera.

Warsaw Concerto. A popular selection for piano and orchestra (not a concerto in the proper sense of the term) composed by Richard Addinsell for the English motion picture *Dangerous Moonlight* (released in the U. S. as *Suicide Squadron,* 1942).

Water Music. An orchestral suite by Handel, probably composed about 1715 for a festivity taking place in boats on the Thames River. It consists of about twenty movements, somewhat like a Baroque sonata (see under *Sonata*) followed by a suite.

Water organ. See *Hydraulis.*

Wedge Fugue. Nickname of Bach's great organ fugue in E minor, so called because of the increasingly widening intervals of its subject.

Weihe des Hauses (G.). See *Consecration of the House.*

Weihnachts Oratorium. See *Christmas Oratorio* (1).

Wellington's Victory (G., *Wellingtons Sieg oder Die Schlacht bei Vittoria*). A "battle symphony" by Beethoven (op. 91, 1813), written in celebration of Wellington's victory over Napoleon. It consists of English and French fanfares, settings of *Rule Britannia* and *Marlborough s'en va-t-en guerre*, the Battle (punctuated by the English and

French guns), a Charge, and, in the second part, a Victory Symphony containing a quotation of *God Save the King*. It was originally written for a mechanical instrument invented by Mälzel, but was orchestrated by the composer.

Well-tempered Clavier, The (G., *Das Wohltemperierte Clavier*). A famous work by Bach, consisting of forty-eight compositions, each a prelude followed by a fugue. It is divided into two parts (*WTC*, I, 1722; *WTC*, II, 1744), each containing twenty-four preludes and fugues, one for each major and minor key (in chromatic order): C major, C minor, C♯ major, C♯ minor, D major, etc. "Well-tempered" refers to a system of tuning, *equal temperament (G., *wohltemperierte Stimmung*), which made it possible to use all tonalities. The system was a novelty in the early 18th century, and Bach's collection was the first complete realization of its possibilities. The work is often called "The Well-tempered Clavichord," but no restriction to this instrument is implied in the German name *Clavier*, nor in the compositions themselves.

Whistle. A small and simple end-blown flute with six finger holes, made of wood, metal, or plastic.

Whole note. See under *Notes and rests*.

Whole tone. See under *Intervals*.

Whole-tone scale. A scale consisting of whole tones only, hence having six notes to the octave, for example, c-d-e-f♯-g♯-a♯-c′. It lacks three of the most fundamental intervals of traditional music, the perfect fifth, the perfect fourth, and the minor second. Lacking the minor second (for example, b-c′), the leading tone is necessarily absent. All of its triads are augmented (c-e-g♯, d-f♯-a♯, etc.), and it is characterized by an "indecisive" quality since all scale steps are equal. Although used by some of his 19th-century predecessors (e.g., Glinka and Liszt), it was cultivated mainly by Debussy, often as the basis of parallel-chord progressions. See Fig. 122.

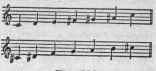

Fig. 122

William Tell (F., *Guillaume Tell*). Opera by Rossini, produced in Paris, 1829. The overture was a popular orchestral concert selection until made banal by association with certain radio programs and motion pictures.

Wind instruments. Generic term for all instruments in which the sound-generating medium is a column of air enclosed in a pipe. The wind instruments of the present-day *orchestra are divided into two groups: brass (trumpets, horn, trombone, tuba, cornet) and wood wind (flute, clarinet, oboe, saxophone, and their relatives). While the brass instruments actually form a unified group (and are all made from brass), the wood winds differ widely in character (and some of them are made from metal, e.g., flute, saxophone). For a proper understanding of the various wind instruments it is necessary to classify them according to different types of mouthpiece. The "brass instruments" form a group, not because they are all made from brass, but because they all have a cupped mouthpiece. In the "wood winds," on the other hand, we have three kinds of mouthpiece; the single reed (see *Reed*), used in the clarinets and saxophones; the double reed, used in the instruments of the oboe family; and the mouth hole, used in the flutes. In instruments with a cupped mouthpiece (a mouthpiece in the shape of a cup or a funnel) the vibrations are set up directly by the lips of the player (hence the scientific name, lip-vibrated aerophones). In the instruments with a reed they are produced by the vibrations of the elastic reed, which is loosely enclosed by the lips. In instruments with a mouth hole the lips are held so as to form a thin stream of air which is directed against the sharp lower edge of the hole.

The sound of a wind instrument depends on the shape of the pipe, whether straight (as in the flute, oboe, clarinet), circular (as in the horn), or wound or bent in any other way. The tone color depends mainly on the mouthpiece and on the inner dimensions of the pipe, whether narrow or wide, cylindrical (in the clarinet, trumpet, trombone), or conical (in the oboe, horn, tuba). The pitch of the sound depends only on the length of the pipe. Properly a pipe of a given length produces only one tone, e.g., a pipe of 8 ft. producing approximately the tone C, one of 4 ft. producing c, etc. (see *Foot*). However, by proper control of the breath and the lips, called *overblowing*, a pipe can also be made to sound a number of higher tones, the °harmonics, which, together with the fundamental tone, form the *natural tones* of a wind instrument, for example, C c g c′ e′ g′ bb′ c″ d″ e″, etc. (the fundamental tone is often difficult to obtain; see *Pedal tone*). They are the only ones available on a "natural" instrument (natural horn, trumpet), i.e., one consisting only of a pipe. In order to obtain the numerous tones between them, means must be provided temporarily to shorten or lengthen the pipe. These are three in kind: a slide (used on the °trombone), °valves (on all other brass instruments), and °finger holes (on all the wood winds).

Wind machine. A device used to imitate the sound of wind, occasionally used for descriptive purposes (e.g., in R. Strauss's *Don Quixote*). It consists of a barrel framework covered with cloth and revolved so that the cloth is in friction against the cardboard or wood of the framework.

Winterreise (VINT-er-REYE-ze: Winter Journey). A cycle of twenty-four songs by Schubert, in two parts, composed in 1827 to poems by Wilhelm Müller. They are romantic pictures of a rejected lover's lonely journey in winter time.

Wohltemperierte Clavier, Das (G.). See *Well-tempered Clavier*.

Wolf. Generally, any disagreeable effect produced by the imperfect tuning of instruments, e.g., by organ pipes not quite in tune. Also, imperfections inherent in certain older systems of tuning, e.g., the difference between G♯ and A♭ in the meantone system. In violins and cellos the term *wolf note* is given to certain tones having a somewhat weak and wobbling sound, caused by the design of the instruments. They occur particularly near the F♯ on the D-string of the cello and near the C♯ on the A-string of the violin.

Wood winds. See under *Orchestra; Wind instruments.*

Word painting. The reflection in musical materials of the ideas resident in or suggested by certain words of a song or other vocal piece. There are two main categories of words lending themselves to such treatment, namely, words implying a natural sound (laughter, wind, birds) or a bodily movement (running, falling, ascending). Both often occur through association of ideas, e.g., "heaven" (ascending) or "death" (falling). Modern composers usually reject the somewhat naive device of word painting which, however, played a prominent role in earlier music, particularly of the 16th century and the °Baroque period. Fig. 123 shows two examples from Bach's Cantatas, nos. 8 (*Ruhstatt*, resting place) and 26 (*Tropfen*, drops). There are, of course, many other ideas which can be "translated" into music. For instance, in Weelkes' madrigal *As Vesta was . . . descending*, two voices, then three, six, and one are used successively for the words, "First two by two, then three by three together, Leaving their Goddess all alone."

Fig. 123

Wozzeck (VOT-sek). Opera in three acts by Alban Berg (to his own libretto, based on G. Büchner's drama of 1836), produced in Berlin, 1925. The story relates the attempts of the desperately poor soldier, Wozzeck (tenor), to provide for his mistress, Marie (soprano), and their young son. Marie, however, yields to the advances of the handsome drum major (baritone) and is murdered by Wozzeck. Unable to forget his crime, Wozzeck returns to the scene of the murder and drowns himself in the nearby lake. The entire score, atonal without adhering to the twelve-tone technique, is organized in abstract musical forms. The first act is a suite in five movements; the second, a symphony in five movements with the usual classical forms; the third, a series of inventions in the form of variations. The opera, recently revived after years of neglect, is widely admired for its musical craftsmanship and emotional appeal.

WTC. Abbreviation frequently used for Bach's °*Well-tempered Clavier.*

X, Y, Z

Xylophone (from Gr. *xylos,* wood, and *phonos,* sound). A percussion instrument consisting of graded bars of hardwood which are struck with hammers. The bars, tuned in a chromatic scale from c' to about c'''' and arranged in a manner similar to the keyboard of the piano, are mounted on taut cords set in a horizontal frame. Underneath each bar there is a cylindrical resonator made from metal. Belonging to the same family of instruments are the °marimba and the °vibraphone.

Yankee Doodle. A popular American tune which, in the course of 150 years, has been used for a great number of texts of a humorous character. The origin of the tune is just as mysterious as that of the words "Yankee" and "Doodle." Its first appearance is in James Aird's *Selection of Scotch, English, Irish and Foreign Airs* (c. 1775), where it is given with its title, but without words. It possibly originated as a tune (a "doodle"?) for the flute. Dvořák used it, somewhat modified, in the last movement of his Symphony °*From the New World.*

Yodel. A special type of singing indigenous to the mountain people of Switzerland and the Tyrol, characterized by the frequent and quick passing from a low chest voice to a high falsetto. It is usually a vocalization, with the low tones sung to the vowels a and o, the high ones to e and i.

Youth's Magic Horn, The (G., *Des Knaben Wunderhorn*). A group of songs by Mahler, based on texts of German folk songs collected and published under the title *Des Knaben Wunderhorn* by Achim von Arnim and Clemens Brentano (c. 1820). The group includes nine songs with pianoforte, and thirteen with orchestra. One of them, *Urlicht,* was incorporated into the °Resurrection Symphony.

Zampogna (tzahm-PO-nyah: It.). A rustic bagpipe or shawm.

Zapateado (tha-pah-tay-AH-ttho: Sp.). A Spanish solo dance in triple time, the rhythm of which is marked by stamping of the heels, frequently in syncopation or in cross-rhythms to the accompaniment.

Zarzuela (thar-THWAY-lah: Sp.). A national type of Spanish opera, usually in the character of a light one-act comedy (*zarzuelita*), but occasionally dealing with serious and dramatic subjects in two or three acts (*zarzuela grande*). The librettos have spoken dialogue and often allow improvised interpolations, e.g., satirical allusions. The name is taken from the royal country palace near Madrid, *La Zarzuela,* where festive representations, called "Fiestas de Zarzuela," were given as early as the 17th century.

Zauberflöte, Die (G.). See *Magic Flute.*

Zigeunerlied (tsee-GOY-ner-LEET: G.). Gypsy song.

Zilafone (It.). Xylophone.

Zimbalon. Same as cimbalom (see under *Dulcimer*).

Zingarese, Alla (AH-lah tseen-gah-RAY-zay: It.). In the style of gypsy music.

Zither. A stringed instrument of ancient origin, consisting of a flat wooden sound box over which are stretched from about 30 to 45 strings. Four or five melody strings, nearest to the player, can be stopped on a fretted finger board and are played with a plectrum held in the right hand. The other strings are plucked with the fingers of the left hand and are used for the accompaniment.

Zoppa, Alla (AH-lah TZOP-pa: It., in a limping manner). Italian term for the inverted dotted rhythm, usually known as Scotch snap (see under *Dotted note*).

Zukunftsmusik (TZOO-kunfts-moo-ZEEK: G.). Music of the future.

Zwischenspiel (TSVISH-en-shpeel: G.). Interlude.

Zymbel (G.). Cymbal.

Perfect English?
Perfect English?
Perfect English??

Communicating is easy
once you have the proper tools.

Develop your speech, vocabulary,
spelling, writing with these excellent language
skills titles from Pocket Books.

____42880	COMPLETE LETTER WRITING, N.H. & S.K. Mager, eds.	$2.75
____82464	ENGLISH VERBAL IDIOMS, F.T. Wood	$2.50
____83230	FASTER READING SELF-TAUGHT, Harry Shefter	$2.95
____83486	A GUIDE TO BETTER COMPOSITIONS, Harry Shefter	$2.50
____82759	HOW TO PREPARE TALKS AND ORAL REPORTS, Harry Shefter	$2.25
____42415	INSTANT VOCABULARY, Ida Ehrlich	$2.95
____43662	MERRIAM-WEBSTER DICTIONARY	$2.75
____43664	MERRIAM-WEBSTER THESAURAS	$2.95

?????